Trinity, Economy, and Scripture

Journal of Theological Interpretation Supplements

MURRAY RAE
University of Otago, New Zealand
Editor-in-Chief

---

1. Thomas Holsinger-Friesen, *Irenaeus and Genesis: A Study of Competition in Early Christian Hermeneutics*
2. Douglas S. Earl, *Reading Joshua as Christian Scripture*
3. Joshua N. Moon, *Jeremiah's New Covenant: An Augustinian Reading*
4. Csilla Saysell, *"According to the Law": Reading Ezra 9–10 as Christian Scripture*
5. Joshua Marshall Strahan, *The Limits of a Text: Luke 23:34a as a Case Study in Theological Interpretation*
6. Seth B. Tarrer, *Reading with the Faithful: Interpretation of True and False Prophecy in the Book of Jeremiah from Ancient Times to Modern*
7. Zoltán S. Schwáb, *Toward an Interpretation of the Book of Proverbs: Selfishness and Secularity Reconsidered*
8. Steven Joe Koskie, Jr., *Reading the Way to Heaven: A Wesleyan Theological Hermeneutic of Scripture*
9. Hubert James Keener, *A Canonical Exegesis of the Eighth Psalm: Y<small>HWH</small>'s Maintenance of the Created Order through Divine Intervention*
10. Vincent K. H. Ooi, *Scripture and Its Readers: Readings of Israel's Story in Nehemiah 9, Ezekiel 20, and Acts 7*
11. Andrea D. Saner, *"Too Much to Grasp": Exodus 3:13–15 and the Reality of God*
12. Jonathan Douglas Hicks, *Trinity, Economy, and Scripture: Recovering Didymus the Blind*

Trinity, Economy, and Scripture

Recovering Didymus the Blind

JONATHAN DOUGLAS HICKS

Winona Lake, Indiana
EISENBRAUNS
2015

Copyright © 2015 Eisenbrauns
All rights reserved.

Printed in the United States of America

www.eisenbrauns.com

Library of Congress Cataloging-in-Publication Data

Hicks, Jonathan (Jonathan Douglas), 1984– author
  Trinity, economy, and Scripture : recovering Didymus the Blind / Jonathan Hicks.
      pages   cm. — (Journal of theological interpretation supplements ; 12)
  Includes bibliographical references and index.
  ISBN 978-1-57506-411-6 (pbk. : alk. paper)
  1. Didymus, the Blind, approximately 313–approximately 398. De Trinitate.
2. Trinity—Early works to 1800. 3. Didymus, the Blind, approximately 313–
approximately 398. De Spiritu Sanctu.   4. Holy Spirit—Early works to 1800.
5. Didymus, the Blind, approximately 313–approximately 398. On Zechariah.
6. Bible. Zechariah—Commentaries. 7. Bible—Criticism, interpretation, etc.—
History—Early church, ca. 30–600. 8. Didymus, the Blind, approximately 313–
approximately 398.   I. Title.
  BT110.D53H53   2015
  230′.14092—dc23
                                                                    2015028991

The paper used in this publication meets the minimum requirements of the American National Standard for Information Sciences—Permanence of Paper for Printed Library Materials, ANSI Z39.48-1984.♾™

To Tesella Elizabeth

True comfort,
Who has steadfastly lived out the meaning of her name
since the day I met her

"But as for me, I am like a green olive tree in the house of God;
I trust in the lovingkindness of God forever and ever"

Psalm 52:8 KJV

TABLE OF CONTENTS

ACKNOWLEDGMENTS	xii
ABBREVIATIONS	xiii
Ancient Texts	xiii
Journals, Sections, Series, Versions, Editions, and Libraries	xiv
INTRODUCTION	1
Theologically-Motivated Recovery	1
On the Place of This Study	4
Retrieval for the Sake of *Praxis*	7
Recovering an Ontology	7
A Baptismal Ontology: Participation in Christ	9
From Ontology to Praxis	11
Summary	13
A Précis of the Study	14
1. DIDYMUS' AUTHORSHIP OF *DE TRINITATE*: STATUS QUAESTIONIS	20
Internal Evidence for a *Terminus post Quem*	22
The Reference to Basil's Death	22
Macedonians and the Intra-Novatian Schism	25
Toward a *Terminus ante Quem*	26
An Anti-Nestorian Argument?	27
Chalcedonian and Proclian Allusions?	32
The Literary Reception of De Trinitate	36
The Date of Didymus' On the Trinity	39
Occasion	39
"Toil and Danger"	40
Didymus' Circle in the 390s	43
Evidence for Provenance	44
"Then Will the Nile's Flowing Be Full"	45
The Arguments for Antioch	47
The Arguments for Cappadocia	51
The Arguments for and against Didymus	53
The Traditional Argument: Its Problems and Strengths	54
The Reference to De Spiritu Sancto	54
The Sources of De Trinitate	57
Style	58
Recent Arguments	64
Christ's Human Soul as a Point-of-Comparison	64
Differing Attitudes toward Philosophy?	66
Conclusion: the Basis of the Attribution	68

2. GOD THE TRINITY: IDENTITY AND ACTIVITY ... 70
The Three *Hypostaseis* ... 70
From the Father's Hypostasis ... 71
The Only-Begotten Son ... 74
Not Created ... 75
Atemporally and Non-Spatially ... 75
Without Suffering or Change ... 76
Immediately ... 77
A Natural Relation with the Father ... 79
Summary ... 80
The Spirit Who Proceeds from the Father ... 80
He Proceeds rather than Proceeded ... 81
Inseparably ... 82
Not from the Father's Activity, by Nature and in Truth ... 83
Summary ... 84
The Begetting Father ... 84
Not the Cause of the Son and the Spirit ... 85
The One Who Begets ... 88
Summary ... 88
The Missions of the Son and the Holy Spirit ... 89
The Father as Sender of the Son and the Holy Spirit ... 89
Freely and Willingly ... 90
Knowingly ... 91
In the Presence of the Father ... 92
The Co-Missions of the Son and the Spirit ... 94
Embracing the Whole Narrative of Scripture ... 96
Divine Activity: Identical or Inseparable? ... 98
A Developing Doctrine ... 100
Indivisibility and Particularity ... 101
"The Same Activity Differently" ... 104
Conclusion ... 107

3. THE ECONOMY AND SCRIPTURE ... 111
The *sine Qua non* of Theological Knowledge ... 111
Beyond the Seeing of the Cherubim ... 113
The Mutual Comprehension of the Hypostaseis ... 115
How then Is God Known? ... 116
Summary ... 119
The Saving Economy of the Trinity ... 120
Salvation: the Gift of the Trinity ... 121
Creation Old and New ... 124
In the Image ... 125
The Loss of the Image ... 129

The Restoration of the Image	130
The Saving Inhumanation	131
The Saving Visitation of the Holy Spirit	133
Baptism and Its Ongoing Implications	135
Sanctification	135
Deification	137
Summary	139
The Authors of Scripture as Participating Witnesses	**140**
The Divine Authorship of the Scriptures	141
The Prophets and Apostles	145
Communicant with the Spirit	145
Illumined	147
Morally Sanctified	149
More than Human	150
Conclusion: a Scriptural Ontology	**153**
4. THE MORAL LIFE AND ITS END	**157**
Humanity and Virtue	**158**
Anthropology: a Brief Sketch	158
On Virtue	161
The Contemplative and the Active Life	163
The Incarnation and the Moral Life	**166**
Clouds and Heavens	166
Building the House of God	170
"My House Will Be Rebuilt in Her"	170
"Let Your Hands Be Strong"	171
"Come to Him, the Living Stone"	173
Crowned with Many Crowns	176
Keeping the Festival	179
Summary	184
Divine Constancy and Human Mutability	**184**
The Earliest Vision	185
"Return to Me, and I Will Return to You"	185
The Man on the Red Horse	186
The Earth Is at Peace	188
Watchtowers Ensuring Salvation	190
Ashkelon: the Praiseworthy Stronghold	190
The Church as Fortress	191
Completing the Tower	192
Summary and Critique	**193**
5. THE CONTEMPLATIVE LIFE AND ESCHATOLOGICAL KNOWLEDGE	**197**
Zechariah: from Word to Vision	**198**
The Stages of the Contemplative Life	**202**

The Vision of the Lamp-Stand	202
The First Treatment of the Vision	203
The Second Treatment of the Vision	205
The Inner and Outer Walls	207
The Former and the Latter Rains	208
Summary	210
Eschatological Vision	**211**
"The Lord Will Be One, and His Name One"	212
Forming a Single Man	213
Lights Illumining Themselves	214
The Humanity of Christ in the Psalms	**217**
He Hands over the Kingdom of His Humanity	218
Not That He Has Wounds	221
Summary and Critique	226
A Composite Sketch of the Dogmatic and the Exegetical	229
The Prophets and the Trinitarian Economy	230
An Instructive Account of Scripture?	231
The Results of the Christological Problem	234
6. "CULLING THE FLOWERS"	**235**
Didymus on Zechariah 3	**236**
Establishing the Interpretive Frame	236
Matters neither Sensible nor Human	236
The Dynamics of Spiritual Struggle	237
Satan as Instrument in the Divine Pedagogy	240
Summary	241
Sketching the Interpretive Skopos	241
The Joshua of the Exile	241
The Vestments of Jesus, the Great High Priest	244
Summary	246
Perfect Holiness, Perfect Vision	247
"Established in Holiness"	247
"Seers"	249
Vine and Fig Tree	250
Summary	251
Retrieving Didymus the Blind	**252**
On the Content of the Literal Sense	252
Israel's High Priest	252
On the Inordinate Pressure of the "Useful"	256
The Sinfulness of Joshua Reconsidered	259
Reasons for Didymus' Limitation of the Literal Sense	261
Summary	263
On the "Mind" of Zechariah 3	264

Sharing in Christ's Victory over Satan — 264
The Problem with the Spiritual Sense — 267
    Conclusion: Divine Economy, Interpretive *Skopos* — 269

EPILOGUE — 273
BIBLIOGRAPHY — 279
    Texts and Translations: Ancient Authors — 279
    Secondary Sources — 283
AUTHOR AND SUBJECT INDEX — 289
SCRIPTURE INDEX — 299

ACKNOWLEDGMENTS

It is a joy to recall the many people who have made this study possible. First of all, I wish to thank my wife, for her joyful and steady labor in the Lord, and our children: Ava, Cohen, Caeli, and Judah, for the profound measure of joy they have brought to our home. I thank my parents for instilling in their children a love for the Lord and his Church, and for their consistent encouragement and prayers in the Lord's work. For your sacrifical example, I give thanks to God. To my siblings Joshua, Alison, and Nathan: I am deeply grateful for your faith and for the many joys of our life together. These latter days with you are even sweeter than those of our happy childhood. And to Stuart and Hsuan DeLorme, I offer up my thanks for your hospitality to us during the past year and your wonderful example of trust in the Lord.

I express my warmest gratitude to Christopher Holmes and Murray Rae for their supervision of my study while I was a doctoral student. At important moments, your words directed me to voices in the Tradition who shed particular light on the great themes discussed by Didymus. Thank you for your love for the One of whom it is your vocation to speak. I thank my examiners: Adam Cooper, Ivor Davidson, and Angus Paddison, and the two reviewers of the manuscript, for their encouragement, astute reading of my work, and many helpful suggestions for the improvement of it. My conversation partners were invaluable: Mark Gingerich, Dillon Thornton, my father Douglas, and my brother Joshua. By your charitableness and desire to seek the truth, you have each given me a picture of what proper discussion about God demands. And I thank the Right Reverend Sam Sahu of Malaita for inviting me to take on the project in preparation for teaching at the Trinity School for Theology and Ministry (Solomon Islands).

I wish also to thank several communities: the church of Holy Trinity, Port Chalmers, for warmly welcoming my family to New Zealand and relaxing my diaconal responsibilities to the parish during the intensive phase of the project. To the scholarly community of Saint Andrew's Greek Orthodox Theological College, Sydney, I also express my gratitude for their encouragement of various presentations and articles that have—in one way or another—made their way into the fabric of this book. Finally, to our friends at Beeson Divinity School and Christ the King Anglican Church (Alabama), Church of the Cross (Boston), Community Fellowship (Montana), The Stony Brook School (New York), and the Diocese of Malaita (Solomon Islands): we owe you an unrepayable debt of love for your prayers on our behalf. May yours be the joy of unending life in the fellowship of the Trinity.

ABBREVIATIONS

Ancient Texts

Adv. Eun.	Pseudo-Basil, *Against Eunomius*
Amb.	Maximus the Confessor, *Difficulties*
Anc.	Epiphanius, *Anchored*
Ant. Apollinar.	Gregory of Nyssa, *Controversial Work against Apollinaris*
Apol.	Eunomius of Cyzicus, *Apology*
Apol. apol.	Eunomius of Cyzicus, *Apology for the Apology*
Asc. Chr.	Gregory of Nyssa, *Oration on the Ascension of Christ*
Bap.	Tertullian, *On Baptism*
Chron.	John Malalas, *Chronicle*
CZ	Didymus, *Commentary on Zechariah*
C. Ar.	Athanasius, *Orations against the Arians*
C. Eun.	Basil of Caesarea, *Against Eunomius*
	Gregory of Nyssa, *Against Eunomius*
C. Nest.	Leontius of Jerusalem, *Treatise against the Nestorians*
C. Ioh.	Jerome, *Against John of Jerusalem*
C. Jul.	Cyril of Alexandria, *Against Julian*
C. Man.	Didymus, *Against the Manichaeans*
Dem. ev.	Eusebius of Caesarea, *Demonstration of the Gospel*
De nup.	Augustine, *On Marriage and Sexual Desire*
Dial. Trin.	Cyril of Alexandria, *Dialogues on the Trinity*
	Pseudo-Athanasius, *Dialogues on the Trinity*
DSS	Didymus, *On the Holy Spirit*
DT	Didymus, *On the Trinity*
EcclT	Didymus, *Commentary on Ecclesiastes*
Ep.	Basil of Caesarea, *Letters*
	Gregory of Nazianzus, *Letters*
GenT	Didymus, *Commentary on Genesis*
Glaph. Ex.	Cyril of Alexandria, *Elegant Sayings on Exodus*
Glaph. Gen.	Cyril of Alexandria, *Elegant Sayings on Genesis*
Hist. eccl.	Eusebius of Caesarea, *Ecclesiastical History*
	Socrates Scholasticus, *Ecclesiastical History*
HiT	Didymus, *Commentary on Job*
Hom. Ezek.	Origen, *Homilies on Ezekiel*
Hom. Gen.	Origen, *Homilies on Genesis*
Hom. Num.	Origen, *Homilies on Numbers*
Hom. op.	Gregory of Nyssa, *On the Making of Man*
Inc. c. Ar.	Pseudo-Marcellus, *On the Incarnation and against the Arians*
In 2 Cor.	Didymus, *Commentary on 2 Corinthians*
In Hab.	Cyril of Alexandria, *Commentary on Habakkuk*
In Ioh.	Origen, *Commentary on John*
In Is.	Cyril of Alexandria, *Commentary on Isaiah*
In Prov.	Origen, *Commentary on Proverbs*

In Zach.	Cyril of Alexandria, *Commentary on Zechariah*
	Jerome, *Commentary on Zechariah*
	Theodore of Mopsuestia, *Commentary on Zechariah*
	Theodoret of Cyrus, *Commentary on Zechariah*
Kat. Pist.	Apollinaris of Laodicea, *Exposition of Faith*
Met.	Aristotle, *Metaphysics*
Or.	Gregory of Nazianzus, *Orations*
Pan.	Epiphanius, *Medicine Chest*
Prin.	Origen, *On First Principles*
PsT	Didymus, *Commentary on the Psalms*
Ps. cat.	Didymus, *Commentary on the Psalms* (catena)
Res.	Methodius of Olympus, *On the Resurrection*
Ser.	Nestorius, *Sermons*
Serap.	Athanasius, *Letters to Serapion*
Synt.	Aetius, *Short Treatise*
Thal.	Arius, *The Banquet*
Thes.	Cyril of Alexandria, *Treasury on the Holy, Consubstantial Trinity*
Vir. ill.	Jerome, *On Illustrious Men*
Vit. Macr.	Gregory of Nyssa, *Life of Saint Macrina*
Vit. Mos.	Gregory of Nyssa, *On the Life of Moses*

Journals, Sections, Series, Versions, Editions, and Libraries

ACW	Ancient Christian Writers
CCSL	Corpus Christianorum: Series latina
CSEL	Corpus scriptorum ecclesiasticorum latinorum
FC	Fathers of the Church
GCS	Die griechischen christlichen Schriftsteller der ersten Jahrhunderte
GNO	*Gregorii Nysseni Opera*
JECS	*Journal of Early Christian Studies*
JTS	*Journal of Theological Studies*
LCL	The Loeb Classical Library
LXX	Septuagint
NT	New Testament
OECT	Oxford Early Christian Texts
OT	Old Testament
PG	Patrologia Graeca, J.-P. Migne, 1857–1886
PTA	Papyrologische Texte und Abhandlungen
RevScRel	*Revue des sciences religieuses*
RSR	*Recherches de science religieuse*
SC	Sources chrétiennes
TLG	*Thesaurus Linguae Graecae*
TU	Texte und Untersuchungen zur Geschichte altchristlichen Literatur
VC	*Vigiliae Christianae*

INTRODUCTION

What follows is an exercise in the recovery of Didymus the Blind's understanding of Scripture and the practices of reading Scripture that are generated by this understanding. In articulating the linkages between these two aspects of Didymus' thought, my primary concern has been to bring together the dogmatic and the exegetical aspects of his program. The preponderance of my exposition of the Alexandrian teacher lies in the description of these linkages. And yet, my interest in this exercise is not finally, or even primarily, descriptive. As a *recovery* of Didymus, the study will—it is hoped—prove a stimulant to the Church's own thinking about her confession of what Holy Scripture is and her task in the reading of it.

The goal of the study and the manner of its pursuit are not accidental. Didymus was, during the course of his long and fruitful lifetime, communicant with the Church and a confessor of its creed. He read and commented on Scripture with his school because he desired for his students to know Christ in the only way such knowledge was possible: by becoming conformed to him. He read in the hope of the beatific vision of the Trinity. His polemical excursuses were largely motivated by the concern to illustrate how Apollinaris, Eunomius, or Mani—in making false claims about Christ, the Trinity, or the soul—had jeopardized the course of the spiritual life for those who were swayed by them. His interests in Scripture were, in other words, irreducibly theological and spiritual. I attempt to do justice to both of these interests—which are really a demonstrable unity—by engaging with Didymus' claims about God, humanity, and Scripture in an orderly way.

Theologically-Motivated Recovery

In signaling the above intent, it is well to recognize both its limitations and its promise. As with all fields of study in which there is a human element involved in the subject matter, the study of another person's exegesis of the Bible involves numerous considerations. Among these, some of the more significant are the pedagogical formation of the interpreter and, in turn, his own pedagogical aims. Both are materially significant in how the text of Scripture is rendered and in what kinds of questions are asked of it.[1] The interpretation

---

1. The most important work done on the question of Didymus' own formation is Richard Layton's *Didymus the Blind and His Circle in Late-Antique Alexandria: Virtue and*

of Scripture is also socially and historically located, involving the interpreter in a web of often-latent assumptions about the interpretive enterprise. Sometimes these assumptions strike the late modern student of patristic exegesis as almost wholly alien: e.g., Didymus' extended discussions of numerology and animal anatomy or behavior in interpreting difficult passages. An appraisal of Didymus' use of such tools in the reading of Holy Scripture would require both an exploration of the inter-relationships between the various pedagogical disciplines as they were conceived in the various schools in late antiquity and some account of why these disciplines are no longer connected to one another in the same way in late modernity.

At the literary level, a chief consideration is the interpretive genre of choice: homily, commentary, scholia, dogmatic treatise, etc.[2] The scope and mode of the exegesis under scrutiny is significantly determined by whether the interpreter is writing for a sympathetic audience at leisure to explore the finer details of the text or for an audience hostile to the interpreter's broad confessional position. Recently, attention has been drawn to the importance of textual form as well. How the Scriptures are presented in scroll, codex, or (later) printed book form carries with it important implications for how the task of interpretation is conceived.[3]

In stating my intent to focus on the theological dimensions of Didymus' acts of interpretation, I do not imply that a summative account of these acts can be a monistic affair. Indeed, Frances Young has warned us against concluding that every dispute about proper interpretation among Christians is reducible to issues that are strictly theological.[4] Yet it is often impossible, in reading Didymus or Theodore of Mopsuestia for example, to get at the reasons for their many divergences by appealing to non-theological or theologically-neutral "methods" of reading.[5] Theodore thinks that taking Zechariah's "man

---

Narrative in Biblical Scholarship (Urbana, IL: University of Illinois Press, 2004). For a thorough, but less analytical assessment of his use of secular learning, see Anne Browning Nelson, "The Classroom of Didymus the Blind," (PhD diss., University of Michigan, 1995).

2. For a consideration of most of these elements with respect to Didymus, see Blossom Stefaniw, *Mind, Text, and Commentary: Noetic Exegesis in Origen of Alexandria, Didymus the Blind, and Evagrius Ponticus* (Frankfurt: Peter Lang, 2010).

3. For the significance of the shift from the papyrus roll to the codex in early Christian circles, see Frances Young, *Biblical Exegesis and the Formation of Christian Culture* (Cambridge: Cambridge University Press, 1997), 9–16.

4. "The Rhetorical Schools and Their Influence on Patristic Exegesis," in *The Making of Orthodoxy: Essays in Honour of Henry Chadwick* (Cambridge: Cambridge University Press, 1989), 182–199.

5. For similar points, see Rowan Greer, *The Captain of Our Salvation* (Tübingen: Mohr (Siebeck), 1973), 4–5. Greer notes that a reduction of the Antiochene-Alexandrian controversy centering around Nestorius to a debate over allegory and typology (or the employment of any other exegetical method, for that matter) is "unwarranted.... The

on the red horse" (Zech 1:8) as a reference to the Incarnate Son is not merely an implausible interpretive move, but also an irreverent one. Didymus the Blind embraces the interpretation with gusto not only because he is a committed allegorist but because he has different operative assumptions about the nature of Trinitarian revelation in OT history. One could classify this particular interpretive disagreement as an inevitable conflict between committed disciples of Diodore and Origen, or between devoted students of *historia* and allegory, but such a classification would likely obscure the irreducibly theological character of the disagreement.[6]

Nor does a theological approach to Didymus the Blind promise only to illuminate some of the more important distinctions between his own interpretive *praxis* and that of his contemporaries. As Brian Daley has reminded us, it is often the "successfully theological" character of patristic exegesis that has most to commend this exegesis to us. Patristic recovery is serviceable to the end of offering us a more coherent vision about the practice of reading Scripture in and for the community of faith.[7] The theological moorings of Didymus' interpretative *praxis*—his pervasively-spiritual reading of Scripture—are most instructive in helping the Church think critically about the significance of its own confessional commitments and how certain practices inhere within this confession. The approach taken here suggests, from the very beginning, that one cannot do justice to Didymus as an interpreter of the Church's Scriptures without taking his confession of the Church's faith seriously. Likewise, it offers to bring Didymus into conversation with the Christian Tradition precisely on these terms.[8] Conversation is a two-way street. In the course of engaging Di-

---

method, when narrowly applied, fails to take seriously enough the role of theological principles both in forming and in applying exegetical methods."

6. One can, in other words, belie what is central to scriptural interpretation by approaching the *praxis* through a methodological lens. One could illustrate this point severally with respect to other fourth-century debates. For instance, Athanasius' interpretive methodology is, in numerous respects, not so very different from Arius'. His *hypothesis* of Scripture, his discernment of its "mind," is far more significant for his interpretation of it than his appeal to grammatical techniques that were by and large the common currency of his day (Young, *Biblical Exegesis*, 29–45).

7. See Brian Daley, "Is Patristic Exegesis still Usable? Reflections on Early Christian Interpretation of the Psalms," *Communio: International Catholic Review* 29 (2002): 214: "A more positive perception of early Christian exegesis, however, as not merely "precritical" but as thoroughly and—in some cases, at least—successfully *theological*, can open our eyes to what seems to be the other, less fulfilled need in Biblical interpretation today: its need to recapture an understanding of its own role within the Church."

8. The aims of the current work differ significantly from those of a recent monograph published on exegesis in Didymus. See Stefaniw, *Mind, Text, and Commentary*, 370–374. In the name of "historical particularity" and "thick description" of the interpretive enterprise, Stefaniw renounces the possibility of recovering noetic exegesis for contemporary practice. The study is driven by the goal of providing a non-confessional

dymus theologically for the benefit of contemporary confession and *praxis*, both positive appraisal and critique are indispensible.

On the Place of This Study

The study fills two lacunae in Didymus scholarship. First of all, a sustained examination of the question of exegetical normativity has never been a central one in the scholarship on Didymus. When the question is raised, it is considered briefly and almost exclusively on the far side of the descriptive task.[9] I hope to pursue this question more or less from the beginning. In order to do so without interrupting Didymus' exposition unnaturally, I have tried to make it clear both where I am endorsing a particular judgment and where there are reasons for parting company with the Alexandrian. I go about this task in a more focused way at the end of chapters 3–6, providing a brief evaluation of Didymus before proceeding on with the trajectory of his discussion in the next chapter. Following these summaries is important for understanding the composite sketch that I offer in the final chapter, where all aspects of the exegetical task canvassed in the study are recapitulated in reference to Didymus' exegesis of Zechariah 3.

---

account of the exegetical practice of Origen, Didymus, and Evagrius. Consonant with this aim, Stefaniw explicitly eschews "see[ing] any particular significance—for our understanding of their interpretive assumptions—in the fact that [these] three commentators . . . are all Christian" (p. 43). Stefaniw successfully isolates aspects of their thinking that are amenable to comparison with late antique schools involved in the "noetic exegesis" of authoritative texts. However, the burden of demonstrating the thesis becomes unbearable in her discussion of how the text relates to the sensible and intelligible orders that it describes. In a particularly obvious instance of this, she observes that Evagrius speaks of the final goal of all knowledge as the "knowledge of the Holy Trinity," and concludes her discussion of the passage by noting that Evagrius' interpretive "agenda clearly [!] overrides any concern with generating meanings which conform with Christian doctrines or ethics in general" (pp. 191–192). In Didymus' case, one does not need to read very far in the *Commentary on Zechariah* and the *Commentary on the Psalms* to see how consistently the spiritual order is given particularity by Didymus' vision of Christ.

9. Thus Jo Tigcheler, *Didyme l'Aveugle et l'exégèse allégorique: Étude sémantique de quelques termes exégétiques importants de son commentaire sur Zacharie*, trans. Denise van Weelderen-Bakelants (Nijmegen: Dekker and Van de Vegt, 1977), 182–185. Tigcheler's remarks on the subject are fairly general: Didymus gives one the impression of standing within the line of the NT authors and the authors of the subsequent Christian tradition. He creatively relates the two Testaments in a manner that is not servile to the approach of others before him, but in a manner that extends their approach. Though Tigcheler's study has attempted to relate theological concerns with exegetical method, he has not tried to appraise the appropriateness of "this method and . . . its results for the Christian life of Didymus and his hearers" (p. 184).

As has been recognized by several in the field, basic to Didymus' approach to Scripture is his concern to read every text "in a manner worthy of God (θεοπρεπῶς)," to understand the text's meaning as residing in the divine *skopos*.[10] In line with this *skopos*, God reveals nothing that is without use for our contemplation and (thus) inconsonant with his divinity. Manlio Simonetti has argued that the notion of the text's "usefulness (ὠφέλεια)" (2 Tim 3:16) is the basic criterion of Didymus' approach to each passage of Scripture. Uniting the diverse exegetical literature—the *Commentary on Ecclesiastes* with its occasional resistance to exploring an explicitly anagogical sense and the *Commentary on Zechariah* with its exuberant and at times dizzying endorsement of several anagogical senses at once—is a unifying commitment to drawing the reader's attention to that which is profitable for the soul in its moral and contemplative progress.[11]

These observations call for theological discussion if we are to move beyond description to the question of normativity. Questions like the following beg to be asked. Given that the appeal to "usefulness" is in some sense bound up with the soul's ability to recognize the divine *skopos*, how does Didymus conceive of this *skopos*? How is the criterion of "usefulness" applied, and what does this tell us about what Didymus believes to be the case with God and the soul? Indeed, this appears to be something of a lacuna in patristic exegesis generally speaking. Mark Sheridan helpfully observes that the "presuppositions and implications [of this criterion] have not been developed in any detail."[12] And this is certainly the case with Didymus, where much light has been shed on various aspects of the divine *skopos* of Scripture, but the pieces have rarely been put together into a coherent whole. The study concludes with some reflections about the proper use and misuse of these criteria in Zechariah 3, criteria that are not always stated but that underlie Didymus' decisions in the interpretation of the passage nevertheless.

The second lacuna that the study fills—and one that is concomitant with the pursuit of the task above—is that of relating the dogmatic and the exegeti-

---

10. See, e.g., Peter Steiger, "Theological Anthropology in the Commentary *On Genesis* by Didymus the Blind," (PhD diss., Catholic University of America, 2006), 226, and Richard Layton, "Didymus the Blind and the *Philistores*: A Contest over *Historia* in Early Christian Exegetical Argument," in *New Approaches to the Study of Biblical Interpretation in Judaism of the Second Temple Period and in Early Christianity* (Boston; Leiden: Brill, 2013), 267.

11. This is the closest that Simonetti will come to isolating a *ratio interpretandi* in Didymus. See his "Lettera e allegoria nell'esegesi veterotestamentaria di Didimo," *Vetera Christianorum* 20 (1983): 388–389. The two criteria of "usefulness" and "worthy of divinity" are two sides of the same coin, as Mark Sheridan implies of Philo and Origen: "The Bible as Read by the Fathers of the Church," in *From the Nile to the Rhone and Beyond* (Rome: Studia Anselmiana, 2012), 289.

12. Mark Sheridan, "The Concept of the "Useful" as an Exegetical Tool in Patristic Exegesis," *Studia Patristica* 39 (2006): 253.

cal material in Didymus' corpus. Since the discovery of the Tura papyri, the theologian and the exegete have been estranged.[13] In this study I endeavor to relate the two dimensions of Didymus' labor. I argue that Didymus' exegesis in the commentaries is better understood in light of his theological commitments in the dogmatic work. Simultaneously, his work in the commentaries extends observations made in the dogmatic material toward an audience that is more sympathetic to his pedagogical or anagogical program. The two dimensions of his activity—the dogmatic and the anagogical exegesis—are not estranged. Rather his spiritual exegesis and his dogmatic efforts attest to a vital unity that has yet to be articulated in any significant detail. This study goes some way toward providing such an articulation.

Important gestures have been made in this direction by Wolfgang Bienert, in his study on Didymus' use of "allegory" and "anagogy." Bienert has emphasized the importance of recognizing the vital overlap of the pedagogical program of Didymus' school—with all its numerous borrowings from the philosophical schools of his day—and the divine pedagogy. The trajectory of Didymus' thought throughout the commentaries is always guided toward the one question that is of vital importance to him: how can the soul be guided toward perfect knowledge and spiritual perfection such as these are revealed to us and enabled in the Incarnation of the Son of God?[14] The importance of understanding Didymus' account of this "plan of salvation (Heilsplan)" for a proper articulation of the divine *skopos* mentioned above is evident. I employ the language of "economy" to designate what Bienert here calls "Heilsplan," devoting much of the study to articulating how Didymus understands this economy.

Didymus' exploration of themes relating to psychic participation in this economy—a predominant concern throughout the commentaries—can give the reader the impression that Didymus is predominantly interested in anthropological *topoi*. These would include the nature of and relationship between the body and the soul, the dynamics of human freedom, and the appro-

---

13. So Alasdair Heron, "Some Sources Used in the *De Trinitate* Ascribed to Didymus the Blind," in *The Making of Orthodoxy: Essays in Honour of Henry Chadwick* (Cambridge: Cambridge University Press, 1989), 179, and more recently Mark DelCogliano, Andrew Radde-Gallwitz, and Lewis Ayres, *Works on the Spirit: Athanasius and Didymus* (Yonkers, NY: St Vladimir's Seminary Press, 2011), 34.

14. See Wolfgang Bienert, *"Allegoria" und "Anagoge" bei Didymos dem Blinden von Alexandria* (Berlin: de Gruyter, 1972), 154-162. The allegorical in Didymus is in the service of the anagogical. He is concerned with revealing how human pedagogy is only rightly ordered toward the true, or divine, pedagogy, where "the Incarnation of the divine Logos reveals in all its clarity God's plan of salvation for people. Humanity, which has departed from God, shall through the help of the Logos find its proper end and return to God" (Die Menschwerdung des göttlichen Logos zeigt in aller Deutlichkeit Gottes Heilsplan mit dem Menschen: Der Mensch, der sich von Gott entfernt hat, soll durch die Hilfe des Logos seine eigentliche Bestimmung wiederfinden und zu Gott zurückkehren) (p. 161).

priation of virtue. But Bienert here warns us that the psychic participation that Didymus describes in the commentaries refers us to something larger than itself, something toward and by which this participation is ordered. A clearer articulation of what this economy is promises to situate Didymus' vision of the soul's ascent toward God more appropriately.

Retrieval for the Sake of *Praxis*

Surveying the field of scholars who have been engaged in exercises of this kind would demand a lengthy introduction. Yet it is helpful here to identify several figures in patristic scholarship whose work the present study hopes to extend by including Didymus in the conversation. T.F. Torrance's *Divine Meaning*, which explores dogmatic questions relating to patristic reflection about Scripture and Henri de Lubac's monumental *Histoire et esprit* and *Exégèse médiévale*, touching largely on how a whole theology of Scripture came to be expressed in the doctrine of the four senses, have informed the present study greatly. If the former illustrates how to conduct a study where the goal is not only descriptive but also constructive, the latter is critical in orienting Didymus' work to the Tradition of which it was a part. Though neither engages with Didymus to any significant extent in these works, the latter in particular proves invaluable in appraising Didymus.

Recovering an Ontology

The most extensively realized dimension of the current project is the recovery of a scriptural ontology which—in its broad outlines—is instructive. By ontology I mean to designate an account of Holy Scripture's location in the divine economy and the various relations that obtain between Scripture and other elements within the economy as a result of this location. Particularly instructive is Didymus' attempt to wrestle faithfully with the question of divine limitlessness and accommodation to human modes of knowing. Didymus overcomes the problematic of a divine-human epistemological impasse in the present life not so much by providing a compelling account of a theory of language, but by relativizing his conception of scriptural language to the dynamics of the economy itself. He does so mainly through the doctrine of the "image": 1) by identifying *true* humanity as that which participates by grace in the Son's relation to the Father. On the human side of the epistemological dilemma, he insists that divinized humanity (i.e. humanity that is reformed in the Son's likeness) is true humanity. 2) Because the Son—the true image of the Father—assumes humanity without suffering change to himself, and makes use of human words out of consideration for our lowliness, he raises us to the knowledge of himself. Human language in Scripture participates in the dynamic of the God who condescends without change to himself; it is always over-burdened with the task of witnessing to divine fullness, but because it is used by God to the end of testifying to himself, it is always sanctified and sufficient to this end. It is always truthful, yet always partial.

By such an account, Didymus instructively overcomes the problematic of accounts that assert or imply a unilateral agency in scriptural inspiration and interpretation. His is a non-competitive account of divine and human agency, that works out the *how* question from within the economy. Within this solution, it could hardly occur to him to problematize the very possibility of human knowledge of God, even given his clear insistence on divine incomprehensibility and the noetic and moral problems stemming from human sin.

There has been a renewal of interest in this aspect of pro-Nicene theology in recent years. Scholars have largely recognized the numerous dividends that accrue from locating Scripture in this place, particularly for questions like the above. Torrance attends carefully to the question of how God's "transcendent greatness" and the "conviction that God has created man to know and love him" are reconciled in Athanasius.[15] If God is incomparable (and hence, without analogy) then how can he be spoken of in human words and conceived of in human thoughts? Basic to Torrance's treatment of Athanasius' hermeneutics is his admirable insistence on recognizing that the tension between these two notions is in one very important sense *not* mitigated by the Incarnation. The condescension of God in the Incarnation is expressive of the very height of God's transcendent greatness, and therefore secures us in the confidence that what is required—if we are to know God—is that God make himself known to us. "[T]he incomparability of the Word of God with our word . . . is not explicable from the side of man."[16] Athanasius urges us to recognize that if the Incarnation of the Son makes creaturely knowledge of God possible—as indeed it does—it does so in a singular way, such that true human knowledge of God is irreversibly bound up with learning of God "from him."

Hence Torrance writes:

> Because God became man and communes with him in and through the humanity of Christ, that does not import a general justification of human forms of thought and speech in their application to God. Rather does it mean that in and through Jesus Christ certain human forms of thought and speech are laid hold of and adapted for knowledge of God.[17]

Torrance concludes his reflections on this exceedingly important strand of Athanasius' thinking by noting that in the Incarnation humanity comes to

---

15. T.F. Torrance, *Divine Meaning: Studies in Patristic Hermeneutics* (Edinburgh: T&T Clark, 1995), 245.

16. Torrance, *Divine Meaning*, 246.

17. Ibid., 251.

know God at God's direction without having to leave "human modes of thought and speech behind."[18]

The Athanasian mould of Torrance's own thoughts on the question of the divine-human epistemological impasse is apparent: "the human word in the Bible is in [no] way less than human or somehow superhuman, but rather . . . it is even more fully human inasmuch as it is in touch with the Word which creates and moulds the human and is essentially humanising Word."[19] Torrance reminds us that Athanasius' account of things would problematize any hermeneutic that assumes one can only attend either to divine or human intentionalities, or that one must somehow get to the divine intent through the immanent processes of human discourse. Latent in such a hermeneutic is an assumed competitiveness between the two words that has been decisively overcome in the Incarnation. Torrance is instructive in reminding us that this overcoming takes place in such a way that divinity and humanity are not confused.

A Baptismal Ontology: Participation in Christ

The importance of conceiving of scriptural ontology from this vantage point also has consequences for Didymus in other ways. True theological knowledge, in which the prophets and apostles are participant, arises out of human fellowship with God. They are participants in the economy of which they speak as recipients of the Word and the Spirit of the Father who act inseparably in their inspiration. The function that they serve in this economy—as servants of the Trinity's knowledge- and fellowship-creating speech to humankind—arises out of their own knowledge of and fellowship with God. They are, in short, being conformed to the Son's humanity in the event of inspiration. Because Didymus' account of the economy culminates in one of the sacraments of this conformity (i.e. baptism), his ontology of Scripture has a highly participatory dimension.

---

18. Ibid., 286.

19. Ibid., 13. In support of my reading of Torrance here, see John Webster's placement of the work with Athanasius in light of Torrance's broader concerns ("T.F. Torrance on Scripture," *Scottish Journal of Theology* 65 (2012): 43). He notes that in Torrance "[t]here is a positive relation between the divine Word and the human words of Scripture; there is no *crisis* about the possibility of human text-acts serving in God's personal activity of self-presentation to intelligent creatures. . . . Greek patristic hermeneutics—supremely, of course, Athanasius, the subject of the centrepiece of *Divine Meaning*—had to overcome [the dichotomy between the intelligible and the sensible] in its Platonic version. In modern culture, the same separations surface in what Torrance identifies as "phenomenalism" in Biblical studies: the extraction of the biblical texts from their intelligible connections with the revealing activity of God, and the assumption that because biblical texts are natural entities they can have no ontological depth or backward reference to divine speech."

There is great illuminative potential in Didymus' arguments about the kinds of activities in which the Son and the Spirit are engaged among the OT prophets. Didymus describes, in very fulsome terms, the involvement of the three *hypostaseis* of the Trinity in Israel's history. This is, for him, a crucial theological point undergirding his account of the OT's revelation of the mystery of Christ. Precisely because the OT prophets are brought into fellowship with the Trinity by the missions of the Son and the Spirit among the people of Israel—missions that have a fuller term in the Incarnation of the Son and the Spirit's cooperation in his conception, baptism, and Pentecostal presence among the members of his Body—they are expositors of this mystery. The OT letter holds in it the mystery of the spirit, with which mystery it is already conversant. Didymus recognizes that the fact of prophetic discourse, just as much as the subject of this discourse, is explicable as a unity only within the context of the missions of the Son and the Spirit of the Father.

Exploring the above theme promises to supplement what has already been identified as one of the key themes emerging from recent efforts at the recovery of patristic exegesis. For many of the Fathers, interpretation and participational soteriology are inseparably conceived.[20] The observation is often used to draw out felicitous consequences for the interpretive enterprise, exploring the dynamics of the participation of audience and interpreter in the realities of which the text speaks. The need to locate the inspiration of the authors of Scripture within this framework is frequently rehearsed;[21] however, the dynamics of the human authors' participation in the divine economy is not usually explored in any great depth.[22]

Here, I argue, Didymus is instructive insofar as his ontology of Scripture is significantly invested in such an account. The human authors of Scripture are participant in the very economy to which they testify, such that they are re-

---

20. See, e.g., John J. O'Keefe and Russell R. Reno, *Sanctified Vision: An Introduction to Early Christian Interpretation of the Bible* (Baltimore, MD: Johns Hopkins University Press, 2005), 128–139, Daniel J. Treier, *Introducing Theological Interpretation of Scripture: Recovering a Christian Practice* (Grand Rapids, MI: Baker, 2008), 51–55, and J. Todd Billings, *The Word of God for the People of God: An Entryway to the Theological Interpretation of Scripture* (Grand Rapids, MI: Eerdmans, 2010), 155–162.

21. Billings, *The Word of God for the People of God*, 90–94. For an important voice articulating the importance of this move for dogmatic theology, see John Webster, *Holy Scripture: A Dogmatic Sketch* (Cambridge: Cambridge University Press, 2003), 30–39.

22. So Philip Moller, "What Should They Be Saying about Biblical Inspiration? A Note on the State of the Question," *Theological Studies* 74 (2013): 613–616, who sums inspiration up quite nicely as "a participation in revelation." The concern to explore this *topos* is to "[overcome] the reduction of biblical inspiration to a catena of truths, arrived at by a supernatural knowledge unaffected by the concrete realities of the economy of salvation" and place a renewed emphasis on "the personal, concrete circumstances of the human authors' experience and proclamation of revelation . . . [since they are] imbued with the same conditions of the historical economy."

created in the act of the Trinity's address to them—as intelligent and moral creatures—even as they are made witnesses of this re-creative economy. Didymus offers what can be described as a baptismal ontology of Scripture, which has important implications for our own understanding of the character of scriptural inspiration, even if Didymus does not explore all the facets of this ontology in significant depth. This ontology offers not only to shed light on how we should speak about the experience of the prophets and the apostles, but also forms a bridge between concerns that are too-often held apart in our day: the dogmatic and the anagogical.[23]

From Ontology to Praxis

A final contribution of this study focuses on Didymus' practice of reading Scripture. How he moves from ontology to *praxis* and the transparency with which he does so are questions that I take up in the concluding case study on Zechariah 3. The success of theological reasoning about Scripture is inseparably united with the reading of Scripture. Engaging responsibly in this evaluative exercise implies wrestling with the question of scriptural meaning, and not just remaining in the realm of interpretive theory.

Here undoubtedly the most significant contribution of modern scholarship to the question of scriptural meaning or senses in early and medieval Christianity is the work of Henri de Lubac.[24] In the current study, the place of de Lubac's work is an important one, for it provides my own work with the final horizon—as it were—against which Didymus' *praxis* can be measured. In *Histoire et esprit*, de Lubac traces Origen's reflections on the Holy Spirit's inspiration of Scripture toward the implications of this claim for scriptural meaning.[25] To assert the presence of a "spiritual meaning" in all of Scripture, as Origen and most of the Tradition after him does, is not to make claims to a dubiously-legitimated and utterly subjective field of inquiry. It is rather to claim that the discernment of the intention of the Spirit of Christ is the whole aim of exegesis. In this intention lies the unity of Scripture, which precedes every human attempt at articulating this unity.[26] His defense of Origen's iden-

---

23. I use "anagogical" here because the word is closest to Didymus' parlance. But one could equally use "mystical" or "spiritual" in the sense of that which participates in the revealed mystery of Christ's Body.

24. I engage with both his *Histoire et esprit: L'Intelligence de l'Écriture d'après Origène* (originally published in 1950), now in English translation as *History and Spirit: The Understanding of Scripture according to Origen*, trans. Anne Englund Nash (San Francisco: Ignatius Press, 2007), and with his *Exégèse médiévale: Les quatre sens de l'écriture*, vols. 1 and 2, now in English translation as *Medieval Exegesis: The Four Senses of Scripture*, vol. 1, trans. by Mark Sebanc (Grand Rapids, MI: Eerdmans, 1998) and vol. 2, trans. by Edward M. Macierowski (Grand Rapids, MI: Eerdmans, 2000).

25. *History and Spirit*, 337–384.

26. Ibid., 344–345.

tification of a spiritual sense in the whole of Scripture is disarmingly simple: "there are not two Spirits."[27]

De Lubac develops these remarks about the Spirit's inspiration of Scripture further. The concern about an indeterminate multiplicity of "spiritual senses" in Scripture is misplaced insofar as "there is no spiritual sense of the Bible considered otherwise than as a whole." There is but one spiritual sense. The single "testimony of the Spirit of Christ," that orders the words of the prophets and the apostles, tends toward the "one Logos to which the one Spirit leads."[28] Thus for de Lubac, the meaning of isolated scriptural passages is discerned only in relation to this end: the Christ who is the consummation of the divine intent with Scripture because he is the consummation of God's intent for all creation.[29]

If the intent of the Spirit is to lead us to Scripture's *telos*, which is neither less than nor more than the fullness of Christ, then de Lubac also makes numerous applications of this idea to the proper practice of Christian reading. The above account of scriptural ontology has an interpretive corollary: "[h]e alone understands [Scripture] who, in the unity of its divine intention, carries out the movement of conversion to which God was inviting him through all these words."[30] In the evaluation of ancient and medieval reading, de Lubac warns against the confusion of the interests of "specialized exegesis" with what is taking place in the majority of cases among the Fathers and Doctors of the Church. Their reading of Scripture "was a total exegesis," which insisted on regarding exegesis as theology or spirituality and not as "an auxiliary science of theology."[31] The spiritual sense that they identified with the mystery of Christ was inexhaustible, and only adequately attended to when this mystery had expounded itself in relation to the Christian in all its fecundity.

Critical for our appreciation of what the ancients offer us as exegetes of Scripture—and Didymus is no exception—is to understand the various moral and anagogical movements that they make within their exegesis. De Lubac is helpful here insofar as he recognizes that these movements, where they are performed appropriately, take place within the one spiritual sense. The Church's moral life (tropology) and her eschatological hope (anagogy) in

---

27. Ibid., 337–339. Though de Lubac does not make the point here, it is fair to add that his articulation of the spiritual sense is undergirded by a lively and determinant pneumatology. The objection about interpretive subjectivity in the spiritual sense often arises because of an inoperative or indeterminate pneumatology.

28. Ibid., 346.

29. Cf. a similar passage elsewhere: "Jesus Christ brings about the unity of Scripture, because he is the endpoint and fullness of Scripture. Everything in it is related to him. In the end he is its sole object. Consequently, he is, so to speak, its whole exegesis" (*Medieval Exegesis* I:237).

30. *History and Spirit*, 347.

31. *Medieval Exegesis* II:77.

which she is in some sense now participating, are all given at once in her conversion from the mere letter to the Spirit (allegory).[32] All of these movements are rightly practiced and understood as aspects of the one mystery of Christ latent in all of Scripture.[33]

As de Lubac and others have recognized, Didymus' exegetical terminology does not reflect the standardized usages of later centuries.[34] Efforts at defining his terminology have proven notoriously difficult.[35] However, engaging with de Lubac is important in dealing constructively with Didymus' construal of the senses, which is also basically two-fold. Didymus' handling of the "literal sense" in conversation with the "spiritual" and the consequent transformation of this "literal sense" is one part of the evaluative task for which de Lubac's understanding of the proper relation between the senses proves pivotal. Likewise, we engage with Didymus' exploration of the "spiritual sense," bearing in mind that it rightly encompasses more than intellectual description. Didymus is concerned—as is much of the Tradition as de Lubac describes it—with unfolding the course of the Christian life in conversation with the whole mystery of Christ in this age and, as far as it has been revealed to us, in the age to come.

Summary

The study moves from discerning how Didymus articulates a scriptural ontology in relation to the doctrine of the Trinity, examines the soteriological scope of his claims for the inspired servants of the Word and scriptural interpreters, and concludes by examining the practices and meanings consonant with such an understanding of Scripture. The evaluative task is concurrent throughout the thesis and takes place largely by comparing Didymus with his contemporaries and commending certain of his theological insights to the

---

32. In using the phrase "mere letter" I mean here what de Lubac calls "the letter... whose prophetic character one refuses to recognize" (Ibid., 60).

33. "In passing from history to allegory we passed, as it were, from the letter to the spirit.... The passage from allegory to tropology involves no such jump. After the historical sense, all those that can still be counted belong to one and the same spiritual sense.... The "transfer" takes place henceforward within the mystery, in order to explore its successive aspects" (*Medieval Exegesis* II:127).

34. Ibid., 199.

35. For a helpful test study of all the current theories about Didymus' exegetical terminology, see Hanneke Reuling's *After Eden: Church Fathers and Rabbis on Genesis 3:16–21* (Leiden: Brill, 2006), 49–80. Reuling rightly concludes that there are problems that arise from trying to tie Didymus down too neatly to a technical definition of his exegetical terms. Exceptions to the helpful generalizations offered by Bienert, *"Allegoria" und "Anagoge,"* Simonetti, "Lettera e allegoria," and Tigcheler, *Exégèse allégorique*, may be produced, such that it seems best to allow an overlapping semantic field between certain terms like "allegory" and "anagogy" or "letter" and "history." If they are sometimes effectively distinguished, this distinction is not a permanent feature of Didymus' intellectual landscape.

Church as of continuing value. The contemporary voices that I draw into conversation with Didymus suggest avenues of criticism of a theological character that supplement the concerns and appraisals offered by Didymus' contemporaries.

A Précis of the Study

The study proceeds as follows. In the first chapter of the work, I briefly introduce Didymus and revisit a central issue in his dogmatic corpus. What is the state of the question of Didymus' authorship of *De Trinitate* (*DT*)? At least one of the reasons for the lack of any significant *rapprochement* between the exegetical and the theological literature is the disputed status of this treatise. *De Spiritu Sancto* (*DSS*) is understood to stem from an earlier period than most of the Tura commentaries.[36] *Contra Manichaeos* is fairly brief, and engages more with questions of human freedom and the nature of good and evil than with questions that would encourage a lengthy *rapprochement* on Trinitarian themes. *DT*'s place had been of decisive importance for the Didymean corpus between its discovery in the eighteenth century and the late 1950s. In brief, I argue in this chapter that the current *status quaestionis* of *DT*, on the whole, favors Didymus' authorship. There is a sound—albeit not finally conclusive—basis upon which the attribution rests. Given that the treatise was written within a decade of the established date for the *Commentary on Zechariah* (*CZ*), I argue that, of all the works within the corpus, we can make the strongest case for a synchronic comparison between the dogmatic work and the exegetical with *DT* and *CZ*.

The second chapter is devoted to attending to the broad question of how Didymus, in *DT*, speaks of the *hypostaseis* of the Trinity in reference to their eternal identities as Father, Son, and Holy Spirit. Leaning on the important work done by Gustave Bardy and Louis Béranger,[37] I argue that Didymus conceives of the three divine *hypostaseis* in a manner that refuses any non-correlative claims about the identities of each of the *hypostaseis*. This is especially pronounced in his account of the Father's identity, where Didymus radicalizes the insistence of his correlativity to the Son by refusing the notion that the Father is the "cause" of the Son (since this would imply that the Father is uncaused, and is thus conceptually non-correlative to the Son). I argue that the claim illustrates his conviction, borne out through his treatment of the other two *hypostaseis* as well, that the cataphatic and apophatic tasks of theo-

---

36. A date in the first half of the decade 360–370 seems most likely. For the most recent assessment of the dating issues, see DelCogliano, Radde-Gallwitz, and Ayres, *Works on the Spirit*, 37–42.

37. Gustave Bardy, "La Théologie Trinitaire," in *Didyme l'Aveugle* (Paris: Beauchesne, 1910), 59–109, and Louis Béranger, "Etudes sur la Christologie du *De Trinitate* attribué à Didyme l'Aveugle," (PhD diss., Lyon, 1960), 5–24.

logical discourse are complementary. He could not assert the distinction of causality between the Father and the Son because he would have to negate the notion so completely that it would cease to communicate meaningfully. Instead, Didymus gets at the notion of the Father's priority through the economy of the *hypostaseis*. How he conceives of the eternal relations between the *hypostaseis* is, I argue, critical in understanding how Didymus conceives of their economy in which they act in the world and establish relations to the world in a manner consistent with these identities. Didymus' account of the activities of the *hypostaseis* preserves the unity of the divine essence even as it articulates the importance of eternal distinctions within this essence for Trinitarian activity. In the conclusion of the chapter, I defend Didymus from the charge of inconsistency in articulating a notion of inseparable, yet differentiated divine activity, by arguing that Didymus thereby does justice to the vital connection between the divine being and the economy in which the *hypostaseis* are inseparable in the divine unity and yet eternally differentiated.

Chapter 3 forms the keystone of the argument. The activities of creation and salvation bear a likeness to one another because the *hypostaseis* participate in these activities as an out-flowing of the divine being. For Didymus this binds together the creation and salvation narratives into an organic unity. Using Edward Louis Heston's helpful corrective to Johannes Leipoldt and Bardy's interpretation of the theme of soteriology in *DT* as a springboard, I examine the central narrative of the economy in *DT*.[38] Arguing that Didymus' conception of salvation as re-creation is brought to fullest coherence in his chapters on baptism in Book 2, I argue that the soteriological themes of the treatise *DT* should be read through this lens. When this is done, a fulsome picture emerges of the original creation of humanity which includes the notion of freedom—focused on by earlier scholars—but also (and more critically) the notion of the soul's participation in the goodness of the Trinity by which it attains all that is intended for it in union with the Son. For Didymus, this gift is common to the Trinitarian *hypostaseis*, since it is the Father who wills to receive other sons in the image of his Only-begotten, it is the Son who fashions them in this image, and the Spirit who breathes upon them, rendering them alive. This original creation includes the notions of humanity's filial identity, its illumination and sanctification by the Son and the Spirit, and its teleology in deification.

Tracing the loss of this *telos* and the futile use to which humanity puts the image by disobedience and refusal to participate in divine goodness, Didymus then ties the expulsion from Paradise to the Spirit's departure from humanity. The saving purposes of God are revealed precisely in the reversal of these conditions, and Didymus is at pains to demonstrate that the OT is shot through

---

38. Edward Louis Heston, "The Spiritual Life and the Role of the Holy Ghost in the Sanctification of the Soul, as Described in the Works of Didymus of Alexandria" (PhD diss., Notre Dame, 1938), 13-14. Cf. Bardy, *Didyme l'Aveugle*, 129-144 and Johannes Leipoldt, *Didymus der Blinde von Alexandria* (Leipzig: Hinrichs, 1905), 78-95.

with the missions of the Son and the Holy Spirit, who are ever intimating their presence to Israel and gesturing through the prophets toward the culmination of divine purpose in the Incarnation. The Son once again takes up the work of creation when he becomes incarnate, receiving the Spirit in his baptism and breathing the Spirit upon the disciples—just as he did in the creation of Adam in the Garden. That these themes cluster around Didymus' account of baptism serves to illustrate the centrality of the gift of baptism in becoming incorporated into the new humanity that the Trinity has created in the Incarnation of the Son. We become, like Jesus, receptive to the Spirit and sons of his Father in our baptism. We participate in the recreating economy of the Trinity when we are divested of our Adamic humanity by the Spirit and raised to new life—the life of conformation to Christ by participation in him.

In *DT* the prophets and the apostles are repeatedly appealed to as witnesses to this economy. But Didymus appeals to them in such a way that it becomes clear that he considers them participant in the very realities to which they testify. They experience the inspiring presence of the Trinity precisely within this economy about which they speak, and therefore precisely as those who are drawn up out of the futility of Adamic humanity to the humanity that is revealed in Christ. They are illumined; they are sanctified; they are deified. At the end of this chapter I argue that Didymus' account of divine and prophetic speech assumes no competition between the divine and the human, but that it raises some concerns about the extent to which the prophets and the apostles are said to be conformed to the image of God in Christ. For answers to these questions, I turn to the *CZ*.

In chapter 4 I take up the question of moral sanctification in the *CZ*. I begin with a brief examination of the literature on Didymus' anthropology and the discussions of the relation between the moral and the contemplative life in Didymus. Noting the asymmetrical relationship between contemplation and ethics in Didymus—that the contemplative life governs the active—I then seek to locate the contemplative basis of the active life. Didymus is consistent in arguing throughout the *CZ* that the ethical life is revealed to us by the contemplation of the doctrine of the Incarnation, in which the Son takes up a morally and ontologically perfect humanity. The proper pursuit of the moral life consists in recognizing the virtues as they are revealed in the Incarnation. The moral life may be summed up by the imitation of Christ. I query several aspects of this imitation. How does it proceed? To what extent does Didymus think it is possible to attain this in the present life? How does Didymus tie this to the main theme of the *CZ*: the attainment of stability in the face of evil? Didymus' account of the imitation of Christ steers wide of the Pelagian problematic in several respects. It is always with the help of God—by participating in the virtues of the Trinity—that the virtuous life proceeds. Didymus is, however, keen to argue quite explicitly that moral perfection is not only possible in this life but essential in overcoming the fundamental problem sketched in the beginning of the commentary: the soul's instability in the face of evil.

There are reasons in the CZ to tie this concern to the recovery of a state that the soul possessed in its pre-existence. The prophets and those who are held up as examples to imitate in their writings are those who—if they have not arrived at this state—are yet competent to declare to us the course of the soul's upward journey toward conformation with Christ: the pursuit of the likeness of God.

In chapter 5 I turn to Didymus' account of illumination, or the sanctification of the human intellect. I query the stages of Didymus' account of the illumined, or contemplative, life as they are presented in the CZ. He is consistent in identifying three stages of contemplation which have important consequences for understanding the various levels at which Scripture is read. These are the contemplation of the world in light of God's "providential care (πρόνοια)" for it, the contemplation of the Son's Incarnation, and the immaterial contemplation of the Trinity. With the summit of the contemplative life so identified, I examine how the acquisition of such participatory knowledge is attained, and note that, as with the moral life, Didymus also identifies a *telos* beyond which further progress in this knowledge is no longer possible. This *telos* is usually identified with life in the age to come.

Given that the knowledge of the Trinity is mediated to us by the Son in his assumed humanity, I then examine Didymus' account of the role of Christ's mediation in the age to come. The *Commentary on Zechariah* is not as forthcoming on the theme as the *Commentary on the Psalms*, but it suggests quite strongly that Didymus envisions a time when the Incarnation will no longer serve in this capacity in the age to come, since in the *eschaton* it will have fulfilled its illuminative function. Two passages from the *Commentary on the Psalms*, to which I turn, confirm Didymus' insistence that the illuminative role played by the Son's humanity must come to an end in the eternal Kingdom toward which he is leading us. In one of these passages, Didymus identifies the "kingdom of the Son's humanity" as having a definite *terminus*; in another, Didymus explicitly denies the material aspect of the Son's ascended body.

The observations from chapters 4 and 5 serve to round out the picture of Didymus' ontology of Scripture. I argue in the conclusion to chapter 5 that Didymus' eschatological vision and his doctrine of perfection have a distortive effect on his reading of Scripture. Given that he rightly understands the age to come as a reality in which we are already—because of Christ's ascension—participant, the denial of Christ's material body has consequences for the service of human words in the divine economy. Words, for Didymus, signify corporeal realities, but indicate incorporeals improperly or iconically. Given that the corporeal dimensions of the age to come are radically called into question by the denial of Christ's material body, it is understandable that Didymus in some sense subordinates the sensible referents of scriptural language. This is especially the case when he is dealing with the advanced stages of the contemplative life.

In chapter 6 I bring the ontology developed at length throughout the study to bear on a concrete instance of Didymus' interpretation: Zechariah 3. Following Didymus' argument throughout an entire vision reveals several aspects of his exegetical *praxis* that I commend as of ongoing usefulness to the Church. Didymus is at his best in speaking of the importance of recognizing Trinitarian activity in the OT for a true account of the meaning of that history. He is likewise instructive in recognizing that the christological focus of Scripture is not an optional addendum for Christian reading of the OT, but is the *sine qua non* of a Christian reading. In this christological emphasis, Didymus is also instructive in overcoming the barrier between "interpretation" and "application" that afflicts contemporary exegesis and homiletics. His participational ontology of scriptural witness has a corollary in the reception of the Word which eschews the division. We only interpret rightly when we hear the Scriptures in their irreducibly baptismal character: that is, we only hear rightly in repentance and faith before the victorious Christ, who offered himself to be sin for us so that we might become in him the righteousness of God (2 Cor 5:21).

Yet there are also important reasons to part company from Didymus in several ways. His implausible reading of the "literal sense" is—I argue—born of his desire to render Joshua the high priest "useful" for Christian imitation. Didymus' desire to read Joshua as a typical representation of Christ serves to downplay the ascription of moral failure in Joshua. Cyril will later call Didymus' identification of the type into question. Didymus' doctrine of progress toward moral perfection clearly colors his reading of the "literal sense" of Zechariah 3, causing him to avoid recognizing the text's fairly clear predication of guilt to Joshua by re-framing the vision into a discussion about temptation. Readings by Theodore, Theodoret, and (in some way at least) Jerome, raise the question of whether Didymus has done justice to this aspect of the "literal sense."

Just as importantly, I argue, Didymus' treatment of the "literal sense" has adverse ramifications for his treatment of the "spiritual sense" of the vision. Since Didymus rightly regards the senses as conversant—with the anagogical elements of the "literal sense" being clearly linked to those developed in the "spiritual sense"—his treatment of the mystery of Christ's assumption of the priesthood suffers. In two respects, Didymus' development of the "spiritual sense" fails to articulate the dimensions of this mystery that a more theologically-astute reading of Zechariah 3 would give us. 1) Christ's ministration of the priesthood in the OT in the place of Joshua (and Aaron, etc.)—to which the "literal sense" points us—should serve to underline Christ's unique performance of the priestly service, such that his obedience is offered in security for us, who though striving to imitate him will inevitably in this life have need of repentance. 2) By identifying the assumption of the priesthood with the overcoming of the consequences of sin, Didymus directs us away from the ongoing significance of the Incarnate Son's priestly mediation in the age to come. However, we have firm reasons to hope that his assumed humanity will not be extrinsic to the Trinitarian mystery, but central to God's ongoing self-exposition to us. By downplaying the material dimensions of Christ's revelation of the kingdom of heaven in the Gospels, Didymus misses another dimension of the mystery of Christ that is latent in Zechariah 3. I conclude with a brief recapitulation of the main points of the argument, and gesture toward some of the promising trajectories of Didymus' scriptural ontology and exegetical *praxis*.

1

DIDYMUS' AUTHORSHIP OF *DE TRINITATE*: *STATUS QUAESTIONIS* [1]

Didymus of Alexandria spent the whole of his life in the environs of this city. Born in 313, he suffered the loss of his sight before the age of six, and spent his early years in the pursuit of learning. In recognition of this learning and the even more acclaimed purity of his life, he was given charge over the operations of a school in Alexandria by Athanasius the Great, and held this post until his death in 398. Whether this is the selfsame Catechetical School of Alexandria—the existence of which contemporary scholarship continues to debate—is unclear. What is certain is that Didymus the Blind counted some of the more famous men of the age as his students or visitors, entertaining such notables as St Antony of Egypt, Jerome, Palladius, and Rufinus in his cell. He is widely reputed to have commented on nearly every book of Holy Scripture, and to have written numerous dogmatic and polemical treatises, the majority of which have been lost, no doubt owing to the condemnation of his works in the sixth century. Among these lost treatises was a three-volume work *On the Trinity*.

In 1769, J.A. Mingarelli published an acephalous work that he had discovered in Cardinal Passionei's personal library in 1758. After some years of indecision about its title and its author, he credited the work to Didymus the Blind under the title *De Trinitate*.[2] The attribution, widely accepted, would serve as the touchstone of Didymus scholarship for the next two centuries. Held to be

---

1. This chapter addresses the historical question: did Didymus write Mingarelli's *DT*? Doubtless patristics scholars will have the patience for it. However, to those whose interest in this book is primarily related to Didymus' understanding of and practice of reading Scripture, I advise briefly visiting the summary (pp. 20–22) and conclusion of this chapter (pp. 68 and 69) before moving on to chapter 2.

2. Dubbed *Passioneianum* by Mingarelli, the codex is housed in the Biblioteca Angelica (Rome) as ms. gr. 116. The question of authorship arises because the treatise is missing its title page. For a lively retelling of the discovery of the manuscript by Mingarelli, see Louis Doutreleau, "Vie et survie de Didyme l'Aveugle du IVe siècle à nos jours," *Le Mardis de Dar El-Salam 1956-1957* (1959): 50–56.

the blind teacher's *magnum opus*, *DT* provided scholars with important resources for re-assembling a large, but scattered theological corpus.[3]

However, the renaissance of Didymus the theologian was eclipsed by the unexpected discovery of his commentaries in 1941. Some of the editors of the Tura papyri, troubled by stylistic and material inconsistencies between the accepted theological corpus and the commentaries, would raise the question of Didymus' authorship of *DT* afresh.[4] In light of differences in style and content between *DT* and the newly discovered *Commentary on Zechariah*, Louis Doutreleau reconsidered the basis upon which Mingarelli had constructed his argument for Didymean authorship, concluding that it was no longer tenable. As a result of his efforts, subsequent scholarship tended to regard *DT* as outside Didymus' authentic corpus. In turn, the exegetical works replaced the dogmatic treatises as the focal point of Didymus scholarship.

This chapter contains an examination of the *status quaestionis* of the authorship of *DT*. I do not attempt to add anything new to the discussion, save where it is a matter of responding to recent arguments not addressed by the important studies on the question in the 1960s and 1970s. Beginning with the text itself, I argue with others that internal considerations and reception history impose discernible limits upon the date, occasion, and provenance of the work that are entirely in concert with Didymean paternity. Next I examine the history of attribution, considering the arguments in favor of Didymus' authorship of *DT* and those opposed, and conclude that there are considerable, unanswered arguments in favor of Didymus' authorship. Although there are certain aspects of the authorship question that remain incompletely addressed, I consider that the arguments adduced in this chapter form a sufficient basis from which to conclude that Didymus was very likely the author of the work.

---

3. The most important addition to this corpus is Pseudo-Basil's *Adversus Eunomium* (Books 4 and 5). Didymean paternity was argued for at first by Anatoly Spassky (in Russian) and then by F.X. Funk independently of the former. See F.X. Funk's "Die zwei letzten Bücher der Schrift Basilius d. Gr. gegen Eunomius," in *Kirchengeschichtliche Abhandlungen und Untersuchungen*, vol. 2 (Paderborn: Schöningh, 1899), 291–329 and his 1907 defense of his position in volume 3 of the same work: pp. 311–323. The argument, based largely on comparisons between the texts of *Adversus Eunomium* 4-5 and *DT*, received additional impetus from Joseph Lebon's discovery that a Syriac manuscript tradition had credited Didymus with the polemical treatise. See Lebon's "Le Pseudo-Basile (*Adv. Eunom.*, IV-V) est bien Didyme d'Alexandrie," *Le Muséon* 50 (1937): 61–83. The argument provided Funk's thesis with much-needed external support. However, the status of the work is still contested. For a more contemporary summary of the arguments, see F.X. Risch, "Einleitung," in *Pseudo-Basilius, Adversus Eunomium IV-V: Einleitung, Übersetzung und Kommentar* (Leiden: Brill, 1992), 3–12. Weighing in on the question is beyond the scope of this thesis.

4. For the decisive study on this viewpoint, see Louis Doutreleau, "Le 'De trinitate' est-il l'œuvre de Didyme l'Aveugle?" *RSR* 45 (1957): 514–557.

This conclusion has important consequences for my argument. In the first half of the study, I investigate *DT* as an important resource for discerning Didymus' account of what the Scriptures are, and hence of how he conceived of his own task as an exegete of sacred Scripture. In short, reckoning with Didymus' more focused description in *DT* of how the Trinity inspires sacred Scripture may better situate us to appreciate what he offers to us as an exegete in the *CZ*, both written within the last eleven years of his long life.

Internal Evidence for a *Terminus post Quem*

The present investigation commences by engaging with evidence internal to *DT* that relates to the treatise's date. Happily, on the issue of a *terminus post quem* there is widespread agreement. All who deal with the question place the work no earlier than the early 380s. The key texts used in making this determination are discussed below. I begin with the reference to Basil's death in conversation with a recent interpreter of it who—while affirming the same *terminus post quem*—has argued that the passage needs to be read as a piece of evidence for a rather later date than the traditional one that had been almost unilaterally assigned to it by other readers of *DT*.

The Reference to Basil's Death [5]

The absolute *terminus post quem* of *DT* is, beyond any doubt, 378/9. Basil of Caesarea died sometime between September 378 and January 379,[6] and the author of *DT* refers to this event when he calls the deceased "one of the fathers among the saints." In the midst of a discussion about whether the Son's appar-

---

5. *DT* 3.42 (920AB). All citations of *DT* come from PG 39 for the sake of consistency. The reader who possesses a copy of both Jürgen Hönscheid, *Didymus der Blinde: De Trinitate, Buch 1* (Meisenheim: Anton Hain, 1975) and Ingrid Seiler, *Didymus der Blinde: De trinitate, Buch 2, Kapitel 1-7* (Meisenheim: Anton Hain, 1975) should have little trouble following the references in these editions since both provide the PG quarter-column referencing system in the margin. However, for the sake of those using *TLG*, where I cite Books 1 and 2.1-7 in PG 39 I also add the paragraph numbers assigned by Hönscheid and Seiler, which do not interfere with but further subdivide *DT*'s own referencing system. Only where their readings challenge, edit, or render *DT* differently do I refer to the page number of their texts.

6. The traditional date is January 1, 379, though a revisionary thesis advancing a date in 377 was proposed in the 1980s. On the merits of both sides of the discussion, see Philip Rousseau, "Appendix 3: The Date of Basil's Death and of the *Hexaemeron*," in *Basil of Caesarea* (Berkeley: University of California Press, 1994), 360-363. Rousseau's discussion, sympathetic to the revisionist theory, nevertheless suggests that there are several things it does not yet explain. On the balance of things, he stays with the traditional date. A moderate position of September 378 is the current emerging consensus. For a complete discussion, see Anna Silvas, *Gregory of Nyssa: The Letters: Introduction, Translation and Commentary* (Leiden: Brill, 2007), 32-39.

ent ignorance of the last day (Mark 13:32) is evidence of his having inferior knowledge to that of the Father, the author of *DT* offers a solution to the difficulty. As is his custom, he multiplies what he takes to be orthodox solutions to the aporia, in the process appealing to Basil's authority. He writes: "Or it is even possible to read this passage, "No one knows that day or hour, neither the Son, except the Father," as a certain father among the saints who was full of wisdom taught non-syllogistically (ἀσυλλογίστως)—Basil was his name."

The importance of this text in the discussion about authorship has recently been brought to the fore by Panayiotis Tzamalikos. 1) He takes the phrase τις τῶν ἐν ἁγίοις πατέρων to mean "one of the ancient 'saintly fathers'," suggesting that such a remark excludes the possibility of Basil's being a contemporary.[7] 2) He interprets the passage as an intended "rebuke" to Basil's poorly-conceived opinion that the Father is the cause of the Son's knowing.[8] The second argument hinges on the meaning of the word ἀσυλλογίστως, which Tzamalikos takes to mean "thoughtlessly" or "not reasoning justly."[9]

Both arguments are difficult to sustain. In the first case, the translation offered by Tzamalikos, adding the word "ancient" before the phrase, makes too much of the language. There are numerous precedents for calling deceased contemporaries by such terms as those used here. Gregory of Nyssa, for example, eulogizes his brother as: "Basil, mighty among the saints (ὁ πολὺς ἐν ἁγίοις Βασίλειος),"[10] and reminds his younger sibling Peter of their saintly brother with the words: "Basil, our shared father and teacher (Βασίλειος, ὁ κοινὸς ἡμῶν πατὴρ καὶ διδάσκαλος)."[11] Gregory the Theologian, Basil's exact contemporary, also refers to him as "saint Basil."[12]

Interpreting the word ἀσυλλογίστως as a rebuke is also difficult since the author of *DT* proceeds to provide other instances of "divine ignorance" in the Scriptures that support Basil's thesis.[13] The word ἀσυλλογίστως is patient of a translation that coheres better with this immediate context. The exegetical argument advanced by Basil, focusing as it does on the precise grammatical force of the dominical saying, is argumentation of a different kind than the one that immediately precedes it. Before introducing Basil's reading, the author of *DT* argues for the Son's knowledge of the last day from two premises:

---

7. Panayiotis Tzamalikos, "Appendix 2: Pseudo-Didymus' *De Trinitate* is Cassian's Work," in *A Newly Discovered Greek Father: Cassian the Sabaite Eclipsed by John Cassian of Marseilles* (Leiden: Brill, 2012), 460.

8. Tzamalikos, *Newly Discovered Greek Father*, 458. This point plays an important part in Tzamalikos' overall argument insofar as it suggests that the author of *DT* was relatively independent of his Christian sources.

9. Ibid., 458 and 460.

10. *Vit. Macr.* 14.1-2 (SC 178:188).

11. *Hom. op.* Prologue (PG 44:125B).

12. *Ep.* 115.3 (Gallay, 10).

13. *DT* 3.22 (921AC).

that the Son knows the Father and that it is greater to know the Father than what belongs to the Father. The greater guarantees the lesser; the Son, knowing the Father, must also know the last day.[14] Given the fact that this argument (a syllogistic one) is proposed immediately before Basil's grammatical argument, the more likely interpretation of the word ἀσυλλογίστως is that its author means to contrast his syllogistic argument with Basil's non-syllogistic one. Mingarelli is therefore not taking too great a liberty with the word when he renders it "simply (simpliciter)."[15]

The author of DT regards Basil's interpretation to have established that the Son cannot be ignorant of the last day, since the Father is not ignorant of it. On this basis, he summarizes Basil's argument by quoting the Gospel and supplementing it with the Savior's imagined interpretation of his own words:

> "If the Father does not know, neither does the Son know (εἰ μὴ ὁ Πατὴρ οἶδεν, οὐδὲ ὁ Υἱὸς οἶδεν)." From this it follows that since the Father knows, not only am I aware [of when it is] but I do not say [when it is] . . . since I do all things according to the Father's will, and it is not the Father's will for you to know this.[16]

According to the author of DT, Basil's reading trades on the versatility of the expression εἰ μή. Depending upon whether it is functioning in an indicative or a conditional construction, it may be rendered either "except" or "if not." By reversing the order of the two clauses, he transforms what his opponents regard as an indicative statement—the Son is ignorant—into a contrary-to-fact conditional: if the Father is ignorant (and how could this be the case?), then so is the Son. In his epistolary correspondence with Amphilochius, this is precisely what Basil had argued.[17]

---

14. DT 3.22 (920AB): "If it is one thing to know the Father, and something different to know the things that belong to the Father, it will prove (ἔσται) greater to know God the Father than to know the things that belong to him, which includes the last day as well, inasmuch as each one is himself greater than the things that belong to him."

15. DT 3.22 (919B). The translation is supported by Béranger, "Etudes," 42: "simplement."

16. DT 3.22 (920B).

17. Ep. 236.2.29-32 (Courtonne, 50): Τὸ δὲ Μάρκου, ἐπειδὴ φανερῶς δοκεῖ καὶ τὸν Υἱὸν ἀπομερίζειν τῆς γνώσεως, οὕτω νοοῦμεν ὅτι οὐδεὶς οἶδεν, οὔτε οἱ ἄγγελοι τοῦ Θεοῦ, ἀλλ' οὐδ' ἂν ὁ Υἱὸς ἔγνω, εἰ μὴ ὁ Πατήρ· τουτέστιν ἡ αἰτία τοῦ εἰδέναι τὸν Υἱὸν παρὰ τοῦ Πατρός. "And the text from Mark, since it evidently seems to exclude the Son from the knowledge [of the last day], we understand in the following way. No one knows, not even the angels of God, but the Son would not know if the Father did not. That is, the cause of the Son's knowing is from the Father". Basil's reading inserts the particle ἄν into the apodosis of the conditional to ensure that it is read as such. On the whole, the author of DT does not appear to be rebuking Basil for claiming that the cause of the Son's knowledge is in the Father. Tzamalikos' conclusions that the author of DT

The above considerations suggest that the author of *DT* was appealing quite accurately to the authority of one whose reputation he held in high regard. The tone of the reference suggests that he considered Basil's reputation to carry a certain gravitas with the intended audience of the treatise. While the report of Basil's death certainly puts the treatise after September 378, the appeal to Basil as an authority need indicate a date no later than a few years after his death. The saint's reputation was secured as early as the Council of Constantinople (381).

Macedonians and the Intra-Novatian Schism

Other indications within the treatise confirm a date after 381. Leipoldt and Bardy note that the numerous references to Μακεδονιανοί probably demand a date after 381, since this name was popularized in the wake of Constantinople.[18] Their argument is borne out by the paucity of references to the party before the 380s. In the mid-370s Epiphanius, for instance, mentions the group in conjunction with the Pneumatomachians in his introductory letter to the heresies that he will address in his *Panarion*.[19] But curiously, this is the only reference to them in the entire work. In contrast, the usage made of the term by the author of *DT* is far more frequent, suggesting that he is thinking of an identifiable party.

Of similar import is a reference by the author of *DT* to the "inhumanity of Novatian and Sabbatius."[20] The latter reference is undoubtedly to the Sabbatius whose ordination was the prequel to the intra-Novatian schism in the surrounds of Constantinople. The ordination took place during the sixth year of the reign of Theodosius I.[21] The charge of inhumanity, in itself too vague to attach to a particular action on the part of Sabbatius, is elucidated by the context. The author of *DT* has in mind Sabbatius' rigorist attitude toward participation in the mysteries. Expounding St Peter's confession and Jesus' response in Matthew 16, our author argues that the keys of heaven are to be understood as a reference to baptism. This gift was given to the saint, not for the purpose

---

"took this statement entirely out of context" because he had no direct knowledge of Basil's letter (suggesting that he had probably only heard of Basil's argument from 6th-century contemporaries) is unwarranted (*Newly Discovered Greek Father*, 459).

18. See Leipoldt, *Didymus der Blinde*, 12–13, and Bardy, *Didyme l'Aveugle*, 30–31.

19. See *Pan.* Proem. 1.4.7 (GCS, n.F., 10:159). They do not make an appearance in *Pan.* 74 (GCS 37:313–332) where Epiphanius treats the Pneumatomachians.

20. See *DT* 1.30.19 (420A). The argument is suggested by Hönscheid, "Einleitung," in *De trinitate, Buch 1*, 5n9a.

21. Socrates, *Hist. eccl.* 5.21.1–6 (SC 505:212). On this evidence, Sabbatius could have been ordained presbyter by Marcian no earlier than 384. Socrates' testimony to these events is to be privileged over the reference to the Sabbatian sect by the Seventh Canon of Constantinople, since the latter was written in a later period. For this discussion, see Hermann Vogt, *Coetus Sanctorum: Der Kirchenbegriff des Novatian und die Geschichte seiner Sonderkirche* (Bonn: Hanstein, 1968), 248–249.

of excluding the lapsed, but with the goal of restoring the repentant. Hereby, our author reflects, the Son pre-emptively "cast down the inhumanity of Novatian and Sabbatius."[22] This charge comports well with the report of Socrates. Sabbatius aired his dissatisfaction with the state of those who partook unworthily of the sacraments.[23] Sabbatius is known to the author of DT for actions that post-date his ordination; this places the treatise no earlier than 384.[24]

In conclusion to this section, there are sufficient grounds to confirm the scholarly consensus regarding the *terminus post quem* of Mingarelli's DT. No scholar, dealing with the question of DT's authorship, has suggested a date earlier than the early to mid-380s.[25] The references to Basil's death, the Macedonian party, and the disruptive action of Sabbatius in the Novatian church suggest a date after 379, 381, and 384 respectively. We establish 384 as our working *terminus post quem*.

Toward a *Terminus ante Quem*

Establishing a *terminus ante quem* for the treatise proves a more challenging task. The limit is generally more difficult to establish in most cases, since conspicuous omissions provide at best an argument from silence. Furthermore, before Doutreleau's seminal article challenging Didymus' authorship of DT, studies in its reception history were concerned solely with gauging Didymus' influence on later authors.[26] None were interested in proving that DT was used by later authors as a means of verifying DT's accepted date. Since

---

22. DT 1.30.12–19 (417B–420A). In using the charge of "inhumanity" in this way, the author of DT is preceded by Eusebius of Caesarea, *Hist. eccl.* 6.43.2 (LCL 265:114–115). He reports that the rigorist party of Novatian is accused of harboring an opinion that is both "brother-hating" and "most inhuman". The Roman synod that meets on the question of apostasy during times of persecution acknowledges that "the medicines of repentance (τοῖς τῆς μετανοίας φαρμάκοις)," i.e. the sacraments, are intended precisely for the healing and restoration of the lapsed.

23. Socrates, *Hist. eccl.* 5.21.8 (SC 505:214).

24. Vogt takes the conjunction of the two names as an indication that the Sabbatians had already become a separate sect (*Coetus Sanctorum*, 247). He then argues that the reference to the sect indicates that the author of DT penned his work between 390 and 395. This is possible, though the wording of DT demands no more than the acknowledgment that Sabbatius was known to the author as one who held a rigorist attitude to the reception of the sacraments.

25. Even those with serious reservations about Didymean authorship posit a date in this window of time. See, *e.g.*, Béranger, "Etudes," 2n1, and Michael Ghattas, *Die Christologie Didymos' des Blinden von Alexandria in den Schriften von Tura: zur Entwicklung der Alexandrinischen Theologie des 4. Jahrhunderts* (Münster: Lit, 2002), 37.

26. See especially Jacques Liébaert, *La doctrine christologique de Saint Cyrille d'Alexandrie avant la querelle Nestorienne* (Lille: Facultés Catholiques, 1951).

some recent arguments have advanced the thesis that the author of *DT* made use of fifth- or sixth-century sources, the aim of this section is three-fold: 1) to consider the weight of the most serious arguments in favor of radically relocating the discussion about the date of *DT*,[27] 2) to consider two important studies that argue for *DT*'s use by subsequent authors, and 3) to propose a *terminus ante quem* on the basis of this examination.

An Anti-Nestorian Argument? [28]

Tzamalikos has recently argued that the author of *DT* has Nestorianism in his sights when, in Book 3, he treats the scriptural aporia: "God made (ἐποίησε) him both Lord and Christ, this Jesus whom you crucified" (Acts 2:36).[29] In relation to this Scripture, the author of *DT* implies that the orthodox have been accused of positing two distinct agents: an eternal Son and one who becomes incarnate. Mingarelli had considered the possibility that this argument stemmed from a Nestorian milieu, but found earlier precedents for it.[30] Tzamalikos thinks that the earlier scholar falsely associated these words with these earlier controversies. The mainstay of his argument is *DT*'s use of the expression "ineffable economy (ἄφραστος οἰκονομία)" in connection with this discussion. For Tzamalikos, the use of this phrase in such a context demands an author from the sixth century.[31] I suggest that his argument is unsupported for the following reasons: 1) the stated opponents of the treatise are Arians or Neo-Arians,[32] 2) all the elements of *DT*'s argument in relation to this text have precedents within the literature of the Neo-Arian controversy, 3) the passage does not seem to have figured very prominently in the Nestorian controversy, and 4) Tzamalikos' claims for the expression ἄφραστος οἰκονομία are falsifiable.

---

27. In the interests of keeping this chapter within a reasonable limit, I have had to select what I deem to be Tzamalikos' most serious argument in this regard.

28. *DT* 3.6 (841B–844C).

29. *Newly Discovered Greek Father*, 453–455.

30. See Mingarelli, PG 39:843D–844Dn30. The Apollinarian context raised by Mingarelli is a possibility, but a more remote one than the Neo-Arian context, since the author of *DT* seems to regard the Son's divinity rather than the reality of the (complete) Incarnation as the crucial point.

31. *Newly Discovered Greek Father*, 454.

32. Given this fact, it is surprising that this controversy is not even raised as a possibility in Tzamalikos' argument. For heresies against the Son, opponents mentioned in the treatise are predominantly opponents of a subordinationist kind: Eunomius (*DT* 2.3.30 (477C); 2.12 (673B)), Eunomians (2.11 (661B); 2.12 (688B); 2.15 (720A)), Arius (2.7.3.17 (576B); 2.8.1 (613C); 2.8.2 (620C); 2.10 (648B); 2.10 (649A); 2.12 (673B); 3.30 (949B)), Arians (2.10 (633A); 2.11 (661B); 2.12 (688B); 3.21 (904A)). *DT* includes reference to other kinds of heresies on the Son, but they are far rarer. See for example the single reference to Sabellius (3.23 (924C)).

In the passage under discussion, the author of *DT* begins by locating the critical point of disagreement between himself and his opponents. They often refer scriptural statements about Jesus to the eternal οὐσία of the Son when these statements clearly beg for an interpretation in light of the Son's Incarnation. It is by virtue of his being conformed to our humble estate that the Scriptures predicate exaltation, being pierced, or being born on a particular day of the Son. Some statements are predicated of the Son in relation to his divine οὐσία; others are predicated of him in relation to his οἰκονομία. A two-fold pattern of speech is thus appropriate.

> We talk in this way so as to indicate by a certain conception (ἐπινοίᾳ) his ineffable economy (ἄφραστον ... οἰκονομίαν) and to avoid the blasphemy that contends against his divinity; nor do we believe that the Son from the Father is one, and the one who became flesh and was crucified another, since divinity can never be divided from itself nor suffer change.[33]

In summary, this Scripture must be read in reference to the "economy (οἰκονομία)" so as to prevent casting aspersions on the Son's "divinity (θεότης)"; this does not imply that the eternally pre-existent Son is someone other than the one who becomes flesh and dies, since this would require either division or change in his divinity. The author of *DT* appeals to axioms shared by his opponents: the divine nature is simple—i.e. incapable of division into parts—and immutable. The burden of his exegesis of this text is to put a hedge around the divinity of the Son. Consonant with the concern detectible throughout *DT*, it is primarily subordinationist interpretations of the Son's οὐσία that are at issue.[34]

Secondly, this text enjoys a long history in the course of the Neo-Arian controversy.[35] Eunomius employs it as evidence that the Son's essence is

---

33. *DT* 3.6 (844AB).

34. With Béranger, "Etudes," 4–5: "With respect to the Son, the first concern [of the author of *DT*] is to demonstrate that He is equal to the Father.... [A]mong the adversaries that our polemicist intends to refute ... are, above all, the Arians, who held the Word to be a lesser and subordinate deity. (En ce qui concerne le Fils, le premier souci de [l'auteur du *De Trinitate*] est de montrer qu'Il est égal au Père.... [P]armi les adversaires que notre polémiste se propose de confondre ... se trouvent en premier lieu les Ariens, qui tenaient le Verbe pour un dieu inférieur et subordonné.)"

35. Just prior to Eunomius' rise to prominence, Athanasius had noted that the Arians were deceived about the "mind (διάνοια)" of this text when they insisted on claiming that it revealed the Son's creaturely status (*C. Ar.* I.53.1-2 (*Athanasius Werke* I/1:163)). In his fuller discussion of the text (*C. Ar.* II.11-12 (Ibid., 187–189)), Athanasius distinguishes between "made" and "begotten." The latter is used of the Son's οὐσία, the former of his οἰκονομία insofar as he was "made man on our account" (*C. Ar.* II.11.1 (Ibid.,

"something made (ποίημα)."³⁶ Basil notes that his opponent has made an unwarranted move in substantivizing the verb in the Acts passage as a summary description of the Son's essence.³⁷ The intent of the passage is to describe the economy, not to offer an account of the pre-eternal substance of the Word. Basil then distinguishes between two modes of description in Scripture: the one pertaining to the οἰκονομία, the other pertaining to θεολογία.³⁸ This text, he argues, functions in the former mode, and he defends the claim by pointing out that the object of the verb ἐποίησε is the phrase "this Jesus." Jesus is an acquired name for the Son.

Gregory Nyssen informs us that the Eunomian response to Basil focuses a great deal of energy on dismantling Basil's distinction between οἰκονομία and θεολογία. Eunomius accuses him of positing two Christs or two Lords: one who does not change—the eternal Son—and another who suffers and dies.³⁹ According to Gregory's quotation,⁴⁰ the Cyzican sought to complicate Basil's solution to the aporia by querying whether the same subject ("this Jesus") was the one who "took the form of a slave" (Phil 2:6–7), and in parallel fashion, whether it was "the Word of God" who was made "Lord." Either response is problematic. If his opponent says "yes" then Eunomius can mock him for speaking nonsensically: a human became a human; God became God. If "no" then Eunomius can suggest that Basil envisions a situation in which there are two separate subjects: the eternal Son and the Son who becomes incarnate and dies.

The key moves in our author's argument are anticipated by the above. With Basil, our author distinguishes between two kinds of statements: those relating to the Son's οὐσία and his οἰκονομία.⁴¹ He then takes this text as an example of the latter, connecting the verb ἐποίησε with "the one who is crucified." With Gregory of Nyssa, our author is aware of the need to defend himself from the charge of positing two subjects, and does so by appealing to divine simplicity and immutability. The Son becomes flesh without becoming a different Son; he becomes flesh "without changing (ἀτρέπτως)."⁴²

---

187)). Most of these moves are made by the author of DT. Athanasius, however, does not respond to a charge about positing two sons.

36. *Apol.* 26.10–15 (Vaggione, *Extant Works*, 68–71).

37. *C. Eun.* 2.2 (FC 122:132–133).

38. *C. Eun.* 2.3 (FC 122:133–134).

39. For a reconstruction of Eunomius' reply to Basil in *Apol. apol.* 3.4, see Richard Paul Vaggione, *Eunomius: The Extant Works* (1987; reprint, Oxford: Clarendon Press, 2002), 119: "Basil preaches two Christs, the one divine and the other human."

40. *C. Eun.* 3.3.15–25 (*GNO* 2:112–116).

41. *DT* 3.6 (841BC). Incidentally, the author uses the same distinction that Athanasius does (between οὐσία and οἰκονομία) rather than Basil's precise terminology; however, the import is much the same.

42. For further comparison see the even more striking resemblance in argument between *DT* and *Adv. Eun.* 5 (PG 29:704C–705A) on this text. The author of the latter ar-

Thirdly, in contrast, the passage does not seem to have featured as prominently in the Nestorian controversy. Cyril treats the text only in the context of his early dogmatic writings on the Trinity, writings that pre-date his polemics against Nestorius.[43] The text is not extant in the Nestorian fragments,[44] although Nestorius cites earlier portions of St Peter's speech as proof-texts against Apollinaris and Arius, with whom he is keen to associate the views of those who advocate the use of the Marian epithet *Theotokos*.[45]

Leontius of Byzantium, a more proximate source for Tzamalikos' proposed author[46] and one who weighs in on the controversy to a significant extent, never treats the passage as a disputed text.[47] Leontius of Jerusalem, on the other hand, does acknowledge a Nestorian argument in relation to Acts 2:36. His *Against the Nestorians* is variously dated either to the same period as Tzamalikos' proposed date for *DT* or to the early part of the seventh century.[48] Leontius' argument is worth following in this regard. Though his opponents are irked with his insistence on calling Christ "God" *tout court*, they cede the point in order to raise a new question. What of Jesus? "If he too is God," they argue, "then it is evident that Christ is not always God, for this Jesus—whom you call God—God *made* both Lord and Christ." The argument proceeds in this fashion, with Leontius' opponents multiplying the subjects, until they can ac-

---

gues that the phrase is to be understood to refer to the Incarnation, adduces the same Lukan text about the day of the Lord's birth, and argues that the two-foldness of orthodox speech about such matters is a division in conception alone (κατ' ἐπίνοιαν). In *DSS* 230, Didymus the Blind employs a similar mode of argument with respect to Christ's reception of the Holy Spirit: "We ought to take these statements in a spirit of piety.... It is not the case that "Lord" is one thing and "Man" another. Rather, we must reason about one and the same subject as if he were one thing according to the nature of God and another thing according to the nature of man. Furthermore, we must do this because God the Word, the only-begotten Son of God, admits of neither alternation nor increase, since he is the fullness of good things" (DelCogliano, Radde-Gallwitz, and Ayres, *Works on the Spirit*, 214).

43. Cyril, *Thes.* 21 (PG 75:364A–368C) and *Dial. Trin.* 4 (PG 75:909C) and 6 (PG 75:1021CD).

44. See Friedrich Loofs, "Verzeichnis der von Nestorius angeführten Bibelstellen," in *Nestoriana: die Fragmente des Nestorius* (Halle: Niemeyer, 1905), 392–394.

45. Nestorius, *Ser.* 10 (Loofs, 268–269).

46. Tzamalikos asserts a personal friendship between the two (*Newly Discovered Greek Father*, 5).

47. These works are gathered together in Brian Daley, "Leontius of Byzantium: A Critical Edition of His Works, with Prolegomena," (PhD diss., Oxford, 1978), 1–225.

48. See Patrick Gray, "Introduction," in *Leontius of Jerusalem: Against the Monophysites: Testimonies of the Saints and Aporiae* (Oxford: Oxford University Press, 2006), 1–43, and Dirk Krausmüller, "Leontius of Jerusalem, a Theologian of the 7th Century," *JTS* 52 (2001): 637–657.

cuse him of constructing a *hypostasis* for the Savior composed of three humans and two gods.[49]

Leontius' response is telling: John the Theologian informs us that the Holy Spirit confesses only one Jesus—he who came in the flesh (1 John 4:2). And in his Gospel, the same confesses of this same one that the Word became flesh (John 1:14). Given that both Jesus and the Word become flesh, "it is evident that [John] acknowledges Jesus to be the same as Christ, and Christ the same as the Word."[50] What of the critical verb: God *made* (ἐποίησε) Jesus to be Christ? Leontius replies that his opponents will be put to the test if they insist on arguing, on the basis of this word alone, that Jesus cannot always be Christ. When God said that he would make (ποιῆσαι) man in his image, will we understand him to be saying that there was first a man, and then that he only afterward *became* the image of God?[51] Leontius' response, in defending the singular subject of the Incarnate Logos, reveals that he is not primarily concerned, as is the author of *DT*, with securing the ontological equality of the Word with the Father. On this, Leontius and his opponents agree. He is concerned rather with upholding the integrity of the Incarnate Savior's person. *DT*'s approach to the aporia is fundamentally different in orientation.

Finally Tzamalikos' argument about a late date for the phrase "ineffable economy" cannot be sustained. He bases his argument on two premises: 1) that the phrase "ineffable economy" is a later by-product of the phrase "ineffable union", and 2) that the phrase "ineffable union" is employed mainly by authors from the fifth century forward. He concludes: "Quite simply, the idiom "ineffable oikonomia" bespeaks an author later than [the] fifth century. There is no way to associate this author with Didymus' era."[52] However, the phrase does not appear to achieve the idiomatic status that Tzamalikos claims for it.[53] What is more, it is difficult to explain why Cyril, Didymus' younger contemporary, uses the purportedly later phrase in a work that dates to the early fifth century and is considered among his earliest: the *Commentary on the Twelve Prophets*.[54]

In conclusion, there is no need to hypothesize the Nestorian controversy as the context for our author's remarks about two separate agents: the eternal Son and the Incarnate. The elements of his treatment of the aporia of Acts 2:36

---

49. Leontius of Jerusalem, *C. Nest.* 5.5 (PG 86:1729BC). The text is not quoted in full as a disputed *locus*, but its language is clearly used in the argument.
50. *C. Nest.* 5.5 (PG 86:1729CD).
51. *C. Nest.* 5.5 (PG 86:1732AB).
52. Tzamalikos, *Newly Discovered Greek Father*, 454.
53. A *TLG* search reveals that, apart from the author of *DT*, no other author uses the phrase more than once until the sixth century (two uses by Basil of Seleucia).
54. Cyril, *In Hab.* 2 (Pusey, 118). For the dating issues see Alexander Kerrigan, *St Cyril of Alexandria: Interpreter of the Old Testament* (Rome: Pontifical Biblical Institute, 1952), 12–15. The commentary was certainly complete before 425.

are well within the bounds of the discussion as it stands in the literature produced by the Eunomian controversy. These considerations advise against radically re-dating of the treatise on the basis of this text.

Chalcedonian and Proclian Allusions? [55]

István Perczel proffers two arguments bearing on the date of *DT*: 1) that the author of *DT* alludes to the Chalcedonian Definition and 2) Proclus' *Theology of Plato* and *Elements of Theology*.[56] On the strength of these allusions, Perczel posits a date in the second half of the fifth century as the *terminus post quem*. From here, he hypothesizes that the author of *DT* is responsible for at least part of the Pseudo-Dionysian corpus.[57]

There is an apostrophe in Book 2 of *DT* that consists of an address to the angels. In the midst of it, the author speaks first to Gabriel as general of the heavenly armies and then to Michael as chosen messenger of "the mystery of the ineffable economy." As each of these angels was given a unique gift, so too each member of the angelic hosts is uniquely gifted. The author of *DT* adds to the above observation that there are some gifts given only to the human race. He then justifies the latter claim:

> For God the Word did not become (ἐγένετο) an angel because of the angels who sinned, but because of men in sin became a man without changing, without confusion, sinlessly, ineffably (ἀτρέπτως, ἀσυγχύτως, ἀναμαρτήτως, ἀφράστως), as he knew and willed, from the Virgin both according to her flesh and that of us all, while he remained what he was and is and will be, one and the same.[58]

These christological affirmations seem to come out of nowhere. In the immediate context, the author of *DT* is not engaging explicitly in any polemics,

---

55. István Perczel, "The Pseudo-Didymian *De trinitate* and Pseudo-Dionysius the Areopagite: A Preliminary Study," *Studia Patristica* 58 (2013): 83–108.

56. Perczel, "Pseudo-Didymian *De trinitate*," 89–95.

57. The longer enumeration of arguments in favor of a Pseudo-Dionysian authorship (see Perczel, 89) is largely undefended in the article (by design), awaiting further development. Here I treat only two of Perczel's three main arguments, for the simple reason that only these two bear on a radical relocation of *DT*'s traditional dating. The third argument—suggesting that *DT* is the missing Pseudo-Dionysian *Outlines of Theology* (pp. 95-108)—leans heavily upon these earlier two. For example, Perczel argues that *DT*'s reference to "Macedonians" is a Pseudo-Dionysian cipher for a much later polemical target. The more obvious referent (the fourth-century group rejecting the consubstantial divinity of the Holy Spirit) is rejected as an interpretive possibility on the basis that it is "unbelievable once one realises that the *De trinitate* could not have been written before the second half of the fifth century" (p. 99). The third argument requires the first two.

58. *DT* 2.7.8.9 (589AB).

and so the four adverbial qualifiers of the Word's "becoming" have a kind of formulaic feel. Perczel believes that the passage is a carefully modified recapitulation of the Chalcedonian Definition. For Perczel, we can conclude from a careful comparison of this text with the Definition that: "1. the author of the *De trinitate* wrote after Chalcedon; 2. as to his Christology, he was an Antiochian dyophysite; 3. he was a Christian Platonist who believed in the preexistence of Christ's human nature/soul."[59]

Perczel offers little in support of the first conclusion, beyond stating that it would be "rather impossible" for the author to be "a precursor of Chalcedon." The weight of his argument rests on the second claim. Here Perczel notes that the author of *DT* repeats several elements of the Definition: namely, four adverbs "qualifying the union" (the first two of which are shared), the phrase "one and the same," and the teaching that the Virgin birth renders the Word's humanity like our own. He goes beyond these similarities, however, in observing that where the author of *DT* alters the Definition or paraphrases it, he takes care to eliminate the Alexandrian concessions. For instance, the author retains the two adverbs meant to exclude a miaphysite interpretation of the Definition (ἀσυγχύτως and ἀτρέπτως) while replacing those meant to exclude "an Antiochian interpretation of the union" (ἀδιαιρέτως and ἀχωρίστως). He also intentionally "omits the Alexandrian term Theotokos."[60] For Perczel, the author hereby tips his hand against Cyril and in favor of the dyophysite position.

This argument has several problems. In the first place, the adverbs as they are used by the author of *DT* do not strictly "qualify the union" of the human and the divine in the Savior, as they do in the Definition. The grammatical subject of the whole passage is God the Word who, though becoming human, nevertheless remains what he was before this becoming (namely, God). The "becoming" does not signal a loss of divinity, and the author marshalls these adverbs in defense of this point. The same point tells, incidentally, against Perczel's third argument as well. If the author were making a case for the preexistence of Christ's human soul, this would be a very awkward way of doing so. The author's point here is simply that the Word was, is, and will be God (and not that he was Word-and-man before the Incarnation). His divinity is not made less so in his becoming human.

Secondly, if the author of *DT* is a studied anti-Cyrillian, then it is difficult to explain why he adopts the use of the word "Theotokos" elsewhere in the treatise.[61] If he is a dyophysite, then it is strange indeed to find him never

---

59. Perczel, 92.
60. The argument is briefly advanced. See Ibid., 91–92.
61. See, for example, *DT* 1.31.2 (421B); 2.4.6 (481C); 3.6 (848C). In each of these instances, the author approves of the epithet. Perczel makes much of the point that this Chalcedonian language is dropped here because the author is anti-Cyrillian (see also p. 108).

speaking of two natures in Christ. His language—as was noted above in the anti-Eunomian text—is much less developed than that of the controversialists after Chalcedon. The two notions expressed by the adverbs common to the Chalcedonian Definition—that the divine nature suffered neither change nor confusion when the Word became human—are attested in christological discussions in the fourth century.[62] These considerations warn against a facile association of *DT* with the text of Chalcedon.

As it stands, our text suggests not a primary concern with the manner of the union of the two natures in Christ. These two natures are nowhere acknowledged as such. Rather, the author of *DT* continues to attest to his primarily anti-subordinationist concern throughout the treatise. In all the activities of the Word, including the economy of his Incarnation, he acts in no way to the detriment of his divinity. The accent is placed differently in the Definition of Chalcedon, and the overlapping material identified by Perczel is too tenuous to suggest that the author of *DT* was relying on it.

Perczel also argues that the author of *DT* alludes to Proclus; the argument, if credible, would place the writing of *DT* in the latter half of the fifth century.[63] In two passages of *DT*, the author argues that scriptural language used of the Spirit's relation to the Father ought to be understood as intimating a common nature between the Holy Spirit and the Father. The Holy Spirit proceeds atemporally and consubstantially from the Father; the same holds for the Father's begetting of the Son.[64] In the first of these passages, it is argued that the Spirit and the Son "went forth (προῆλθον)" from the Father not by way of his creative act, but in such a manner that they may be said to "be brought back (ἀνάγονται) to the same one." In both passages the author of *DT* asserts that things begotten or proceeding are like and equal to the things that beget them or cause them to proceed.

Perczel finds some intriguing parallels with the Proclian literature. On the one hand, Proclus asserts that in the divine orders of being there exist certain

---

62. Gregory of Nyssa, in *Adv. Apollinar.* 21 (*GNO* 3:160), sustains the notion that though the Word became man, he did not become so "because of the alteration of his substance. . . . [I]n this manner he humbled himself, by becoming human without changing (ἀτρέπτως)." For the notion that the divine is not confused with the human in the Incarnate Word, see Epiphanius, *Pan.* 78.24 (GCS 37: 475). Citing an earlier letter he himself wrote, he enjoins his audience to think of Christ not as "two, but as one, united not into a confusion (συγχύσιν), nor into non-existence, but into a great economy of grace." We note here the same lack of conceptual and linguistic precision that we find in the *DT*.

63. Perczel, 92. Perczel refers to "citations of and allusions to Proclus." However, his argument nowhere identifies a citation, at least in the usual sense of the term. There is neither direct quotation, nor identification of a source, nor even an acknowledgment that a source is being used. The verbal parallels, such as they are, at most indicate a possible allusion.

64. *DT* 2.2.21-22 (460AB) and 3.38 (976AB).

higher causes—or henadic gods—that proceed or emanate from the One. This manner of derivation occurs according to their likeness with the One, and it is on the basis of this likeness that these higher causes may also be said to return to the One and to be the principle of the return of their products to the One. Here we find two thoughts that have some kind of similarity with what is written by the author of DT: 1) procession implies return and 2) procession (or emanation) implies a certain kind of likeness to that from which the procession occurs.

The similarity of the ideas is stronger than the verbal parallels that Perczel identifies.[65] And yet, on my reading of DT, the author is making two claims that would be difficult to draw from the above summary. 1) The language used of the Son and the Holy Spirit—namely, generation and procession—has a limited analogy among creaturely referents. We do not ordinarily use this kind of language to speak of a mode of derivation between two substances of different essences. A carpenter does not "beget" a table. On the other hand, fathers beget sons while both share the same essence. Likewise when we say that a river proceeds from its source, we are not claiming an ontological difference between the two. The source consists of water, just as the river does. Any priority between the two is conceptual rather than ontological, although such priority cannot be absolutized, since "source" is a correlative word, demanding as its correlative the "river" whose source it is. The same is true of begetting. DT's argument then is that there is a kind of limited analogy here between the properly creaturely and the properly divine. Among the divine *hypostaseis*, the use of such language as procession and begetting implies *consubstantiality* rather than mere *likeness* (Proclus' argument).

2) The conceptualities surrounding the word "return" are not the same. When the author of DT uses this kind of language to speak of the "processions" of the Son and the Holy Spirit, he is indicating that the language of "procession" ought to be understood advisedly, as suggesting the lack of any spatial or ontological separation involved in the procession of the divine *hypostaseis*.[66] But in Proclus, the higher causes and their products are ontologically and (at least in the case of the products) morally separate from their Cause, reliant upon their likeness to the One in order to attain to the Goodness that subsists perfectly in the One. This allusion would be an embarrassment to DT's argu-

---

65. For example, Perczel (p. 94) claims a direct appropriation of the Proclian phrase: μάλιστα δὲ ἐν τοῖς θείοις διακόσμοις in the author of DT's phrases: μάλιστα δὲ διαφερόντως ἡ ἀπὸ τοῦ ἑνὸς πατρὸς καθ' ἕνωσιν τῆς ἑαυτοῦ θεότητος γέννησις καὶ ἐκπόρευσις and καὶ διαφερόντως ὁμοουσίως ἐγένετο ἡ ἀπὸ τοῦ θεοῦ γέννησις τοῦ υἱοῦ καὶ ἐκπόρευσις τοῦ πνεύματος αὐτοῦ. Is the lone word μάλιστα (and its synonym διαφερόντως in the second quotation) meant to signal the allusion?

66. For precedents of this second argument, see DSS 111. I develop both of these ideas in chapter 2.

ment. The "return" envisioned by Proclus is removed *toto caelo* from that envisioned by the author of *DT*.

Given the lack of any direct citation, of any persuasive verbal parallel, and the complicated character of the purported allusion, we conclude that the allusion is not supported by a comparison of the texts. To his credit, Perczel recognizes that the author of *DT* has altered Proclus in a Nicene direction. But surely the simpler explanation of *DT*'s argument is preferable to the notion that he is appealing to Proclus' notion of the henadic gods. For his argument on the Spirit's procession, the pro-Nicene author of *DT* capitalizes on a point that has been well- and frequently-made with respect to the Son. First of all, procession, like begetting, implies consubstantiality on the basis of the common usage of these terms when used of sensible referents. Secondly, *divine* procession, like *divine* begetting, implies the negation of certain creaturely notions associated with these terms: such as spatial or temporal separation. Neither of these points is made in the Proclian passages cited by Perczel. Both are commonly made in the Trinitarian literature of the fourth century.

The Literary Reception of De Trinitate

Although there has not been anything like a comprehensive study of *DT*'s reception, nevertheless, the important work done on it provides necessary support to the idea that *DT* was written no later than the earliest quarter of the fifth century. In this section, I will investigate the claims of earlier scholars regarding the literary relationship between *DT* and the works of Cyril.[67]

Jacques Liébaert's study on the early Christology of Cyril (before 428) investigates Cyril's sources for the *Thesaurus*, the *Seven Dialogues on the Trinity*, and the *Commentary on the Gospel of John*. Although Liébaert finds numerous close resemblances between Cyril's work and *DT*, his conclusions about Cyril's use of *DT* are largely negative. Apart from chapter 8 in the *Thesaurus*, which uses terms that are fairly common in *DT* and that Cyril does not use elsewhere in the work, there are few reasons to suspect that Cyril used *DT* as a source in his early writings.[68] Oriented as his study is toward christological themes, Liébaert suggests that Cyril may have made use of *DT* in the later chapters of the *Thesaurus* (on the Holy Spirit).[69]

Robert Grant's study on the use of *DT* as a source in Cyril is more promising. In *DT* 2, our author investigates whether there are secular antecedents for the doctrine of the Word and the Spirit's consubstantiality with the Father.

---

67. The two studies that examine *DT*'s influence on Latin authors uncover little. These are by Berthold Altaner, "Augustinus und Didymus der Blinde: eine quellenkritische Untersuchung," *VC* 5 (1951): 116–120 and Theodor Schermann, "Didymus der Blinde: de Trinitate ll. III und de Spiritu sancto," in *Die griechischen Quellen des hl. Ambrosius in ll. III de Spir. s.* (Munich: Lentner, 1902), 70–87.

68. Liébaert, *La doctrine christologique*, 60–61.

69. Ibid., 63.

Possibly availing himself of a philosophical anthology of sorts,[70] our theologian locates arguments for the divinity of the Holy Spirit and his relationship to God (the Father). The chapter appears to have attracted Cyril's attention in the course of preparing his monumental work *Against Julian*.[71] The parallels are so close as to suggest that Cyril in some cases borrowed not only *DT*'s quotations but also its transitional remarks. The passage in *Against Julian* to which Grant refers indeed contains not only the same quotations, but also the same (or similar) introductory formulae, and similar exposition.[72] Cyril announces that he is to begin investigating the philosophers' teachings on the Holy Spirit, before launching into a section with several similarities to *DT*. (See Table 1.)

Two points are worth making in regard to these parallels. First, in parallel 3, we are fortunate to have testimony to the same Hermetic passage cited independently by John Malalas. Noting that Cyril had made use of this text, Malalas proceeds to cite it with two crucial differences: 1) he does not break the citation as our author and Cyril do, but proceeds as if it is a continuous quotation and 2) cites it at greater length, revealing that he has independent knowledge of the text.[73] By way of contrast, Cyril ends the quotation exactly where our author does, and breaks it exactly where he does, moving between the two sections of the quotation with a formula of identical length, structure (conjunction-prepositional phrase-verb), and nearly-identical meaning. These considerations, in conjunction with the other clustered parallels, demonstrate that one author was quoting the other.

Second, variants between the two works suggest that one is not reduced to slavishly copying the other's citations. In parallel 2, Cyril's citation reveals more precisely where the Hermetic quotation can be found. His quotation of the text is different enough from *DT*'s to suggest that he has access to a different manuscript tradition. This argues against the hypothesis that Cyril and the author of *DT* are simply employing the same anthology in their research. If this were the case, it would be difficult to understand why their quotations would differ as they do. Given that Cyril's quotations and citations are on the whole more precise than those in *DT* and that an author would more likely correct his source toward rather than against greater precision, it is most likely that Cyril is using *DT*. Grant argues that Cyril used sources like *DT* to get to others. The use of *DT* by Cyril places *DT* no later than 429.[74]

---

70. Bardy, *Didyme l'Aveugle*, 223.

71. Robert Grant, "Greek Literature in the Treatise *De Trinitate* and Cyril *Contra Julianum*," *JTS*, n.s., 15 (1964): 271–275.

72. *C. Jul.* 1.47–50 (SC 322:200–206). Cf. *DT* 2.27 (753A–761B).

73. *Chron.* 2.4 (Thurn, 19–20).

74. On the dating of *Against Julian*, see Paul Buguière and Pierre Évieux, "Introduction," in *Cyrille d'Alexandrie: Contre Julien*, vol. 1, SC 322 (Paris: Cerf, 1985), 10–15. The

Table 1: *De Trinitate* and Cyril

De Trinitate 2.27	*Contra Julianum* 1.47-50
1) The author opens the chapter by exhorting his audience to pay attention to "those among the Greeks who received a perception of the equality of the Son, the Word, and the Spirit with God the Father." He will attend to two kinds of texts: those that assert this equality and the Spirit's procession. (733A)	1) Having expounded the philosophers' opinions on the Only-begotten Word of God, Cyril considers it necessary to set forth "also the things said by them concerning the Holy Spirit." (1.47)
2) The author cites a passage from the *three books* of Hermes Tresmegistus to Asclepius, prefacing the quotation: ἐρομένου τινὸς τὸν ἀγαθὸν δαίμονα, περὶ τοῦ τρισαγίου Πνεύματος ἔχρησεν οὕτως· (756B)[75]	2) Cyril cites the same passage from the *third book* of Hermes Tresmegistus to Asclepius, prefacing the quotation: ὡς ἐρομένου τινὸς περὶ τοῦ θείου Πνεύματος, φησὶν οὕτως· (1.49)
3) He cites two more Hermetic passages, moving between them with the phrase: Καὶ μεταξὺ ἄλλων ἐπάγει· (757B–760A)[76]	3) Cyril cites the same two passages, moving between them with the phrase: Καὶ μεθ' ἕτερά φησι· (1.48)
4) The first of the citations is expounded by identifying the Father, Son, and Holy Spirit. The second citation is taken as evidence that all things are under this "indivisible power, the one creating source of all things." (760AB)	4) The first citation is expounded by identifying the Son and the Spirit (the Father is left implicit in the "light from light" language). The second citation is taken to assert that nothing is outside the divine superiority or "power ... and that all things are ordered by it and because of it." (1.49)
5) The author of *DT* cites Porphyry, "expounding on an opinion of Plato's" (Πλάτωνος ἐκτιθέμενος δόξαν). (760B)[77]	5) Cyril cites the same text of Porphyry, noting that he is "expounding on an opinion of Plato's" (Πλάτωνος ἐκτιθέμενος δόξαν). (1.47)

date of the treatise's publication falls between 434–437 or 439–441. The research for it was completed before 429, when Cyril became embroiled in the Nestorian controversy.

75. The two passages are of identical length. The only differences between the citations are the author of *DT*'s μοι, as compared to Cyril's με, and *DT*'s τοιοῦτος ἔρως κατεῖχεν, as compared with Cyril's νῦν ἔρως τοιοῦτος κατεῖχεν.

76. The first passage has one variant between the two texts: *DT* has αὐτῷ, whereas Cyril has ἑαυτῷ. The second passage is identical.

77. *DT*'s text has an additional γάρ and an ἔφη Πλάτων, whereas Cyril's text has neither. Cyril's other citation of this text in *Against Julian* restores the γάρ and the ἔφη Πλάτων (*C. Jul.* 8 (PG 76:916B)). The difference here is probably due to Cyril's judgment

The Date of *Didymus'* On the Trinity

The window of time above, established without recourse to Didymus, allows comparison with the possible time-frame in which Didymus would have compiled his own *On the Trinity*. The sole reference of import to the writing of the treatise by Didymus appears in Socrates Scholasticus' *Ecclesiastical History*. Socrates informs us that, in addition to various other works, Didymus "dictated . . . three books *On the Trinity* (ὑπαγορεῦσαι . . . τὰ περὶ Τριάδος τρία βιβλία)."[78] Socrates does not permit us to reach any conclusions about chronology. In 392, however, Jerome was busy writing his *On Illustrious Men*: a list of works written by the important figures of the age. Didymus makes an appearance therein, but *On the Trinity* is absent.[79] Jerome had visited Didymus in 386, staying with him for just under a month.

Although it is an argument from silence, it is hard to imagine that Jerome would have been uninformed of a three-volume work *On the Trinity* if Didymus had written it before then. As far as we can hypothesize, Didymus had not yet completed his *On the Trinity* by Jerome's visit. Perhaps the work was still being composed in the 390s, during or after Jerome's completion of *On Illustrious Men*. We conclude this section treating the date of the treatise *DT* only with the recognition that Didymus' *On the Trinity* was written at some point during the first fifteen years of the window that we have established by evidence internal to the treatise (384-398) and that there are reasons to favor the view that Didymus wrote the work in the early 390s.

Occasion

DT is a polemical treatise. The author is concerned, above all, with positing arguments that defend the consubstantiality of the Trinitarian *hypostaseis*. Those who worship the Son and the Holy Spirit are not worshipping "created gods." These *hypostaseis* are not inferior to the Father in essence. Our author advances positions that are, for the most part, consistent with those of other theologians sympathetic to the Nicene and Constantinopolitan confessions.

However, there are two instances in the treatise that tell against locating the concerns of the author purely in relation to the arguments of the heterodox. Although the author of *DT* has eyes mainly for such opponents, occasionally we find him glancing backward over his shoulder, as if he is persuading a secondary audience. Two passages that illustrate this feature of the treatise deserve treatment, since they reveal several important things about the author's circumstances.

---

that, having just prefaced the phrase with the line: "setting forth Plato's opinion," saying Plato's name again just five words later would sound redundant (as the text of *DT* sounds).

78. *Hist. eccl.* 4.25.6 (SC 505:104–106).
79. *Vir. ill.* 109 (TU 14:50).

"Toil and Danger"

There are two prayers of significant length in Book 2: the Prayer to the Angels (earlier mentioned) and the Prayer to the Trinity. Prior to the first prayer the author distinguishes between the way angels and the Holy Spirit act in delivering or interpreting the divine oracles. Macedonian arguments against the Spirit's divinity highlighted similarities between angels and the Holy Spirit. So the author of *DT* points out that the angels are dependent upon the Trinity for knowing what messages they are to deliver, while the Holy Spirit inspires and interprets divinely.[80] For the author, there are two unequal, but significant dangers to be avoided in this discussion: 1) suggesting that the Holy Spirit is an angel by nature or 2) belittling the angelic order so that one may elevate the Holy Spirit in light of the contrast. But the author of *DT* is sure that he has navigated the straits; the faith he confesses with the orthodox has erred in neither direction.

There follows a lengthy apostrophe in which he appeals to the angels Michael and Gabriel to vindicate him on this point.[81] In the midst of it, he says:

> For you know—let all things be said with God's help—that I have acted in accord with you and with those from our nature who have become saints and make intercession,[82] so that no one as yet, even until the present day, has obtained leave to bring anything like a charge against me and to convict me with slander in regard to you, who are our advocates, who possess the honors befitting your stature from all. Nor has anyone called me by name into a dispute and judgment on this matter, even though there can be found those who bring false accusations.

After a space, he concludes the thought:

> For I consider every toil (πόνον) and danger (κίνδυνον) that I took on behalf of the one who created and saved us, if it was necessary, as the greatest and eternal gain for myself and my children (τῶν ἐκ ἐμοῦ) and our friends (τῶν σὺν ἡμῖν), and [I consider] that I judged and acted humanely on account of him who is Father, Son, and Holy Spirit.

---

80. *DT* 2.7.8.1–7 (581B–588B).
81. *DT* 2.7.8.8–13 (588B–593A).
82. Cf. Seiler, *De trinitate, Buch 2*, 239. She provides a helpful gloss of the phrase. The prayer acknowledges the company of the saints "who have come from our nature (namely, human) and (after their bodily death) make intercession for us" (die aus unsrer (d.h. der menschlichen) Natur gekommen sind und (nach ihrem leiblichen Tod) für uns Mittlerdienste tun).

He concludes by asking those who intercede for the race of men to beseech the Trinity on his behalf that he would "keep his opinion in this matter immoveable,"[83] so that all might benefit from his orthodox confession.

This apostrophe affords us several suggestive pieces of information. 1) The author of *DT* composes the treatise in response to heretical doctrines on the Trinity, but also as a means of vindicating himself from "false accusations" which have yet to reach the pitch of a formal indictment. 2) These accusations are not directed against his doctrine of angels. 3) The author is insistent that he has judged rightly on the matter of the Trinity, and asks that his faith in the same be kept immoveable. 4) He has undertaken to respond to the charges laid against him in the company of others, whom he calls "my children (οἱ ἐκ ἐμοῦ)" and "our/my companions (οἱ σὺν ἡμῖν/ἐμοί)." The possible referents of this language will be examined in due course, but it is difficult at this juncture to avoid the conclusion that the author of *DT* is responding to false allegations in relation to his doctrine of the Trinity, for which he and his circle have suffered toil and danger. The author of *DT* also appears to conceive of his role in combating these charges as a mediating one: it is for the sake of those near to him and finally for the sake of all people that he asks for his confession to be kept unshaken. His orthodoxy in this matter will have beneficial effects on others.

That most of these ideas resurface in the final chapter of Book 2 adds impetus to the theory that the author of *DT* constructed the treatise at least partially as a defense of his teaching on the Trinity.[84] In the preface to his concluding prayer, he asserts that he and those with him who shared in "daily ... gatherings (παρ' ἡμέραν ... συνουσίαι)" could attest that his "remembrance (μνήμη)" of the Trinity at these gatherings "always bestowed good things, subtracted nothing [from the Trinity], and did not occasion reproach."[85] The author takes pains to assert that he is orthodox precisely in connection with this doctrine, and that there are those with him who can attest to this. As the means of blessing to his dependents, he appeals to God for vindication.[86]

These passages are windows on the external circumstances that occasioned the writing of the treatise. In light of the final chapter of Book 2, we

---

83. *DT* 2.7.8.13 (589D). The "matter" of which he is speaking is the recognition that the Trinity is higher than all created natures. Cf. Seiler, *De trinitate, Buch 2*, 241n1.

84. My treatment of this passage is more abbreviated, preceded as it is by the careful reading offered by Ludwig Koenen in "Ein theologischer Papyrus der Kölner Sammlung: Kommentar Didymos' des Blinden zu Zach. 9,11 u. 16," *Archiv für Papyrusforschung* 17 (1960): 80–105.

85. *DT* 2.27 (761B–764A). Koenen edits Mingarelli's text at this point, removing the comma between Τριάδα and τῆς διδούσης (*DT* 2.27 (761B)) and arguing that the genitive case of the latter is attracted to μνήμης. It is specifically the author's "remembrance (μνήμη)" of the Trinity "that mediates the blessing (welche den Segen vermittelt)" to his hearers (Koenen, "Ein theologischer Papyrus," 83–84n1).

86. *DT* 2.27 (764B–769A).

may add the following circumstances to the list: 1) the author of *DT* is apparently an old man, 2) working in the midst of a community that assembles daily for the purpose of study. Immediately before the prayer, the author says: "I pray for myself and my children (τῶν ἐξ ἐμοῦ), and their children present and future (τῶν ἀπ' αὐτῶν ὄντων τε καὶ ἐσομένων)" and follows this remark with a quotation from the Psalter that concludes with the words: "Do not cast me away at the time of old age; when my strength deserts me do not abandon me" (Ps 70:18 LXX).[87] The remark is one of several intimating that the author is an old man at the time of writing.

Koenen argues, on the basis of the introduction to the prayer, that the above-mentioned "assemblies (συνουσίαι)" are best understood in relation to the work of a teacher with his school. There are other possibilities: 1) a father with his household, 2) an abbot with his monks,[88] or 3) a presbyter catechizing his congregation. However, the context of a school makes best sense of the passage and the evidence of the treatise as a whole. As for the first possibility, the author's reference to children is paralleled by other remarks in which he refers to the children of others.[89] Few since Mingarelli have seriously espoused this interpretation.[90] The third possibility also seems unlikely; one would not expect daily gatherings in church assemblies to have included the study of pagan literature.[91]

These daily gatherings for the purpose of study best fit the context either of a monastic group committed to the study of texts or a school. The author

---

87. *DT* 2.27 (764A and C). In addition to the citations in the earlier apostrophe to the angels, see also *DT* 3.1 (784A) in which the author refers to "the children whom (God) gave to me and my children's children, for whose sake we labor while we live."

88. Tzamalikos argues for this point-of-view (see *Newly Discovered Greek Father*, 448–450).

89. These are the "children" or "disciples of Macedonius (Μακεδονίου . . . παῖδες)" (*DT* 1.34.18 (436C)) and those of the Greeks ('Ελλήνων παῖδες) (3.4 (833B)). The author of *DT* uses the name in a figurative sense; the children of his opponents are their disciples, their spiritual progeny.

90. Here Mingarelli is probably motivated by faulty external evidence. He had considered the references to the author's children (all contained in the Prayer to the Angels (*DT* 2.7.8), the Prayer to the Trinity (2.27), and the Prologue to Book 3 (3.1)) to lend support to his argument for Didymean authorship, since he had wrongly associated some epistolary correspondence speaking of the children of another Didymus with the blind teacher (*Commentarius* 10 (154D–158C)).

91. The translation is suggested by Bardy, *Didyme l'Aveugle*, 11, who treats the phrase in isolation from its context as evidence that Didymus carried out his work in close connection with the life of the Church. Although Bardy's broader point seems to be borne out elsewhere, Koenen points out that the daily gatherings of a church-congregation for the study of pagan literature is hardly consonant with what we know about the frequency and purpose of church-gatherings ("Ein theologischer Papyrus," 86).

has just promised that, God permitting, he will continue to expound further arguments from the "books of the Greeks" with those who have gathered around him. Although the possibility of a monastic community cannot be altogether excluded, Koenen helpfully notes that "in DT, asceticism is never emphasized, and the monastic is never mentioned."[92] On the balance of the evidence, a school is the most likely context of the final remarks in Book 2. The author's "children" are most likely his students. Having learned the faith from him, they have become his spiritual progeny. And he has had the good fortune of living long enough to see his students take on disciples of their own. He continues to labor on their behalf. Not only is he in danger of being discredited, but they are as well since they never found fault with his doctrine of the Trinity, the point at issue in the recent dispute with his unnamed opponents.

Didymus' Circle in the 390s

Before progressing further, the question must be raised: considering the dearth of information available to us about Didymus' *curriculum vitae*, is there a window of time in which the above circumstances were likely to obtain? Again, it is possible. The events leading up to the First Origenist Controversy were precipitated by Epiphanius, bishop of Salamis, who visited Palestine in 393.[93] By 394, Epiphanius' disregard for John of Jerusalem's authority within his own see had reached an intolerable pitch, forcing John to appeal to the powerful, neighboring patriarch of Alexandria. In 396 Theophilus attempted (unsuccessfully) to intervene.

Among the earliest casualties of Epiphanius' campaign against the Origenists were relations between monasteries: notably, the Bethlehemite and Olivet monasteries of Jerome and Rufinus. That these persons and their followers had strong connections with Alexandria is evident. Rufinus spent several years under Didymus' tutelage. In 386–387, Jerome was busy requesting and receiving commentaries from Didymus after the Latin's brief visit with him. As fluid and well-connected as these monastic communities were, it is almost certain that a dispute of such magnitude in Palestine would have made waves in Didymus' circle in Alexandria.[94] Theophilus' attempt to pacify the anti-Origenists in Palestine could have had the added benefit of securing harmony

---

92. "In de trin. ist die Askese nirgends betont, und nirgends hört man den Mönch sprechen" (Koenen, "Ein theologischer Papyrus," 86). The difference between Tzamalikos' "Caesarius/Cassian" and the author of *DT* is pronounced at this point.

93. Doutreleau, "Vie et Survie," 37.

94. For the social factors involved in this conflict, see Elizabeth Clark, "Elite Networks and Heresy Accusations: Towards a Social Description of the Origenist Controversy," *The Origenist Controversy: the Cultural Construction of an Early Christian Debate* (Princeton: Princeton University Press, 1992), 11–42.

between the same factions in his own see.[95] *DT*'s remarks about a rising tension between some churches and the members of the school could well reflect the general mood in Alexandria in the mid-390s.

To this it should be added that the charge of Trinitarian heterodoxy was a weapon that was ready to hand in the anti-Origenist's arsenal. Epiphanius argues that Arians and Anomoeans furnished themselves with matter in Origen supple to their impious intent, producing as his first example Origen's affirmation of the Father's invisibility to the Son and the Son's invisibility to the Spirit.[96] Jerome—somewhat disingenuously, it must be said—accuses John of Jerusalem of being the world's leading authority on Arian theology and then reprimands him for responding to the charges laid against him as if he is on trial for Arian views.[97] It is Origen's Trinitarian "heresy," not Arius', for which he is under examination.[98] The author of *DT*'s view on the *topos* of divine invisibility is decidedly affirmative of Nicene orthodoxy (the *hypostaseis* of the Trinity are mutually known to one another, the Father to both Son and Spirit no less than vice versa), even while he insists on maintaining that the divine *hypostaseis* do not see one another with corporeal eyes.[99] This is entirely consistent with the response given by others who sympathized with Origen.

Because of the dearth of evidence available to us about the closing stages of Didymus' career, it is best to hold out as a possibility that Didymus was implicated in the early stages of the First Origenist Controversy. Too little is known, however, about the situation in Alexandria and Didymus' circle during the years between the eruption of conflict in Palestine and the full-blown controversy of 399 to say if this is the case for sure.

Evidence for Provenance

Until relatively recently, discussions concerning *DT* assumed an Egyptian, and often more specifically an Alexandrian provenance. Revisionist suggestions have expanded this field of inquiry to Antioch (and environs) and Cappa-

---

95. In 399 monks, leaving the Nitrian desert for the metropolis, forced Theophilus to recant his "Origenist" assertion that God was incorporeal.

96. *Pan.* 64.4.2–3 (GCS 31:410).

97. *C. Ioh.* 3 and 5 (CCSL 79A:8 and 11).

98. *C. Ioh.* 8–9 (CCSL 79A:14–17). The text under discussion is Origen's *Prin.* 1.1.8 (Butterworth, 13–14). (See also *Prin.* 2.4.3 (Butterworth, 98–99) in which the Marcionite position on the visibility of the God of the OT and the invisibility of the God of the New involves them in serious difficulties).

99. See *DT* 2.6.16 (544AC), especially: ὁ δὲ μονογενὴς καὶ τὸ ἅγιον πνεῦμα διὰ τὸ ταὐτὸν τῆς θεότητος ὁρῶσιν οὕτως, ὡς ἔστιν ὁ ἀμεγέθης καὶ ἀνείδεος θεός (Seiler, *De trinitate, Buch 2*, 162). The "seeing" of the Son and the Spirit, a seeing that is utterly complete, does not involve the comprehension of the Father's magnitude or form (for magnitude and form are only categories of corporeal realities).

docia.¹⁰⁰ Before examining these suggestions, the internal evidence of DT demands prior attention, since there is a reference within the treatise that argues strongly for an Egyptian setting. After examining this text, I will inquire on what basis the revisionist proposals advise relocating the discussion to other regions.

"Then Will the Nile's Flowing Be Full" [101]

The author of DT closes Book 2 with a prayer that discloses not only several helpful pieces of information about the occasion for the treatise (discussed above), but also one piece of information relating to the work's place of origin. Prefacing his conclusion to the book with a relatively brief defense of his continuous devotion to the Trinity, he launches into a prayer that concludes the book.

Nearing the end of the prayer, the author petitions God on behalf of his circle, that there would be a cessation of conflict so that they might live among books and be no longer separated from the Church's assemblies. He prays that they would no longer be defamed but that the "concord (συμμετρία)" between virtue and all knowledge, this "concord" that was their teacher from the beginning, would be praised by others around them.¹⁰² Calling upon God to bless him and his followers, the author then turns his attention to the "external commonwealth (ἡ ἑξῆς πολιτεία)," praying that it would be "more prudent (σωφρονεστέρα)" than the commonwealth of old, insofar as it is being perfected by the "Christian law." The reference to the Nile follows:

> Then let sweet light arise and be radiant, and good government and peace will be deep in every sense and measure throughout all the land and the sea, and the stream of the Nile will be full and there will be an abundant harvest (καὶ μεστὸν τοῦ Νείλου τὸ ῥεῖθρον καὶ εὐετηρία πλείστη), and a great and complete scarcity of those who hanker after positions of power.¹⁰³

The prayer for the Nile and for the state is interwoven into the prayer that the author is offering on his own behalf.

The text is treated more fully here because it is necessary to illustrate that the author is concerned both with the needs particular to his own community and those pertaining to the world around him. Tzamalikos, however, reads the reference to the Nile in a purely metaphorical way, arguing that the author of

---

100. Tzamalikos espouses the former view (*A Newly Discovered Greek Father*, 525–536), while Manlio Simonetti proposes the latter ("Ancora sulla paternità Didymiana de De Trinitate," *Augustinianum* 36 (1996): 385).
101. DT 2.27 (768B).
102. DT 2.27 (768A).
103. DT 2.27 (768B).

DT is asking God to grant him "the lips of orthodox theologians standing as staunch defenders of orthodoxy." The flow of the Nile is, on this reading, a metaphor for "a flow of upright theological pronouncements."[104]

Such a reading, however, is improbable. The author of *DT* tells us that he is praying "on behalf of myself and my children . . . and again indeed on behalf of all" as one who is "commanded by the Savior Christ to pray on behalf of others." The turn from his own situation to the needs of the world around him is therefore anticipated in the preface to the prayer. Moreover, a similar turn occurs earlier. The author prays that his community "will be delivered from the psychical and bodily people who have sinned against [them] in knowledge and ignorance" and follows this with a prayer that the Lord will grant "to all people a desirable . . . dwelling in each city." Thereafter mundane requests (e.g., the freedom to travel, to remain at home, to farm, and to attend the festivals) are mixed in with requests of a more spiritual nature (e.g., that all would remember the Trinity).[105] The reference to the Nile need not be allegorized.

As Koenen had earlier argued, it seems best to understand the prayer as one in which the author understands his situation to be intrinsically linked with the welfare of the state and even the created order around him.[106] He is not concerned with personal vindication for its own sake, but rather for the sake of the Church and the world. And he conceives of his role as that of a mediator, through whom the Trinity bestows his blessing on others.[107] Thus, the most natural reading of the request about the Nile and the harvest dependent upon it is a literal one: the author of *DT* understands his own faithfulness to the Trinity as part-and-parcel with God's desire to bless the land in which he lives.[108] The reference clearly suggests an Egyptian setting.

---

104. Tzamalikos, *Newly Discovered Greek Father*, 456.

105. In summary of *DT* 2.27 (764A–765B).

106. "Out of the fullness of grace that has been granted to him and his party because of his "remembrance of the Trinity," there follows—according to the old style of prayer—his certainty that . . . grace will be poured out on himself, his followers, and on the whole world. . . . So he asks, in the confidence that it will be granted to him, for a new age of peace on the earth." ([A]us der Gnadenfülle, welche sich aus der μνήμη τῆς Τριάδος für ihn und die Teilnehmer . . . ergeben hat, folgt nach altem Gebetsstil seine Gewißheit, daß . . . die Gnade auf ihn, die Seinen und die ganze Welt ergießen wird. . . . So bittet er in der Gewißheit, daß es ihm gegeben wird, um eine neue Friedenszeit auf Erden.) So Koenen, "Ein theologischer Papyrus," 84.

107. Ibid., 85–86.

108. It is worth noting that very similar sentiments are expressed in *CZ* I.264–270, in which Didymus connects peace of a cosmic order with the triumph of his disciples over the "cosmic powers of darkness" by the virtues of the contemplative and the active life. I employ the book-paragraph citation form for *CZ*.

The Arguments for Antioch

Arguments for Antiochene provenance have been recently advanced by Tzamalikos.[109] The primary argument he advances in relation to this point is the exegesis of the lamp-stand text in the Zechariah Commentary and the very different interpretation given to the same passage in DT. Though Tzamalikos is not alone in raising this objection to Didymus' authorship, he is alone in using it as an argument for Antiochene provenance.[110] He supports the exegetical argument with several others of a lexical variety. Among the more significant of these are the following:[111] 1) that DT's author styles Christ by the title δεσπότης with some consistency, 2) that he calls David "melodist" (μελῳδός), and 3) that his exegetical terminology has greater kinship with Antiochene rather than Alexandrian authors.

Let us turn to the first argument. Tzamalikos claims that persistent use of phrase δεσπότης Χριστός is something of an Antiochene tendency. If he means that we are to look for frequent occurrences of the phrase δεσπότης Χριστός as an indication that a work is likely from Antioch (the phrase that predominates among the uses of the word δεσπότης in Theodore of Mopsuestia's *Commentary on the Twelve Prophets*, for example), then the instances of the word δεσπότης in DT do not bear the argument out. Of the "more than eighty instances where the term δεσπότης is ascribed to Christ," only four actually occur within the phrase δεσπότης Χριστός.[112] If, however, one interprets Tzamalikos to mean that the title is applied to the second Person of the Trinity on numerous occasions, it should be noted that the application of the title to Christ is not unique

---

109. "Antioch," in *Newly Discovered Greek Father*, 525–565. As far as I am aware, Tzamalikos is the first to have made this suggestion. Christoph Bizer places much of DT's source material in Antioch, but does not challenge Alexandria as its place of origin. See his "Studien zu pseudoathanasianischen Dialogen der Orthodoxos und Aëtios" (PhD diss., Bonn, 1970), 228–235.

110. For the use of this argument see Doutreleau's "Le 'De trinitate'," 547–553. This is the chief problem raised against Didymean authorship by Bizer as well ("Studien zu pseudothanasiansichen Dialogen," 34). The amount of time required for an author to change his mind about the exegesis of the text does not obtain for him between the writing of CZ and DT.

111. Some of Tzamalikos' other arguments are easily dismissed. For example, connecting the author of DT with the Antiochene Caesarius on the basis of a common idea and citing only one example of this idea (later than the fourth century), he writes: "[n]o author did ever make the point about a dove having no bile" (*Newly Discovered Greek Father*, 619n908). The passage is DT 2.14 (693B). Mingarelli (695CDn28) had drawn attention to the fact that this passage about a "dove lacking bile" appears in Tertullian's *Bap.* 8.3 (Evans, 18-19), and that Tertullian's treatise—in Greek translation—has served as a source for DT 2.14 (692D–693Dn21). Latin sources are almost entirely absent from Tzamalikos' considerations, as is most of the secondary literature.

112. Tzamalikos, 527. These are DT 2.5.20 (500B), 2.6.4.2 (516B), 2.6.19.3 (548C), and 3.34 (961A).

to Antiochene authors. Counter-examples are readily produced, from Alexandria no less. Athanasius, for instance, employs the title more often in reference to the Son than he does to all other referents combined.[113] The use of δεσπότης for the Son seems too unwieldy a criterion to establish an argument for Antiochene provenance.

David is termed "melodist" by the author of *DT*. Tzamalikos argues that numerous Antiochene authors employ the epithet, and that it is not very common outside this milieu. A similar ambiguity to that above, however, hampers the argument. Tzamalikos specifically denies to authors like Origen, Eusebius, and the Cappadocian Gregories the use of the word μελῳδός as a description of David, but cites their use of its cognates.[114] He then contrasts this with the use of the word among Antiochene and Sabaite monks, Palestinian dependents, and other eminent Syrians. However, based on the examples produced, it would appear that the author of *DT* is almost alone in using the word μελῳδός to refer to David. Of the numerous examples Tzamalikos produces, only one contains the word his argument leads us to expect.[115] Broadening the search somewhat to include the association of David with μελῳδία or descriptions of him "making melody" (μελῳδέω) reveals that Theodoret of Cyrus makes the connection frequently. (Of all the authors surveyed by Tzamalikos, only he can be said to have made habitual use of the association). However, Cyril of Alexandria uses the notion three times (only one less than *DT*'s author) between his *Glaphyra* and the *Commentary on Isaiah*.[116] Once again, the argument is too unwieldy.

---

113. If one sets aside the *spuria* and places in which Athanasius is quoting others, Athanasius uses the term most often of the Son. In a *TLG* search of the title, I count more uses of the word in Athanasius' undisputed corpus where the application of the title to the Son is unambiguous than uses where he is referring either to the Father or to God as Creator or Ruler of his creation. The former use predominates in the *Orations against the Arians*, *On the Incarnation*, and the epistolary literature, the latter in *Against the Pagans*. One sees here that the subject matter of the texts plays a significant role in Athanasius' use: where he is expounding the doctrine of the Son, the reference to Christ is quite normal. Where he is dealing with polytheistic opponents or addressing God in prayer, δεσπότης appears to be used of the Godhead or of the Father.

114. The appearance of the language in Origen is dismissed as the result of the compilation of his *catenae* in Antioch; the point is made but not defended (see Tzamalikos, 529n530).

115. Ibid., 530nn532–534. Among the twenty-one citations he lists, only the citation from Asterius of Antioch possesses the word μελῳδός itself, in the vocative case. None of the participle forms he produces is substantivized: "the *melodist* (μελῳδῶν) David"; they are all used adverbially: e.g., "making melody, the blessed David said [the following]" (μελῳδῶν ὁ μακάριος ἔφη Δαβίδ).

116. *Glaph. Ex.* 2.2 (PG 69:429B), and *In Is.* 2.4 (PG 70:473A) and 5.2 (PG 70:1217BC).

Tzamalikos' third argument is somewhat more successful, at least from a descriptive point of view.[117] *DT*'s exegetical terminology is fairly restrained. There is one insignificant use of the word ἀλληγορία and one insignificant use of a cognate in *DT*, and no use at all of other terminology that appears with some frequency in Didymus' exegetical work (τροπολογία and ἀναγωγή). The point about exegetical terminology is a fair one to make. However, the absence of such terminology is not altogether surprising, given the genre of the treatise. *DT* is primarily a dogmatic work intended to vindicate the author from charges that he considers specious. Polemic concerns are hardly in keeping with prolonged figural interpretations of Scripture! Didymus' undisputed dogmatic corpus is—with one exception that Didymus does not capitalize upon—free of such terminology.[118] Tzamalikos' point tells us little more than that *DT* is not a commentary. A fuller portrait of the author's teaching on Scripture is surely required to sustain the claim that he is not an Alexandrian.

The final, and most important, argument in favor of Antioch and against Didymean paternity revolves around *DT*'s rendering of Zechariah 3:8–4:10.[119] Tzamalikos largely repeats Doutreleau's observation that *DT* and Didymus' *CZ* differ significantly on the exegesis of this passage; however, Tzamalikos extends the argument further by noting that *DT* shares a number of close similarities with Theodore of Mopsuestia and Theodoret of Cyrus.[120] Some of the purported similarities are quite tenuous. For example, the remarks on the "tin stone" in the hand of Zerubbabel (4:10) are different. Theodore and Theodoret content themselves with remarking on the metal's weakness, relating this point to the apparent weakness of God's people who stand in need of divine help. The author of *DT*, on the other hand, observes that tin is used for the restoration of metal vessels, but "the notion of restoration of the people of

---

117. Tzamalikos, 533–535.

118. Didymus mentions allegory once in his undisputed dogmatic corpus. See *DSS* 68: "Now if *thunder* and *the dawn and the foggy mist* and the creation of *spirit* are understood through the cloud of allegory [nubilum allegoriae], they will not indicate the thing itself but a figurative interpretation [figuratam interpretationem]" (trans. DelCogliano, Radde-Gallwitz, and Ayres, *Works on the Spirit*, 164). After providing a lengthy interpretation of Amos 4:13, Didymus introduces the possibility that the text could be taken allegorically, but does nothing with this observation, remaining committed to providing an exposition of the plain sense (see *DSS* 69). In his *Against the Manicheans*, Didymus uses ἀνάγω (the verbal cognate of ἀναγωγή) in the general sense of "instructing" children, but not in its exegetical sense. See *C. Man.* 13 (PG 39:1101C).

119. Tzamalikos, 535–565.

120. In the instances cited by Tzamalikos, there are no correspondences between *DT* and Theodoret that are not shared by Theodore. This is perhaps unsurprising given that Theodoret's most proximate source for his *Interpretation of the Twelve Minor Prophets* was Theodore. For a discussion of Theodoret's relation to his sources, see Robert Hill, "Zechariah in Alexandria and Antioch," *Augustinianum* 48 (2008): 323–327.

God" does not come into view.[121] However, several of the resemblances are quite close: the similarity of several passages suggests at least that the author of *DT* was familiar with Theodore or that both were appealing to the same exegetical tradition.[122]

Yet there is one major discrepancy between the two authors that Tzamalikos does not address. Pneumatological concerns are clearly what bring the author of *DT* to this passage in Zechariah in the first place. Adducing testimonies to the Spirit's work in baptism, the author of *DT* appeals to the sevenfold dipping of Naaman the Syrian in the Jordan (4 Kgdms 5:10, 14), and follows this with a discussion of the number seven. As the full and perfect number, "seven" intimates the divine Spirit. To defend the claim, our author appeals to Isaiah's enumeration of the seven gifts of the Spirit (11:1–3). It is by this route that he arrives at Zechariah's stone with the seven eyes. The seven-eyed stone is introduced in the first citation of Zechariah (3:8–9) and the discussion of seven returns again at the end of the author of *DT*'s brief exposition of the passage (4:10). The development between the two citations largely serves as a summary of the Zechariah text. Our author moves from the description of the Lord's words to Zerubbabel and Joshua, to descriptions of the items seen in the vision, to the angel's awakening of the prophet to look again "with more precise comprehension"[123] at the things that would be shown. He cites the pneumatologically explicit text: "Neither by might nor power, but by my Spirit" (4:6), and concludes the argument: "The seven eyes that survey the whole of creation are the aforementioned marvellous gifts of the Holy Spirit."[124] The burden of the author in bringing this passage into his discussion is pneumatological.[125]

---

121. Cf. Tzamalikos, 548.

122. The strongest of these connections discussed by Tzamalikos include the following: 1) the comments on Zechariah 3:9. Both interpret the phrase: "I am digging a trench . . . and I will remove all unrighteousness from that land in one day," to mean that God will bring death or destruction upon "the enemies by the military office of Zerubbabel." 2) In connection with the stone upon which Joshua's face is fixed (also Zech 3:9), both remark that Zerubbabel receives the aid of Joshua's prayers, while Joshua receives the benefits of Zerubbabel's exercise of kingship. 3) Both note in reference to Zechariah 3:10 that people will "invite one another to feasting" (in nearly identical language) at the ensuing peace. 4) Both note that the golden lamp-stand (Zech 4:2) joins together things earthly with things heavenly in very similar language (though they disagree as to its referent).

123. *DT* 2.14 (704B).

124. *DT* 2.14 (705A).

125. See *DT* 2.14 (700B–701A). Hence the argument is not, strictly speaking, "a long digression" ("une longue digression") as Doutreleau suggests in "Le 'De trinitate'," 547. Nor is Tzamalikos right in claiming that the passage "seems irrelevant" and that there is "no obvious reason" for it (*Newly Discovered Greek Father*, 533).

This theme is entirely absent from both Theodore and Theodoret's discussion of the same text. In his discussion of the number "seven", Theodore avoids dwelling on its significance beyond remarking that it reveals that God will certainly render Zerubbabel capable of ruling the kingdom.[126] Returning to the notion again at the end of the discussion of the "seven eyes" of the Lord, Theodore speaks of God's abundant supervision, administration, and salvation. Here "seven" denotes "perfection."[127] Even in the text where the prophet mentions the Spirit by name (4:6), Theodore, like Theodoret after him, avoids bringing the Holy Spirit into the discussion. Indeed, the word πνεῦμα is not even discussed by Theodore. But this is a strange omission. The pneumatological theme is not lost on Jerome, for instance, who associates the seven eyes with Isaiah 11.[128] Didymus repeatedly draws the connection.[129] If the author of DT is following carefully in the footsteps of his Antiochene predecessors, then what explains this significant interpretive difference?

Taken as a whole, the argument for Antiochene provenance does not appear sufficient as a revisionist proposal to dislodge the widespread scholarly consensus in favor of Alexandria. There is some evidence that the author of DT is conversant with Antiochene texts, as Christoph Bizer has argued.[130] Tzamalikos has demonstrated that there are certain similarities between the interpretations of the author of DT and Theodore on Zechariah 3–4. But, considering the significant divergences between the two authors on other matters highlighted above, nothing more conclusive than this can be said.

The Arguments for Cappadocia

Manlio Simonetti, offering a different proposal, likewise denies the possibility of attributing DT to Didymus the Blind, citing his use of the terms ὑπόστασις and οὐσία in the Tura Commentaries. Therein Didymus never distinguishes between the two terms, even when he is afforded the occasion. For Simonetti, the author of DT regularly distinguishes the terms in the manner that they are distinguished by the Cappadocians.[131] Given the lack of consensus about authorship, might this not suggest the working hypothesis that the

---

126. Theodore, *In Zach.* 3:8b–9a (Sprenger, 343.23–27). Cf. Theodoret of Cyrus, *In Zach.* 3:8–9 (PG 81:1896A).

127. *In Zach.* 4:10c (Sprenger, 347.15–16).

128. Jerome, *In Zach.* 1, 3:8–9 (CCSL 76A:775).

129. Didymus, *CZ* I.255–256 cites Isaiah 11:1–3 in connection with the stone with seven eyes and comments that Christ (the stone) saw all things "with counsel and might ... being filled with the Spirit of God." The Holy Spirit of Zechariah 4:6 is the focus of a lengthy discussion in *CZ* I.294–299.

130. For a cautiously positive evaluation of Bizer's arguments for the Antiochene provenance of some of the source material for DT, see Alasdair Heron, "The Two Pseudo-Athanasian Dialogues against the Anomoeans," *JTS*, n.s., 24 (1973): 101–122 (in particular, p. 122).

131. Manlio Simonetti, "Didymiana," *Vetera Christianorum* 21 (1984): 144–145.

author of *DT* hails from Cappadocia rather than Alexandria? Simonetti argues that *DT* has "the air of a work coming from a setting very close to that of the Cappadocians and in any event strongly influenced by them." We cannot argue strongly for a Cappadocian influence on any other work by Didymus, dogmatic or otherwise.[132]

Simonetti adds to the above argument that a turn from the accepted Athanasian vocabulary—then current in Alexandria—would be unexpected for Didymus, and even unlikely given the fact that politically Alexandria and Cappadocia were at loggerheads. It is not until Cyril that one finds an Alexandrian openly employing the Trinitarian language of the Cappadocians.[133]

Three considerations relativize Simonetti's objections. 1) First of all, though Athanasius does not regularly employ the language of three *hypostaseis*, he officially endorses its usage as early as 362, in the *Tomus ad Antiochenos*. It is hard to justify Simonetti's claim that the employment of the formula by an Alexandrian would have been perceived as a betrayal of the Athanasian position in light of this concession. 2) Moreover, the Cappadocian influence on the author of *DT*'s Trinitarian language is uneven; there are notable differences in the accentuation and vocabulary of their Trinitarian theologies. Simonetti rightly notes that the author of *DT* uses ὑπόστασις in the sense of an "individuale (= persona)" and that the use of the formula is a defining characteristic of the treatise.[134] The similarity between *DT* and the Cappadocian vocabulary likewise extends to *DT*'s distinction of the *hypostaseis* according to "individuating marks" or "properties." Yet Bardy, in his study on the meaning of the word ὑπόστασις in Didymus (particularly focusing on *DT*), had noted that the burden of the word, when it is pressed into the service of Trinitarian doctrine, is to

> présenter les trois ὑποστάσεις comme des réalités distinctes, subsistantes, plutôt que mettre en relief leurs caractères distinctifs. Chez les Cappadociens, chez Grégoire de Nazianze surtout, ce sera ce dernier sens qui sera le plus développé: les mots ὑπόστασις et ἰδιότης seront interchangeables. Le pensée de Didyme est encore loin d'avoir acquis ce degré de précision.[135]

---

132. Simonetti, "Ancora," 385: "*DT* abbia tutta l'aria di un'opera proveniente da ambiente molto vicino a quello dei Cappadoci e comunque da loro fortemente influenzato."

133. Ibid., 384-385n25.

134. Ibid.

135. He is using the word "to establish the three *hypostaseis* as distinct realities, subsistent, rather than to measure their distinctive characteristics by contrast. For the Cappadocians, for Gregory of Nazianzus in particular, it will be this latter sense that will be the most developed: the words *hypostasis* and *idiotēs* will become interchangea-

There is a distinction in accent between the two in their usage of the same vocabulary.

More significantly—and a point that is taken up in the following chapter—the author of *DT* is far less sanguine about the possibility of doing justice to the distinguishing characteristic of the Father's *hypostasis* than are the Cappadocians. Though the full significance of this point is examined in greater detail later on, its importance to the present discussion consists in the fact that it demonstrates *DT*'s independence from ideas that were fairly standard in the Cappadocian literature.

3) Finally, the argument in support of a Cappadocian hypothesis is likewise relativized in light of *DT*'s occasion. The author of *DT* is responding after 381 to detractors from his Trinitarian orthodoxy. Were he composing a treatise in more irenic circumstances, one could expect less rigorous conformity to the terminology of the imperially-sanctioned orthodoxy. Given the occasion of the treatise, the use of such language is hardly surprising.

In conclusion, it does not appear that the revisionist arguments adduced for a non-Egyptian provenance are sufficient to overturn the internal evidence (which Simonetti does not address), and widespread scholarly consensus in favor of it. That the author of *DT* is aware of various exegetical traditions is beyond dispute. That he employs Trinitarian language that is in some sense indebted to the Cappadocians is likewise indubitable. The author has surely spent some time rehearsing the arguments of others in making his defense. In any case, the revisionist arguments do not satisfactorily address the significance of the geographical reference internal to the treatise. Egypt remains the most plausible place of writing.

The Arguments for and against Didymus

On the basis of the above then, we can conclude with certainty that the author of *DT* wrote the treatise between 384 and 429. As far as we can tell from the available catalogues of Didymus' works, Didymus wrote his *On the Trinity* in the 390s. We can conclude that the author was writing in Egypt at a time when he was not under official examination but had been accused of promoting unorthodox opinions on the Trinity. He is an old man at the time of composition. The most plausible interpretation of his remarks at the end of Book 2 is that his immediate audience is comprised of students who gathered daily to hear him. These are the hard facts, as it were, of the case, of which the arguments for and against Didymean authorship must make sense. In this final section, then, I consider the strength of the various arguments raised for and against the attribution to Didymus.

---

ble. The thought of Didymus is still far from having acquired this degree of precision" (Bardy, *Didyme l'Aveugle*, 80).

The Traditional Argument: Its Problems and Strengths

Mingarelli based the attribution of *DT* to Didymus upon numerous arguments, many of which must be regarded as supporting rather than primary.[136] The primary arguments have rightly constituted the focal point of the more recent debate about Didymus' authorship. These are as follows: 1) there are references within *DT* to an earlier λόγος on the Holy Spirit.[137] Mingarelli took these to be references to Didymus' *De spiritu sancto*, a work that is extant in Jerome's Latin translation. As Jerome's prologue to the translation and his remarks in *On Illustrious Men* testify,[138] *DSS* is unquestionably by Didymus. If the author of *DT*'s references to his earlier work on the Spirit were references to *DSS*, little more would be needed to secure the attribution. 2) There is also the testimony of Socrates Scholasticus to Didymus' having written three books *On the Trinity*. 3) The author of *DT* employs the rare word ἀμεγέθης in relation to God's οὐσία; the word appears elsewhere in Didymus' corpus.[139] 4) Stylistically, the author of *DT* and Didymus have several similarities.[140]

The Reference to De Spiritu Sancto

The first argument in favor of Didymus' authorship was based on a distinction made by Mingarelli between λόγος and βιβλίον.[141] The former, he argued, referred to a self-enclosed work or treatise while the latter referred to a book or volume within a larger work. The distinction permitted Mingarelli to hypothesize that the two references in the text to an earlier "book (λόγος) on the Holy Spirit" were in fact references to a separate treatise: Didymus' *DSS*. The terminological distinction between λόγος and βιβλίον would enjoy a long role in arguments relating to the possibility that the author of *DT* was referring to yet another identifiable treatise when he mentioned his "first book (πρῶτος λόγος)."[142] F.X. Funk argued that these referred to the polemical treatise *Adversus Eunomium 4-5*.[143] Funk's conclusions found a mixed reception, though all agreed at the time that the πρῶτος λόγος was certainly a reference to another work.[144]

---

136. For the arguments, see Book 1 of his *Commentarius* in PG 39:139B–176B. These are summarized in the prologue (141C–142A).

137. See *DT* 3.16 (872B) and 3.31 (949C). Mingarelli points this out in *Commentarius* 1.1 (142B–144D).

138. *Vir. ill.* 109, 135 (TU 14:50, 55–56).

139. *Commentarius* 1.12 (159B–160A). The scope of this claim is too limited; the argument is untreated here.

140. I have repeated the order of the arguments as they are found in Doutreleau, "Le 'De trinitate'," 516.

141. *Commentarius* 1.1 (143A–144D).

142. There are fourteen references in *DT* to a πρῶτος λόγος.

143. Funk, "Die zwei letzten Bücher," 317–329.

144. Leipoldt, *Didymus der Blinde*, 11–12, thought Funk's explanation impossible. Bardy, *Didyme l'Aveugle*, 27–28, favored Funk's argument.

Doutreleau, although still assuming that Mingarelli's linguistic analysis of the terms was correct,[145] was the first to question whether these two purported references to *DSS* were as sound as Mingarelli had supposed.[146] Comparing *DT* 3.16 (872B) with the relevant passages in *DSS* (paragraphs 181 and 194), he was hardly encouraged by the results. For the author of *DT* quotes St Paul (1 Tim 5:6) and notes that he has already provided an explication of the passage to similar effect in the book on the Holy Spirit.[147] Although there are similar overlapping ideas between *DT* and *DSS* in relation to the theme under discussion, *DSS* offers no examination of the passage at all and does not even cite it.

Mingarelli also claimed that the author of *DT* was referring to *DSS* 65–73 in a second reference. Later in *DT* the author once again refers to an earlier work on the Holy Spirit.[148] *DT*'s author mentions that the heretics adduce certain texts to disparage the Holy Spirit (John 12:49, 16:13; Rom 16:27). He mentions these texts "in addition to the others set forth in the book on the Holy Spirit." Then he sets forth the pneumatological aporia par excellence: Amos 4:11–13, since his opponents have made use of this prophecy to argue "that the Holy Spirit of God is a creature."[149]

Most of the above pneumatological texts are indeed discussed in *DSS*. But then, argues Doutreleau, this is the case with numerous others who wrote on the doctrine of the Spirit in the fourth century. Doutreleau rightly insists on establishing the citation on a more secure basis than that both authors refer to the same texts. In their discussion of Amos 4:11–13, he notes that both authors employ the argument that the definite article is missing, which suggests that the Holy Spirit is not the referent here.[150] But Doutreleau finds that the author of *DT* employs a different strategy with the text than Didymus does. In *DSS* 65–73, Didymus is basically concerned with eliminating the aporia by denying any reference to the Holy Spirit whatsoever. The author of *DT* overcomes the aporia by placing the whole text not in the mouth of the Father but in the

---

145. Doutreleau, "Vie et survie," 81.

146. Doutreleau, "Le 'De trinitate'," 519–527.

147. He writes: καθὰ ἤδη ἐν τῷ περὶ τοῦ Ἁγίου Πνεύματος ἐξηγήθη λόγῳ. Doutreleau overstates his case with respect to the word ἐξηγήθη by claiming that the word and its cognates always relate to the interpretation of Scripture ("Le 'De trinitate'," 519n9). The author of *DT* uses the word in relation to the explanation of other things, such as giving an account of the divine generation of the Son (*DT* 1.15.48 (309C)) or of the reasons behind the Holy Spirit's bestowal of eternal existence on created nature (*DT* 2.4.1 (516A)). In context, however, his interpretation of the word is sufficiently credible.

148. *DT* 3.31 (949BC). For Mingarelli's comments, see PG 39:950–951n45.

149. *DT* 3.31 (949C–952A).

150. Likely both are preceded in this by Athanasius, *Serap.* I.4.1–4 (*Athanasius Werke* I/1:456–458). However, there are reasons to suppose that Didymus in *DSS* is relatively independent of Athanasius. See Mark DelCogliano, "Basil of Caesarea, Didymus the Blind, and the Anti-Pneumatomachian Exegesis of Amos 4:13 and John 1:3," *JTS*, n.s., 61 (2010): 646–655.

mouth of the Holy Spirit.¹⁵¹ Doutreleau concludes the matter: these references are too loose to conclude that the author of *DT* has *DSS* in mind.

Béranger would take Doutreleau's critique of Mingarelli a step further. Every attempt to associate *DT*'s "λόγος on the Holy Spirit" or "first λόγος" with a discrete treatise had been inconclusive. Might the reason for this lie not so much in the incompleteness of Didymus' theological corpus, as was earlier assumed, but rather in the assumption that Mingarelli's linguistic analysis of the terms λόγος and βιβλίον was correct? Béranger questions whether the references to a "first λόγος" or a "λόγος on the Holy Spirit" are better understood as references internal to the treatise itself.¹⁵² Taking up Doutreleau's argument about the references to the "λόγος on the Holy Spirit" and their insufficient basis in *DSS*, Béranger notes that Book 2 of *DT* is a far likelier candidate for the reference. Book 2 is entitled "On the Holy Spirit" (Περὶ τοῦ ἁγίου Πνεύματος). In this Book, our author cites 1 Timothy 5:6 and provides the same exposition of it as the reference in Book 3 had led the reader to expect.¹⁵³

Béranger then notes with Doutreleau that the intention of the second reference (in *DT* 3.31) is somewhat vague. The author of *DT* only notes that he has already dealt in his earlier "λόγος on the Holy Spirit" with several texts that the heretics have raised as objections to the Spirit's divinity. He does not claim to have dealt with the texts he mentions, but only notes that these texts have been used by the heretics "in addition to the others already set forth in the λόγος on the Holy Spirit." It is to the first reference that one must turn if one is to control the reference to the earlier λόγος.

Without further evidence, Béranger's thesis can only be regarded as an intriguing possibility. Though he places greater weight on the clearer reference, the second of the two reveals a greater correspondence with *DSS* than with *DT* Book 2. Béranger therefore brings home his argument by comparing the occurrences of λόγος and βιβλίον, and notes that many of the references to the "first λόγος" can be found in Book 1, a greater percentage in fact than the references to the "first βιβλίον." Moreover, of the four references to the "first λόγος" that could not be found in Book 1, two of them cited chapters that were missing. Thus, only two out of thirteen or fourteen references to the "first λόγος" are unaccounted for, whereas two of five references to the "first βιβλίον" are unaccounted for.¹⁵⁴ It would be illogical to continue to suppose (as Mingarelli had) that λόγος refers to a separate book, whereas βιβλίον refers to a section within a work.¹⁵⁵ Finding that the author of *DT* could use both

---

151. Doutreleau, "Le 'De trinitate'," 524.
152. Louis Béranger, "Sur deux énigmes du *De Trinitate* de Didyme l'Aveugle," *RSR* 51 (1963): 255–267.
153. *DT* 2.6.3.1–6 (512B–513A).
154. Book 1 of *DT* is lacunose and missing several chapters.
155. Béranger, "Sur deux énigmes," 263–264.

words in both senses, he concluded that it was most natural to take the references to the "first λόγος" and the "λόγος on the Holy Spirit" as references to Books 1 and 2 of DT.[156] These considerations, widely accepted by scholars on both sides of the debate,[157] removed from Mingarelli his most important argument in favor of Didymean authorship. The author of DT does not refer to an earlier treatise on the Holy Spirit, but rather refers to the self-same treatise DT throughout.

The Sources of De Trinitate

Nonetheless, in spite of this critique, Doutreleau noted that Mingarelli was not wrong in finding numerous points of contact between the texts of DSS and DT. Though DT did not refer to DSS by name, it certainly made use of the work. Doutreleau argues that DT's dependence on DSS is, of all the arguments advanced by Mingarelli, the strongest support for Didymus' authorship.[158] Alasdair Heron extends the discussion in this direction, investigating the similarities between DT and Didymus' undisputed dogmatic works (especially DSS). He also casts his net somewhat more broadly, asking if there might be reasons to suppose that its use of parts of the pseudo-Athanasian corpus could shed light on crucial aspects of DT's composition. Of course, resemblances between these sources and DT would need to be interpreted "in light of other evidence for/against his authorship."[159]

As well as examining the literary relationships between DT and the pseudo-Athanasian corpus, namely the *Dialogues, De Trinitate et Spiritu Sancto,* and *De Incarnatione et contra Arianos* (sometimes attributed to Marcellus) and pseudo-Basil's *Adversus Eunomium 4-5,* Heron documented numerous connections between DSS and DT. Arguments from DSS, *De Trinitate et Spiritu Sancto,* and *Adversus Eunomium 4-5* are employed by DT. Quite apart from their use by the author of DT, all of these texts stand in some kind of literary relationship to one another. But Heron summarizes his conclusions in the following manner: DT has certainly made use of each of these texts directly.[160]

The importance of this latter statement for the discussion of the authorship of DT is two-fold: 1) the author of DT has made direct use of Didymus' DSS, rather than dealing with an argument common to DSS and other works on the Holy Spirit. 2) The extent of DT's reliance upon DSS is even more well-founded and more extensive than Mingarelli (and, following him, the earlier Doutreleau) had supposed.[161] It is precisely this point that the later Doutreleau found

---

156. Ibid., 264–267.
157. See Heron's positive assessment of Béranger's argument ("Studies," 2).
158. See Doutreleau, "Le 'De trinitate'," 527–532.
159. Heron, "Studies," 12.
160. Heron, "Studies," 176.
161. Doutreleau later addresses some of these points of dependency in several footnotes in his *Didyme l'Aveugle: Traité du Saint-Esprit,* SC 386 (Paris: Cerf, 1992).

most persuasive, when he recanted his former position against Didymean authorship and restored the work to Didymus.[162]

Space does not permit a detailed examination of the numerous points of comparison between *DSS* and *DT*. However, it is worth noting that Simonetti's article questioning Doutreleau's later shift to defending Didymean authorship is far from complete in dealing with the resemblances between the two. In the article, Simonetti treated only those parallels that *did not appear* in Doutreleau's earlier article, and also overlooked Heron's work completely.[163] In short, the resemblances between the two works remain almost as unanswered as they are numerous.[164] Heron's work, responding as it was to the important questions raised by Doutreleau and Béranger's analysis of Mingarelli's traditional argument, offered a mitigating conclusion to the status of *DT*'s relationship to *DSS*. The author of *DT* is certainly very familiar with Didymus' theological work. We know that a major source for our author was Didymus himself.

Style

Taking up another important argument advanced by Mingarelli, Doutreleau notes several stylistic differences between *DT* and *CZ*. Doutreleau followed Mingarelli's arguments about the author's style in light of his work with the *CZ* and compared the two works on several points.[165] On several points, Mingarelli's stylistic observations are vindicated: Didymus, like the author of *DT*, has a habit of citing himself, he is conscious of his limitations and readily admits them, he enjoins his readers to search specific passages of Scripture in their reading as a supplement to his exposition, he abounds in epithets for the writers of Scripture, frequently employs imperatives, and often appeals to the formula: "no one is so daft as to suppose" or an equivalent phrase.[166]

---

162. Doutreleau notes this change of position in *Traité du Saint-Esprit*, 204–205n1. Of his earlier article contesting Mingarelli's conclusion, he writes that he had been too conclusive at the end of the article, that stylistic considerations had played too large a role, and the whole ensemble of the book too small of one: "I admit having been too severe: the analyses of this article—on the whole correct in detail—depend upon a quantity of stylistic elements, small in comparison to the great ensemble of the book, and the conclusion, which I did not formulate without a measure of reservation . . . exceeded in certainty the hesitations expressed within the article. (Je reconnais avoir été trop sévère: les analyses de cet article—justes ordinairement en détail—portent sur une quantité d'éléments stylistiques, infimes par rapport au grand ensemble du livre, et la conclusion, que je n'ai pas formulée sans une certaine réserve . . . dépasse en fermeté les hésitations exprimées dans l'article.)"

163. See "Ancora," 378–383.

164. For the most important of these, see Heron, "Studies," 107–111, 135–139, 146–148, 156–161, and 163–166.

165. Doutreleau, "Le *De Trinitate*," 536–537.

166. Ibid., 543–546.

However, Doutreleau also lists no less than twenty-one points of divergence between DT and CZ.[167] These may be placed into three categories: 1) true contrasts between DT and Didymus' corpus, 2) contrasts between DT and CZ where DT is supported by other writings in Didymus' corpus, and 3) falsifiable contrasts. To the latter category belongs only Example 4, in which Doutreleau argues that the precise terminology of DT in relation to treatises or parts thereof contrasts with Didymus' casual usage of the same or similar terminology in CZ. (Doutreleau's article is written prior to Béranger's helpful study on this terminology, discussed above.) Examples belonging to the other two categories appear in Table 2 where, unless otherwise indicated, DT's distinctive feature precedes CZ's. (See Table 2 on the following pages.)

As the Table illustrates, Doutreleau's work, accurate in the main, suffers from being too narrow. Stylistic habits are best established in relation to a whole corpus,[168] especially when different genres are being compared. Of twenty-one points of contrast between DT and CZ, only twelve of these are supported by the corpus as a whole. Of these, two (Examples 10 and 21) rest on single occurrences of words, hardly enough evidence to establish a habit peculiar to an author. However, in the case of the other ten genuine contrasts, Doutreleau's work serves to underline important stylistic differences between DT and the Tura Commentaries. These demand careful attention, and it is to these that we turn.

Examples 14–17 demonstrate a puzzling tendency toward a more polished style in DT.[169] The author is more concise, more measured in his vocabulary choice, more varied (and more proper) in his grammatical construction, and avoids phrases that are more at home in conversational Greek. The Didymus of the Tura Commentaries, on the other hand, occasionally rambles, employs too many genitive absolutes, and uses conversational language. Yet these stylistic differences, as Koenen pointed out,[170] can be explained. In light of some important work that post-dates Doutreleau's article, it is apparent that there are significant stylistic differences between the commentaries themselves. These differences are largely due to different processes of redaction.

---

167. Ibid., 538–543.

168. Those who responded to him were quick to point this out. See, *e.g.*, Μάρκος 'Ορφανός, Ἡ ψυχὴ καὶ τὸ σῶμα τοῦ ἀνθρώπου κατὰ Δίδυμον Ἀλεξανδρέα (τὸν τυφλόν) (Thessaloniki: Patriarchal Institute of Patristic Studies, 1974), 20.

169. The argument is considered the chief one against attribution by Bärbel Kramer, "Didymos von Alexandrien," in *Theologische Realenzyklopädie*, vol. 8 (Berlin: de Gruyter, 1981): 743.

170. Koenen, "Ein theologischer Papyrus," 80.

Table 2: Doutreleau on Style

True Contrasts	Relative Contrasts
Example 3: Abounds in emphatic adjectives vs. very few emphatic adjectives	Example 1: Use of καθά to introduce citations or compare earlier discussions vs. no use of the above (instead καθώς or ὡς)[174]
Example 5: Use of the dual vs. no use thereof	
Example 9: Different terminology for OT/NT and other books of the Bible[171]	Example 2: The phrase "that is to say" expressed by τοῦτ' ἔστιν vs. no use made of it (instead ὅ ἐστιν)[175]
Example 10: Use of adjective θεϊκός for the Holy Spirit vs. θεῖος[172]	Example 6: Formulas of excuse used vs. none[176]
Example 11: The use of the phrase οἱ ἔξω to designate pagan authors vs. no use of the phrase (instead τὰ ἔθνη)	Example 7: Unafraid of neologisms vs. seldom used[177]
Example 12: Use of term θεοτόκος vs. no use of it[173]	Example 8: Use of first person singular vs. a more impersonal tone[178]

---

171. Apart from one use of νέα with διαθήκη (PsT 107,27) the Tura Commentaries and DT differ on this vocabulary. However, Doutreleau's rendering of κοσμογονία as the book of Genesis is a very debatable reading of DT 1.15.47 (309B). Cf. Mingarelli's translation of the term by *creatio mundi* (310C) and Hönscheid's "Weltentstehung" (*De trinitate, Buch 1*, 63). The names for the Psalter (one example in DT) and Acts of the Apostles (several examples in DT) are unprecedented in the corpus.

172. However, there is only example in CZ where Didymus uses θεῖος to modify πνεῦμα. Didymus will use the word θεϊκός to refer to divine persons or the divine substance elsewhere. See EcclT 105,23 (θεϊκὸ[ν] πρόσωπόν ἐστιν τὸ δι[ὰ τ]οῦ προφήτο[υ ἀπαγ]γέλλον) and PsT 3,12; 149,12 (the Son being the exact imprint of "the divine substance (τῆς θεϊκῆς ὑποστάσεως)").

173. There is one use in his fragments on the Psalms in the catenae. See his *Ps. cat.* (Fragment 693A) in Ekkehard Mühlenberg, *Psalmenkommentare aus der Katenenüberlieferung*, vol. 2, Patristische Texte und Studien 16 (Berlin: de Gruyter, 1977), 69.

174. In CZ, Didymus never uses the word καθά in such circumstances. The same tendency is common to both the EcclT and the PsT. Numerous counter-examples can, however, be produced from the other two Tura Commentaries. See, among many others, HiT 25,13; 176,20; 185,2; 250,26; 259,3 and GenT 27,20; 39,11; 46,10; 227,9; 230,13. In the latter there are no less than thirty-four uses of the word καθά in the situation described.

175. τοῦτ' ἔστιν or τουτέστιν is employed on numerous occasions in all the other Tura Commentaries; it occurs most frequently in the PsT.

176. Judging by his examples, Doutreleau interprets "formules d'excuse du type εἰ θέμις εἰπεῖν rather broadly ("Le 'De trinitate'," 539). Similar formulas of excuse are

Table 2, continued

Example 14: Lack of characteristic particles of speech in *DT* Example 15: Less use of genitive absolute vs. frequent use and abuse of the construction Example 16: Less use of ὡς or ὥστε with the infinitive vs. frequent use of the same construction Example 17: Generally brief and orderly in style, with a more exact and useful vocabulary vs. a wearying style with clumsier vocabulary Example 18: ἱεροφάντης used indiscriminately vs. used of Moses alone Example 21: *DT* mislabels Zechariah "the last of the prophets" vs. correct label	Example 13: Equal use of both οἰκονομία and ἐνανθρώπησις to indicate the Incarnation and infrequent use of ἐπιδημία vs. no use of οἰκονομία in this sense and frequent use of ἐπιδημία and cognates [179] Example 19: Twelve citations of secular sources vs. no direct citation[180]

encountered in Didymus' dogmatic work (e.g. "ut ita dicam" (*DSS* 97, 115, and 133)). They seem to occur where Didymus realizes that he is saying something that is beyond speech or that could be misunderstood.

177. See Koenen, "Ein theologischer Papyrus," 101n2. Koenen points out that most of Doutreleau's "neologisms" are not in fact so. And he cites other places in the corpus where Didymus employs them.

178. Many of *DT*'s uses of the first person singular are found in the prayer sections, a fact that skews the evidence somewhat. Didymus' voice is very apparent in *PsT* and *EcclT*, which contain numerous instances of phrases like πολλάκις εἶπον and λέγω δέ (see Nelson, "The Classroom," 16). (Doutreleau's *Example 20* largely repeats this point.)

179. In relation to οἰκονομία, the argument is fairly weak. Especially in *PsT* the word is given its more specific definition: Incarnation. See, *e.g.*, *PsT* 328,19 (οὐκ ἀλλοιωθεὶς κατὰ τὴν θεότητα, ἀλλὰ κ[α]τὰ τὴν οἰκονομίαν, κα[τὰ τ]ὴν ἐνανθρώπησιν), where the terms are treated interchangeably. For other counter-examples, see Leipoldt, *Didymos der Blinde*, 132 (in many of these the reference is unambiguous, joined as the word is to the modifying prepositional phrase like κατὰ σάρκα). The word ἐπιδημία has a higher rate of occurrence in the Tura Commentaries as a whole than it does in *DT*.

180. *CZ* is somewhat anomalous in this regard. Other Tura commentaries contain direct citations.

As Jerome tells us, *CZ* was dictated at his request. Didymus sends him a copy.[181] The work was thus prepared for the purpose of dissemination. *PsT* and *EcclT* are, by contrast, copies of lectures given by Didymus to an audience. Complete with student questions and occasional arguments, these commentaries give us a more accurate glimpse of the day-to-day activity of the school. As lecture notes, they differ stylistically from the commentaries that are intended for publication: namely *GenT*, *HiT*, and *CZ*.[182] In her important contribution to the study of Didymus' classroom, Anne Nelson points out that the occurrence of conversational language tends to decrease in relation to the work's readiness for publication.[183] *CZ*, *HiT*, and *GenT* were apparently copied from Didymus' lectures and then re-worked before their dissemination.

The writing of *DT* represents a heightening of this tendency, already a consistent feature within Didymus' accepted exegetical corpus. Doubtless the occasion of the treatise and the importance of the topic under consideration encouraged this tendency further. The opening section of Book 2, for instance, as well as the prayer that concludes it, are written in a more highly stylized form.[184] Clearly the author of *DT* spent a great deal of time in preparation for certain sections, not only researching orthodox arguments and sources for his response to Arian, Heterousian, and Macedonian objections, but also formulating these stylized sections. Stylistic infelicities, like the overuse of the genitive absolute, are easily limited by the formational and redactorial processes of the composition.

But it is important not to over-state the response to Doutreleau. Several dissimilarities remain. Some of these are relatively easy to explain. For example, the increased use of emphatic adjectives in *DT* (Example 3) is skewed by the fact that the author of the treatise is constantly searching for predications for the Holy Trinity. Phrases like οἱ ἔξω (Example 11) have near-equivalents in the Commentaries.[185] But other features (Examples 5, 9, 12, and 18) certainly

---

181. Doutreleau gathers Jerome's several testimonies to this fact in his "Introduction," in *Didyme l'Aveugle: Sur Zacharie*, vol. 1, SC 83 (Paris: Cerf, 1962), 23–24n1. While in Alexandria in 386, Jerome had asked Didymus to complete the works that were unavailable to him from Origen, among which he included Hosea (Origen's short book on the prophet was in bad condition) and Zechariah. These Didymus dictated at his request.

182. See Ludwig Koenen and Wolfgang Müller-Wiener, "Zu den Papyri aus dem Arsenioskloster bei Ṭurā," *Zeitschrift für Papyrologie und Epigraphik* 2 (1968): 42–43.

183. Nelson, "Classroom," 15n26. E.g., there is a "striking increase" of the expression ἀμέλει γοῦν in the Psalms and Ecclesiastes commentaries over the published commentaries. Koenen notes that the word ἀμέλει is more at home in speech than in literature ("Ein theologischer Papyrus, 100").

184. See Seiler, *De trinitate, Buch 2*, viii–xiii.

185. *HiT* 288,14–17: "For not only saints, but even those who are outside the true preaching accept concerning the human soul that it is immortal (οὐ γὰρ ἅγιοι μόνοι, ἀλλὰ καὶ οἱ ἔξω τοῦ κηρύ[γμ]ατος τῆς ἀληθείας περὶ τῆς ψυχ[ῆς] τῆς ἀνθρώπου ὡς ἀθανάτο[υ ἐ]κλαμβάνουσι(ν))."

represent almost total departures from Didymus' habitual language. The use of the word Θεοτόκος in particular is curious. We may suggest possibilities, of course, but these remain speculative.[186] Certainly the author of *DT*'s nomenclature for the books of Scripture or the epithets given to their authors is more varied. These points being granted, they are not very damaging to the argument for Didymean authorship.

As noted in the responses to Doutreleau's work, the comparison between *DT* and *CZ* is limited by the fact that Doutreleau is comparing two different genres. The aim of *CZ* is to interpret Scripture with the goal of assisting Didymus' students in psychic ascent toward God, whereas the aim of *DT* is the defense and exposition of Trinitarian orthodoxy. Primarily polemical in intent, *DT* does not appeal as readily to controversial assumptions about the allegorical character of many of Scripture's utterances. Nor should one be surprised that Didymus' *CZ* does not limit itself to the scope of *DT*: Scripture was not written with the sole intent of providing fodder for argumentation! Though there are significant differences of interpretation on the same scriptural passages from Zechariah, the comparison is once again inconclusive, since the aims of both works are markedly different.

To conclude this section on the traditional argument, it appears that Doutreleau and Béranger were right to query whether some aspects of Mingarelli's argument for attribution were sound. Mingarelli's arguments about the references to *DSS* are, in particular, based on problematic interpretations of *DT*'s terminology. However, recognizing the indebtedness of *DT* to *DSS* was well-founded, as Doutreleau recognized. Heron's work on this question—which has received too little attention—extends this indebtedness significantly, such that one may conclude that *DSS* is a major source for the author of *DT*. Though it is not self-evident that Mingarelli's three-volume work is Didymus' three-volume work *On the Trinity*, the occasion of the work suggests that the work we are dealing with here was probably called *De Trinitate*.[187] Finally, Doutreleau's arguments from style seem to have overshot the mark somewhat. When compared with Didymus' whole corpus, and bearing in mind the occasion of the work, *DT* has much more in common with Didymus' writings than Doutreleau had assumed.

---

186. Didymus is a bit of an exception here. His contemporaries use the word on many occasions, especially in anti-Arian polemic. Heron has extensively documented *DT*'s indebtedness to the pseudo-Athanasian *De Incarnatione et contra Arianos* (sometimes attributed to Marcellus). Very reminiscent of Didymus' own doctrine of the two begettings and *DT*'s language, cf. the latter's ὁ γὰρ γεννηθεὶς ἄνωθεν ἐκ Πατρὸς Λόγος ἀρρήτως, ἀφράστως, ἀκαταλήπτως, ἀϊδίως, ὁ αὐτὸς ἐν χρόνῳ γεννᾶται κάτωθεν ἐκ Παρθένου Θεοτόκου Μαρίας (PG 26:996A). Even if Didymus' only other use of the term Θεοτόκος (apart from *DT*) is in the catena, the sources for *DT* certainly made use of the term.

187. Cf. Doutreleau, "Le 'De trinitate'," 532–533.

Recent Arguments

Before offering our conclusion, we look at arguments that have taken on the question from angles other than those determined by Mingarelli's work. Among these, two in particular deserve consideration: arguments from the material in the *Commentary on the Psalms* (*PsT*) and from *DSS* have been raised against Didymean authorship of *DT*.

Christ's Human Soul as a Point-of-Comparison

Shortly after the discovery of the Tura Commentaries, Didymus scholarship quickly turned toward themes that had figured less largely in his extant dogmatic work. Perhaps the most significant of these themes was Didymus' Christology.[188] Christ's human soul in particular, it was noticed, played a significant role in *PsT*, revealing Didymus' alertness to the threat posed by Apollinarist conceptions of the Incarnation. Employing the notion of the "forepassion (προπάθεια)," Didymus could account for Jesus' "experience" of human passions such as fear, anger, or grief without implicitly charging him with sin. He could also reveal the significance of this for soteriology: by "experiencing" passion in his soul without sinning Jesus springs the trap, as it were, of our enslavement to the various passions.

Adolphe Gesché in particular argued that this represented a genuine development on earlier discussions in relation to Christ's human soul, since Didymus not only affirmed the existence of this soul but made it central to his theological system.[189] The importance of this claim for our discussion of *DT* lies in the degree to which Didymus in *PsT* asserts that Christ *experiences* passion without doing so sinfully.[190] Apollinarist denial of a rational soul (λογικὴ ψυχή) in the person of the Incarnate Logos occasioned in the Didymus of *PsT* the need to provide an account of why the existence of the intellective soul (νοῦς) was critical if Jesus was to share in an ontologically complete humanity. Gesché had noted that the author of *DT* likewise affirmed the presence of this

---

188. This was especially true in the 1960s. See, e.g., Adolphe Gesché, *La christologie du 'Commentaire sur les Psaumes' découvert à Toura* (Gembloux: Duculot, 1962); Stephen C. Reynolds, "Man, Incarnation, and Trinity in the *Commentary on Zechariah* of Didymus the Blind of Alexandria" (PhD diss., Harvard, 1966); and Béranger, "Etudes," 1960. More recently Ghattas has rendered the inestimable service of gathering up the various christological discussions with respect to the whole Tura corpus in his *Die Christologie*, 2002.

189. Gesché, "Un document nouveau sur la christologie du IVe s.: le Commentaire sur les Psaumes découvert à Toura," *Studia Patristica* 3 (1961): 206.

190. The language of "experience" must be carefully guarded, however, even in reference to the Psalms Commentary. Didymus develops an account of how Christ can be said to triumph over the passions by experiencing προπάθειαι ("forepassions"). In the Commentary, he can only be said to "experience" passion in a circuitous way: by refusing the herald of the passions, the προπάθεια.

soul and had ascribed to this soul the function of enduring the "passions of the soul (πάθη ψυχῆς)."[191]

Béranger scrutinizes the latter notion.[192] In his study of the critical section in *DT* that deals with questions relating to Christ's soul and his experience of passion,[193] Béranger concludes that while the author of *DT* clearly affirms the existence of Christ's human soul and argues for the significance of this in response to Arian conceptions of the person of Christ (of the σάρξ ἄψυχος variety), the author of *DT* can at best only be shown to argue that Christ *manifests* the passions of the soul. In his words: "selon [notre auteur], le Christ ne les a pas éprouvés."[194] Béranger is not concerned with taking on the authorship question directly, but he is concerned with posing the question: how does one explain two different emphases on the same christological question, especially considering the fact that the Christology of *DT* seems less developed in relation to this question than the Christology of the Psalms commentary (which was assumed by Béranger to be the earlier work)?

Heron responds at length to Béranger's objection. Noting that the relevant chapters of *DT* (3.21–22) are primarily anti-Arian rather than anti-Apollinarian in tone, Heron agrees with Béranger that there is some difference between the understanding of Christ's soul advanced in the treatise and that advanced in *PsT*. But he is careful not to overstate this difference. Even in *PsT*, "Christ, in virtue of the possibility of his soul, suffers προπάθεια—but he does not suffer πάθος as Didymus expressly says."[195] True, there is more description given in *PsT* about what it might mean for Christ, by virtue of his full humanity, to grapple with temptation, but the position staked out in *DT* is not so radically different. Moreover, the psychology of Christ is not really the main theme of these chapters of *DT*. The author of *DT* is more concerned with multiplying orthodox (i.e. anti-Arian) interpretations of the relevant portions of Scripture than he is with developing a coherent account of Christ's soul in its "experience" of human temptation and weakness.[196]

Heron's chief argument, however, consists in noting that in this section of *DT*, the author has drawn from older material that 1) was recognizably orthodox and 2) tended to soft-pedal the ascription of fear and ignorance to

---

191. Gesché, "L'âme humaine de Jésus dans la christologie du IVe s. Le témoignage du Commentaire sur les Psaumes découvert à Toura," *Revue d'histoire ecclésiastique* 54 (1959): 416–418.

192. First in "Etudes," 45–102, and again in his article expanding on this chapter of his thesis: "L'âme humaine de Jésus dans la christologie du *De Trinitate* attribué à Didyme l'Aveugle," *RevScRel* 36 (1962): 1–47.

193. *DT* 3.21–22 (900A–921C).

194. Béranger, "Etudes," 100: "According to [our author], Christ has not *experienced* them."

195. Heron, "Studies," 219.

196. Ibid., 215.

Christ.¹⁹⁷ Adding to the list of possible sources employed at this juncture, Heron includes Epiphanius' *Ancoratus*.¹⁹⁸ The importance of this point for Heron is that *DT*'s argument is akin to texts that pre-date the Apollinarian controversy. This reveals that the author of *DT* is concerned with bringing earlier orthodox voices to bear on the task of refuting Arian Christology. He does not need to adduce his account of "fore-passion" into this discussion, since it is sufficient for his purposes to note that the Scriptures assign human passions to Christ, thus assuming in him a medium (the soul) because of which these passions may be truly predicated of him. This is enough evidence to state his case against Arian Christology: Christ has a human soul.

Differing Attitudes toward Philosophy?

A final argument that has enjoyed a fairly long role in the discussion against attribution of *DT* to Didymus is that advanced by Bienert.¹⁹⁹ In Didymus the Blind's *DSS*, there is a statement that suggests an altogether different attitude toward the philosophical tradition than that on display in the latter chapter of *DT* Book 2. In Book 2 of *DT*, Didymus draws liberally from philosophical sources, producing instances where the philosophers have spoken truthfully about the Godhead and about the Spirit's procession from God the Father. In *DSS*, however, Didymus writes:

> The designation [appellatio] "Holy Spirit" and the substance which is indicated by this designation are altogether unknown to those who do philosophy outside of Sacred Scripture. For only in our writings, as much in the new as in the old, is reference made to both the idea and name of the Holy Spirit.²⁰⁰

How can these two differing attitudes be explained if the works are by the same author?

In the first place, *DT* post-dates *DSS* by at least two decades. Secondly, the two statements are not as contradictory as a casual reading of the texts would suggest. In the chapter where the author of *DT* takes up secular sources as testimony to his doctrine of the Trinity, he promises to set forth verses of Greek poetry in which the poets had received a "perception (συναίσθησις)" of the Son, the Word, and the Spirit.²⁰¹ The language is somewhat guarded; they did not *know* the Holy Spirit. He proceeds to cite passages that refer to the Holy

---

197. Cf. *DT* 3.21 (917B and 920AB) and *Adv. Eun.* 4 (696C and 696BC). *DT* 3.22 borrows from Basil, as noted above.

198. "Studies," 216–218. See Epiphanius, *Anc.* 31–39 (GCS, n.F., 10:39–49).

199. Bienert, *"Allegoria" und "Anagoge,"* 19–20. The argument is repeated by Bart Ehrman, *Didymus the Blind and the Text of the Gospels* (Atlanta: Scholars, 1986), 28, and by Ghattas, *Die Christologie*, 38.

200. *DSS* 3 (DelCogliano, Radde-Gallwitz, and Ayres, *Works on the Spirit*, 144).

201. *DT* 2.27 (753A).

Spirit under the following names: πνεῦμα (five times) and ἡ τοῦ κόσμου ψυχή (once). Though the author of DT clearly thinks that the Holy Spirit is the referent of these names, nowhere does he make reference to a secular source that actually uses the appellation πνεῦμα ἅγιον, which would in fact constitute a contradiction of what Didymus says in DSS.

As it stands, however, this is at least part of Didymus' point in DSS: no philosophical source can produce both the idea and the name of the Holy Spirit. Didymus' second sentence in DSS 3 can be read as epexegetically related to the first. What does he mean by claiming that the Holy Spirit, in name and substance, is unknown to the philosophers? That only in sacred Scripture is "*both* the idea of him *and* his name mentioned (et notio et uocabulum eius refertur)."[202] The DSS text therefore admits the interpretation that DT endorses: while the philosophers may have some sensation of the idea of the Holy Spirit, they do not know his proper name. To know both is the birthright of those who claim the Scriptures as their native writings.

In the second place, DT's positive review of certain Greek philosophers and poets is roughly equivalent with the reviews given to the same authors in Didymus' undisputed corpus. Hermes Tresmegistus is twice positively assessed for his teaching on necessity: those who know God and are wise in him become freed from it.[203] Porphyry suffers predictable scorn, faring only a little worse than he does in DT, where the author admits that he says something sensible about God either because he was forced to by the sheer coercive power of the truth or because of his regard for Plato.[204] Aristotle is, on the whole, upheld as an authority throughout his work.[205] Indeed, as Richard Layton asserts, the "Tura commentaries suggest firsthand knowledge across a wide range of the Aristotelian corpus."[206] On the whole, the corpus is far more generous to the philosophical tradition (as DT is) than the remark in DSS leads us to believe. But after all, in this programmatic remark in DSS—which may very well be a

---

202. Presumably, Jerome's "et . . . et" translates a καί . . . καί rather than an ἤ . . . ἤ construction.

203. See EcclT 167,15-17 and PsT 88,12-14.

204. DT 2.21 (760B). Cf. HiT 280,21-28; PsT 308,13-14; EcclT 281,17-22. In the latter two texts, Porphyry is held up as an example of someone who does not grasp the significance of Scripture's two-fold sense.

205. DT 3.1 (776B); 3.5 (840BC). Cf. EcclT 69,12-17; 90,25-91,2. The reference in EcclT 116,14 is lacunose. The only exception to this would appear to be Didymus' citation of Aristotle in PsT 77,8-12 as a foil for the dominical teaching about love for one's enemies. Michael Gronewald, noting that the saying (as quoted by Didymus) is not extant, discusses the possible sources of the citation in Aristotle. See his "Anmerkungen," in *Didymos der Blinde: Psalmenkommentar 2* (Bonn: Habelt, 1968), 248-249n2.

206. Layton, *Didymus the Blind and His Circle*, 137. See pp. 137-141 for a fuller discussion of Didymus' debts to Aristotle.

borrowing from Origen[207]—Didymus is concerned with establishing the parameters in which he will undertake his study of the Holy Spirit: he will restrict his investigation of a question so fraught with peril to the Scriptures.

Conclusion: the Basis of the Attribution

The most significant of the arguments raised against Didymean authorship elucidates the partial inadequacy of the traditional case in favor of it. This inadequacy has been largely overcome by studies revealing the extent to which *DT* is dependent upon *DSS*, a dependence that is most naturally explained by assuming a common author. Other arguments underline differences in approach to the same theological *topoi* between *DT* and parts of the exegetical corpus. But in the most significant of these cases (the argument about Christ's human soul), it has been demonstrated that 1) *DT* has different opponents in view and 2) that its argument is based on earlier sources. In short, the arguments against Didymean authorship, on balance with those in favor of it, seem to call for revisiting Mingarelli's conclusion.

Didymus is known to have composed three books *On the Trinity*. This treatise, though missing its title page, deals with the Trinity and is composed of three books. A compelling case can be made for the title *On the Trinity*. *DT* was written at some point between 384 and 429. The clearest deduction we can make from those who wrote about Didymus' work is that the blind theologian wrote his *On the Trinity* during the same window of time, between 384 and 398. At this same point the author of the work *DT* was 1) embroiled in controversy and 2) an old man. Didymus was certainly the latter, and could well have been the former, since at this period in his life his circle was involved in the early stages of the First Origenist Controversy. The author of the work is living in Egypt, as Didymus did throughout his life. The author of the work presides over the daily assemblies of a school, as Didymus does. Consonant with this office, the author has a habit of alluding to his own work, as does Didymus. The author of *DT* composes his work in the presence of an audience. We know that this was Didymus' daily habit. He enjoins his audience to search specific passages of Scripture in their reading as a supplement to his exposition. So does Didymus. *DT*'s closest debts, in terms of sources, are works that either belong to Didymus' corpus or (as with *Adversus Eunomium 4-5*) are still not settled, with some external manuscript testimony to support Didymus' authorship. *DT* is deeply indebted to Didymus' extant theological corpus, more so than even Mingarelli had originally assumed.

---

207. *Prin.* 1.3.1. Origen asserts that God's Son was known to the Greeks, but that they did not realize there was a Holy Spirit: "But no one except those who are familiar with the law and the prophets ... could have even a suspicion of the personal existence of the Holy Spirit" (Butterworth, 29).

The argument, as it now stands, is not entirely conclusive. And yet, the weight of the evidence points in favor of Didymus' authorship. Until there are clearer reasons to the contrary, the work ought to be considered again in relation to his corpus. The study thus far certainly suggests that an attempt at synthesizing Didymus' exegetical work with his theological cannot safely ignore a treatise that nearly two centuries of scholarship regarded as his greatest achievement. To this task we turn.

2

GOD THE TRINITY: IDENTITY AND ACTIVITY

In this chapter I treat, in a thematic way, Didymus' account of the *hypostaseis* of the Trinity in relationship to the activity of the Trinity. The Father, Son, and Holy Spirit are who they are in relation to one another. The Son is the divine *hypostasis* who is begotten by the Father. The Holy Spirit is the divine *hypostasis* who proceeds from the Father. The Father is the *hypostasis* from whom these other two *hypostaseis* are begotten and proceed.

The missions of the Son and the Spirit of God reflect their identities as the only-begotten and only-proceeding from the Father. Thus, the divine identities of the *hypostaseis* are determinative of the activity of the Trinity in and toward the created world. Co-inhering in the unity of the Trinity, the divine *hypostaseis* never act alone in reference to the creation. All of the divine *hypostaseis* share in the same activity. And yet the several identities of the *hypostaseis*, I argue, are related to the particularity afforded each of the *hypostaseis* within the one activity of the Trinity. In the creation and recreation of the world, this particularity is seen with greatest clarity in *DT*: the Father wills, the Son fashions, and the Spirit sanctifies.

This discussion will serve mainly to elucidate the subject matter of the next chapter: the activities of the *hypostaseis* in the economy of re-creation and the implications of this activity for Didymus' account of Scripture. The present chapter, however, has some immediate consequences for Didymus' account of the divine use of human language. In *DT*, Didymus does not provide us with material for re-constructing his philosophy of language. He does not weigh in on the *thesis-physis* debate. His attitude toward the use of human words in the service of theology unfolds very much in the course of his exposition of his main theme: the nature and identities of the divine *hypostaseis* and the activities by which they are known to us. In this chapter I argue that attending to Didymus' account of the identities of the *hypostaseis* reveals two basic convictions: 1) that human language is relativized by its contact with divine reality 2) yet in such a way that it maintains some purchase on this reality.

The Three *Hypostaseis*

The treatise *DT* is written largely with the goal of defending the consubstantial divinity of the Son and the Holy Spirit with the Father. In order to accomplish this goal, Didymus occupies himself largely with revealing the extent to which the Son and the Holy Spirit share in all the activities, names, and essential properties of the Father. If these are held in common—save the few names reserved to distinguish the *hypostaseis*—there is a strong presumption in favor of the Son and the Spirit's consubstantiality with the Father. Hereby, Didymus challenges the accuracy and scope of Eunomius' claim that the names of the *hypostaseis* are different. Throughout, Didymus is concerned with illustrating the sheer multitude of the names that are common to all three *hypostaseis*: their ἐπίκοινα ὀνόματα.[1]

My treatment of the identities of each of the divine *hypostaseis* in DT assumes the background of their consubstantiality. The divine *hypostaseis* share the same nature.[2] None of the *hypostaseis* are excluded from the worship that creatures are to offer up to God. The scope of the present study demands that attention be paid to the ways in which Didymus speaks of what is unique to each of the divine *hypostaseis*. Toward this end, I commence with the Son, continue with the Holy Spirit, and conclude with the Father. The decision to proceed in this manner is mainly a formal one: beginning with the Son and moving to the Holy Spirit reflects the manner in which the treatise unfolds. But it holds an additional benefit as well, since Didymus' treatment of the Father (barely a separate *topos* within the treatise)[3] develops naturally alongside his treatment of the other two *hypostaseis*.

From the Father's Hypostasis

Didymus' understanding of the generation of the Son and the procession of the Holy Spirit from the Father has run afoul of contemporary scholarship since Leipoldt. Before addressing the significance of the Son's generation and the Spirit's procession for the missions of these *hypostaseis*, it is important to deal with a terminological or conceptual issue that is highlighted with some frequency. It is Didymus' normal custom in DT to speak of the Son's generation and the Spirit's procession from the *hypostasis* of the Father. The significance of this move lies in its uniqueness. Didymus does not follow the Athanasian and Nicene vocabulary of the Son's begetting from the Father's οὐσία.[4] Nor

---

1. Cf. Eunomius, *Apol.* 18 (Vaggione, *Extant Works*, 54–57) and DT 1.11.1–6 (293A–296A). See also DT 3.21 (928BC).

2. For the best discussion of Didymus' use of terms like οὐσία and φύσις (and derivations like ὁμοούσιος and ὁμοφύης), see Bardy, *Didyme l'Aveugle*, 74–93. Béranger adds a helpful correction to Bardy's treatment of the word συμφυής and its cognates, discussed below.

3. In DT 1.34–35, Didymus acknowledges this limitation of the treatise. His goal throughout has been to contend that the Son and the Holy Spirit are divine "without injuring in thought the ineffable glory of God the Father" (1.35 (437B)).

4. For this discussion, see Leipoldt, *Didymus der Blinde*, 105–106 and Bardy, *Didyme l'Aveugle*, 78n2.

does he speak in a noncommittal fashion of the begetting ἐκ τοῦ πατρός. Didymus far more commonly speaks of the Son's being begotten ἐκ τῆς ὑποστάσεως τοῦ πατρός.⁵ The only exception to this language in the treatise occurs in a place where Didymus' language is heavily indebted to his source and the terms of his opponent's argument.⁶

The language has drawn frequent criticism. Leipoldt criticizes Didymus here for having little facility with the speculative aspect of the theologian's task, proving awkward when he undertakes to invent new formulae. This particular formula, he avers, involves Didymus in the contradictory assertion that the Father transfers that which separates him from the Son to the Son (namely, the Father's own *hypostasis*).⁷ Not that Leipoldt charges Didymus with such a serious doctrinal error; it is his terminology, not the substance of his confession, which Leipoldt deems infelicitous.

More recently, T.F. Torrance has drawn attention to the inadequacy of the formula in a more nuanced way. He situates the production of such formulae within neo-Nicene discussions of the relationship between the divine οὐσία and its internal relations. Caught between the desire to do full justice to the Son's and the Spirit's principle of individuation in the Father, and to avoid any subordinationist distinctions between the Persons on the basis of the Father's role in this individuation, Didymus asserts hypostatic derivation but not essential derivation from the Father.⁸ To communicate this idea, Torrance argues, Didymus normally articulates the generation and the procession from the Father's *hypostasis*. Torrance argues that this solution has the unfortunate consequence of rendering the divine "essence" as an abstraction, clearly separate from the intra-Trinitarian relations of the *hypostaseis*.

Bardy's solution to the difficulty is the most nuanced, more closely tied to the way that Didymus uses his terms. He notes with Leipoldt that the phrase under discussion seems to involve Didymus in a contradiction. But he cautions against leaning too heavily on the formulaic aspect of Didymus' articulation of this relationship: "La prédilection de Didyme pour la formule ἐκ τῆς ὑποστάσεως τοῦ πατρός ne suppose pas autre chose qu'une définition plus précise du terme οὐσία réservé exclusivement à l'unique substance divine."⁹

---

5. For a sampling, see *DT* 1.15.39 (308C), 1.36.7 (440D–441A), and 3.3 (817B).

6. This is *DT* 1.10.8 (293A), in which Didymus is answering Aetius' argument that the Son cannot be generated from the Father's οὐσία (*Synt.* 8 (Wickham, 541)). Didymus draws his response almost verbatim from the pseudo-Athanasian *Dial. Trin.* 2 (PG 28:1181A).

7. Leipoldt, 106.

8. T.F. Torrance, *The Trinitarian Faith: the Evangelical Theology of the Ancient Catholic Church* (Edinburgh: T&T Clark, 1993), 325.

9. Bardy, 78n2: "Didymus' predilection for the formula ἐκ τῆς ὑπόστασεως τοῦ πατρός assumes nothing other than a more precise definition of the term οὐσία referred exclusively to the one divine substance [i.e., of the Father]."

Bardy understands Didymus to be specifying that the generation is from the Father's essence, but that this relationship of generation is one that the Son has only in relation to the Father.[10] I argue, following Bardy, that understanding Didymus' use of the word ὑπόστασις is critical in appraising his formula.

Leipoldt rightly recognizes two basic meanings for the term in Didymus' corpus as a whole: "personality (Persönlichkeit)" and "that which is actually existent (das wirklich Vorhandene)." The former use is exceedingly rare;[11] it does not feature in DT. In DT then, Didymus speaks of the non-existence of the light that has no radiance in such terms: "if . . . there was a time when the radiance was not, where is the existence (ὑπόστασις) of the light that causes it to radiate?"[12] Didymus regularly employs cognates of the word ὑπόστασις that emphasize the existence or non-existence of things or persons in actuality.[13] Transposed into a Trinitarian key, the notion of "actual existence" obtains;

---

10. This raises the question as to whether Didymus implicitly endorses a "from the Father alone" understanding of the Spirit's procession. Torrance's attempts to circumvent this possibility by documenting passages in which Didymus affirms a procession of the Spirit "from the Son's *hypostasis*" are not convincing. See *The Trinitarian Faith*, 225n166. Of the eleven citations that he lists, only two of these are possible references: DT 1.15.76 (320A) has a reference to the Spirit's procession from "his *hypostasis*" in which the referent of αὐτοῦ is grammatically ambiguous. However, the argument indicates that Didymus is emphasizing the immediacy of the Son and the Spirit's derivation from the Father, since he is asserting their equality with the Father in time and essence. DT 2.1.1 (448C) provides the only example where the referent of αὐτοῦ could be taken either of the Father or the Son, and should therefore be harmonized to Didymus' clear uses throughout the rest of the treatise.

Though it is the case that Didymus seems to affirm by this formula the Spirit's procession from the Father alone, Torrance cites other passages in which Didymus seems to expand on this notion in a way that discourages such a facile conclusion. See, for instance, DT 2.2.22 (460B), which speaks of the generation and the procession "from the one Father in the unity of his divinity (ἀπὸ τοῦ ἑνὸς Πατρὸς καθ' ἕνωσιν τῆς ἑαυτοῦ θεότητος)." In context, the phrase expresses the difference between created generations or processions and divine ones. In the former case, these generations or processions reveal *equality* of essence between the generator and the generated; in the latter, they reveal *identity* of essence, since the Father is not *essentially* who he is in the one Godhead without the one who proceeds and the one who is generated from him. When one moves beyond the formulaic, Didymus cannot be easily pressed into service on either side of the *filioque* debate. H.B. Swete appears to recognize this with respect to DT as well in his *On the History of the Doctrine of the Procession of the Holy Spirit, From the Apostolic Age to the Death of Charlemagne* (1876; reprint, Eugene, OR: Wipf and Stock, 2004), 93-95.

11. Leipoldt, 104. Bardy follows him closely in *Didyme l'Aveugle*, 79-80.

12. DT 1.15.36 (308B).

13. See ἐνυπόστατος/ἐνυποστάτως in DT 1.16.44 (337B); 1.26.15 (384C); 2.1.7 (452A); 2.1.9 (452B); 2.8.1 (616A); 2.10 (648A); 3.19 (892A); 3.37 (972B), and ἀνυπόστατος in 1.16.38 (337A) and 1.18.53 (356C).

ὑπόστασις is used of the Three to indicate that each is really subsistent. The Word and the Spirit are not the properties or energies of the Father.

Given that this is Didymus' primary emphasis in the use of the vocabulary, Leipoldt's criticism of Didymus' formula seems somewhat misplaced. As Bardy maintains, Didymus does not appear to be saying that the Son and the Holy Spirit derive what is unique to themselves from that which is unique to the Father. The point of the affirmation is that the Spirit and the Son do not come forth from the Father's will or from his activity, but rather from his very Person. Didymus speaks of the Son and the Spirit proceeding from the Father's *hypostasis* primarily as a way of affirming that they are joined in a natural relation to one whose existence *as* Father is never under threat. This being so, the generation of the Son and the procession of the Spirit are intrinsic to the Father's existence as such. They exist in concrete actuality in distinction from the Father, just as he exists in concrete actuality in distinction from them.

The Only-Begotten Son

For Didymus, as for the other authors in the late fourth century, the sharing of the Son in the Father's essence demanded an account of how to admit real differentiation without threatening the unity and (hence) simplicity of the divine nature. As far as the Son is concerned, Didymus' most significant opponents in DT are Eunomian. In developing an account of the Son's identity, Didymus establishes the Son's relationship with the Father in terms that reveal the problematic assumptions behind the Arian or Eunomian thesis that the Son is a creature of the Father. It is to this argument that we must attend if we are to understand Didymus' account of that which differentiates the Son's *hypostasis* from the *hypostaseis* of the Father and the Spirit.

Though the *hypostaseis* of the Trinity share most names in common, each of the *hypostaseis* possesses certain names that are not shared: the proper names of the *hypostaseis*. The Father is always Father; the Son is always Son; the Holy Spirit is always Holy Spirit. The Son is also—in distinction from the Father and the Spirit—the Word. He is the "Only-begotten (μονογενής)," a name that he possesses because of the reality to which the name attests: the Son is the only *hypostasis* who is begotten of God the Father by nature.[14] The adjective serves as a substantive in DT, communicating the numerical unity of the Son and thus differentiating him from the Holy Spirit (who is not begotten) and from created sons who by grace come to call his Father their own.[15]

---

14. See DT 1.11.5 (293B–296A).

15. Bardy (p. 99) notes that the term is regarded by Didymus as a synonym of ὁμοούσιος in DT 3.9 (853A). However, the phrase μονογενῆ, ὅ ἐστιν ὁμοούσιον should be taken to mean that consubstantiality is implicit within (rather than synonymous with) the affirmation that the Son is the only Son of the Father. I say this because μονογενής is more frequently used by Didymus to affirm the numerical unity of the Son (cf. 1.15.59 (313A) and 3.2.2 (788B)). It is possible to connect this adjective closely with the argu-

The un-shared names given to each of the *hypostaseis* serve to illustrate that they truly subsist in real distinction from one another.[16] In the case of the Son, the property that distinguishes him from the other two divine *hypostaseis* is his generation (γέννησις) from the Father.

Not Created

Most of what Didymus says about the generation serves to prevent its being understood in creaturely terms. Didymus takes pains to distinguish generation from creation. His Eunomian opponents ask whether it is the case that "the whole universe is from God [i.e. the Father]." If Didymus responds in the negative, then he posits two (or more) first principles for the cosmos; if he responds affirmatively, he calls the Son's unique relationship to the Father into question. Didymus answers "yes," but with the caveat that the universe is not from God "by way of generation (γεννητῶς), as the Son is."[17] The distinction between the two modes of being from the Father is the distinction between creaturely being and divine being. What comes forth from God by his act of creation is not God, but the one who comes forth from God by generation is God the Only-begotten Son. Since the Word's being begotten in the manner of a son (υἱϊκῶς) is to be distinguished from the creature's production in a creaturely way (δημιουργικῶς), Didymus can affirm that "there is no discrepancy in being, power, and glory between the Only-begotten Son and God the Father, and every difference, if it is fitting to say this, [between the Son] and the creature."[18]

Atemporally and Non-Spatially

The Son's generation does not belong to the created world. Ingredient within this affirmation is the concern not to couch the generation of the Son in categories drawn from the investigation of the created world. Temporal categories in particular are regularly imported by opponents of the orthodox into the doctrine of the Son's generation. When asked, "When was the Son begotten?" Didymus is ready with his cheeky reply: "At the same time that the Father was not begotten."[19] How ludicrous the attempt to measure the Creator

---

ment made about the numerical unity of the Holy Spirit in his *hypostasis*, a point that Didymus regards as an important one in defense of his divinity. Cf. *DT* 2.4.7 (484A), 2.6.21 (553AB), and 2.8.1 (620B). The latter reference informs us that Didymus had used this argument in Book 1 (in the missing chapters), possibly in reference to the Son.

16. See *DT* 1.15.2 (296B) and 2.8.1 (608D). In 1.18 (341B heading), Didymus employs the abstractions πατρότης, υἱότης, and ἐκπόρευσις to speak of what is "proper to each *hypostasis* individually (ἴδιον ἑκάστης ὑποστάσεως ἰδίως)."

17. *DT* 1.9.2 (280A). In addition to the verb γεννάω, Didymus employs the following cognates of the noun γέννησις: the adjectives γεννητικός (2.2.41 (464C)) and γεννητός (3.5 (841A)), the adverbs γεννητῶς (1.9.2 (280A)) and γεννητικῶς (1.35 (437C)).

18. *DT* 2.2.41 (464C).

19. *DT* 1.8 (280A). Didymus perhaps borrows this remark from Gregory Nazianzen's *Or.* 29.3 (Wickham and Williams, 246).

of time by his own creature!²⁰ So the Father begot the creating Son without beginning (ἀνάρχως).²¹ The Son, who in time would enter into the world to be born without the contribution of a father, was begotten above atemporally (ἀχρόνως) without a mother.²²

If temporal categories are problematic for Didymus, so are attempts to understand the generation of the Son in spatial ones. The words "above" and "below" are, strictly speaking, concessions to human habits of speech. Being incorporeal, the divine *hypostaseis* are not bound by the limitations associated with the possession of bodies. Neither are they like the spiritual beings enumerated among the creatures of God, who are merely "incorporeal to us" but in actuality possess heavenly bodies.²³ This being the case, the location of the generation of the Son from the Father is unsearchable,²⁴ since such a conception of the generation of the Son would imply both the Father and the Son's confinement by spatial limitations. The Author of space and magnitude (the Son) cannot be measured in terms that derive their meaning and existence from him.²⁵ Un-circumscribed by the thoughts of spiritual beings,²⁶ it follows that the divine *hypostaseis* cannot be circumscribed by the sensibly-perceived boundaries of the spatial world.

Without Suffering or Change

Certainly, there are certain created analogues that illuminate one aspect or another of the divine generation. According to Didymus, Heterousian interpretations of the Son's generation fail in a strange way to follow certain aspects of these created analogues. What son is of a difference essence than his father? Begotten substances are not unlike the substances that beget them.²⁷

---

20. Cf. *DT* 1.15.39–41 (308C–309A).

21. *DT* 3.2.4 (789A).

22. See *DT* 1.15.79 (321A).

23. *DT* 2.4.4 (481B). With Origen, Didymus asserts that only the Trinitarian *hypostaseis* are bodiless.

24. *DT* 1.9.5 (280AB), though lacunose, presents the above ideas. Cf. Hönscheid, *De trinitate, Buch 1*, 26n17.

25. *DT* 1.16.10–11 (332C). Didymus concludes the thought: "For where among the highest, beyond incorporeal (ὑπερασωμάτοις), and superior *hypostaseis* is magnitude?"

26. *DT* 2.4.8 (484A). This is the chief epistemological distinction between divine being and spiritual beings for Didymus; the latter are comprehended by those who are pure in their thinking, even if they are unable to be conceived in strictly material categories. The latter are subject to limitation (πέρας) and quantity (ποσότης). Divine being is defined or circumscribed by neither one (cf. *DT* 2.6.2.1 (509A) and *DSS* 21–23).

27. See *DT* 1.16.6 (332B): Adam and Eve, though not begotten (and thus possessing a different mode of generation than ours), are equal in nature to us who are from them; 1.16.41 (337A): Seth is not ἑτεροούσιος from Adam; 1.34.19 (437A): those who confess the Son to be a creature might as well be spouting the nonsense that sons are not "of the same race (ὁμογενεῖς)" as their own fathers. For additional passages on this theme, see Bardy, *Didyme l'Aveugle*, 96–97.

But Didymus recognizes that attempts to follow this analogue in every direction are bound to run into terminal difficulties. When a man begets a firstborn son, he becomes that which he was not prior to the begetting: namely, a father. Creaturely begetting involves the begetter in change. The close connection between change and passibility likewise implies that creaturely begetting always involves the begetter in suffering. But neither changeability nor passibility may be attributed to the divine nature. Being immutable (ἄτρεπτος), the Father begets the Son impassibly.[28] In connection with this doctrine, Didymus is fond of remarking that the "generation below" provides a helpful indication that the Father's generation of the Son was "without suffering": the Mother of God gives birth to her Child and remains a virgin.[29]

Immediately

A final qualifier of the generation of the Son occurs with some frequency in DT. Didymus argues that the Son is begotten ἀδιαστάτως.[30] The word is variously rendered "continually" or "immediately."[31] Didymus regularly uses the term in connection with the light-radiance analogy that he employs to illustrate certain aspects of the relationship between the Father and the Son. In the section where he develops the analogy to the greatest extent, he is responding to Aetius' argument that the Father, being un-begotten in essence, by definition cannot beget a Son who shares in his essence.[32] The Heterousian argument takes two tacks: 1) If, while God is un-begotten in essence, he begets a Son who shares in his essence but is begotten, then the essence of God is found to be compounded: it is both un-begotten and begotten at the same time. 2) If, however, the essence of God is transformed into a thing begotten when God begets the Son, then the essence of God is itself changeable. The Homoousian argument, argues Aetius, involves the essence of God in one of two impossibilities: complexity or change.

Didymus responds largely along lines developed before him.[33] To the first argument he notes that even among created things, there is some analogy for the Homoousian position. Light, he argues, is wholly generative, and yet no one supposes that the radiance that it generates is of another essence than it is. The light neither adds the radiance to itself from some external source nor acquires it; the radiance exists inseparably with the light. They are distinguishable; yet they both belong to the same essence. Didymus summarizes his argument about light by qualifying the verb γεννάω with the use of the word ἀδιαστάτως. God the Father begot the Son in the same manner: ἀδιαστάτως. To

---

28. DT 3.2.9 (792A).
29. See especially DT 3.2.20 (793CD).
30. DT 1.10.3 (292B); 1.15.76 (320A); 1.32.37 (429C); and 3.2.9 (729A).
31. See Hönscheid, *De trinitate, Buch 1*, 75 and 219, who takes the phrase to mean "without delay (ohne Verzug)" and "without interruption (ohne Unterbrechung)."
32. Aetius, *Synt.* 8 (Wickham, 541).
33. DT 1.10.3–4, 6–8 (292B–293A).

the second argument above, Didymus points out that the light does not undergo change in order to become radiance but rather remains what it is while it produces the radiance as something that is wholly perfect. Yet this takes place in such a way that both remain "organically one (συμφύτως)."[34]

The relationship between the Father and the Son is one in which the Father always has his Only-begotten. For Didymus, the light-radiance analogy illustrates both the immediacy and perfection of the two terms. Light that exists without radiance is not real light. Both exist perfectly and immediately together. A later occurrence of the word further clarifies the idea:

> For since it is impossible for the Father not to be eternally and truly Father—since he did not acquire this name in time nor as an epithet—so it is impossible for the Son, the Word, and his [i.e. the Father's] Spirit not to be eternally and by nature from his *hypostasis*. For at the same time that the Father exists—permit me to speak in this way—the one is begotten immediately (ἀδιαστάτως), and the other proceeded. He is not deprived of being the Father of the Only-begotten and of having his Spirit proceeding from him, and because he is Father, he differs from his Son and his own Spirit neither in time nor in essence. For if he were to beget later, he would be changed, or would become something different (which is foreign to divinity), since he is found to be God at some time when he is not called, or rather, actually is not Father, because he has not yet begotten.[35]

In the above argument, it is the immediacy of the generation that is stressed. To be Father means to have a Son without delay. Immediacy, rather than continual action, is the sense of Didymus' exposition. Later arguments also suggest that Didymus does not conceive of the generation of the Son as an activity of the Father that is ongoing. This squares with Didymus' distinction between the created wisdom that comes into existence when God makes creatures wise and the divine wisdom who is his Only-begotten Son. Didymus plays on the present tense of the verb γεννάω in Proverbs 8:25 to make the distinction. If this were a reference to the Son, he argues, it would employ the aorist (ἐγεννήθη), since he is "no longer being begotten (οὐκ ἔτι γεννᾶται)."[36]

---

34. Béranger, "Etudes," 12–13, helpfully points out that Didymus employs the adjectival form of this word only of the divine *hypostaseis*, improving on Bardy's assertion that it is a synonym of ὁμοφυής (*Didyme l'Aveugle*, 91). συμφυής, in Didymus' usage, emphasizes co-inherence within the same specific nature, rather than equality within the same nature.

35. *DT* 1.15.76–77 (320A).

36. *DT* 3.3 (813BC).

In a closely related analogy, Didymus notes that the fruit trees in Paradise came into existence in a manner that images the eternal relation of Father and Son. The root was present at the same time as the fully-formed fruit (Gen 1:11–12 and 2:9). If this takes place among temporal things, why is it so unbelievable a thing then that the eternal Father should be ever "ripe (ἔγκαρπος)" with his own Son?[37] The Son is immediately present with the Father, and between the Father and the radiance of his glory nothing can be thought.[38]

A Natural Relation with the Father

In a passage that is particularly helpful in distinguishing between divine and created natures, Didymus argues that "what is born by the creature is begotten in the fellowship (κοινωνίαν) of one to another and is not naturally united (συμφυές) with its begetter, nor did it come forth as perfect immediately and impassibly. With the Divinity, it is the opposite."[39] Among creatures, the begotten and the begetter share in the same generic nature; this point is affirmed throughout the treatise. But unlike creatures, the Son and the Father do not merely share in the generic nature of divinity. If this were the case, then there would be three Gods (extending the sharing to the Holy Spirit). Both are "naturally united" in the one nature that they share. The use of συμφυής indicates that Didymus cannot merely speak of a relational unity such as could be termed "fellowship." Their individuation, in which they are truly "one" and "another," is an individuation that is expressed purely in terms that refer to one another.

This is perhaps the most important distinction that can be made between the Father's begetting of the Son and all other kinds of begetting. When a human father begets a son, that son will surpass his father with respect to appearance or strength or some other quality.[40] Accidents accrue among substances of the same generic nature such that wild discrepancies exist between the virtuous and the vicious. But this is not the case with the Father and the Son. In every possible way, Didymus is at pains to note that the individuation of the Father and the Son is an individuation that is always linked in the closest possible way with the unity of the *hypostaseis*.

What may be said positively about the generation of the Son is said in relation to the Father. The Father begot the Son consubstantially and truly.[41] He begot him by nature.[42] That is, the Son is the natural and genuine Son of the

---

37. DT 1.15.47 (309BC). Mingarelli's proposed emendation (310Dn62) does not change the sense of the passage, which is abundantly clear (Hönscheid, 63n5).

38. See DT 1.8.17 (281C–284A). The context of this latter remark is Didymus' argument against the position that the will of the Father is a mid-term between the Father and the Son.

39. DT 1.15.54–55 (312B).

40. DT 1.16.34 (336C).

41. DT 3.5 (841A). For "truly," see also DT 2.6.20 (552A).

42. See DT 1.9.19 (284A), 1.11.5 (296A), and 1.32.37 (429C).

Father, who does not come to his Sonship by adoption or any other means; he *is* the Son because of his own natural relation (φυσικὴ σχέσις) to the Father.[43] The Son is the true image of the Father (2 Cor 4:4 and Col 1:15).[44]

Summary

Didymus reveals that he is committed to developing an account of the Son in ways that guard against importing creaturely categories into the account of his generation from the Father. If an analogy is taken up from the created order, he is quick to illustrate its inadequacies in certain respects. The cataphatic moment in his account of the Son tends to focus on the revealed names of his *hypostasis* and the analogies suggested by Scripture (light, radiance, fruit, etc.); the apophatic moment consistently qualifies these analogies by paring away what could cause the analogy to be misconstrued. The dialectic intends to honor two givens: 1) the Son has revealed himself to us in his eternal identity as the Son of the Father and 2) the Son who has revealed himself to us is of the one uncreated being that is beyond human definition and comprehension.

The Spirit Who Proceeds from the Father

Book 2 of *DT* is devoted to defending the consubstantial divinity of the Spirit with the Father and the Son. The Holy Spirit, or the Spirit of God as he is more commonly known in the treatise, is the name proper to his *hypostasis*. Didymus avers that "whatever the Father is, so his Spirit is, without of course being Father."[45] As such, the Spirit of God is demarcated from created spirits with qualifiers such as "all-holy" or "divine."[46] As the only-Begotten of the Father is separated from the adopted sons who come to be such only in a relation of grace, Didymus makes much of the notion that the Holy Spirit is unique in his *hypostasis*, possessing his unique identity in one *hypostasis* alone. Such a situation never arises among creatures, even among the higher echelons of the angelic host.[47] There are multiple *hypostaseis* who share in the name of archangel; there is only one Holy Spirit.

In an argument that closely parallels the one he develops in relation to the generation of the Son, Didymus argues that divine procession is the mode of the Spirit's derivation from the Father. This serves to distinguish the Holy Spirit's *hypostasis* from the Son and from created spirits. He is the Spirit of God

---

43. The phrase "natural relation" is used in *DT* 1.26.21 (385A).

44. This is Didymus' most frequently employed analogy for the Father and the Son. See *DT* 1.15.35 and 95–98 (308B and 328B), 1.16.28–35 (336AC), and 2.5.26 (504B).

45. *DT* 1.15.71 (317A).

46. For πανάγιον, see *DT* 2.7.3.8 (569A), and for θεϊκόν and θεῖον respectively, see 2.7.3.8 (569B) and 1.30.4 (416C).

47. See *DT* 2.6.21 (553AB): "The creation has nothing that exists in one *hypostasis* or in one person (πρόσωπον) ... but the oracles show us that the Holy Spirit is one and the same, since he is not enumerated within creation." Cf. 2.4.7 (484A) and 2.8.1 (620B).

"by procession."[48] The language that he uses in relation to the Spirit's procession is far more varied than that employed of the Son, however. He will speak most frequently of the Spirit's "procession (ἐκπόρευσις)" from the Father's *hypostasis*,[49] and will also speak of the Spirit's "issuing forth (πρόοδος)"[50] or simply "going forth (προέρχομαι)"[51] from the Father. Of similar import are affirmations of his being "breathed forth,"[52] "manifest (ἐκφαίνω),"[53] and "shining forth (ἐκλάμπω)" from the Father.[54]

He Proceeds rather than Proceeded

Didymus argues for the atemporal character of the Spirit's procession just as he argues for the same with respect to the Son. But, curiously, he draws attention to this point in a different way. Producing a different grammatical argument to that developed in relation to the Son, he notes on separate occasions that Scripture never once uses the phrase "he proceeded (ἐξεπορεύθη)" to describe the Spirit's eternal procession.[55] Expounding the significance of this observation more fully in the Book on the Spirit, he writes that the word ἐκπορεύεται, "being indeterminate (ἀόριστος), signifies the eternity and inseparability of his nature with that one from whom he goes forth ineffably."[56] The exposition Didymus offers here reveals that he conceives of the procession of the Spirit neither as an event that happened in time and then was finished, nor as an ongoing or continual event; rather, that it is spoken of indeterminately signifies that he is eternally and inseparably with the one from whom he has his procession. A very similar point is made in a passage where he is reflecting less on the aspect of the above verb than its meaning: "'He proceeds from the Father' means that he was produced without beginning and consubstantially from the Father's *hypostasis*, since every issuing forth (πρόοδος) is accomplished by things that are equal and alike."[57] As in his de-

---

48. *DT* 2.8.2 (621A).

49. The use of the word ἐκπορεύομαι and cognates is most frequent.

50. *DT* 2.2.22 (460B); 2.12 (673B); 3.38 (976A).

51. There are several instances. See *DT* 2.4.8 (484A) for an example. Note that this language is also used once of the Son (1.36.7 (441A)).

52. See *DT* 2.2.22 (460B) and 2.6.6 (524C).

53. See, for example, *DT* 3.38 (976A), where the notion is related to the Spirit's procession rather than his mission into the world.

54. *DT* 2.5.11 (496B).

55. *DT* 1.15.42 (309A). Recall the significance he attaches to the present tense of the verb γεννάω in not reading Proverbs 8:25 as a reference to the Son. On one occasion (2.5.10 (496A)) Didymus renders ἐκπορεύεται with ἐξεπορεύθη, but in this instance he appears only to be attempting to harmonize the quotation about the Spirit with that written of the Son (ἐξῆλθον).

56. *DT* 2.8.1 (620B).

57. *DT* 3.38 (976A). For an almost identical passage see 2.2.22: "For all begetting and proceeding are realized by beings that are equal and like each other. But in the most distinctive way, generation and procession from the one Father take place according to

scription of the Son's generation, Didymus describes the Spirit as proceeding "without beginning" and "immediately" from the Father.[58]

Inseparably

If the language of generation has potentially problematic connotations relating to corporeality (passibility and change), the doctrine of the Spirit's procession presents difficulties related to the idea of locality. Hence Didymus emphasizes that the procession of the Spirit does not involve separation, as we have already witnessed above. The Spirit is not separated from the one who breathed him but remains "inseparable (ἀχώριστον)" from the Father, just as this inseparability likewise includes the Son.[59] But Didymus clearly intends more by this than merely to affirm that the procession cannot be conceived of in spatial terms. The inseparability of the Spirit and the other two *hypostaseis*, secured by the Spirit's divine identity as the one breathed by the Father, is what gives Didymus license to speak in this passage of all three *hypostaseis'* involvement in creation. The natural inseparability of the *hypostaseis* is the ontological reality behind the unified activities of the *hypostaseis* in the world. It is impossible for the Spirit to be absent from the Father's act of creating through the Son when he is inseparable from the Father who breathed him in the divine essence.

Didymus' favorite analogy for the relationship between the Father and the Spirit is that of a spring and the water that flows from it. How felicitous, he notes, that the "sacred preachers" liken the Spirit to living water (John 7:38)! The Spirit is living water because "he proceeds in a manner such that he is united in nature (συμφυῶς) with the Paternal spring that is immortal, life-producing, and is not created." He draws two additional points from the analogy: 1) the water that flows from the spring is consubstantial with it. 2) The Spirit is the living water who attends upon the waters of baptism. Since these things are true of him, "he cannot be separated (διασπασθῆναι) by nature from the spiritual spring [i.e. the Father], as a river and its headwaters [are] also [inseparable]."[60] The consubstantiality of the Spirit with the Father cannot be conceived of on the analogy of two bodies of water that share the same generic essence but are separate in actuality. It is not a generic nature in which the Spirit shares—again, there are not three Gods—but rather, He is inseparable from the Father in the one divine nature. To this end, Didymus notes that Scripture also speaks of the Spirit's being poured out from the Father (Joel

---

the unity of his divinity" (trans. Brian Daley, "The Fullness of the Saving God: Cyril of Alexandria on the Holy Spirit," in *The Theology of St Cyril of Alexandria: a Critical Appreciation* (London: T&T Clark, 2003), 123).

58. *DT* 2.1.1 (448C).
59. *DT* 2.7.3.6 (568A).
60. *DT* 2.6.22.1–2 (553BD).

2:28). This too is well said, he argues, for both water and divine unction proceed consubstantially from themselves.[61]

Another kind of analogy is also employed by Didymus to get at the notions of inseparability and consubstantiality. Exploring the anthropological analogy of the relationship between a person and his "spirit (πνεῦμα)," Didymus argues that speaking of persons in separation from their spirits is impossible. Just as a spring does not create the water that flows from it, so no "person is the creator of himself . . . or [his own] spirit." A person could hardly create the animating principle of his own life.[62] Rather, just as when one conceives of a person, the person's spirit is never absent from this conception, so it is with the Father and his Spirit. Even when the Spirit is not mentioned together with the Father in Scripture, he is implicitly present with him as "his Spirit."[63]

As is the case with the analogy of a father and a son, there are of course aspects of this anthropological analogy that Didymus is keen to approach through negation. In the analogical site that Didymus is exploring, persons may be said to be lifeless without the presence of their animating principles. The Father, on the other hand, is the ever-living God, even though he is never this in isolation from the life-giving Spirit, and from the Son who calls himself "the Life." The analogy intends to affirm the notion that the Father and the Spirit are inseparable.

Not from the Father's Activity, by Nature and in Truth

The idea of consubstantiality is Didymus' most frequent way of qualifying the procession. Phrases like "by nature" or "in truth" or "consubstantially," appear with some regularity and with apparently little difference in meaning.[64] Of critical importance in the defense of the Spirit's divinity is countering the Macedonian charge that the Holy Spirit is produced by the Father's activity, the way creatures are. The procession is not an operation of the Father; the Breath of the Almighty is not diffused into the air like some insubstantial breath. The Spirit is ever in existence, subsisting as the Holy Spirit of God.[65] The Spirit is therefore proper to the Father's own identity as Father, without whom the Father would be deprived of his own Spirit, his own Breath. The Father distinguishes between created spirits and the Spirit when he calls the Spirit his own, the Spirit who is proper to him.[66]

---

61. *DT* 2.2.10 (456B).
62. *DT* 2.22 (553C). Cf. 3.2.35 (800C).
63. *DT* 2.6.19 (548C). Cf. also 3.2.28 (797B): "because the Father is there, there too is his Spirit."
64. See, for instance *DT* 2.8 (608D); 2.14 (705B); 2.26 (752A).
65. Cf. *DT* 2.1.9 (452B).
66. Didymus is emphatic in *DT* 2.2.7 (456A). "The Most High Father in Ezekiel calls the spirit that is ours "our spirit" but the Holy Spirit he names as his very own, proper to him (τὸ δὲ ἅγιον Πνεῦμα ἴδιον ἑαυτοῦ ἐξονομάζει)." (See Ezek 36:26–27 and 37:14.)

Summary

We see in Didymus' treatment of the Spirit's eternal identity similar concerns to those expressed of the Son. As in the case of the Son, Didymus explores scriptural analogies (e.g. river, unction, living water, spirit) as opportunities to express important affirmations about the Holy Spirit. The Spirit is inseparable from the Father and the Son by nature, sharing in the same specific essence that belongs to them. As such, however, the Spirit who proceeds from the Father, in the eternal mode of his derivation from the Father, is of that self-same being which is beyond human thought. We predicate titles, attributes, and activities of him in a similar way that we predicate these things of the other two divine *hypostaseis*.

The Begetting Father

As we noted earlier, it is with respect to the Father's *hypostasis* that Didymus is least committed to giving a unified account of that which differentiates him from the other two *hypostaseis*.[67] There are reasons why this is unsurprising: 1) Didymus' opponents assume the divinity of the Father. The Father, as Didymus notes in the latter chapters of Book 1, is not the direct object of the heretics' impiety. He even recognizes that they have in some measure been concerned precisely with safeguarding the Father's incomparability. 2) "God" is occasionally used in Scripture as the Father's name. It is by linking the generation of the Son and the procession of the Spirit to the Father that arguments for their divinity proceed.

However, Didymus is insistent throughout that his opponents have pursued their goal of honoring the Father "beyond Scripture." Their insults against the Son and the Spirit are a grief to the Father whom they intend to glorify.[68] Frequently, Didymus queries whether the statements his opponents make about the Son and the Holy Spirit do not reflect rather poorly on their doctrine of the Father. Didymus argues at length that the Father is irreducibly Father. And to make this claim is to insist that the Father does not come to this name in time. When one says God and then adds the phrase "the Father," the added words are no epithet. They do not suggest that the divinity is prior to the Fatherhood, either in time or in conception. This is the name proper to his *hypostasis*, a name that he does not share with the other two *hypostaseis*.[69]

---

67. Cf. Bardy, *Didyme l'Aveugle*, 100.
68. DT 1.35 (437C).
69. Didymus addresses a possible counter-example to this in DT 1.27.26–27 (397C). Isaiah calls the Son "Father of the age to come," meaning that he is the Creator of the ages. "He called him "Father" then of what is created, and not of the uncreated nature, since there is one Father of the uncreated and consubstantial Son." Didymus' quotation of Isaiah 9:5 includes the lengthy variant known to Codex Alexandrinus and a scribe who supplemented Codex Sinaiticus.

Not the Cause of the Son and the Spirit

Two aspects of Didymus' doctrine of the Father are of particular interest in the context of late fourth-century arguments. 1) Didymus shares with the neo-Nicene adversaries of Heterousian theology the conviction that ἀγεννησία is not the definition of the divine essence or the formula of divine being. However, unlike several prominent neo-Nicenes, Didymus studiously avoids the term and its cognates in describing the distinguishing property of the Father's *hypostasis*.[70] 2) Unlike many of his pro-Nicene contemporaries, Didymus also refuses to understand the Father's relationship to the Son and the Spirit in terms of causality.[71] These features of his doctrine of the Father are, I will argue, both significant to his account of the Father's *hypostasis* and closely related to one another.[72]

Every use of the word "unbegotten" in the treatise is drawn from the arguments of his opponents.[73] In the most important of these instances for our purposes, Didymus discusses the Eunomian thesis that the Father, being unbegotten, is incomparable with and greater than the Son.[74] Eunomius appeals to biblical testimony in which the Son appears to assert the Father's superiority: namely John 14:28. Throughout the chapter Didymus passes over the Eunomian premise that the Father is unbegotten in silence, without contesting it. Even if it were the case that the Father was unbegotten, and the Son begotten, this would not imply unlikeness. Are we, for instance, to suppose that Adam and Eve who are not begotten are of a different race than their descendants who come from their loins? Didymus argues throughout the chapter that

---

70. Cf. Gregory of Nazianzus, *Or.* 25.16 (SC 284:198): the unique property of the Father is his ἀγεννησία.

71. For Basil the Great's use of the notion of causality in Trinitarian relations, see *C. Eun.* 1.20 and 2.12 (FC 122:120–121 and 145–146). The Father is accounted the cause of the Son as the one who is conceptually (not temporally) prior to the Son. Gregory of Nyssa repeats a similar notion of causality in his own *C. Eun.* 1.1.691 (GNO 1:224–225), but expresses the idea earlier in 1.1.280 (GNO 1:108–109) that the Spirit is distinguished from the Son in his mode of derivation from the Father. The Spirit is mediately derived through the Son, whereas the Son is derived without mediation from the Father. For further discussion of the theme of causal differences between the *hypostaseis* in Gregory's other works, see Lucian Turcescu, *Gregory of Nyssa and the Concept of Divine Persons* (Oxford: Oxford University Press, 2005). In a helpful summary, Turcescu writes: "[Gregory] distinguishes the person who is "the cause" [the Father] ... from the person who is "from the cause" ... or "directly from the first" [the Son] ... and from that who is "by that which is directly from the first" [the Holy Spirit]" (p. 68).

72. My account of the Father's identity is complementary to Bardy's (*Didyme l'Aveugle*, 100–102); I extend the argument by relating the discussion of the Father's distinguishing mark to the discussion of causation.

73. *DT* 1.10.2 (292A) and 1.16.1 (332A). See also 1.26.33 (385D).

74. Cf. Eunomius, *Apol.* 11.11–16 (Vaggione, *Extant Works*, 46–47). Didymus' summary of the argument is a distillation of the ideas in this passage.

Eunomius' assertion of the Father's incomparability and greatness in comparison with the Son remains unfounded, even if one grants the initial terms of his argument. There are simply no measurements with which we are acquainted by which the comparison might be established.[75] Thus far Didymus' rebuttal of the thesis runs along fairly well-established lines.

Didymus then insists with some forcefulness on an idea that sets his doctrine of the Father apart. He refuses to allow that the Father can be called "greater than" the Son on account of his being the cause of the Son. Throughout the treatise, Didymus argues for the notion of the Son's causelessness. The word "was" in John 1:1 establishes that the Son is "causeless (ἀναίτιος)." In such a context as it is placed, the word denotes an existence that is beyond time and without beginning.[76] But in the passage under discussion above (John 14:28), Didymus makes it clear that he is not merely applying the concept in a general way to the Son's distinction from everything that is created as one of the Trinity. Didymus is specifically rejecting the notion of causation in his account of the Son's relationship to the Father. The Father is not greater than the Son as his cause, "for he is not the cause of him."[77] One may add to this that, in his extensive quotation of the pseudo-Athanasian *Dialogue on the Trinity*, he excludes only one significant detail from this text: that in which the light is said to be the cause of the radiance.[78]

Didymus appears to apply the same concept to the Spirit when, early in the extant portion of Book 1, Didymus chides his opponents for inquiring into mysteries that are well beyond human comprehension. Referring to the generation of the Son and the procession of the Spirit, Didymus argues that the mode of these things as well as the difference between them is hidden from us; moreover, "it is brash to render an account of the causes of those who are beyond every cause and thought."[79]

---

75. See *DT* 1.16.1–26 (332A–336A). For a very similar argument, see Basil's *C. Eun.* 1.25 (FC 122:127). Basil, however, explains the comparison ("the Father is greater than I" (John 14:28)) in connection with the Father's being the "cause and principle" of the Son. Eunomius' detractors loved to point out that it was inconsistent to speak both of the Father's incomparability with the Son and then to say that the Father was "greater than" him. See, for instance, Basil's humorous remarks at the end of Book 1 (*C. Eun.* 1.27 (FC 122:130)).

76. See, especially, *DT* 1.15.6–7 (297A–300B). Cf. also 3.3 (825B).

77. *DT* 1.16.16 (333A).

78. Cf. *DT* 1.10.8 (293A) and *Dial. Trin.* 2 (PG 28:1181A). The former has: εἰ δὲ οὐ μεταβληθὲν τὸ φῶς ἀπαύγασμα γεγέννηκεν, μεῖναν καὶ αὐτὸ φῶς καὶ <u>ἔχον τὸ ἀπαύγασμα συμφύτως ἐξ αὐτοῦ τέλειον</u>, καὶ ὁ Θεὸς μένει ἀτρέπτως Θεός. The latter runs as follows: εἰ δὲ οὐ μεταβληθὲν τὸ φῶς ἀπαύγασμα γέγονεν, ἀλλὰ καὶ τὸ φῶς μένει φῶς, <u>καὶ ἀπαυγάσματός ἐστιν αἴτιον</u>, καὶ ὁ Θεὸς μένει Θεός. Didymus has expunged the notion of causality from his rehearsal of the argument.

79. *DT* 1.9.12 (281B). Gregory Nazianzen notes a similar reservation, *Or.* 31.8 (Wickham and Williams, 283): "What, then, is "proceeding"? You explain the ingeneracy of

Coupled with his rejection of causality as a viable notion in describing the Father's relationship to the Son, Didymus' complete silence on the question of the word "unbegotten" appears to be a significant omission. Against the positions advanced by other pro-Nicenes, Didymus commits himself to a doctrine of the processions in which the Father is not understood as the cause of the divinity of the other two *hypostaseis*. He appears to be motivated by two concerns: 1) avoiding subordinationist-sounding concessions to his Heterousian opponents and 2) rendering an account of the Father in which his individuating mark cannot be conceived of in abstraction from the identities of the other *hypostaseis* of the Trinity.

That Didymus appeals to Aristotle's *Metaphysics* to explain a similar concept elsewhere (that the Lord calls himself the "beginning" (ἀρχή))[80] suggests the possibility that Didymus would conceive of the claim to causality within the Trinity along lines developed by him. Aristotle argues that the principle (αἴτιον) of an eternal thing is 1) truer than the principle of what is derivative from it and that 2) the principle of an eternal thing is incapable of being defined,[81] since this would lead to an infinite regress. First principles are those things which are for their own sake and are not as they are because of others.[82]

If Didymus is thinking of the claim along these lines—as appears likely—then the wish to avoid causal language within his account of the Trinity is understandable because it would imply that the Son is in some sense less divine than the Father; the Father, having the cause of his divinity within himself alone is more truly so.[83] According to Aristotle's understanding of causality in eternal things, an admission of causality would also be tantamount to suggesting that the Son's divinity is somehow patient of some kind of explanation while the Father's is not.[84] Didymus, clearly rejecting a notion of temporal causality, also appears to be rejecting notions of conceptual causality as well. The Son's identity as Son is ultimately as incomprehensible as the Father's identity as Father; both are equally distant from creaturely comprehension.

---

the Father and I will give you a biological account of the Son's begetting and the Spirit's proceeding—and let us go mad the pair of us for prying into God's secrets."

80. See *DT* 3.5 (840B–841A).
81. *Met.* α.1 (993b.23-31 (Jaeger, 34–35)).
82. *Met.* α.2 (994a.1-18 (Jaeger, 35)).
83. Eunomius, *Apol.* 26.3-4 (Vaggione, *Extant Works*, 68–69), separates the Unbegotten God from all else by calling him "superior to every cause, being the cause of all things that exist."
84. The doctrine of the Son's "incomprehensibility (ἀκατάληπτος)" and "imperceptibility to the mind (ἀπερινόητος)" is one that Didymus insists on with particular vigor in *DT* 1.15 (the chapter prior to this one).

The One Who Begets

The above explanation accords well with Didymus' ordinary way of speaking of the Father's identity in the treatise. Though he does not as regularly identify the Father's distinguishing property as the Son's and the Spirit's, there are a few notable instances in *DT* in which he does so. The Father is called, in distinction from the Son, the "begetting God."[85] Characterizing the three *hypostaseis* together in the final chapter of Book 1, Didymus speaks of the Father as the one who begets in contrast to the Son who is begotten and the Spirit who proceeds.[86] Once again distinguishing the Father from the Son and the Spirit, Didymus writes that "the Father alone is called "Father" because he alone begets in his *hypostasis*."[87] Even when he is speaking about the relationship between the Spirit and the Father, Didymus calls the latter the "begetter."[88]

Didymus speaks in less committed terms of the Father as the self-originate (αὐτογενής) one.[89] And although he never employs such an adjective in reference to either of the other two *hypostaseis* it is clear that Didymus uses the language with hesitation. On one occasion he even apologizes for its inadequacy.[90] In every case, Didymus is quick to qualify the word immediately by affirming either that the Son co-exists eternally with the self-originate Father or that the Son is conjoined to him. The import of these passages seems to lie in affirming the eternal co-existence of the Son with his Father, and not so much in identifying any distinction between the two *hypostaseis*.

Summary

In describing the generation of the Son and the procession of the Holy Spirit, Didymus largely focuses on negating created categories: especially

---

85. *DT* 1.9.16 (281C).
86. *DT* 1.36.7 (440D–441A).
87. *DT* 2.6.20 (552A).
88. *DT* 2.12 (673C). It is difficult to tell whether Didymus means this in an improper sense or if it should be read in parallel to εἰς τὸν Πατέρα (above it). If the latter, then the argument for γεννῆσαι as the differentiating property of the Father is all the stronger. Perhaps at a loss to know how to encapsulate the Father's role in the Spirit's procession in a single word, Didymus falls back on language he has used of the Father in relationship to the Son. This tendency may also be in play in *CZ* IV.249, a difficult text that Doutreleau amends by adding the word "giver (δοτήρ)" into the text, when the uncorrected manuscript asserts that the Father is Father of God the Word and of the Holy Spirit. Cf. Doutreleau, *Didyme l'Aveugle: Sur Zacharie*, vol. 3 (Paris: Éditions du Cerf, 1962), 932–933n2.
89. See *DT* 2.1.1 (448C), and 3.2.20 (793C). Cf. 1.30.10 (417A) in which the Father is described as the self-originate root of the organically-united and co-eternal branch of God (the Son).
90. *DT* 1.15.9 (300A), using Hönscheid's punctuation and translation of the text (*De trinitate, Buch 1*, 48–49).

those related to time, space, and materiality. By employing carefully-selected and qualified analogies (mostly, if not entirely, from Scripture), Didymus is able to draw conclusions from the generation and the procession that have important consequences. 1) The *hypostaseis* are inseparable from one another by nature. 2) The *hypostaseis* of the Son and the Holy Spirit are distinct from one another by virtue of their mode of "coming forth" from the Father; both are known as they are in relation to the Father. 3) The *hypostasis* of the Father is known only in relation to these *hypostaseis*. The latter argument, we will argue at the end of the chapter, raises the most questions.

The Missions of the Son and the Holy Spirit

Didymus' account of the identities of the *hypostaseis* of the Trinity supports his account of the missions whereby the Trinity acts in and toward the world. In this section of the chapter, I provide an outline of the way that Didymus speaks of the missions of the Son and the Holy Spirit in relation to what has gone before. I also seek to establish the groundwork for speaking about Trinitarian activity, since the missions of the Son and the Holy Spirit provide the context of divine activity in and toward the world. It is by virtue of what has been said above about inseparability in essence, that the activities of the Son and the Holy Spirit are also attributed to the Father, as Didymus frequently reminds his audience.[91] Of particular importance is the way 1) that he speaks of the missions as stemming from the identities of the *hypostaseis* of the Three, 2) that he relates the missions of the Son and the Holy Spirit, and 3) speaks of these missions in fulsome terms that encompass the entire narrative of Scripture. The above provides a platform for speaking of differentiation within the one activity of the Trinity.

The Father as Sender of the Son and the Holy Spirit

Macedonian exegesis tended to interpret the Father's sending of the Holy Spirit as evidence of the essential subordination of the latter. Arian and Heterousian exegesis regarded the Son's mission in the world in parallel fashion. Didymus counters these tendencies by insisting that Scripture tends to differentiate the missions of the divine *hypostaseis* from the missions of angelic beings, prophets, and apostles in several ways. Though the Father is to be regarded as the sender of the Son and the Holy Spirit, this is not to be taken as evidence that he is superior in nature to them. Rather, that they agree in will,

---

91. See, e.g., *DT* 2.6.4.9 (520B): "[One who is so inclined] may learn that every activity and gift of his Only-begotten Son the Word and of the one Holy Spirit, [everything] that is both creative, good, perfect, and common to them, is also wholly attributed to the one, from whom and with whom these blessed *hypostaseis* shined forth unspeakably." Later in the same sentence, Didymus reminds his audience that he has frequently made this argument. Cf. also later in the treatise: 2.8.1 (613B).

authority, and knowledge with the Father in these missions is evidence of their consubstantiality.

Freely and Willingly

The Son, as Creator, does not bring his creatures into existence either as a servant or an intermediary. He acts in accordance with his divine nature which "possesses freedom (αὐτεξούσιος)," bringing all things into existence "willingly (ἐθελουσίως)" and with all the authority of one who has but to assent to something for it to be accomplished.[92] Likewise, in the Passion at Golgotha, the Son suffered as "as he knew and willed"; he was crucified upon the prophetic ladder in Jacob's vision "freely (ἑκουσίως)."[93] The notion of a free will extends to the Holy Spirit as well, since the Holy Spirit does not bestow his gifts as a servant, but by his own power.[94] He apportions his gifts to whomever he pleases.[95] His appearance in the world is "free, superior, and most serene."[96] At the giving of the Holy Spirit near the conclusion of John's Gospel (John 20:22–23), the Son tells the disciples that the giving of the Spirit is the *sine qua non* of their own authority to forgive sins. Hence they do so "in his name and by his power." This too, Didymus argues, reveals the free will and authority of the Spirit, who bestows forgiveness to those who believe in him.[97]

This argument would seem to be relativized by Didymus' claims that human beings also possess free will. Didymus encounters such an objection in a chapter in which he engages with a dialogue between an Orthodox and a Macedonian, wherein he distinguishes between "the symbols of divine power and nature" and those that are said of created nature.[98] In this same argument, he notes that it is not the phrase "free will" alone that establishes the distinction between the Holy Spirit and creatures, but rather the way in which divine freedom is qualified.[99] Humans are described in the treatise as free in the

---

92. *DT* 1.15.91–92 (325A–328A).

93. *DT* 1.15.89 (324B) and 1.15.103 (329AB).

94. *DT* 2.8.1 (600A).

95. See *DT* 1.18.33–34 (349BC). Didymus is fond of referring to Hebrews 2:4 as evidence of the Spirit's freedom in the distribution of his gifts, taking the grammatically ambiguous "his" in the phrase "according to his will" in reference to the Holy Spirit rather than referring it back to θεός. Whatever the reference in Hebrews 2:4, Didymus has iron-clad authority for the notion that the Spirit apportions the gifts in 1 Corinthians 12:11 (a text he employs to similar effect in *DT* 1.19.22–24 (368C–369A)).

96. *DT* 2.1.11 (452C). The passage is taken from the Prose-Hymn in chapter 1. It reads: ἡ αὐτεξούσιος καὶ ὑπερβάλλουσα γαληνοτάτη ἐπιφάνεια. For the triadic structure of the lines in the hymn see Seiler, *De trinitate, Buch 2*, 13.

97. *DT* 2.7.6.1–2 (577C).

98. *DT* 2.8.1 (604CD).

99. The Macedonian strategy, a *reductio ad absurdum*, was to argue that the names and activities given to the Holy Spirit were shared with creatures (the word under discussion here is the verb "operates (ἐνεργεῖ)" (*DT* 2.8.1 (605AC))). "Homonymy" was a

sense that they, like the angels, have the choice between doing good or evil.[100] Hence, goodness is not predicated of either in an absolute sense, since it is subject to corruption.[101] Divine freedom, Didymus notes, is never described as subject to corruption. This implies that the *hypostaseis* always act in ways consistent with their nature by a power that is not foreign to them but rather is their own.

The missions of the *hypostaseis* therefore flow from the agreement of the *hypostaseis* in the one will of the Trinity. In his helpful discussion of the formulas of unity in *DT*, Béranger argues that the author of *DT* insists on unity of will within the Trinity "simplement exclure la possibilité d'opposition morale entre des volontés réellement distinctes" rather than to "repousser la distinction proprement ontologique des volontés."[102] In the Trinity, there is no possibility of any of the *hypostaseis* exercising their freedom of will in a manner that suggests any opposition between the wills of the *hypostaseis*. Any such opposition of will would demand a denial of the hypostatic identity of each Person, whose identity is given only in relation to the others. Moreover, any such opposition would imply a definition of freedom that is unworthy of God.

Knowingly

Likewise, the *hypostaseis* of the Son and the Holy Spirit are not ignorant of the Father's will. What they perform in accordance with the Father's will is not unknown or unforeseen by them. Scripture testifies that the Son says what the Father tells him to (John 12:49) and that the Holy Spirit does not speak from himself but receives from the Son what he proclaims to others (John 16:13–14). This language informs us, not that the Son and the Spirit are ignorant of the Father's will, but rather that there is a "union of nature (ἕνωσις τῆς φύσεως)" and an ineffable "harmony (συμφωνία)" in the Holy Trinity, as well as that all the teachings of the Trinity are common. Not so among creatures.

> For every creature, if it is rational, has its own will. [This will], as it is written, remains silent in order that the will of God might speak. Wherefore at one time [the creature] speaks and does its own things, at another time [it speaks and performs] the things of God. . . . God the Word, being Mighty One and Wisdom, and the Holy Spirit of God proceeding from him [i.e. God], who according to the Apostle searches out his depths and alone knows the things of God, bestowing the di-

---

grammatical argument frequently advanced by both sides in this controversy: the use of the same word did not prove that the same signification was intended.

100. *DT* 1.9.34–37 (288A). For the angels, see 1.17.4 (341B).
101. *DT* 2.6.3.2 (512C), 2.6.4.13 (521B), and 2.6.8.1–2 (529BC).
102. Béranger, "Etudes," 14–15: Didymus insists on a unity of will "simply to exclude the possibility of moral opposition between wills that are really distinct" rather than "to reject the properly ontological distinction between the wills."

vine gifts with authority, does not wait to hear and thus to say or to do, as creatures do who are not only ignorant of God's will but sometimes fail to do it.[103]

The *hypostaseis* of the Trinity do not require the use of words or hearing to know and to foreknow all things; nor do they require these means to make themselves heard and known.[104] The *hypostaseis* of the Trinity are fully present to one another and, by virtue of the commonness of their nature, fully disclosed to one another. The Holy Spirit, therefore, is not like the angel who reports the messages of God as the herald of a superior. The angel is taught the message he communicates. The Holy Spirit, on the other hand, "utters a divine message divinely (χρηματίζει θεϊκῶς)." "Like the Father he sees whatever the Father and the Son will with the sleepless eyes of divinity."[105]

In the Presence of the Father

If the former two aspects of the missions of the divine *hypostaseis* reflect primarily the notion of their ontological equality with the Father, the aspect of their missions treated under this heading reflects the specificity of their identities. The missions of the Son and the Spirit take place in the presence of the Father.[106] Didymus reflects on the crucial passage in John's Gospel that speaks of the coming of the Paraclete and his sending from the Father (John 14:16). Macedonius had embraced the word πέμψει ("he will send") with particular relish, arguing that it connoted the Spirit's inferiority.[107] Didymus responds by treating several different passages within John's Gospel, noting that 1) sending in Scripture does not always imply inferiority and 2) that the sending is predicated of one who is present everywhere *before* his Pentecostal mission.

Didymus proves the first point by adducing the testimony of Isaiah 48:16, which speaks of the Spirit and the Father as co-senders of the Son. The latter point he defends by appealing to scriptural testimony to the Spirit's presence in the whole world (e.g., Wisdom 1:7). At the conclusion of the chapter he adds significantly:

> So the Spirit of the God and Father is not sent according to the apostolate of the apostles or prophets, but [is sent] as his Spirit, and neither [does he go] from one place to another

---

103. *DT* 3.19 (888BC).

104. *DT* 2.1.2 (448D).

105. *DT* 2.7.8.3 (584B).

106. In the interests of space, this section will proceed almost solely in connection with the Spirit's mission from the Father, since it receives the clearest and lengthiest exposition in the treatise. That the same dynamic is at work in the mission of the Son is evident in passages like *DT* 3.21 (912D–913A), in which the Son is served by angels as a superior since the Son is always in the Father (ἐν τῷ Πατρί) and in the presence of God (πρὸς τὸν Θεόν), even in the Incarnation. Cf. John 1:2.

107. *DT* 3.38 (977B).

(μεταβατικῶς), since the Father from whose *hypostasis* the Spirit is, is not circumscribed by boundaries.[108]

This latter argument is significant for Didymus' account of the missions of the *hypostaseis*. The Spirit who is sent by the Father as the Father's peer in all things save the Fatherhood does not leave the Father's presence in order to carry out his mission. Such a conception is unworthy, above all, of the Father's own relationship to the cosmos. Like the Spirit, the Father is present in and to the world that he created. The missions take place in the presence of the omnipresent Father.

Didymus develops this notion particularly by insisting on the "return" or the "ascent" of the Son and the Holy Spirit to the Father as inhering within their missions. Indeed, in the following quotation, the ideas of mission and procession are so closely linked as to occasionally become intertwined. Didymus takes Jesus' words to Nicodemus—"you do not know whence he comes (ἔρχεται), and whither he departs (ὑπάγει)" (John 3:8)—as a reference to the Holy Spirit's inspiration of Scripture.

> He was not saying this for the benefit of Nicodemus alone, but was pre-emptively accusing Arius, Eunomius, and Macedonius as well, who hear the voice of the Holy Spirit through the Scriptures and do not understand that he comes (ἔρχεται) as the one who proceeds without beginning from the Father and remains at all times in every place, and departs (ὑπάγει) to him. [They do not know] that, as his Spirit, he is inseparable in the Divinity, since he went forth from him by nature ineffably and is returned to him. He possesses both an issuing forth (πρόοδον) from the Father since he proceeds from him, and an abiding in the Father since he is one and the same thing [with him].[109] He returns to the Begetter (τὸν γεννήσαντα) when he goes forth, since he belongs to one and the same essence and is unable to come outside of the Paternal co-existence.[110]

The value of this passage for the present discussion lies in the way that it binds together two themes: 1) that the mission of the Spirit is a consequence of his procession from the Father, and 2) that the mission of the Spirit demands to be understood as a mission in which the Father is fulsomely present.

In the beginning of the quotation, Didymus asserts two notions discussed above: that the Spirit comes not as one subordinate to the Father and that he

---

108. See *DT* 3.38 (976D–977C, citing 977C).
109. Didymus means this in the sense of their oneness in the Godhead; he is far from endorsing a uni-personalist creed.
110. *DT* 2.12 (673BC).

comes in a way that does not imply his crossing from one place to another. Didymus then asserts the Spirit's inseparability and union of nature with the Father from whom he proceeds. The consequences of this for the mission of the Spirit are that the Spirit abides in the one from whom he proceeds and from whom he is sent. The Spirit whom we meet in the waters of baptism[111] and whose voice we hear in the words of Scripture (the Spirit sent by the Father) is none other than the Spirit who exists in eternity in the presence of the Father from whom he was sent. The Spirit's presence to us is the guarantee of the Father's presence to us.[112]

Treating the passage in which the Son confesses that he is sent by the Father (John 14:28), Didymus thinks that such language is finally a concession to mortal reason, since like the Holy Spirit the Son is present everywhere, and by virtue of his divine nature remains "in the Father" who sends him (John 14:11). The sending of the Son is an indication not that he takes up residence in a place where he formerly was not present, but that he takes up the "form of a servant" in accordance with the Father's will, even while he remains in the presence of the Father.[113] The Incarnation—the mission of the Son *par excellence*—is the inauguration in time of the Father's will to restore the creation through his mission and the mission of the Spirit who is sent with him.

The Co-Missions of the Son and the Spirit

Didymus is relatively silent on the question of the eternal relationship between the Son and the Holy Spirit. In attempting to describe this relationship such as Didymus conceives of it, one can only point to a handful of passages. Didymus speaks of the three *hypostaseis* in relation to one another on one occasion by the analogy of utterance, speech, and mind.[114] In connection with the same family of analogies, Didymus argues that the procession is without beginning and that the one divine Spirit is therefore consubstantial with the

---

111. Cf. the context of the discussion: 673A.

112. In the Prose-Hymn at the beginning of the Book on the Spirit, Didymus asserts something similar when he writes: "Through [the Spirit] and because of him the God and Father abounds toward us. With [the Father, the Spirit] is in the heavens while he remains near to us" (*DT* 2.1.8 (452A)).

113. *DT* 3.18 (880A–881C). Didymus argues here that Scripture secures the Father's character as a "lover of humankind (φιλάνθρωπον)" against Manichean divisions between the Father and the Son by showing that the Son's mission does not come out of nowhere, but that it is a function of his relationship to the Father who in every way agrees with the Son in saving humanity.

114. "In whatever way the Son is called "Word" (λόγος) in Scripture because of his co-existence with the Father, in the same way too Scripture called the Holy Spirit "Utterance (ῥῆμα) of God," and "Spirit of his mouth," and "Breath of the Almighty," since he shined forth from him co-existently, lest anyone assume that he is external to the divinity of the Father or of his Word. For the utterance (ῥῆμα) is proper to speech (λόγος), and speech to the mind (νοῦς)" (*DT* 2.5.11 (496AB)).

Only-begotten Word. Appealing to "natural reason (φυσικὸς λόγος)," he notes that "no word is begotten or produced unless a breath moves together and comes forth together with it."[115] Elsewhere: "the Father is in the Son, and the Son remains in the Father, and . . . the Spirit proceeds from the Father and remains in a divine way (θεϊκῶς) with the Son."[116] The Son is never without the Spirit, who always rests upon the Son.[117] The two come forth from the Father together.

Though Didymus is less forthcoming on the question of the eternal relationship between the Word and the Spirit, he provides a more fulsome account of the supplementary character of their missions. The Holy Spirit perfects the creative work of the Son: sanctifying it and giving it life, working with him inseparably.[118] In this connection he is fond of quoting Psalm 32:6 against those who deny the Spirit's involvement in creation: "By the Word of the Lord the heavens were established, and by the Spirit of his mouth all their powers."[119] The Son is never without the Holy Spirit, who continually remains upon him; this is seen in the "economy (οἰκονομία)" with particular clarity.[120] The Spirit is the generative principle of the Son's birth from the Virgin.[121] The Son recognizes the Spirit as the one who anoints him and accompanies him in his earthly ministry.[122] The Word of God, conversely, causes "*his* Holy Spirit" to dwell in the soul through his breathing (φύσημα).[123] By his "ineffable Incarnation (ἀνέκλεκτος ἐνανθρώπησις)" the natural Son and heir of the Father makes us co-heirs with himself, and the Spirit of adoption sets his seal upon this work of the Son by crying out in our stead: "Abba, Father!"[124]

This latter example is of paramount importance for Didymus, whose exposition of the baptismal event majors on the coordination of the missions of the Son and the Holy Spirit. Didymus employs a scriptural analogy felicitously in connection with this idea. The Son is called the "exact impress (χαρακτήρ)" (Heb 1:3) and the "image (εἰκών)" (Col 1:15) of the Father. Likewise, the Holy Spirit is called the Father's "seal (σφραγίς)" (see 2 Cor 1:22 and Eph 1:13). As

---

115. DT 2.27 (761AB). The Migne text misleadingly capitalizes Λόγος and Πνεύματος here.
116. DT 1.31.16 (425A).
117. See DT 3.36 (968A), citing Isaiah 59:21 and Luke 4:18 (citing Isaiah 61:1).
118. DT 2.7.3.3–6 (565C–568B). Cf. 2.8.1 (616A).
119. See DT 1.9.7 (280B) and 2.7.3.14 (573B).
120. See DT 3.36 (968A) and 2.2.5 (456A). οἰκονομία is often short-hand for Incarnation in DT. The Incarnation, as the culminating expression of the divine plan, is God's economy *par excellence*. The word also has a broader definition, inclusive of all of God's purposes for the creation from the beginning until the *eschaton*.
121. See DT 2.7.3.10 (569C–572A).
122. DT 2.25 (748B).
123. DT 3.1 (780A). Didymus is consistent in speaking of the Son's breathing of his Spirit to the human soul in creation and restoration (as we will see in the next chapter).
124. See DT 2.12 (676BC).

such both reflect the Father, the "archetype (ἀρχέτυπος)," perfectly.[125] Since this is the case, it must also be the case that the Only-begotten is "imaged (ἐξεικονίζεται)" perfectly by the one Holy Spirit.[126] Within the narrative of creation and re-creation that serves as an outline of the economy, the missions of the Son and the Spirit are mutually implicating at every juncture. In the missions, the Son and the Spirit remain inseparably joined together. Torrance sums this up nicely: in Didymus "the experience of the Holy Spirit and filial relation to the Father through the Son [are] inseparably associated."[127]

Embracing the Whole Narrative of Scripture

As implied by the above discussion, it is clear that Didymus conceives of the missions of the Son and the Holy Spirit in quite fulsome terms. The missions are not limited to the appearance of the Son in the flesh or the sending of the Holy Spirit after his resurrection. These moments within the divine economy have a particularly important role to play insofar as they reveal the meaning of all that went before and inaugurate what God is irrevocably committed to accomplishing on behalf of creation because of the Incarnation. But it is as a culmination that they are best understood. The NT economy is not an utter *novum*. The Word and the Spirit of God are continually sent by the Father into the world to accomplish what the Trinity wills in common on the world's behalf. Because of who the Father is in eternity, he enters into human history—or rather, human history unfolds in his presence—in union with his Word and his Spirit. Thus Didymus will speak of OT history in unapologetically Trinitarian terms.

The Son and the Holy Spirit share together in the work of creation.[128] The Only-Begotten is the very angel of the Lord who speaks to Abraham, requiring from him the sacrifice of his son. And it is he who swears by himself, offering himself in Isaac's stead: the true son of Abraham.[129] God the Word is present as "angel" to the patriarch Jacob, intimating to him his coming salvation on the cross, and delivering him from evil.[130] During the sojourn of the children of Abraham in the land of Egypt, the Son appears to Israel as the "true and free light," saving the nation and training it to recognize him after its long period of polytheistic syncretism in Egypt.[131] Didymus notes that the activities of the Son and the Spirit were here—just as they are in the Incarnation—mutually implicating. When the Lord led the people out of Egypt, Paul and Jude attest

---

125. *DT* 1.16 (336AB).
126. *DT* 2.5 (504B).
127. *The Trinitarian Faith*, 225.
128. *DT* 2.8.1 (616A).
129. *DT* 1.26.57–59 (392BC).
130. *DT* 1.15.102–107 (328D–329C).
131. *DT* 1.9.16 (276A). Cf. the reconstructed text of Hönscheid (*De trinitate, Buch 1*, 20).

that the leader of the people was Christ; Isaiah, without in any way compromising the testimony of the apostles, tells us that "a Spirit from the Lord descended and led them."[132] Conversely, the Holy Spirit speaks through the prophets and the apostles, inspiring them.[133] Zechariah, the father of John, recognizes the Spirit to be the God of Israel, speaking in the prophets. But this is in no way inconsonant with Paul's own confession that Christ speaks in him.[134]

It would be possible to provide a much fuller account of the missions of the Son and the Holy Spirit in the OT from *DT*. The above testimonies are merely indicative of a robust acknowledgment that the OT is imbued with Trinitarian activity. The above examples illustrate also that Didymus conceives of this OT economy not as something separate from the New, nor merely as an economy which in some ways extrinsically anticipates what will be revealed in the NT. Rather, the appearances of the Son and the Holy Spirit in Israel's history are, for Didymus, part of the very same economy that has its culmination in the Incarnation. The Son and the Spirit, in other words, do not merely predict the Incarnation and the Pentecostal life of the Church. The Son, precisely as the angel of the Lord who *delivers* Abraham, Jacob, and the nation of Israel, intimates his coming salvation. He does not merely speak about this deliverance to come; he enacts it, albeit on a less universal scale.

It is in this context that one should understand Didymus' remarks about the new knowledge granted to the faithful in the NT. On the one hand, Didymus speaks on occasion almost as if the NT introduced the knowledge of the Son and the Holy Spirit to the faithful. He writes, for instance, that "the New perfected the Old Covenant because of faith in the Son and the divine Spirit."[135] The Church's law, he argues, has precedence over the older law, since the newer includes "the saving message that concerns Christ and the Holy Spirit."[136] The Church's worship is superior to that of the synagogue because the latter invokes and glorifies God the Father alone.[137] Didymus, not averse on occasion to interpolating his text, speaks of the "*new* faith working through love" (Gal 5:6); Christ's appearance revealed this faith to all humanity.[138] On this account of things, the faithful are able only after the advent of the Son in the Incarnation to discern that this same one was active with the Spirit of God in the biblical history.

---

132. *DT* 1.19.13–18 (365C–368B). Didymus cites, among other passages: 1 Corinthians 10:4, Jude 5, and Isaiah 63:13–14.
133. *DT* 2.1.10 (452B).
134. *DT* 1.21.1–4 (373B). See Luke 1:68, 70 and 2 Cor 13:3.
135. *DT* 1.30.4 (416C).
136. *DT* 1.7.4 (272B). See Hönscheid, *De trinitate, Buch 1*, 14–15.
137. *DT* 1.25.7 (380B).
138. *DT* 1.7.12 (276A). Mingarelli (275Dn24) notes that the word καινή has been introduced "for the sake of the exposition (*explicationis causa*)."

On the other hand, Didymus orients himself toward the OT in such a way that renders the above paradigm far too facile. The prophets are appealed to with regularity as authorities on the identities and missions of the Son and the Holy Spirit. Didymus speaks of the Holy-singer of the Psalms, of Jeremiah, and of Isaiah as those who are "especially conversant with the divine Spirit."[139] The teaching about Christ in the OT was only ignored by some of the Hebrews "because of the abiding observance (ἔναυλον . . . μνήμην) among them of Egyptian polytheism."[140] Jewish agnosticism or denial of the deity of the Son and the Holy Spirit for the sake of honoring the Father alone is not equated with the attitude of the saints of the OT. Rather, such denial is treated in the same chapter in which Didymus says that those who deny the divinity of the Son and the Holy Spirit "probably (τάχα) do not even believe in the Father."[141]

Didymus' distinction between the Testaments is primarily a distinction between hiddenness and openness. He affirms that the saints of the OT knew of the Spirit and the Son and spoke of them, albeit in terms less forthcoming than those on display in the New. If we "inquire" of the authors of the OT, we learn that the Son, just as much as the Father, is the God of the forefathers.[142] But the Son, who is active and present in the events of the OT, and who is recognized by the saints and prophets who wrote of his glory, is nevertheless "widely known" among men "from the time of the economy."[143]

The missions of the *hypostaseis* of the Son and the Holy Spirit are the means whereby the Trinity sustains the cosmos. These missions embrace the whole history of God's relation to the world, and therefore encompass the bringing of the world into existence and its restoration into life in God's presence (salvation). God is therefore known in all his works toward his creatures. In the missions of the Son and the Holy Spirit, all three *hypostaseis* will the same purposes on behalf of creatures; moreover, the Son and the Holy Spirit are never separated in these missions from one another, and by virtue of their relationship to the Father, are always with the Father.

Divine Activity: Identical or Inseparable?

It is time to bring what has been said thus far about Didymus' understanding of the eternal identities and missions of the *hypostaseis* to bear on the question that is of chief importance for the next chapter. How should one speak of divine activity? For in the treatise as a whole, it is usually Didymus' custom to speak as if all of the actions of the Trinity are shared in equally by the *hyposta-*

---

139. *DT* 1.18.44–46 (353AB).
140. *DT* 1.7.16 (276AB).
141. See *DT* 1.34.5 (436A). Cf. 1.34.19 (437A), where Didymus asserts that such confessions render the Fatherhood of the first person highly suspect.
142. *DT* 1.27.14 (396D–397A).
143. *DT* 1.27.26 (397C).

seis. Didymus asks: does the Father govern the world by his power? So do the Son and the Holy Spirit. The purpose of this kind of observation is clear: to defend the consubstantial divinity of these *hypostaseis* by insisting on inseparability in activity. By virtue of the hypostatic identity of the Father, he never acts without them. This raises a question that is of fundamental importance for speaking about Trinitarian activity: do we do justice to Didymus' concern better by speaking of identical or of inseparable activity?

It has been pointed out with some regularity that Didymus is not always consistent with himself in his reflections on the "unity of operation (μία ἐνέργεια)" in the Trinity. Bardy notes that Didymus is not very precise in his endorsement of the doctrine, sometimes failing to uphold in practice what he subscribes to in numerous places in the corpus.[144] Heston engages with this aspect of Didymus' work in greater detail. He notes that Didymus'

> inconsistency verges on . . . two extremes: when he is concerned with the unity of the Three Persons of the Trinity, Didymus insists on absolute unity of operation, . . . when he is intent on establishing the real distinctions of the Persons of the Trinity, he defends diversity of operation just as energetically, and then warns his readers against concluding that this diversity of operation implies also diversity of nature—seemingly unmindful of the argument he exposed with such conclusiveness [earlier].[145]

Heston seeks to account for this inconsistency by arguing that it is not really a material one. On the one hand, in Didymus we find a consistent emphasis on the sharing of all the *hypostaseis* in every activity of the Trinity; on the other, we find that each of the *hypostaseis* is occasionally credited with a particularity in this activity that is not ascribed to the other *hypostaseis* (the chief example for Heston being the Holy Spirit's role in the sanctification of the soul).

Employing categories standardized by later dogmatics, Heston explains that the two positions are harmonious insofar as the Trinity is the efficient cause of every activity of the *hypostaseis*, whereas an individual *hypostasis* of the Trinity is the quasi-formal cause of the same.[146] For example, the entire Trinity effects the sanctification of the soul by the Holy Spirit who "communicates to the soul His own divine substance, and thus unites the soul with the Father and the Son." Heston is less successful in appraising Didymus than he is in describing him, however. Keen as he is to defend Didymus from the charge of positing that the operations of the Trinity are divisible, Heston notes that this particular activity of the Holy Spirit in no way implies division of activity,

---

144. Bardy, *Didyme l'Aveugle*, 83–84. See especially 84n1.

145. Heston, "The Spiritual Life," 37. The language is somewhat misleading, as I discuss below.

146. Ibid., 53.

since the Spirit's self-communication to the soul "is not, strictly speaking, an operation."[147] Explaining with greater clarity what he means, he argues that the Spirit's work in the sanctification of the soul is not a "veritable *opus ad extra* in the fullest sense of the term. Through the gift of supernatural life, however, the soul is elevated to a supernatural sphere and thus shares to a certain extent, in the intimate life of the Trinity."[148] To speak in this way, however, is to threaten to abuse the notion of the *ad extra*, wherein creaturely being, however elevated to the "supernatural sphere," remains *ad extra* unless it is to be subsumed into divine being.

In the section that follows I agree with Heston that Didymus' understanding of the activity of the Trinity in *DT* is defensible. However, it is important to point out what Didymus is doing with greater specificity. In *DT* he argues that 1) the activities of the *hypostaseis* of the Trinity are inseparable and that 2) the roles of the *hypostaseis* within this indivisible activity are not identical. He defends these positions successfully by ascribing activity to *hypostaseis*, thereby guaranteeing that hypostatic identity plays a significant role in the way that the Trinity acts in reference to all that is not God (Heston's *ad extra*). Recognizing this affords a more ready solution to an issue that Heston's account of the Spirit's work makes problematic: the prominence afforded the Son in the work of creation.[149]

A Developing Doctrine

Before examining the critical texts in *DT*, it is important to observe that Didymus' position on the activities of the *hypostaseis* undergoes development or clarification between his writing of *DSS* and *DT*. He does employ a similar argument throughout both treatises: one activity bespeaks one essence.[150] However, in *DSS*, when Didymus is addressing the Johannine text that speaks of the Holy Spirit's being sent as "another Comforter" (John 14:16), he struggles to maintain the argument. He insists that the "otherness" mentioned here does not imply that the Holy Spirit is of a different nature than the Son. Rather, he urges his audience to understand the text in question as implying only a difference in activity: the Savior comforts as our mediator while the Holy Spirit comforts the downcast. Realizing what he has said thus far about

---

147. Ibid., 54.

148. Ibid., 57.

149. The activity of creation must surely, by any standard, be considered an *opus ad extra*. Heston's argument that the sanctified soul, by sharing in the divine life, is not truly external to the Trinity, renders problematic the distinction between "being" and "participating" in Didymus. Only God who is not a creature gives life to creatures; only creatures who are not God may share in the life of God. Deified creatures are still creatures, even though we will have cause to query certain aspects of Didymus' account of eschatological participation in the divine life.

150. See *DSS* 81, 105, and 145. Cf. *DT* 2.8.1 (601A), 2.8.2 (624C), and 2.15 (717A).

the identical activity of the *hypostaseis*, Didymus is then forced to backtrack quickly, warning his readers not to conclude that the natures differ because of this diverse activity. Consequently, he then produces examples in which the Holy Spirit comforts as an ambassador and the Son comforts the grieving.[151]

The whole text gives one the impression, as Heron observes, that Didymus "remains uncomfortably committed to the *diversa operatio*."[152] Didymus' approach to the same text in *DT* is much more satisfactory. The "otherness" is predicated not of the Holy Spirit's activity but rather of his *hypostasis*.[153] In *DT* Didymus is prepared to speak in such terms, because he is more forthcoming in the 380s/390s with respect to the question of the *differentia* of the divine *hypostaseis*. And it is interesting to note that in conjunction with this difference between the works, there also seems to be a corresponding willingness in *DT* to differentiate the roles of the *hypostaseis* within the activity of the Trinity without apologizing for this differentiation.[154]

Indivisibility and Particularity

The thesis of the treatise, the consubstantial divinity of the Son and the Holy Spirit with the Father, is defended largely by attending to the numerous activities shared by these *hypostaseis*. Didymus' affirmation of the μία ἐνέργεια in *DT* is serviceable to this purpose. The one activity of the *hypostaseis* of the Son and the Holy Spirit in baptism indicates that they are one in essence.[155] It is severally spoken of the Father, the Son, and the Holy Spirit that they raised Christ from the dead; this is an indication to us of their "sameness in the Godhead and of the one activity."[156] The Lord speaks of the coming of the Spirit as one whose appearance will be equal to his own, "because of the one Godhead and activity."[157] In each of these instances, Didymus is intimating that the unity of the activities of the divine *hypostaseis* reflects their organic unity in the divine nature. We infer from the activities of the *hypostaseis* that which is

---

151. *DSS* 120–123.

152. Heron, "Studies," 139. *Contra* Heston, 37. The passage under discussion does not give one the impression that Didymus is "energetically" defending diversity of operation; his hesitation to do so indicates that he is well-aware of his earlier argument.

153. *DT* 3.38 (973C–976A).

154. See Jaroslav Pelikan, *The Christian Tradition: A History of the Development of Doctrine 1: The Emergence of the Catholic Tradition (100–600)* (Chicago: University of Chicago Press, 1971), 218: "The apparent inconsistency of Didymus's first arguing that there was a correlation between the operation of Father, Son, and Holy Spirit and their ousia, and then maintaining that one could not conclude a difference of nature between them on the basis of the diversity of their operations, could not be clarified without a full-scale doctrine of the Trinity, in which both the unity and the diversity could be precisely formulated."

155. *DT* 2.7.7.2 (581A).
156. *DT* 2.7.2 (561C–564A).
157. *DT* 2.17 (725A).

common to their nature: their power, goodness, holiness, authority, freedom, etc. This inferential argument inveighs almost exclusively against subordinationist interpretations of the Son and the Holy Spirit's nature.

While the above argument is a customary one for Didymus, it is not the only mode in which he speaks of divine activity. With some frequency, Didymus also differentiates the roles of the *hypostaseis* within the activity of the Trinity. Most frequently, he does so in relation to creation. The following example illustrates the two ways of speaking of divine activity in close conjunction with one another. Speaking of the Creator's incomprehensibility to creatures, Didymus writes:

> For how could the things of the Trinity not be incomprehensible to all, when [the Trinity] is the Creator (γενεσιουργός) of them all and is far superior to every rational, indeed even every spiritual creature, and when behind [the Trinity] and beyond it there is nothing whatsoever, but rather all things are under it, and [exist] because of it and under its feet as creatures? For, being well-pleased (εὐδοκήσας) the Father began (προκατήρξατο) it, and the Only-begotten created (ἐδημιούργησεν), while the Spirit of God sanctified, and by his sanctification brought it to perfection (ἐτελείωσεν), illumined, empowered, and gave it life.[158]

The Trinity is the Creator of all things. And yet this creation takes a certain form: the Father is credited with inaugurating the creative work of the Trinity in his good pleasure, and the Son is in some sense the focal point of this creative work, while the Holy Spirit brings the work of the Trinity to completion by sanctifying it. Within the one Trinitarian activity of the creation of the world, at least some kind of particularity is afforded each of the *hypostaseis*.

The Holy Spirit's role is highlighted with greatest clarity above. Didymus further develops his role later on in the treatise. Once again assigning the activity of creation to the Word, Didymus notes that God distributes his gifts to creation through the Spirit. And it is arguably "more useful (συμφορώτερον)" for the creature to receive the "providential care (προνοεῖσθαι)" of the Spirit than it is to be created *tout court*.[159] By bestowing upon the creatures his gifts, the Spirit raises the creature from lifelessness to life, from powerlessness to freedom, from subjection to sin to the former and better pattern of life.[160] The

---

158. *DT* 2.1.6 (449AB).

159. *DT* 2.8.1 (616AB). It is a rhetorical moment; Didymus' point is not that the Spirit's role is somehow more important than the Son's but that creation without sanctification is of little benefit to the creature. Judas is the primary example of such a creature for Didymus, since he destroyed sanctification (see 616C and 2.6.3.4 (513A)).

160. Cf. *DT* 2.7.3.7 (568BC).

Holy Spirit completes the work of creation by "filling, sustaining, sanctifying, and giving life" to that which the Father and the Son create.[161]

Didymus affords prominence to the Son in the work of creation. When he is not using the word to speak of the Trinity, Didymus most frequently employs the word "Creator (δημιουργός)" of God the Word alone.[162] In a similar vein, when he is giving a Trinitarian interpretation to the text that speaks of the creation of humanity (Gen 1:27–28), Didymus assigns the "making (ποιέω)" particularly to the Son and the "blessing" (which he interprets to mean "sanctifying") to the Holy Spirit.[163] In the case of the Word of God, Didymus understands the word "create" to mean that he is the one through whom God the Father wills to bring creation into being out of non-existence.[164] Hence, although all three *hypostaseis* are rightly termed "Creator," the Word is credited particularly with the role of establishing the universe in existence, with giving it being, and fashioning or ordering it in accordance with the Father's will.

The Father, as the lengthy quotation above showed, is prominent in the inauguration of the activities of the Trinity. He begins the work of creation, and continues it through his Word and by his Spirit. The word that most often appears in connection with the Father is that spoken by him at the baptism of his Son, echoing his satisfaction at the completion of his good creation: εὐδοκέω, "I am well-pleased." Didymus consistently describes this "beginning" of the activities of the Trinity in these terms. The Father is well-pleased to do all that he does through his Word and by his Spirit. It is precisely through his "good pleasure (εὐδόκησις)" that he enters into the work of creation as "co-creator (συμποιητής)" with his Son and his Spirit.[165] Likewise, with the other *hypostaseis* of the Trinity the Father enters into the work of baptism as one who is well-pleased to renew us by the gift of his Spirit.[166]

There are frequent examples of this tendency.[167] The most important instance of it for our understanding of the role of the Father deserves to be quoted in full. Didymus quotes an argument from his opponents in which they speak of the Father being "well-pleased" for everything to be created by the Son.[168] By focusing solely on the Son's agency in creation, the Macedonian argument means to exclude the Holy Spirit from this activity. Didymus responds that the Holy Spirit cannot be excluded from this activity since he is

---

161. *DT* 3.23 (924D–925A).

162. See *DT* 1.32.19 (428B), 2.6.4.9 (520B), 2.7.3.6 (568A), and 2.7.3.16 (573D). The latter reference, in the context of the argument, refers to the Son.

163. *DT* 2.7.3.3 (565C).

164. *DT* 3.23 (925A). Cf. 2.8.1 (616A).

165. *DT* 2.7.3.15 (573C).

166. *DT* 2.12 (680A).

167. See *DT* 1.9.42 (289A) (in relationship to the Son's work of salvation), 2.1.6 (449B), 3.28 (945A) (in relation to the Spirit's bestowal of good things).

168. *DT* 2.6.4.9 (520AB). See Seiler, *De trinitate, Buch 2,* 125n2.

ever a "co-worker (συνεργόν)" with the creating Son, just as the Father is. In fact, "every activity and gift of his Only-begotten Son the Word and of the one Holy Spirit that is creative, good, perfect, and common to them both is attributed (ἀνάγεται) to the one from whom and with whom these blessed *hypostaseis* shined forth unspeakably."[169] In short, when Didymus comes to explain what is meant by the language of the "good will" of the Father, he argues that no activity either of the Son or the Spirit can be understood as taking place without the agency of the Father, to whom all divine activity is attributed. The particularity afforded to the Son or the Holy Spirit does not exclude the Father, since they do all things at his good pleasure and are ever present to him.

"The Same Activity Differently"

Now that the portrait of Didymus' teaching on the inseparable, yet particular, activity is nearly complete, we are in a position to suggest the reason for its expression. For Didymus, the "oneness" of the divine activity points primarily to the *hypostaseis'* common agency in this activity. In no case is it appropriate to speak of one of the *hypostaseis* of the Trinity undertaking a work that is reserved exclusively to his own *hypostasis*. Creation, like salvation, is the common gift of the Trinity. If it could be shown that any of the *hypostaseis* acted alone in this sense, then there would be reason to suggest that the *hypostaseis* belonged to different natures. That this is never the case secures the Homoousian argument in favor of confessing the one nature of Father, Son, and Holy Spirit.

Yet this "oneness" of activity does not exclude in Didymus' mind the notion of particularity. As long as it is understood that the Son is not the only one who may be termed "Creator," Didymus is comfortable speaking of the prominence of his role in relation to this activity. Likewise, the title "Sanctifier" cannot serve as a replacement for the Holy Spirit's name, since the Son and the Father also sanctify. Nevertheless, in the work of sanctification the Holy Spirit achieves a certain degree of prominence. Finally, the Father is not alone in willing the divine activity, since the Son and the Holy Spirit share the one will of the Father. Nevertheless, the Father in all divine activity is accorded the role of inaugurating it by his good pleasure.

What then is the basis for expressing Trinitarian activity in this way? This question may be answered by attending to two passages in particular. In the first, Didymus responds to a Eunomian argument that the Scriptures regularly separate the Father, the Son, and the Spirit by prepositional phrases like "from whom (ἐξ οὗ)," "through whom (δι' οὗ)," and "in whom (ἐν ᾧ)."[170] For the Heterousians, the language is taken to refer to the Father's primacy over the

---

169. *DT* 2.6.4.9 (520B).

170. See *DT* 3.23 (924AB). Didymus produces texts like 1 Cor 8:4–6 ("one God the Father *from whom* . . . one Lord Jesus Christ *through whom*"), Eph 4:30 ("the Holy Spirit of God *in whom*"), and Rom 14:17 ("joy *in* the Holy Spirit").

Son; if all things come into existence from the Father, then this "all," they argue, must include the Son as well. All things subsequent to the Son himself, including the Holy Spirit, are brought into being through the Son.[171] Didymus' response to the argument is instructive. Rather than focusing on dismantling their scriptural exegesis, he notes that in the Corinthians-text Paul does not enumerate the one Lord through whom all things come with the "created gods" but rather joins him in unity with the Father from whom are all things. He then reflects on the positive significance of the passage:

> Rather, this was said[172] in this way so that we might not perceive any confusion (σύγχυσιν) between the divine *hypostaseis*, but [might understand] that each is thoroughly distinguished (διευκρινηθῆναι). And this was said so that by the phrase "One God the Father," Greek polytheism might be cast aside, and that by the phrase "One Lord Jesus Christ" Jewish rejection of Christ might be as well, by the phrase "one," and "one," and "one," the foolishness of Montanists who would come to worship as one person (πρόσωπον) the three *hypostaseis* worthy of all praise and finally the excessively mindless madness of Sabellius, who dreamed that God the Word is like the utterance that is released and dispersed in the air.[173]

Didymus then produces Ephesians 4:6 as evidence that the Father is not understood to be absent from creation when the text says that he is "over all things," though it is God the Word "through all things" who brings creation into being, and the Spirit of God "in all things" who "fills, sustains, sanctifies, and gives it life."[174]

We learn two things from the above discussion: 1) Didymus develops his account of the particularity of divine activity in an anti-Eunomian direction that also (quite explicitly) steers clear of uni-personalist or modalist accounts of the *hypostaseis*, and 2) that in this context Didymus is happy to repeat the distinction between the activities of the *hypostaseis* in connection with the notion that the *hypostaseis* are in fact not confused and clearly distinguished. The connection between separate *hypostaseis* and separate roles within the one divine activity of creation is quite strong. There are, on the basis of this pas-

---

171. The argument is presented in very brief form in Eunomius, *Apol.* 26.16-20 (Vaggione, *Extant Works*, 70–71).

172. Lampe ("διευκρινέω," p. 367) proffers the emendation εἴρηται for the text's εἴρηνται. Perhaps the plural form reflects the overall structure of the sentence, which has as its subject both τοῦτο μέν and τοῦτο δέ. In any case the referent is the same (the whole Pauline passage), which argues that Lampe's emendation—even if it does not identify the original word used—does justice to the intended sense.

173. *DT* 3.23 (924BC).

174. *DT* 3.23 (924C–925A).

sage, clear reasons for supposing that Didymus associates differences in activity with eternal distinctions in hypostatic identity. The doctrine of individuated roles within the one activity of the Trinity complements and safeguards the doctrine that the *hypostaseis* really are distinct, and are not merely manifestations of the same uni-personal deity.

In a second example, Didymus is advancing several theses for the sake of his orthodox audience. Lest they conclude that the interpretation of Scripture is a veritable minefield for all but the most experienced, Didymus fittingly concludes Book 1 by listing several rules for interpreting difficult Trinitarian passages. Toward the middle of this list, Didymus writes:

> Whenever the same deeds teach that both *hypostaseis* do the same activity differently (διαφόρως), [this is] because of what was said before [namely, "because of the equality in honor and power, the consubstantiality and real distinction (εὐκρινίαν) of the *hypostaseis*"]. Whenever, though each *hypostasis* is capable of creating and doing all things, the God and Father was well-pleased for all things to be established through the Son and God, and to be sanctified through the Holy Spirit, this is because of the one will of the Trinity, and because it is shown that all good things are bestowed from it, and because we send up thanksgiving and worship (δοξολογίαν) that is common to it and equal.[175]

Once again Didymus ties together the notion of distinction within activity to the real distinctions between the *hypostaseis* that he has defended at length. As we have come to expect of him, Didymus illustrates the idea by appealing to the roles of the *hypostaseis* in the creation of the world. These roles, differenti-

---

175. *DT* 1.36.4–6 (440BC). Mingarelli translates the text as it stands, but suggests in the notes that the word διαφόρως is corrupt. On the basis of much of Didymus' argument, one expects ἀδιαφόρως, he argues (440Dn27). Mingarelli's proposal would place the two sentences in contrast with one another. However, this reading is difficult to sustain since it is unclear what connection there would in Didymus' mind between saying that the *hypostaseis* do the same activities without any distinction (ἀδιαφόρως) and his conclusion that this teaches us to acknowledge their real distinction (εὐκρινίαν). (The "aforementioned reasons" of 1.36.4.13 (440C.3) refer backward to 1.36.4.11 (440B.11–12), a passage I have inserted within the quotation). Hönscheid, *De trinitate, Buch 1*, 236, preserves the reading of the manuscript. He argues that the point is primarily an anti-Eunomian one, meant to outflank the Eunomian argument that any difference in activity assumes a difference in essence. Didymus appears to grant that the *hypostaseis* work differently, but not that their activities are separable. E.g., the Son creates all things with the Father and the Spirit though his role in this activity is not identical to that of the other two *hypostaseis*. Hönscheid's reading has the support of the manuscript and makes better sense of Didymus' overall argument (Ibid., 237n3).

ated though they are, nevertheless reveal the unity of nature that exists within the Trinity.

These examples illustrate that Didymus is ready to deal with the consequences of insisting on true distinctions within the Godhead. If the Three really are truly and eternally distinct from one another in their *hypostaseis*, then their activities must also reflect such distinctions. However, because the distinctions between them are not distinctions in nature or essence, and because Didymus understands that the missions of the *hypostaseis* necessarily indicate the presence of all of the *hypostaseis* in the activities of each one, it is impossible to suggest that the *hypostaseis* act alone. Their differentiated activity reveals that the Three are truly distinct, but also that there is an underlying unity of will, power, nature, and essence in the Trinity, since this activity is never out of tune and diverse.

Conclusion

Assessing Didymus' doctrine of the Trinity first of all demands the recognition that he undertakes to articulate it in a manner that does justice to the sublimity of his subject and the limitations of human speech and thought. He is, for example, aware that when he is speaking of the "begottenness" of the Son he is using human language to speak of that for which human language is manifestly inadequate. Thus he uses parabolic speech for that which is "beyond comparison," conveying what is "beyond thought" to the mind, "inferring that which is great . . . from the small."[176] He is continually qualifying his arguments about the mode of existence of each of the *hypostaseis* with phrases that disavow the attempt at exhaustive understanding: "For if it is comprehended, it is not incomprehensible, neither is it a mystery if it is understood, nor is it divine if it is contained."[177] He frequently warns against attempts at providing exhaustive definition, especially given the fact that even the scriptural parables about divine reality are themselves beyond our grasp.[178] Hence a significant emphasis of Didymus' theological method is apophatic; by clarifying what aspects of the scriptural analogy do not apply in the case of the Son's begetting or the Spirit's procession, one sees more clearly that which is being affirmed about these things. "Speech (λόγος)" is subordinate to "reality (πρᾶγμα)."

Nevertheless, and instructively so, he is not reduced to agnostic silence in the presence of these singular facts, since he is aware that God himself is the

---

176. *DT* 1.15.35 (308A).

177. *DT* 1.15.56 (312C).

178. See *DT* 1.15.57 (312C): "When we hear concerning the Father: "You are, from one age even unto another," and "his truth reaches the clouds," we do not impose a limitation (ὅρους) upon him, but we believe in the eternal one, for the age is not the same age as he is."

one who speaks to us of such matters. Didymus therefore remains closely tied to these words in adding his testimony to that of which the Word has spoken. The move is instructive in contemporary theological parlance inasmuch as it affirms that 1) epistemological limitations are of material significance in the pursuit of divine knowledge. We must indeed beware of importing human categories into our thoughts about God, of construing God in our own image. Equally important, however, and a point that is sometimes missed where the above is made, is Didymus' conviction that 2) these epistemological limitations are not grounds for abandoning the specificity of divine revelation in the words of the Scriptures, but rather grounds for highlighting their irreplaceability. If Didymus recognizes that he must often resort to analogies, he recognizes that these must have some purchase on divine reality, since they are the very terms in which God has spoken of himself.

Didymus' account of the identities of the *hypostaseis* remains closely tied, therefore, to the language in which God has expressed himself to us. My study thus far does not alter the picture of Didymus as essentially conservative in his dogmatic writings. It has been fairly noted that Didymus remains closely tied to scriptural language in speaking of the inner mysteries of the Trinitarian life, that his efforts at speculative theology are largely conservative.[179] There is, for instance, almost nothing original in his account of the hypostatic identities of the Son and the Holy Spirit. However, Didymus should be attended to in raising the question of how the Church ought to conceive of the hypostatic identity of the Father and his role in the economy.

In the first of these, Didymus puts his finger on an issue of some importance. He is somewhat unique in refusing to use the word "unbegotten" to characterize the Father. Other pro-Nicene theologians likewise de-centralized the word under pressure from its abuse in Arian and Eunomian discourse. They highlighted its inadequacy in conveying the meaning of the scriptural term "Father." Didymus represents an extreme example of this tendency, only using the term when he is summarizing his opponent's argument or responding to the terms that he has been given. More significantly, in the company of this guarded silence is also Didymus' explicit refusal to speak of causality in giving an account of Trinitarian relations. What is the significance of these moves?

First of all it should be noted that Didymus—like other pro-Nicenes—acknowledges a certain kind of priority to the Father, especially in relation to Trinitarian activity. This is highlighted by Didymus' language of "beginning" or "willing" the activities of the other two *hypostaseis* in the economy. In these instances, a kind of passivity or receptivity is discernible both in descriptions of the Son and the Holy Spirit in their cooperation in the works of the Father.

---

179. See, e.g., Daley, "Fullness of the Saving God," 122–123, and Frances Young, *From Nicaea to Chalcedon: A Guide to the Literature and its Background*, 2nd ed. (Grand Rapids, MI: Baker, 2010), 100–101.

And it is for this reason that Didymus can speak, as Gregory of Nazianzus frequently does, of all Trinitarian work, and indeed, of the *hypostaseis* of the Son and the Spirit themselves, being "referred back" or "attributed to" the Father.[180] For Didymus, in other words, the economic priority surely gestures backward to something in the eternal life of the Trinity. The point at issue in his refusal of any notion of causal priority is therefore not whether but how this priority should be spoken of.

To speak of the Father as cause of the Son and the Spirit is, for Didymus, to characterize the Father in contrast to them as the one who is uncaused. The distinguishing marks of the Son and the Holy Spirit are given only in relation to the Father from whom they, respectively, are generated and proceed. The distinguishing mark of the Father would, in contrast, be defined in abstraction from these relations: he is "without cause (ἀναίτιος)" or "unbegotten (ἀγέννητος)." To absolutize ἀγεννησία as the Father's distinguishing mark is surely to guarantee the distinction between the Father and the Son, but to do so at the risk of giving an account of the Father's identity in terms of a distinction in which the Son is not conceptually necessary to the Father's identity.[181] Didymus offers a doctrine of the Father that is surely less developed, but one that avoids the problematic of articulating a causal priority which can be construed in conception alone.

Didymus' attitude to such a formulation, to speculate somewhat, would likely be two-fold: 1) using causality to describe intra-Trinitarian relations runs the considerable risk of being filled with content drawn from creaturely categories. All of the enumerated definitions of ἀρχή in *DT* 3.5 (840BC) are unworthy descriptions of the intra-Trinitarian relation of the Father and the Son. Although Didymus is happy to draw on some of them to describe the Son's relation to the creation, they are too bound to the material order to be used to the end of giving an account of a relation that is properly divine. 2) If the word was used anyway without any identifiable referent, it would be a word that described "in conception alone," a word that pushed theological language beyond the bounds of apophatic qualification into the realm of the purely apophatic. Didymus' silence at this point—God alone knows how the Father is said to be greater than the Son—is instructive. This mystery is, for Didymus, reserved for God and the *eschaton*.

---

180. See *DT* 2.2.21 (460A) and 2.21 (660C). On Gregory, see Christopher Beeley, *Gregory of Nazianzus on the Trinity and the Knowledge of God* (Oxford: Oxford University Press, 2008), 206n55.

181. My argument is sympathetic to DelCogliano's assessment of Athanasius' and Basil's reasons for decentralizing the term "unbegotten" in relation to the Father. The term "correlates inappropriately." See Mark DelCogliano, "The Influence of Athanasius and the Homoiousians on Basil of Caesarea's Decentralization of "Unbegotten"," *JECS* 19, no.2 (2011): 213-214. Didymus takes the above tendency further.

In this chapter I have argued that the Father is involved in all the missions of the Son and the Spirit by virtue of this hidden priority in the Trinitarian life. The Son, as the Only-begotten of the Father, is the true image of the Father, having the same authority, will, and power. Just as the Son comes forth from the Father as one begotten, so he always dwells with the Father. The Holy Spirit proceeds from the Father as the Father's seal, joined to the image (the Son) inseparably. The missions of the Son and the Spirit are in every way mutually involving, so that the Son always has the Spirit of his Father resting upon him, and so that the Spirit is always with the Son. All the *hypostaseis* act inseparably in all the activity of the Godhead; yet, because of the distinctions in their *hypostaseis*, all take on recognizably-consistent patterns of activity in relation to this one activity. The consequences of this distinction-in-unity of Trinitarian activity will be spelled out in the next chapter.

3

THE ECONOMY AND SCRIPTURE

The inspiration of Scripture is ingredient within the self-presentation of God to creatures. Given the ontological and epistemic divide between divine and created being, God must reveal himself to humanity if he is to be known. In the first part of this chapter I argue, with Didymus, that such a situation necessarily privileges divine activity within the human *ordo cognoscendi*. God's activity toward us is the basis of all our speech about and knowledge of God.

The second—and most significant—portion of this chapter is devoted to articulating what God has done in overcoming human ignorance of and alienation from him. God overcomes creaturely ignorance and alienation in his gracious economy, in which the *hypostaseis* of the Trinity cooperate in restoring the filial identity of humanity. It is as children of God, regenerate in the waters of baptism, that humans can be said to know God and to see him as he is. The knowledge of God is a function of the recreated identity of the Christian, and is therefore relationally conceived.

Scriptural ontology cannot be abstracted from such an account. In the third portion of this chapter, I argue that locating Scripture at this place has two clear implications for Didymus for its reading. 1) Christian reading of Scripture proceeds by the sanctifying (or purifying) work of the Spirit, who thereby conforms the Christian into the likeness of the Son. This sanctifying work has clear moral overtones in Didymus' vocabulary. 2) Directed toward the Son by the Spirit, the Christian is illumined by the divine *hypostaseis* so that she is given the mind of Christ. Christian reading of Scripture involves a reorientation of the intellect so that the reader thereof reads with Christ.

The *sine Qua non* of Theological Knowledge

Homoousian theology in general faces a significant epistemological dilemma. Confessing an absolute equality of essence between the *hypostaseis* of the Trinity, pro-Nicene theologians as a whole faced the consequences of abandoning an account of theological epistemology that had played a prior role in the Christian tradition. The Homoousian confession rendered impossible the notion that one *hypostasis* of the Trinity was more proximate to human comprehension than another because his *ousia* was nearer to our own. It could not be sustained, for instance, that the Word mediates the knowledge of the incomprehensible Father to human creatures by virtue of his being by nature more amenable to human limitations. Such a conception of things would, in any case, raise the question of whether the Son could really know the Father fully.[1]

Moreover, though Arius resolved the tensions within the earlier tradition in a rather one-sided manner, there were some grounds for the inference within the tradition. Origen, for instance, endorsed at least some kind of epistemological distinction between the absolute unknowability of the Father and the relative proximity of the Logos as the Wisdom by which the universe receives its own ideational structure.[2] The Father is "altogether one and simple (πάντη ἕν . . . καὶ ἁπλοῦν)," but the Son of God establishes a plurality of relations with creation.[3] While this secured the essential character of the Son's mediation of the Father, it raised the question of the Son's own knowledge of the Father. And there are some passages in Origen that raise the question of whether he was ready to speak of the *complete* epistemic disclosure of the Father to the Son.[4]

Didymus moves in a consistently pro-Nicene direction on the doctrine of the Trinity, departing from or modifying Origen where subordinationist accounts of the Son in his own day demanded clearer expression of the Son and

---

1. See, for instance, Arius, *Thal.* (Williams, 103): "What scheme of thought, then, could admit the idea that he who has his being from the [a?] Father should know by comprehension the one who gave him birth? For clearly the one who has a beginning is in no way [in a position] to encompass in thought or lay hold upon the one without beginning as he is [in himself]."

2. See Rowan Williams, *Arius: Heresy and Tradition*, rev. ed. (Grand Rapids, MI: Eerdmans, 2002), 139–140.

3. See *In Ioh.* 1.19.109–20.124 (FC 80:56–59). The point illustrates Origen's commitment to understanding the Logos both in relation to the Father and in relation to the universe. Origen prioritizes the name Wisdom over Word, since it is as Wisdom that there is a basis for his communication to rational creatures as Word.

4. For a helpful introduction to Origen's theological epistemology, see Peter Widdecombe, "The Revelation of the Son and the Names of God," *The Fatherhood of God from Origen to Athanasius*, rev. ed. (Oxford: Clarendon Press, 2000), 44–62. Widdecombe's helpful portrait of Origen's epistemology does not adequately deal with the consequences of his clear affirmations of the Father's transcendence over the Son, though he successfully secures the importance of an epistemology that anchors the knowledge of the Father in the Son's mediation of (and thus possession of) this knowledge. Though Widdecombe points out that it is unclear whether the notion of the Father's more fulsome self-knowledge is tied to Origen's use of Plotinian categories, he rather preemptively dismisses the tensions identified by Williams (*Arius*, 140) in his account of the Son's knowledge of the Father (pp. 42-43). Origen—whatever his reasons for doing so—articulates at least some quantitative distinction between the Father's self-knowledge and the Son's knowledge of the Father. Though the Son's knowledge of the Father is deemed "perfect" and though only he "can contain the whole reflection of the full glory of God," Origen nevertheless notes that the Father's "contemplation of himself . . . surpasses the contemplation of the Son" (*In Ioh.* 32.28.345–353 (FC 89:407–408)).

the Spirit's equality with the Father in all things.[5] We have already seen him insist, against Eunomius and Macedonius, that the Son and the Holy Spirit are by nature as incomprehensible as the Father, and that all three know one another fully. The proportion between the creature's unknowing of the Father's essence and its unknowing of the Son and the Holy Spirit's essence is equal. The treatise *DT* trades significantly on this concept; indeed, Didymus' cosmology supports distinctions between the rational or spiritual creation and the Creator of the world that call into question the very possibility of the kind of knowledge—knowledge of God's essence—that is claimed by his opponents.

Beyond the Seeing of the Cherubim

Repeatedly throughout the treatise, Didymus warns that confession is not to be confused with investigation. The attempt to provide a rational explanation for all the *data* of divine revelation is not only futile but dangerous. There is safety to be found rather in marvelling at the divine in reverent fear and in limiting the scope of one's speech about God to what we are able to speak about as creatures.[6] His opponents frequently transgress these boundaries. They are constantly demanding definitive description of God's being or explanation of the eternal relationships between the *hypostaseis*. They continually fail to recognize that the economy proceeds "for our sake," that the activities of the Son and Spirit in this economy are not to be facilely taken as evidence of their substantial subordination to the Father. Arguing against such a conclusion in the face of the Son's manifestation of human frailty in the Gospels, for instance, Didymus appeals to the maxims of secular authorities: "Do not shake (σάλευε) the secret things; do not investigate God";[7] "Believe in God and pay him homage, but do not examine him."[8]

The epistemic gap that stands between the Creator and human creatures is widened by the disordered dispositions of the soul. Subjected to the experiences and desires of the body that threaten to lure the creature away from the contemplation of God, human creatures are necessarily clouded in their interior vision.[9] Bound up by these limitations, humanity is unable to contemplate God as he is. Didymus frequently frames the difficulty of obtaining true knowl-

---

5. It is consistently noted that Didymus diverges from Origen most notably on the doctrine of the Trinity. However, there is evidence for the view that he is concerned with illustrating the pro-Nicene trajectory of Origen's thought. See, for instance, Alasdair Heron's "The Holy Spirit in Origen and Didymus the Blind: A Shift in Perspective from the Third to the Fourth Century," in *Kerygma und Logos* (Göttingen: Vandenhoeck and Ruprecht, 1979), 307.

6. *DT* 1.9.12 (281B). Cf. 1.15.48 (309C).

7. *DT* 3.21 (916C). The sense of σαλεύω here is tied to the shaking down of goods for the purpose of measurement.

8. *DT* 3.2.1 (788A).

9. See *DT* 3.1 (773B–777A).

edge of God against that of obtaining true knowledge of angelic beings. Angelic beings are invisible to the eyes of our body, he argues. Such beings lack the properties that would make sensory experience of them possible. The angels, however, possess "heavenly bodies." Thus, they are circumscribable by thought and place, in contrast with the limitless Spirit of God.[10] Although these spiritual beings are invisible to our eyes, however, they are not "beyond the reach (ἀνέφικτοι)" of human understanding. They are visible to the eye of the soul; they are seen "in the apprehension of a knowledgeable insight (κατὰ ἀντίληψιν θεωρίας ἐπιστημονικῆς)."[11] This does not imply that one can provide a definition of the essence of these spiritual substances, but Didymus is confident that the mind can impose definite limits upon them by which it can advance to some understanding of the angelic nature conceptually. Angelic freedom is, for instance, closely analogous to human freedom: as creatures, both angels and human are mutable. Change is predicated of beings that come into existence and not of divine being that simply *is* and does not become.[12]

On the basis of this observation, Didymus can sustain the notion that the epistemic gap between angels and the divine is infinitely larger than that between the lower rational order (humanity) and the higher (angels). After affirming the notion of the mental visibility of souls and angels, Didymus writes:

> God, however, is beyond invisibility, even beyond what is most hidden, and is beyond every thought; not only is he not subject to vision and every other sense, but neither is he visible to the thinking of angels themselves because he is incomprehensible and inaccessible. For that there is a God is well-known to everyone, but what (τί) he is or how (πῶς) he exists is utterly beyond the comprehension (δυσαλωτότατον) of all natural things.[13]

If the divine is by nature inaccessible to all created beings, then it follows that even angels do not comprehend God. The angels see the face of the heavenly Father, but they are not granted a vision that comprehends him in all his magnitude (ὅσος . . . ἐστιν) nor are they able to comprehend how he is (οἷός ἐστιν).[14] The Trinity is uncircumscribed by the vigilant, sleepless eyes of the seraphim.[15] For this reason, the Incarnation has a revelatory function even among the angelic hosts. Before it, the Son was invisible to them because of his

---

10. On the spatial limitation of angelic beings, see *DSS* 21–24. Cf. *DT* 2.4.4 (481BC) and 2.6.2. (509A).
11. *DT* 3.16 (873AB).
12. Cf. *DT* 2.6.3.7 (513AB).
13. *DT* 3.16 (873AB).
14. See *DT* 2.6.16 (544B).
15. See *DT* 2.1.5 (449A). Cf. 1.36.1 (440A): the grasp (διάληψις) of God himself is beyond even the sensation (αἴσθησις) of archangels.

"limitlessness (ἀπειρία)" and "formlessness (ἀνειδεότης)."[16] The angels acquire new "knowledge of God (θεογνωσία)" at the birth of the Savior, marking the festive occasion together with the shepherds in Bethlehem.[17]

The Mutual Comprehension of the Hypostaseis

No epistemic gap, such as that described above, exists between the *hypostaseis* of the Trinity. The knowledge that the Son has of the Father is equal to the knowledge that the Father has of the Son. Didymus produces the text: "No one knows the Father except the Son, nor does anyone know the Son except the Father" (Matt 11:27), adducing as an interpretive device the philosophical axiom that substances of different natures cannot acquire mutually complete knowledge of one another. If two *hypostaseis* know one another fully, they must also possess the same nature.[18] The creature acquires its knowledge of the Father from the Son; the Son, however, needs no one to reveal the Father to him.[19]

Because of his knowledge of the Father, the Son is ignorant of nothing. We have already witnessed Didymus interpreting statements in the Gospels that predicate ignorance of the Son by appealing to the category of feigned ignorance for our benefit, ignorance "on our account (δι' ἡμᾶς)." As for the last day, the Son knows it, but chooses not to disclose what he knows to us. After all, how could "the one who is in the Father and [who] has the Father in himself" not know the day of his own making? "If the Father who knows all things is in him, he himself also knows who sees all things in the Father." The Son who knows the Father knows all things.[20]

As for the Holy Spirit, Didymus defends the same notion just as vigorously. The Macedonians are fond of mentioning the Scripture that speaks of the Holy Spirit as one who "searches out the depths of God" (1 Cor 2:10). St Paul speaks of the Spirit searching out the hidden things of God, they say, because the Spirit is ignorant of them. Once again Didymus counters by appealing to the above axiom: hetero-substantial beings cannot acquire the same knowledge. Only one who is "of the same essence and knowledge as God" can "know the things of God just as God knows them."[21] Didymus then offers his own counter-interpretation. The divine Spirit does not search God out as though ignorant of him but rather searches as the one who is "united (ἡνωμένον) to him by nature." The searching out is a searching that takes place in and for us.

---

16. *DT* 1.27.56 (404BC).

17. See *DT* 3.6 (844A).

18. *DT* 1.26.33–34 (385D–388A). Cf. 2.6.16 (544A): to see "God the Father just as he is" is impossible for the creature, "since this is beyond the reach (ἀχώρητον) and endurance (ἀβάστακτον) of a nature different [than God's]."

19. *DT* 3.2.11 (792B).

20. See *DT* 3.22 (917B–920B).

21. Summarizing *DT* 3.37 (969AC) and quoting 969B.

"Concretely existing (ἐνυποστάτως)" as God's hidden wisdom, the Holy Spirit is the source of its revelation to us.²² The Holy Spirit is never ignorant of all that the Father does, having knowledge in every way equal to him. As Lord, the Holy Spirit is unlike the servant who is ignorant of his master's affairs (cf. John 15:15).²³ Wholly uncircumscribed as the Father is, the Spirit comprehends the Father utterly.²⁴

Only the Son and the Holy Spirit are said to see or to know God the Father as he is in all his fullness. And because of their "singularity" and "sameness" (τὸ ταὐτόν) of Godhead, the Son and the Spirit—who are themselves beyond quantity and form—see "just as the unquantifiable (ἀμεγέθης) and formless (ἀνείδεος) God is."²⁵ Didymus does not leave any room at all for any differentiation of degrees of knowing within the Trinity. Just as it is the immeasurable and eternal glory of the Son and the Holy Spirit to know the Father, so also the Father's greatness is secured "because he knows the Son."²⁶

How then Is God Known?

Given the fulsome character of the mutual comprehension of the divine *hypostaseis* and that such comprehension remains by nature beyond the capacity of every created thing, three closely related questions follow: 1) Can creatures be said to know God at all? 2) If so, what kind of knowledge can creatures have of God? 3) And how is this knowledge of God obtained?

In Didymus' mind, the answer to the first question is a resounding "yes." In seeming contradiction to the repeated affirmations of divine incomprehensibility, Didymus repeatedly affirms that human creatures do become partakers of divine knowledge. The vision of God is the goal of human existence. Hence Didymus pleads with the Macedonians to take up the prayer of Moses: "Show yourself to me; let me see you as you really are" (Exod 33:13). "For as it seems," he writes, "they do not yet really know what many prophets and kings desired to see and hear and did not. We, however, not only hear but see as well."²⁷ And what is it that Didymus claims to hear and see? He repeats the same language about seeing and hearing in relation to "what is proper to each of the *hypostaseis* (τὸ ἰδικὸν τῶν ὑποστάσεων)." At the baptism of Jesus, we hear the Father's word about the Son and see it corroborated by the Spirit's

---

22. *DT* 3.37 (972BC). Cf. 3.2.37 (801A). Creatures acquire and then forget knowledge. Not so with the Spirit who reveals the wisdom and knowledge of God the Father. For Didymus, the nature that reveals wisdom and knowledge in an absolute sense (that is, without receiving this revelation from another) is necessarily the very substance of that revelation.

23. *DT* 3.2.38 (801AB).
24. See *DT* 2.2.24 (460BC).
25. *DT* 2.6.16 (544AC).
26. *DT* 1.15.73–74 (317B).
27. *DT* 3.36 (968B), echoing Luke 10:24.

descent upon the Son in the form of a dove.[28] Adducing the same Lukan text echoed above, Didymus expounds it by reflecting on the sacraments: "We who are spiritual not only see and hear, but we are even illumined freely by the Holy Spirit and enjoy [these things] when we partake of Christ's body and taste the immortal font."[29]

How can Didymus assert such things and remain consistent in affirming divine invisibility and incomprehensibility? On the one hand, it is clear that Didymus avoids suggesting that we know God's essence the way we might attempt to delimit a created essence discursively. The creature never comprehends the kind of being that God is in this sense, since the human creature is deprived of the necessary criteria for determining the answer to this kind of question. On the other hand, it is clear that Didymus is not overly distressed about needing to break off such an investigation before it even properly begins. In being given the understanding of the Trinity sacramentally—i.e. by partaking of God in faith in the Eucharist and baptism—the Christian has been given something infinitely more precious. She is brought into the deepest recesses of the divine being and participates by grace in the divine *hypostaseis* themselves. Didymus is convinced that we know the divine *hypostaseis*, even if we do not have immediate access to the divine nature.

That Didymus does, on the basis of his knowledge of the *hypostaseis* in their activities toward us, predicate the divine nature itself with goodness, holiness, the love-of-humanity, etc., is significant. It reveals two things: 1) claims to divine incomprehensibility do not utterly relativize all claims about the divine essence. 2) By proceeding in this fashion, Didymus subordinates our knowing of God to the manner in which God reveals himself. Though Didymus is consistent in affirming that natural reason can arrive at the fact of God's existence, the knowledge of God himself is utterly dependent upon the manner in which God discloses himself to us. Furthermore, and this is of paramount importance, the purpose of divine revelation is not merely that we may speak and think appropriately to the object (or rather, the Subject) of our knowing, but rather that we both "see and hear" and "taste and drink." By linking epistemic and sacramental language so closely, Didymus is intimating that true knowledge of God is inherently participatory.

That such knowledge is a gift, Didymus likewise maintains. The creature is not left to itself to find God. Didymus gets at this notion in several different ways. Here I examine three of them, each of which serves to highlight a different aspect of the divine economy. 1) Early in the treatise, Didymus produces a raft of scriptural texts that warn against the Heterousian investigation of eternal mysteries that God has concealed from us. In the midst of these texts, Didymus repeats his observation about God's infinitude and creaturely limitation. He then says: "If it [namely, divine knowledge] was not revealed by the

---

28. *DT* 1.18.49 (356A).
29. *DT* 2.14 (717A).

Scriptures, it would be unknown to the creature."[30] For Didymus, natural notions are sufficient to affirm the existence of God but are not reliable in disclosing who God is and what he is like. For this, one needs the Scriptures.

2) In his first thesis of the second chapter in Book 3, Didymus proposes that the Son's uncreated divinity is assured on the basis of the scriptural designation: "true God" (1 John 5:20). Being himself "true," he writes, the Son is the "genitor of the truth (ὁ τῆς ἀληθείας γενέτης)." Didymus is keen to assert that this truth is absolute and thus unable to be grasped by human understanding. However, he reins in the epistemological crisis that would ensue on a reckless interpretation of his words—namely, how can truth be known at all?—arguing: "Since he himself is the genitor of the truth, he could not be comprehended by a human mind unless, being filled by his truth [the human mind] could kindle for itself a lamp from this [truth] for its searches."[31] The creature is dependent upon the self-revelation of God; only by being filled by the object of its search can it come to know that for which it is seeking. The Truth for which the creature seeks is the One who illumines the path leading to himself. He does this by giving himself to the creature.

3) In each of the instances above, divine activity is the occasion of divine self-disclosure. God reveals the knowledge of himself through Scripture; God illumines the path that leads to himself. Nowhere else in the treatise, however, is the notion of divine priority in self-revelation given such formal precision as in Didymus' discussion of the activities of the Spirit. He reflects on the numerous activities of the Holy Spirit as evidence of his cooperation with the Father and the Son. Because of these activities, the Holy Spirit takes on numerous relational designations (e.g., the "sanctifying Spirit").[32] Didymus observes:

> There is nothing strange, if though he is one and always remains the same (ἀεὶ ὡσαύτως ἔχον), he is glorified by diverse designations. For since his inexpressible divinity is incomprehensible in mortal terms, in order to celebrate the activities that take place among ourselves—as far as we are able (κατὰ δύναμιν)—we make use of different names as well.[33]

---

30. *DT* 1.9.10. Cf. Hönscheid, *De trinitate, Buch 1*, 29. See also p. 28n21 for the reconstruction of the *lacuna*. ἠγγ[οεῖτο] is surely correct.

31. *DT* 3.2.1 (788B). This is a difficult passage in the manuscript. *Passioneianum* has the reading πληρωθῇ σαφῶς (cf. 788Dn31). But the aorist subjunctive here is clearly problematic, since 1) it demands αὐτός (the Son) as subject (making nonsense of the argument) and 2) renders the final clause untranslatable. Mingarelli's solution is elegant and convincing: πληρωθεῖσα φῶς is identically pronounced and the emendation solves both the above problems at once. 1) The participial phrase takes διάνοια as its subject (as the argument demands), and 2) the second optative (ἀνάψειεν) completes the idea of the first (ληφθείη).

32. *DT* 2.3.1-32 (465A-480B).

33. *DT* 2.3.19 (473BC).

Didymus perceives the need to offer a pre-emptive warning to his audience. The sheer multiplicity of designations for the Holy Spirit raises the possibility that Didymus' opponents will charge him with compromising divine simplicity or immutability. Didymus replies that a multiplicity of names does not imply multiplicity in the Spirit's nature or divinity, but rather that the Spirit in his divine nature is free to be a relational absolute. The names that we ascribe to him by virtue of his activities are names that he takes on because of the relationships that he establishes with us. He is, for instance, the light "in which and by which we are illumined."[34]

In this passage, Didymus makes two fundamental moves based on the original epistemological dilemma: the Spirit, in his divinity or essence, is incomprehensible to us. 1) The Holy Spirit is known to us in his activities toward us. 2) We have need of multiple terms or conceptions in apprehending that which the Holy Spirit reveals about himself in his activity. It would be a stretch to claim that this is the later Byzantine distinction between the unknowable essence of God and the knowable activities. What is clear is that human understanding of God proceeds above all by attending to divine activity, insofar as God is only revealed to us through his activity toward us.[35] Divine activity is the basis of human knowledge of the divine being and the means whereby God reconstitutes the human knower into one who, in Didymus' language, becomes worthy of knowing God.

Summary

The above illustrates that for Didymus the notion of creaturely limitation and sinfulness both play a role in humanity's ignorance of God. However, though we have yet to examine the reasons for this, these limitations are no barrier to speaking in quite fulsome terms of recreated humanity's knowledge of God. Though Didymus regularly denies direct apprehension of the divine essence, he is quite sanguine about the possibility of speaking and thinking

---

34. DT 2.3.18 (473AB).

35. Herein lies one of the critical differences between Homoousian and Heterousian theology. The Eunomian account of divine being largely brackets it off from intra-mundane activity. The unbegotten Father creates the Son outside the cosmos; the Son undertakes the activity of creating the cosmos on behalf of the unbegotten Father, but not as one who shares the Father's divinity. Divine activity—in the sense of consubstantially divine activity—is therefore not a category that the Eunomian can claim to know much about. The activity of the mediating Son and Spirit are not, strictly speaking, the activity of God. If there is greater clarity for the Eunomian about the account of the divine nature, there is much less that can be said of divine activity. The Son does the will of the Father, but the Son's activity is not by nature the Father's activity. Rather, it mirrors the Father's activity. We see here also the importance of Didymus' insistence that all of the activities of the Son and the Spirit are attributed to the Father. He does not mean this in the highly qualified sense in which the phrase could be affirmed by a Eunomian.

about God in a manner that has some purchase on the reality of God. Language can function analogously—as we have seen in the last chapter. The apophatic accents of Didymus' thought are rightly understood as an acknowledgment that creaturely limitation has a happy function to play in restricting our confession to the vast scope of what has been accomplished and revealed. We are, in short, to know God as he wishes for us to know him.

This is only possible for the creature because the Father is utterly disclosed to the Son and the Holy Spirit, whose missions among us are both the occasion and substance of divine self-disclosure to us. God enacts the revelation of himself, and it is to this activity that we must attend. True knowledge of God proceeds in this way. We also see here how misleading it would be to investigate Didymus' account of theological knowledge from a purely theoretical point-of-view, as if it were purely a matter of discerning how creaturely language and thought conform to the reality that they seek to convey. For him, the fact of human knowledge of God is most fulsomely affirmed in the context of human participation in the sacraments. We will come to see the reasons for this in the context of the whole treatise.

The Saving Economy of the Trinity

If we would then follow Didymus' account of divine knowledge, we must attend to divine activity, to the economy of the Trinity. Central to Didymus' account of our knowledge of God is his description of the work of the *hypostaseis* in salvation or re-creation: the restoration of the image of God in mankind. In brief, Didymus understands this restoration in terms of human assimilation to the Son by the work of the Holy Spirit at baptism. There, the Spirit of adoption regenerates us and renews us so that the image of our Creator is restored in us. In this new identity, we are henceforward recipients of all the gifts of the Spirit and become partakers of the divine nature, realizing our *telos* as creatures. Human knowledge of God proceeds as 1) the creature is conformed to the Son and 2) deified by this conformation. The knowledge of God implies assimilation to God.[36]

In describing Didymus' account of the economy in this way, I enter into conversation with three of Didymus' earlier interpreters. Leipoldt, Bardy, and Heston have all essayed to provide an account of Didymus' central soteriological concern. Leipoldt and Bardy—the latter leaning heavily on the former—isolate the forgiveness of sins as the central idea.[37] Heston, responding primarily to Bardy, opts for the view that salvation is for Didymus more ade-

---

36. This need not imply that there is a loss of creaturely identity, or that there are not important distinctions that remain between the knower and the object of her knowledge.

37. Leipoldt, 78–95. Cf. Bardy, *Didyme l'Aveugle*, 129–144.

quately described in terms of "the infusion of a new life."[38] In the section below, I argue that Heston provides a helpful corrective to the standard monographs on Didymus. I seek to demonstrate and extend this corrective by arguing that Leipoldt and Bardy's treatment of the theme suffers from three weaknesses. 1) Both fail to appreciate the significance of Didymus' claim that all Trinitarian activity, including salvation, is both unified and differentiated (the argument of the last chapter). 2) The consequence of this failure is a lack of engagement with the pneumatological dimension of Didymus' soteriology.[39] 3) Both carry out the investigation of the theme too narrowly, restricting themselves to the treatment of σωτηρία (and cognates) in Didymus' corpus.[40]

In the following sections, I aim to re-situate the discussion about salvation in Didymus by suggesting that 1) even a study of σωτηρία-cognates in *DT* reveals a more thoroughgoing Trinitarian accent in Didymus' soteriology than Leipoldt and Bardy acknowledge. 2) The saving activity of the Trinity is expounded with greater breadth in relation to the over-arching narrative of creation/renewal that provides Didymus with his outline of Trinitarian activity in the created world. Salvation involves not only the overcoming of sin but also the recovery of humanity's filial identity and the full realization of its *telos* in the *eschaton*.

Salvation: the Gift of the Trinity

It is frequently observed by Didymus that all the *hypostaseis* of the Trinity are involved in bestowing the gift of salvation. Though the Son alone is termed "Savior (σωτήρ)," the Father is referred to as the "compassionate and saving God,"[41] whose fellowship is salvation.[42] Likewise the Spirit too "bestows salvation."[43] The Father's work in salvation is incomplete without the "fullness of the Son and the Spirit," which is both "beneficial and saving (σωτηριώδης)."[44]

All the *hypostaseis* of the Trinity share in this great work, granting salvation to the creature in their common activity of grace. Didymus most frequently affirms that salvation is the gift of the whole Trinity. He does so in one of two ways: 1) he asserts without further specificity that the work of salva-

---

38. Heston, 13–14.

39. Improving on Leipoldt, Bardy (*Didyme l'Aveugle*, 141–142) acknowledges that the sanctifying work of the Spirit is an integral part of Didymus' account of salvation, but makes very little of the observation.

40. Bardy contextualizes "salvation" language more adequately in relation to Didymus' account of humanity's possession of the divine image and human freedom (*Didyme l'Aveugle*, 132–138). However, Bardy leans too heavily on Leipoldt to adequately challenge his interpretation of the theme.

41. *DT* 1.29.2 (413B).

42. *DT* 1.15.25 (304B). See also 3.2.7 (789C), which speaks of the Son and the Father bestowing salvation together.

43. *DT* 3.2.33 (800B).

44. *DT* 2.7.3.11 (572B).

tion, or an aspect thereof, is common to all the *hypostaseis*.⁴⁵ 2) Predicating a saving act of one of the *hypostaseis*, Didymus follows this with the observation that the other two *hypostaseis* cooperate in the accomplishment of this work. So, for instance, he argues that the abiding and protecting presence of the Holy Spirit in the baptized wards off the advances of the enemy, securing their salvation. He follows this claim by noting that this "saving seal (τὸ σωτήριον σήμαντρον)" is given only when Christians are both baptized and sealed (i.e., anointed with chrism) in the name of the Trinity.⁴⁶

That Didymus differentiates the roles of the *hypostaseis* within the work of salvation becomes apparent when we look specifically at what is said of the saving work of the Son and the Holy Spirit. Continuing to restrict ourselves mainly to those passages in which Didymus employs cognates of the word σωτηρία, we observe that Didymus most frequently remarks on the saving work accomplished by the Son. Though the saving activity of the Son is not restricted to the time of his "inhumanation (ἐνανθρώπησις),"⁴⁷ this is his saving work *par excellence*. Didymus therefore speaks frequently of the Son's "saving inhumanation" or uses language that expresses the same thought.⁴⁸ On other occasions, Didymus highlights particular moments during the time of the Incarnation as salvific moments. The Son's conception and birth from the Virgin Mary,⁴⁹ his Passion,⁵⁰ ascension, second coming,⁵¹ and his judgment of the living and the dead are events that are invested with soteriological significance.⁵²

Didymus employs the same vocabulary of the Holy Spirit. The complementary character of the Son and the Spirit's work in creation is revealed in that the creatures of the Son are endowed with the good things leading to salvation by the Holy Spirit.⁵³ Bestowing good upon all things in which he is pre-

---

45. *DT* 2.7.8.13 (592AB), 2.12 (677C and 681A), 2.14 (713A), 2.27 (756A), 3.2.53 (805A), 3.38 (976B), and 3.39 (980A).

46. *DT* 2.15 (717A–721A). Cf. also 1.34.1 (433BC), 2.7.8.7 (588B), and 3.3 (820A).

47. See, e.g., *DT* 1.7.16 (276A) (Hönscheid, *De trinitate, Buch 1*, 20) where Didymus speaks of the saving appearance of the Son in the OT.

48. See *DT* 1.9.42 (289A), 1.15.89 (324B), 1.27.18, 43, and 54 (397AB, 401A, and 404B), 1.29.4 (413C), 2.7.8.1 (581C) (most likely), 3.4 (840A), and 3.10 (857BC). With Bardy, *Didyme l'Aveugle*, 129: "the descriptor "saving" is one of the words that occurs most frequently in connection with terms that serve to refer to the Incarnation" (l'épithète σωτήριος est de celles qui reviennent le plus fréquemment à côté des termes qui servent à désigner l'Incarnation).

49. *DT* 3.3 (817B).

50. *DT* 1.15.89 (324B), 1.27.59 (405A), 3.3 (821A), and 3.6 (844A).

51. *DT* 2.7.8.9 (589B): the ascension is sandwiched between the Son's coming "because of men in sin" and his second coming when he "will judge and will do according to love-of-humanity (φιλανθρωπίαν)."

52. *DT* 1.29.1 (413B).

53. *DT* 2.8.1 (616B).

Economy and Scripture 123

sent, the Holy Spirit saves by opposing the corrupting evil that stems from the choice of the free will.[54] He saves those who have been led astray.[55] The festival of Pentecost is observed in honor of his "saving and venerated visitation (ἐπιδημίας)";[56] as the Lord announces in the Upper Room, the coming (παρουσία) of the Paraclete means nothing less than salvation for his creation.[57] The baptismal event, in which the saving work of the economy extends into the present life of the Christian, is incomplete without the saving chrism of the Holy Spirit.[58]

Thus far, the discussion of salvation language in DT confirms the dynamics discussed in the previous chapter. In all the activities of the divine *hypostaseis* each *hypostasis* takes up a role appropriate to his divine nature *and* his hypostatic identity. Salvation is accomplished by the whole Trinity. It is accomplished by each of the *hypostaseis* in a manner appropriate to his hypostatic identity. In the subsequent section we will investigate the question of the coherence of Didymus' salvific narrative more thoroughly. However, the present discussion serves to reveal that the doctrine of inseparable and differentiated activity in salvation is materially significant for Didymus. Consequently, in contrast to Leipoldt and Bardy, the Pentecostal descent of the Holy Spirit and his activity are to be brought into the category of the soteriological.

Leipoldt acknowledges some of the above features of Didymus' reflections on salvation. Salvation, he notes, is for Didymus the common gift of the Trinity. However, he appears to regard the idea as materially insignificant in his exposition of Didymus' soteriology. In any case, after reviewing two of Didymus' formulations of the doctrine of inseparable saving activity in DT, he bypasses any attempt at articulating a Trinitarian soteriology for Didymus, asserting that Didymus unwittingly contradicts himself.[59] I have shown in the previous chapter that arguments of this kind are conceptually infelicitous. Didymus predicates all divine activity of *hypostaseis* who are hypostatically differentiated and yet one in the divine nature; the doctrine of μία ἐνέργεια is best understood to reflect these distinctions even while it reveals the underlying unity of nature and (thus) will among the *hypostaseis*. Salvation is the work of the Trinity; it is a work in which the roles of the *hypostaseis* are differentiated.

Bardy's work is an improvement on Leipoldt's insofar as he recognizes that there are pneumatological dimensions of Didymus' soteriology. It is regrettable, however, that he does not explore these in any depth.[60] The above

---

54. DT 2.6.8.2 (529BC).
55. DT 2.7.5 (577A). Cf. 3.2.23 (800B).
56. DT 2.16 (721A).
57. DT 2.17 (725A).
58. DT 2.15 (717A).
59. Leipoldt, 84.
60. Bardy, *Didyme l'Aveugle*, 141–142.

passages suggest that no description of Didymus' soteriology is complete without attending to the work of the Spirit. Bardy's claim that "the Spirit does nothing other than implement the power of the salvation accomplished by the death of the Incarnate Word"[61] demonstrates a certain narrowness of scope that 1) focuses too unilaterally on the Son's death as the *locus* of the saving work of the Trinity and 2) thus minimizes the importance of themes relating to the work of the Spirit.

My brief investigation above suggests that a more fulsome picture of Didymus' soteriology in *DT* is possible.[62] To achieve this, I endeavor to explore the central narrative of Trinitarian activity in *DT*: creation/new creation. The study of this narrative reveals that themes like filiation, sanctification, and deification are ingredient in Didymus' understanding of salvation and of the whole economy.

Creation Old and New

Extending the scope of the investigation thus proceeds from the conviction that—to do justice to the economy of salvation—we must examine Didymus' Trinitarian account of creation and attempt to articulate its central threads. In this section, I argue that doing this adequately demands attending to chapters 12–14 of Book 2, in which the echoes from the various themes in the treatise become almost deafening.[63] In them Didymus reflects at length on the baptismal event as the culmination of most of the soteriological themes that he has developed elsewhere. The most far-reaching of these is the theme of re-creation. Didymus conceives of the baptismal event in terms that reveal the narrative coherence of his account of the divine economy. The key features of this narrative are: 1) the meaning of humanity's creation in the image of God in relationship to the Son's *being* this image, 2) the manner in which the image is lost (or corrupted) and recovered, and 3) the ongoing work of the Spirit in putting the image to its proper use.

In this section, I argue that attending to Didymus' soteriology demands recognizing the privileged place that these chapters on baptism hold. They reveal that salvation is conceived of as the restoration of humanity's filial image through the Incarnation of the Son and the philanthropic descent of the Holy Spirit. The Son recreates us in his own image, making us sons of his Fa-

---

61. "[L]'Esprit ne fait que mettre en œuvre la vertu du salut opéré par la mort du Verbe Incarné" (Ibid., 142).

62. Thus far, I have looked almost solely at passages that have included one of the following words: συσσώζω, σώζω, Σωτήρ, σωτηρία, σωτήριος, and σωτηριώδης.

63. See especially *DT* 2.13 (692A): ἔστι γὰρ ἡ κολυμβήθρα τῆς Τριάδος ἐργαστήριον πρὸς σωτηρίαν πιστῶν ἀνθρώπων. Cf. also 2.1.10 (452BC) in which Didymus connects the φώτισμα poetically with the gates of heaven, the entrance of salvation, and angelic citizenship. Didymus recapitulates all these themes in 2.12 (668A–672B). See also 2.13 (692B) and 2.14 (692C, 696B, and 716A).

ther; the Spirit, through the spiritual gifts, brings us into the fullness of this filial identity: deification. I propose that salvation is given its full scope when it is understood in relationship to Didymus' teleological account of the divine image in humanity and hence that the sanctifying and deifying work of the Holy Spirit is soteriologically conceived.

In the Image

The consequences of humanity's reception of the divine image are severally conceived in the treatise, as Leipoldt notes. Acknowledging the other ideas that are aired in Didymus' treatment of the *topos*, Leipoldt canvasses it primarily by speaking of its relation to human sinlessness and freedom.[64] Addressing the issue on one occasion, Didymus says that human sinlessness and freedom are expressive of the image and likeness of God in humanity. Adam was sinless and free, capable of acting in accordance with his proper end as a rational creature of God. In baptism, this protoplastic condition is restored.[65] Bardy's exposition of the divine image and likeness in humanity is restricted to this passage, and he raises it to highlight, quite correctly, that there is a sharp tension in Didymus' corpus over the possibility of exercising the freedom of the will to attain sinlessness.[66] In his exposition as in Leipoldt's, however, two significant ideas receive almost no attention: 1) that being made in God's image carries with it significant relational and teleological implications and 2) that image-language is consistently related to the Son.

To get at these other important dimensions of Didymus' thinking about the divine image in humanity, it is necessary to examine his treatment of the *topos* in the context of the Trinitarian creation of the world. For Didymus, the Father begins the creative work that the Son brings into existence, and the Spirit sanctifies the creation, perfecting or completing the work of the other two *hypostaseis*.[67] Didymus later focuses these activities on the specific case of the creation of humankind: "the great creature."[68] In the triadic structure of the creation of humanity, he argues, the Father addresses the other two *hypostaseis*: "Let us make a man" (Gen 1:26). The Son fashions humanity "in the image (κατ' εἰκόνα)" of his Father. And the Holy Spirit finishes the work of the Trinity by sanctifying the creature.[69] The above reflections on Genesis 1:26 are closely complemented by Didymus' triadic interpretation of the more forthcoming description afforded the creation of Adam in Genesis 2:7. If the Son is implicitly the one who forms Adam from the dust of the earth, Didymus identifies the divine inbreathing into Adam as the moment when the divine image

---

64. Leipoldt, 81.
65. *DT* 2.12 (680AB).
66. Bardy, *Didyme l'Aveugle*, 137.
67. See *DT* 2.1.6 (449B).
68. *DT* 2.7.3.1 (564A).
69. *DT* 2.7.3.3 (565BC).

and likeness are communicated to him.[70] Only with the reception of the Holy Spirit is the image of God received.[71]

Didymus then expands on the ramifications of this reception of the Holy Spirit, noting that with the breathing of the Holy Spirit humanity receives

> the immortal spirit (πνεῦμα) and an intellect (νοῦς) that always considers and directs [it] to what is fitting, and wise thought that is pleasing to the Giver and that is able to become—with faith—the cause of the begetting of children, and [the cause] of life, the raising of the dead, and the removal of mountains. In addition to these things [the phrase "according to the image" means] that we have also partaken (μετειλήφαμεν) of his goodness.[72]

The image of God in humanity may be described in a sense as something that is unable to be lost, inasmuch as the "immortal spirit" is constitutive of human nature.[73] Inhering in the gift of the spirit is the rational and moral agency of the human creature. The protoplasts are free-of-will insofar as they direct their souls to the good intended for them by the Giver of the gift. Moreover, without the experience of sin, they are free from the disordered passions that direct them away from this good.

Leipoldt rightly notes that this passage accounts for the dialectic in which the freedom of the will operates for Didymus. On the one hand, human freedom must be continually affirmed against Manichean notions of cosmic determinism; asserting the agency of the human intellect (as in the quote above) guards against any notion that the image can be completely lost, since the im-

---

70. DT 2.12 (680A). I think it is possible to suggest that Didymus envisions the breather of the Spirit here in the first creation to be the Son. Didymus will, with little encouragement, connect the creative work of the Son upon the soul with the breathing of the Spirit in 3.1 (780A).

71. DT 2.7.3.4 (565C).

72. DT 2.7.3.4 (565CD). Cf. DT 2.20 (737A) for this use of πνεῦμα. Following Mingarelli, Leipoldt, and Seiler, I take the phrase τὸ πνεῦμα τὸ ἀθάνατον as a reference to the human spirit or ψυχή. The word πνεῦμα is sometimes contrasted with ψυχή in Didymus' vocabulary. However, on this occasion Didymus appears to conceive of the νοῦς as the higher "part" of the πνεῦμα that directs it toward its proper ends, thus conflating πνεῦμα and ψυχή. Ὀρφανός notes this use in Ἡ ψυχὴ καὶ τὸ σῶμα, 43 and 51.

73. For Didymus' defense of this point—which was almost commonplace among the Fathers—see DT 3.16 (872B–873A). Didymus argues at length that both souls and angels are immortal "in the indestructibility and incorruptibility of their substance (κατὰ τὸ ἀνώλεθρον καὶ ἄφθαρτον τῆς οὐσίας)" but mortal with respect to their moral faculty (γνώμη) (872A). Soul-death does not denote the dissolution of the soul into nothingness, since it is "incomposite and indestructible" in existence (873A). The death of the soul is its mortification in bondage to evil; but this mortification is not final for Didymus.

age is bound to an irrevocable dimension of human existence: the possession of the immortal spirit.[74] As long as the gift of the spirit is in effect, the possibility of its attainment of the good cannot be written off. On the other hand, Didymus insists elsewhere—in the prior passage on baptismal generation—that without the regeneration of the Holy Spirit, the human spirit is frustrated in its use of this freedom.

However, Didymus' reflections on the divine image extend beyond anti-Manichean interests, as the second half of the quotation demonstrates. There is a relational and teleological dynamic at work in this part of the quotation. It is only with faith in the Giver that his gift is put to its proper use. The fruit of the rational and moral labor of humanity is spiritual fruitfulness, life, and dominion over death. This fruit is made possible, however, only when humans are communicant with God. By faith in God they remain fully receptive to the gifts of divine goodness. It is this latter exposition of the image of God that allows us to affirm that Didymus conceives of the image both ontologically and teleologically. With respect to the former, human beings are given an immortal spirit that possesses free will. With respect to the latter, the human spirit achieves the goal for which it was created when it partakes of God's goodness in faith, becoming spiritually fruitful. If the *locus* of the image is the intellective aspect of human existence, there is no divorcing of this aspect of human existence from its proper end in God. It is by faith in God that the intellect participates in the goodness that is the proper goal of the soul.

With these observations in mind, we are well-positioned to attend to the most important aspect, from a Trinitarian point-of-view, of Didymus' teaching about the divine image in humanity. For Didymus, "image of God" language connotes that humanity bears a certain kind of resemblance to the Son: the natural image and exact imprint of the Father. Thus, immediately following Didymus' remarks about sinlessness and freedom being expressive of the divine image in humanity, there appears a lengthy collection of scriptural citations that Didymus brings to bear in defense of his claim. These include Colossians 3:10, 1 Corinthians 15:49, Romans 8:29, and Ephesians 2:5–6. Each of these citations relates to the Son. He is both the one "who created us" and the one in whose image God foreknew that we would be conformed.[75] Didymus, in speaking of the divine image in humanity, must speak also of the one who is the true image of the Father.

On a later occasion, Didymus is called upon to explain why St Paul calls the only Son of the Father "the first-born of all creation."[76] The aporia is awkward for two reasons: 1) an only-begotten cannot be a first-born and 2) the text clearly identifies the Son with the creation in some sense. Didymus responds to the objection instructively, distinguishing between what is said of

---

74. Leipoldt, 81.
75. *DT* 2.12 (680B–681A).
76. *DT* 3.4 (828C), citing Colossians 1:15.

the Son's divinity (Only-begotten) and that which is said economically (first-born). The eternally Only-begotten Son of the Father becomes the first-born of humanity in the Incarnation.[77] Subordinationist interpretations of this passage—which would conclude the Son's inferior ontological standing to the Father—are not wrong in noting that creaturely existence is really predicated of the Son. The Son is "first-born of all creation," Didymus insists, because he really becomes part of creation by assuming our created nature. By the philanthropic descent of the Son, the Father makes his Only-begotten the first-born of many brothers. Drawing once again on Romans 8:29, Didymus argues that it was the Father's intent from the beginning of the ages that many brothers be "conformed to the image of his Son."[78] Before creation itself, human conformity to the Son was the intention of the Father.

The sheer magnitude of the gift of the image of God in humanity is therefore realized with the coming of the Son: the express image of the Father. The created image is not the Creating, as Didymus makes plain at numerous points. One who sees the Son (the true image) sees the Father as he is. With the rest of us it is different: the one who looks at a "piece of furniture (δίφρος)" does not see the carpenter, but may attain some conception of his greatness and skill analogically.[79] It is essential to distinguish the natures. But this critical distinction between the Son and the race of Adam, highlighted here with particular severity, does not make light of the divine image in humanity. It subordinates it to the Son's being this image and therefore secures it. In an eloquent passage in which Didymus links John 1:16 with the first and second gifting of sonship, he argues that it is out of the sheer "fullness (πλήρωμα)" of the Son's divinity that "we receive the grace of regeneration in place of that grace we had cast off." Forfeiting the former grace and becoming slaves, our filial identity is restored by the Son's own abundance.[80] Revealing the continuity between the two "graces," the Son creates and re-creates humanity in a manner that is mimetic of his own relation to the Father. This is why, of the three names proper to the *hypostaseis*, humanity takes on only one: the name of the Second Person.

The divine image in humanity is therefore conceived of in *DT* in several related ways: 1) it is the gift of an immortal soul, endowed with an intellect capable of moral agency or freedom. 2) This intellect is put to its proper use when it maintains itself in relationship to God in faith and bears (as the fruit of this relationship) the goodness that is God's intent for it. 3) The image is bestowed only by the mutual cooperation of the divine *hypostaseis* and 4) mirrors the Son's relationship to the Father.

---

77. *DT* 3.4 (836C).
78. *DT* 3.4 (837C–840A).
79. *DT* 1.16.44 (337B), appealing to Wisdom 13:5.
80. *DT* 1.27.45–48 (401AC).

The Loss of the Image

The pre-cosmic intention of God is called into question by human transgression of the divine injunction. Through the transgression of the divine command, the protoplasts lose or corrupt the image. The Alexandrian is not entirely clear which of these it is.[81] On the one hand, he speaks of humanity losing (ἀπόλλυμι) "the image and likeness . . . through sin."[82] Humanity is unable to recover "the way that leads to God."[83] On the other hand, he speaks of humanity's being corrupted (φθείρω) by its transgression, being brought to futility (καταφθείρω).[84]

The reason for Didymus' lack of clarity here (is the image lost or only ruined?) seems to be that the image of God in humanity is conceived of both ontologically and teleologically. Ontologically speaking, the immortal soul is not a gift that can be utterly lost. Teleologically speaking, human expulsion from Paradise indicates the servitude of human intellective capacity to vain pursuits and destructive masters. No longer receiving the proper guidance for its journey, the human soul is left to the "counsels . . . of evil men," who deprive it of its proper goal: the knowledge of the good.[85] Deprived of fellowship with God, humanity becomes less than human, dragged earthward like the beasts.[86] The race, prone to corruption and vice, destroys the sanctification and saving fellowship of the Holy Spirit. Significantly, as we have seen in relation to the first creation and as we will see in relation to the re-creating work of the Trinity, Didymus relates this broken fellowship both to the "departure" of the Holy Spirit from humanity in Genesis 6:3 and the transgression of God's command in Genesis 3:6.[87] No longer participant in the goodness of the Spirit, the image—in its teleological sense—is lost.

---

81. See Bardy, 140n5.

82. *DT* 2.12 (680A). Here he echoes Tertullian, *Bap.* 5.7 (Evans, 14).

83. *DT* 3.3 (817B). Cf. 2.14 (697C). The same point is re-iterated in Didymus' allegorization of the story of Elisha and the axe-head (4 Kgdms 6:1–7). The loss of the axe-head "into the obscure depth" signifies "the power of human nature that falls away from the light" when Eve and Adam eat the fruit of the forbidden tree.

84. *DT* 2.7.3.8 (569A).

85. *DT* 3.1 (776A).

86. See *DT* 2.20 (740BC) and 3.1 (776B). Germane to this connection is what Didymus says in the fragments of his commentary on 2 Corinthians. It is only those who preserve being "in the image and likeness of God" who are truly human, he argues (*In 2 Cor.* 2:15 (PG 39:1692B)).

87. For the first view, see *DT* 2.2.40 (464C). This is an important passage, since it reveals that Didymus conceives of John 20:22 as the culmination of an event that takes place in Genesis 6:3. For the departure of the Spirit from humanity at the transgression in Genesis 3:6, see 2.7.6.1 (577C).

The Restoration of the Image

In such a condition, the human creature is dependent upon divine grace: the recreative work of the Trinity. God, out of love for the human race, does not leave it to its own ends. The Father reveals to us his Fatherly care; the Son, our Creator, empties himself and takes our form; the Holy Spirit of God, not overlooking "the lost (ἀπολλυμένην) nature of humanity ... comes of his own accord (ἐφοίτησεν δι' ἑαυτοῦ), leading us, teaching all truth, renewing us, and bestowing the divine gifts" to his creatures "in the image (κατ' εἰκόνα)."[88] Both the Incarnation of the Son and the Pentecostal visitation of the Holy Spirit are necessary to the saving economy of the Trinity on our behalf.

The filial dimension of this restoration is frequently highlighted. In two of the clearest instances of this, Didymus asserts that salvation is a Trinitarian gift and then proceeds to apportion aspects of this work to each of the *hypostaseis*. In the former Didymus is reflecting on the significance of the Only-begotten Son becoming the "first-born" of many brothers in the economy. It is a passage we have already visited briefly, but is now worth quoting in full:

> Let him then be both an only-begotten and a first-born! ... For if the Holy Spirit had not regenerated us because of an inexpressible love-of-humanity, and the God and Father had not received additional sons, and the one of whom the passage speaks, the Only-begotten God, had not become a son of man for the salvation of men, without change and without flux—as he foreknew—he himself would not have been called "first-born among many brothers," nor would the sons of men be called gods and sons of God, since no one is by nature a brother of the Only-begotten Son.[89]

A parallel passage later in the treatise is worth quoting in similar connection. Reflecting on Romans 8:15, Didymus speaks of the Trinitarian shape of adoption:

> Since, as was said many times, the whole of salvation is granted to us in common by the Holy Trinity, the Father called us into adoption; the Only-begotten, true, and genuine Son designated us his brothers, and commanded that God be called our Father; the Holy Spirit indwelt, inspired, and taught us saying, "Abba."[90]

Both passages are remarkable in our context for the admirable clarity in which Didymus sets forth the work of the three *hypostaseis* in salvation. In both, the filial restoration of humanity is emphasized. In the former passage, the Father

---

88. *DT* 2.6.9.1–3 (536AC).
89. *DT* 3.4 (836CD).
90. *DT* 3.39 (980BC).

is well-pleased that others share by grace in the unique sonship of the Only-begotten; the Son assumes their humanity by his Incarnation; the Holy Spirit regenerates the baptized so that they share in the fullness of the divine Son. In the latter passage, the role of the Holy Spirit is highlighted while the same general Trinitarian shape of Didymus' argument is maintained. The Father calls sons into adoption; the Son permits the faithful to address his Father as their own; and the indwelling Holy Spirit speaks the words with us and on our behalf since formerly we were unworthy of using this "form of address (πρόσρησιν)."[91]

The Saving Inhumanation

To this end then, the Son becomes one of the things made: that by his becoming so all things may be remade. Didymus, as we noted above, insists upon the saving significance of numerous events in the Inhumanation of the Son. The recreative activity of the Incarnate Son is conceived of as a transformative exchange: taking our sinfulness and our death upon himself, the Son gives us in return the gift of regeneration.[92] He takes the form of a servant in order that we may become in the image of him who created us.[93]

> By this wondrous obedience of his on our behalf, he abolished our ancient transgression. And in the same way that he suffered, as he knew and willed to do when he descended into our likeness (ὁμοίωσιν), so also by rendering us conformed to himself, he translated us into impassibility (ἀπάθειαν).[94]

The extent of his philanthropy is revealed in that, while remaining wholly good, he even "appropriates to himself (ἰδιοποιεῖται) the sins that are in the works of his hands."[95] Thomas declares him Lord and God because he acknowledges that it could only be the act of the Creator "not only to suffer on behalf of his own creatures, but also to bestow universal—which we also term general—salvation, and that for all time."[96] The resurrection of the Son is not, for Didymus, a gift of grace for the Son, but he receives it from the Father to give us "grace to be raised again in likeness to this resurrection of his."[97]

---

91. See *DT* 3.39 (980A).
92. *DT* 1.27.48 (401BC).
93. *DT* 3.3 (817A): a wonderful summary of Pauline teaching in Philippians 2:6–7 and Colossians 3:10.
94. *DT* 3.12 (860C). For the meaning of ἀπάθεια in Didymus, see Bardy, "Apatheia," in *Dictionnaire de Spiritualité* 1 (Paris: Beauchesne, 1937), col. 734. He concludes that ἀπάθεια is, for Didymus, neither impeccability nor indifference but rather "the tranquillity of the soul which evil desires no longer disturb (la tranquillité de l'âme que ne troublent plus les concupiscences)."
95. *DT* 3.3 (816C).
96. *DT* 1.27.58–59 (405A).
97. *DT* 3.14 (861AB).

Chapter 21 of Book 3 is full of similar examples. If the extent to which the Son can be said to really experience abandonment, fear, weakness, sleep, and other human ailments is somewhat limited in Didymus' exposition—Christ alone knows how he has taken these upon himself—,[98] the effects of his manifestation of these things are admirably expressed. He assumed human "frailties (ἀσθενείας)" to bestow to humans a better condition.[99] Putting death to death by his life-giving death, he delivered all from it: those who lived before his coming from its power and those after his first advent from its fear.[100] By his apparent fear at the coming of death, he guaranteed his victory over it and gave us a share in the victory.[101] By weeping with the sisters of Lazarus, he was bringing to an end "our ancient dirge."[102] His weariness, consequent from the Incarnation, was bringing healing and rest to the weary and heavy-laden.[103] He prayed and "learned obedience from what he suffered" in order to "acquire obedience and erase the ancient disobedience" on our behalf.[104] It is not going too far to say that for Didymus all the events of the Incarnate life of Christ are invested with saving significance.

This is especially the case with the baptism of the Savior. Didymus concludes chapter 13 of Book 2 with a reflection on Psalm 26:10 LXX: "My father and my mother abandoned me, but the Lord received me." "Adam and Eve did not remain alive," writes Didymus, but I was given "the font as mother, as a father the Most High, as a brother the Savior who was baptized for our sake."[105] He who makes the Jordan deigns to "be baptized in the Jordan because of us."[106] By submitting to the baptismal waters of the Jordan, the Lord kills the serpent that lives in its depths.[107] By his baptism he wipes away our filth and forgives our sin, giving us power over the demonic powers arrayed against us, "and teaching all that the re-birth is salvation for men."[108] Didymus notes elsewhere, thinking of the chrism applied at baptism, that "just as the Savior is anointed by the Holy Spirit in the economy, so you also have an

---

98. See Béranger, "Etudes," 101.
99. *DT* 3.21 (904A).
100. *DT* 3.21 (904C–905A).
101. *DT* 3.21 (908AB).
102. *DT* 3.21 (909B).
103. *DT* 3.21 (909BC).
104. *DT* 3.21 (916AB).
105. *DT* 2.13 (692B).
106. *DT* 2.14 (697C).
107. *DT* 2.12 (684AB). Didymus arrives at this interpretation of baptism through a creative interpretation of Job 40:15–23, in which the beast of v.15 is described as "confident because the Jordan will rush into his mouth." This θηρίον Didymus identifies with Satan, who is the first of God's creatures (v.19). For more on Satan as the first of God's creatures, see 1.17.2–4 (341AB) and 3.2.51 (804D).
108. *DT* 2.12 (684AB).

anointing from the Holy Spirit."[109] The Son is sanctified by the Father and sent into the world, where he is anointed with the Spirit, "the oil of gladness," "in order that he may make us partakers of himself and might sanctify us."[110] Jesus' baptism and his reception of the Holy Spirit are central to that which he accomplishes on our behalf. Thereby the consequences of human disobedience in the Spirit's departure from the race are undone.

The Saving Visitation of the Holy Spirit

The Holy Spirit, involved in the creation of humanity by his sanctifying and life-giving breath, reveals the fullness of his divinity in the recreative work of the Trinity. The Holy Spirit cooperates with the Word in the creation of the "servant's form":[111] the humanity of the Son. Indeed, this work of the Spirit is essential in assuring us that the Lord's humanity is real, since the Spirit is (with the Father and the Son) the co-creator of our nature, and since nothing is created without the Holy Spirit.[112] In the Son's labor on our behalf in his own baptism, the Holy Spirit is present; he descends and remains upon the Only-begotten Son. By this descent from heaven, the Holy Spirit assures us not only that he is seated together and reigns together with the Most High, but that we, becoming his temple, are raised heavenward: sitting together with God and reigning together with him.[113] The descent of the Spirit in the form of a dove at the baptism of the Savior symbolizes his "visitation (ἐπιφοίτησιν)" and the "supernal reconciliation" that he communicates to us.[114]

The saving descent of the Holy Spirit acquires its full significance, however, only after the resurrection of the Savior, where the recreative work of the Trinity reaches its zenith in Didymus' mind. At his appearance to the disciples in the Upper Room, Christ with the Holy Spirit breathes into the faces of the disciples "in order to recreate and sanctify the man ruined by disobedience."[115] Here Didymus focuses on the renewing effects of the Spirit's descent. In a more straightforward exegesis of John 20:22, the same event is described equally as effecting the forgiveness of sins.[116] In both instances, the new creation narrative developed throughout the treatise is brought to full coherence. In fact, Didymus goes so far as to say that the first creation and the new creation are precisely analogous in this respect. As Adam was formed by the breath of the Spirit, so now God's new humanity is formed by the same act. Didymus writes: "in the same way that we were created by the blessed Trinity at the

---

109. DT 2.6.23.4 (557C).
110. DT 3.13 (860D–861A).
111. DT 2.7.3.10 (569C–572A).
112. DT 2.7.3.16 (576A).
113. DT 2.12 (684B–685A).
114. DT 2.14 (693B–696A). Didymus connects the appearance of the dove at the baptism of Jesus with the dove that brings the olive-sprig to Noah.
115. DT 2.7.3.8 (569A). See John 20:22.
116. DT 2.7.6.2 (577C).

first according to the saying, "Let us make man," so secondly are we saved by [the Trinity]."[117] The transgression that occasioned the Spirit's departure from humanity (Gen 6:3) is first reversed in Christ's reception of the Spirit at his baptism. But here the Spirit whom he breathed upon Adam is once again breathed out upon those who share in his baptism.[118] With the gift, humanity is re-created into its filial image once more, capable of fulfilling the teleological dimension of its identity as the creature made in the image of God.

Hence Didymus insists regularly on the renewing or re-creative aspect of baptism. The restoration of the image of God in humanity is assigned to baptism, wherein, being sealed by the Holy Spirit, "we are reconstituted into the first image."[119] In an analogous passage, Didymus speaks of the Holy Spirit as the one who "renews us in baptism as God together with the Father and the Son, and from our ugliness leads us back to our former beauty (πρεσβύτερον ... κάλλος)."[120] As in all the other divine activities, the Holy Spirit perfects or finishes the divine work. Baptism is described by Didymus in Trinitarian terms that closely mirror the creation of humanity:

> Descending in the bath at the good pleasure (εὐδοκίᾳ) of the God and Father we are stripped bare of our sins by the grace of his Spirit, laying aside the old man, and by his [i.e. the Spirit's] kingly power we are regenerated and sealed; ascending we are also clothed with the Savior Christ, our incorruptible stole and of honor equal to the Holy Spirit who regenerates and seals us—"for," it says, "as many as were baptized into Christ are clothed with Christ" (Gal 3:27)—and we regain (ἀπολαμβάνομεν) the image and likeness of God of which the Scriptures speak.[121]

Once again, the Father is instrumental in willing the accomplishment of divine activity. The Son accomplishes the form of the new creation, now bringing creation to completion in himself: by his incorruptible and immortal life guaranteeing this life to his creatures who have put him on. Yet again, the recreating work of the Trinity is brought to completion only by the perfecting agency of the Holy Spirit.[122] He regenerates us into our former filial beauty,

---

117. *DT* 2.12 (681A).

118. See *DT* 2.12 (680A). As mentioned above, Didymus is here drawing on Tertullian, *Bap.* 5; the Trinitarian shape of the event is more explicit in Didymus.

119. *DT* 2.15 (717AB). Cf. 3.2.42 (801D): τὸ ἅγιον Πνεῦμα διὰ τοῦ βαπτίσματος ἀναστοιχειοῖ ἡμᾶς εἰς εἰκόνα τὴν πρώτην.

120. *DT* 2.12 (668A).

121. *DT* 2.12 (680A).

122. Cf. *DT* 2.12 (668B). In baptism, the Holy Spirit "makes us spiritual, and partakers of divine glory, and sons and heirs of God the Father, and conformed to the image of

and sets his seal to the baptismal work of the other two *hypostaseis*. So essential is baptism to the re-creative work of God that Didymus can write: "Without being regenerate in baptism by the Spirit of God, and being sealed by his sanctification, and being his temple, no one gains the heavenly goods, even if he is found blameless for the rest of his life."[123]

Baptism and Its Ongoing Implications

Recalling the teleological dimension of the image of God discussed above assists us in understanding what follows. Given the gift of freedom, the human creature is empowered by the indwelling Spirit to realize the *telos* of the gift: spiritual fruitfulness by sharing in the goodness of God by faith. We have also seen Didymus describe this *telos* as utter conformity to the Son. In both of these descriptions of the image, Didymus highlights the importance of conceiving of the restoration of the image in humanity as a process. Even if the image and the likeness are in one sense given to us in the sanctifying and deifying waters of baptism, the restoration of the gift is not a static reality, but one to which the baptized must be continually assimilated.

Sanctification

When believers are renewed and sanctified by the Spirit of God in baptism, they are recalled to "the better and first plan of life (σχῆμα τοῦ βίου)."[124] The "sealing" work of the Holy Spirit at baptism relates closely to the ongoing work of the Holy Spirit in the believer after it. In chapter 15 of Book 2, Didymus speaks of the sealing work of the Spirit in relation to the Savior's promise that the Spirit will lead the disciples into all truth. He likewise evokes the Pauline eschatological schema in which the Spirit seals believers until the day of redemption. Being reformed by the saving seal of the Spirit, there is an ongoing role that the Spirit plays in preserving the soul from its enemies.[125] Those sealed by the Holy Spirit are "those sanctified by him."[126] They are

---

the Son, and his co-heirs, and brothers who will be glorified together with him and reign together with him."

123. *DT* 2.12 (681AB).

124. *DT* 2.7.3.7 (568BC).

125. See John 16:13 and Ephesians 4:30 (*DT* 2.15 (717AC)). Didymus relates the σήμαντρον of baptism to the shepherd's "branding-mark (σφραγίς)" that identifies the sheep as his own possession. The "alliance (συμμαχία)" of the branding-mark prevents the sheep from molestation by wolves. Clearly Didymus is thinking of the soul's protection from demonic adversaries; it is by the Holy Spirit's aid that the believer becomes a participant in the victory that Christ has won on her behalf over these powers.

126. Here we see a key feature of Didymus' distinction between divine and created natures. The proof of possession is in bestowal for Didymus. The Holy Spirit *is* the substantial holiness and goodness that he bestows upon others. For discussions of Didymus' understanding of participation (mostly in reference to his *DSS*), see Lewis Ayres, "The Holy Spirit as the "Undiminished Giver": Didymus the Blind's *De spiritu sancto* and the Development of Nicene Pneumatology," in *The Holy Spirit in the Fathers of*

commanded by St Paul not to depart "out of a certain drunkenness or negligence from his eternal grace that is fixed in us." The grace of which Didymus is speaking is the gift of holiness.[127]

Didymus conceives of this participation in the holiness of the Spirit largely in relation to the creature's reception of the virtues. Immediately before his discussion of sanctification, Didymus argues that the rational creature is receptive (δεκτική) of both virtue and vice. The "divine Spirit is beyond virtue" or rather "is himself the source of the highest virtue."[128] Didymus makes the first claim to show that the Holy Spirit does not "possess" virtue; he is "beyond virtue" in the sense that virtue is not an acquisition for him. Didymus' second claim guards against a possible misapplication of his language; by "beyond virtue" Didymus does not mean to imply that the Holy Spirit's nature cannot be partaken of, that human beings partake of a sanctification that belongs to some order beneath divinity. The only sanctification on offer is that which comes by participating in what the Holy Spirit is.

Hence, we speak "metaphorically (μεταφορικῶς)" when we say that someone is filled with virtue and knowledge (ἀρετῆς καὶ ἐπιστήμης); we speak "with circumspection (τεθεωρημένως)"—i.e. more accurately—when we say that those "who partake completely (οἱ ἀκραιφνῶς . . . μεταλαχόντες) of the grace of the Holy Spirit" are able to produce "the rewards of virtue and knowledge."[129] Since holiness subsists absolutely only in God, it is impossible for the creature to become holy "by its own self-transformation" or "to be sanctified by its own virtue (κατ' ἀρετὴν ἁγιάζεσθαι)."[130] Even the holy angels are made so by a participation in the divine Spirit.[131]

The virtues are not treated in DT with the same depth that they are in Didymus' exegetical work; however, two points germane to the study of the theme may be made from the material in DT. The virtues include both 1) an ethical dimension and 2) an intellective dimension. In reference to the ethical dimension of sanctification, David and Judas serve as examples. In David's case the recreative work of the sanctifying Spirit is manifest in that he renews the heart of the man who was formerly "ruined by sin."[132] Judas is a prime example of the opposite; he "destroys sanctification," making the most absurd

---

the Church (Dublin: Four Courts Press, 2010), 57–72; Heron, "The Holy Spirit in Origen and Didymus the Blind," 298–310; Kellen Plaxco, "Didymus the Blind and the Metaphysics of Participation," *Studia Patristica* 67 (2013): 227–237.

127. DT 2.10 (640C), citing 1 Thessalonians 5:19 and echoing Ephesians 5:18.

128. DT 2.6.5 (524A).

129. DT 1.20.5 (369C).

130. DT 2.6.6.6 (525D–528A). For my translation, cf. Seiler, *De trinitate, Buch 2*, 137: "es unmöglich ist, daß sie durch eigenes Sich-Wandeln heilig ist oder nach ihrer Tugend geheiligt wird."

131. See DT 2.6.6.7 (528AB) and 2.7.8.8 (588C). The point is an important one also in DSS 24–28.

132. DT 2.7.3.8 (569B).

(ἀσυμφορώτατον) choice of all: electing silver over the Life of the world.[133] The presence of the Spirit, lost by Adam and Eve because of their transgression, is that which counters the moral failure of the free will left to its own devices, preventing it from evil and leading it toward doing what is good.[134]

Also involved in the rehabilitation of the will is the reformation of the human intellect: the seat of the will. Thus Didymus sometimes pairs knowledge (or wisdom) with virtue, as its natural complement;[135] sometimes he includes wisdom within the scope of the virtues.[136] On these latter occasions, Didymus includes the sanctifying activity of the Holy Spirit together with his gift of wisdom under the umbrella of "every kind (εἶδος) of heavenly virtue." There is a certain amount of imprecision here—is sanctification one of the virtues or is it a way of speaking of the summative content of divine virtue as it is communicated to humanity?—, but it is clear that Didymus conceives of the sanctifying activity of the Spirit in relation to his rehabilitation of the human mind by the gift of wisdom. The two (holiness and wisdom) are often connected, as in the following example: "the Holy Spirit bestows wisdom and knowledge and sanctifies all that is made."[137]

The sanctifying work of the Spirit is conceived of as the completion of the saving work of the Trinity. Completing the recreative work of the Trinity, the Holy Spirit directs the creature toward the attainment of that which was to be its goal in the beginning: by faith in God bringing forth the rewards of its union with God and participating in the divine goodness. To be sanctified by the Holy Spirit is to be receptive to all his gifts: to be claimed in one's entirety as a moral and intellective being for communion with God.[138]

Deification

We complete our summary of Didymus' account of God's saving economy by examining a final theme, which rightly takes its place at the conclusion of it. The Holy Spirit, in his re-creative activity, deifies humanity. Through the deifying work of the Spirit at baptism, the final element of Didymus' teaching on the divine image and likeness in humanity is brought to its conclusion. The Holy Spirit gives us by grace the very name of the Son, restoring our filial identity and realizing the creative intent of the Father from the very beginning.

---

133. DT 2.7.3.10 (569C). Cf. 2.6.3.4 (513A).

134. See DT 2.6.8.2 (529BC). The Spirit is the one who rehabilitates us from the corrupting evil that stems from our free will: καὶ αὐτὸ [τὸ ἅγιον Πνεῦμα] σώζει πάντα οἷς ἂν παρῇ, ὥσπερ τὸ κακὸν ἐκ προαιρέσεως ἡμῶν συμβαῖνον φθείρει.

135. See the contrast twice in DT 1.20.5 (369C). Cf. 2.27 (768A).

136. See DT 2.6.6.1 (524B) and 3.2.36 (800CD).

137. DT 2.25 (748C). Cf. also 2.6.6.3 (525A), 2.6.8.3 (532AB), and 3.2.7 (789C) (the latter passage speaking of the activities of the Father and the Son and including others among them).

138. Cf. DT 3.34 (960C).

Norman Russell has helpfully summarized some of the defining features of the theme of deification in *DT*. First, he notes that there is one instance in which deification is assigned to the whole Trinity,[139] but that Didymus' normal custom throughout is to assign the work of deification to the Holy Spirit. Second, isolating the most important passage on the theme, he argues that Didymus "connects the Spirit closely with the Father and the Son in the work of restoring the divine image by adopting us as sons and gods."[140] Both points are promising ones for the present study. Extending Russell's insights further, we note here that the theme of deification, where it is elaborated upon in *DT*, is repeatedly connected with the language of adoption or regeneration. Deification, the culminating work of salvation, is given shape specifically in the Spirit's conformation of the creature to its true paradigm in the Son.

In contrast to the angels of God who "neither regenerate us, nor deify us, nor forgive sins," the Holy Spirit does all of these things.[141] The cluster of verbs suggests that Didymus is thinking of the Holy Spirit's activity at the baptismal event, where all three verbs regularly occur.[142] At the baptismal event, the reconstitution of the divine image in humanity is the common gift of the three *hypostaseis*, but it is the Spirit in particular who "by participation is the cause of our adoption and of our becoming gods (τοῦ γίνεσθαι θεούς)."[143] Discussing the texts in Scripture that speak of those who are called gods, Didymus argues that the saints are called "gods" by grace, since they are "rendered worthy of adoption and of this name (προσηγορίας)."[144]

In each of these instances, in addition another passage discussed before—in relation to the Son's becoming a son of man that we might become gods and sons of God—the connection between regeneration/adoption and deification is made. There is but one exception in the treatise, in which Didymus seems to speak of deification in a way that obscures its filial location. Didymus once speaks of deification in connection with the name that sometimes functions as the proper name of the First *hypostasis*: "God." The point is made in connection with the sharing of the names, "God," "Son," and "Spirit" among creatures. Didymus argues that the sharing of the name πνεῦμα with created spirits does not in any way diminish the Spirit's divinity, any less than creaturely sharing in the names "gods" and "sons" on account of "his (sic) goodness and abun-

---

139. *DT* 3.16 (868BC).

140. Norman Russell, *The Doctrine of Deification in the Greek Patristic Tradition* (Oxford: Oxford University Press, 2004), 160.

141. *DT* 2.4.5 (481C).

142. The same can be said for *DT* 2.25 (748C), where Didymus includes the liberating and renewing activities of the Holy Spirit.

143. *DT* 3.2.42 (801D–804A).

144. *DT* 3.24 (937B).

dance (ἀφθονίαν)" diminishes the divinity of the Father and the Son.[145] Whatever the antecedent of the word "his," the polemical context of the argument seems to force Didymus out of his ordinary habit of connecting deification with humanity's relationship to the Son.

What Didymus means to communicate by the concept of deification is decipherable only in two instances, but they are significant. Russell notes that in one of these, Didymus connects the word ἀποθεοῖ with the "deifying property of baptism,"[146] and that this "immortalizes us."[147] In another instance, Didymus writes that those saints who are called gods in Scripture are such because their "citizenship is in heaven from their virtue." As examples of this Didymus chooses Moses and Aaron, whom Scripture speaks of as being the "neighbors (γείτονας) of angels."[148] In the first quotation, the one who is deified shares in the eternal life of God; in the latter, she has reached the point of sanctification in which her virtue is compared to that of the citizens of heaven. In both cases, the soteriological narrative is brought to completion in the life of the baptized. So transformed by the deifying effects of baptism, and so completely conformed to the Son, the soul is firmly on its course toward its true *telos*.

Summary

We see in the resurfacing of these themes of adoption or regeneration at the culminating moment of the saving economy the importance of the earlier claim that humanity, made in the image of God, bears a certain kind of special resemblance to the Son. Our regeneration is a re-birth as sons of God the Father and as co-heirs with the Son. The latter receives our form that we might receive his; he is conformed to us that we might be conformed to him. The gift of salvation is in large measure the restoration of humanity's filial identity and the reception of all that is proper to this identity because of the outpouring upon us of the Spirit of adoption, whom the Christ received on our account in his own baptism in the Jordan. Closely tied together here are Didymus' accounts of θεολογία and οἰκονομία. The eternal identity of the Son is reiterated in time and space by the Son's enacted restoration of the filial identity of humanity. The logic of scriptural "image" language is that conformity to the Son—the exact imprint of the Father's nature—is the goal of human existence. In the gracious economy of God, the Son takes on human nature in order to

---

145. *DT* 2.5.4 (492BC). The occurrence of the singular αὐτοῦ, however, makes the logic of the phrase somewhat unclear. Does Didymus mean to indicate that the reception of both the Father's sometime proper name "God" and the Word's proper name "Son" is made possible precisely because of the goodness of only one of the *hypostaseis* (in which case the antecedent is unclear)? Or does the word αὐτοῦ have a distributive function—that is, it is because of the goodness of each one—in the sentence?

146. Russell, *Doctrine of Deification*, 160.

147. *DT* 2.14 (716A).

148. *DT* 3.24 (937B). Is this a reference to Exodus 7:1?

recreate humanity so that it bears, by grace, his filial likeness to the Father once more.

Just as in the first creation, the work of the Holy Spirit is not incidental to its completion. He always goes forth together with the Son. Without the Spirit, our Adamic humanity would neither be vivified in the beginning nor stripped away so that we could be conformed to the life of the new Adam. At the will of the Father, humanity is created by the Son with the goal of being conformed into his image, a goal made possible by the breathing of the Holy Spirit who bestows upon the filial creature the heavenly blessings of his sanctification. With the loss or corruption of the image, humanity puts the gift to an impossible use, losing its freedom and sinlessness in its enslavement to base passions. The restorative work of the Trinity is accomplished at the good will of the Father by the Son's assumption of humanity. Taking on human sin and death, he offers to humanity instead the abundance of his life as the Son: an abundance so full that he reconstitutes us into his own image by grace. Hence we become sons of God and heirs of the Father. The Spirit sets his seal to the work of the Son, returning to dwell in the humanity that was formerly ruined by its own disobedience. And this takes place at baptism. Henceforth the Spirit bestows upon these re-constituted children of God the gifts of the Spirit, which are nothing less than the goods of heaven.

We are now in a position to fill out the content of the second kind of knowledge that Didymus speaks of in the treatise. The knowledge of God proceeds relationally as the creature is rendered receptive to the activity of the Trinity in the creature's reconstitution in likeness to the Son. It is finally only as children of the Father, conformed to the Son by the sanctifying Spirit, that humans can know God as the divine activities of the Trinity have made him known to us. It is now no surprise to find that Didymus connects baptism with "the knowledge of God" (θεογνωσία).[149] In baptism, the activities of God toward us coalesce with our saving experience of those activities. It is in being reconciled that we both know God and are known by him as sons and daughters of the living God. And it is in this location, I argue in what follows, that the reading of Scripture begins and ends.

The Authors of Scripture as Participating Witnesses

In this third section, I bring to bear what has been said thus far to the question that is at the heart of this study: what are the Scriptures? To get at a sufficiently nuanced answer to this question, it is necessary to see 1) how Didymus speaks of the activity of the Trinity in relation to the inspiration of Scripture. 2) Subsequently, Didymus' characterization of the apostles and

---

149. See *DT* 1.26.52 (389C) and *DT* 2.12 (684A). The cultic worship of the OT makes way for baptism, in which the "perfect knowledge of God" is granted. In baptism humanity is ushered quickly into the knowledge of God.

Economy and Scripture 141

prophets in relation to the activity of the Trinity merits our attention. I argue here that for Didymus the human authors of Scripture are those who are made participant in and witness to God's saving activity. On the basis of the scriptural ontology developed here, I will suggest several themes relating to the interpreter's task that are corollaries to this ontology. These themes will serve as the outline of the remaining chapters of the study.

The Divine Authorship of the Scriptures

Didymus does not provide us with anything approaching a theory of the divine inspiration of Scripture. For him, it is often sufficient only to say that the Scriptures have their origin in the activity of God.[150] If the roles of the *hypostaseis* are clearly differentiated in the narrative of creation-salvation, they are not so clearly defined in relation to the inspiration of Scripture. Didymus speaks sometimes of the Trinitarian authorship of Scripture.[151] Expounding this notion on one occasion, Didymus points out that the Father, Son, and the Holy Spirit are all said to speak to Isaiah in the Vision of the Seraphim.[152] These kingly activities of the Son and the Spirit are attributed to the Father because of their "indistinguishable Godhead" (ἀπαράλλακτον . . . θεότητα) with the one from whom they went forth.[153] Of similar import are places in which Didymus speaks of the Father, Son, and Holy Spirit speaking in the faithful, or of their indwelling of the saints.[154]

On other occasions, Didymus attributes portions of Scripture to the Son or the Holy Spirit. He draws the reader's attention to Paul's assertion that "Christ speaks in [him]" (2 Cor 13:3).[155] Most frequently, he asserts that the Holy Spirit inspires the prophets and apostles or commands them to take up their role in ecclesial governance—in which governance the authorship of Scripture plays a role.[156] Didymus recalls to good effect that the Scriptures are called "God-breathed" (2 Tim 3:16) because the Holy Spirit of God established them.[157] As we noted in the last chapter, he observes that "since there is no distinction between their nature and teaching" the divine Spirit is said to speak in the

---

150. See, for instance, *DT* 1.15.11 (300B) and 1.16.32 (336B).
151. See *DT* 1.23.1–5 (376BC). He has more than casual precedent in Origen for this argument. See Peter Martens' important recovery of this point in his: "Why Does Origen Introduce the Trinitarian Authorship of Scripture in Book 4 of Peri Archon?" *VC* 60 (2006): 1–8.
152. *DT* 1.19.4–10 (364B–365B), citing Isaiah 6:8–9; John 12:41; Acts 28:25.
153. This is to use the language of *DT* 2.11 (660C).
154. *DT* 1.21.1–5 (373BC) and 2.6.7 (529A).
155. *DT* 2.8.1 (604B).
156. See *DT* 2.1.10 (452B), 2.6.11 (537BC), 2.8.2 (624AB), 2.25 (748C), 3.2.44 (804A), and 3.33 (960AB).
157. *DT* 2.10 (644BC).

apostles, and Christ to speak in Paul.[158] Both Christ and the Holy Spirit speak together in Paul and the rest of the apostles.[159]

This divine inspiration of the Scriptures impresses them with a certain character. As the address of the ineffable and invisible God to embodied human creatures, the Scriptures necessarily involve a certain level of condescension. The Scriptures teach things appropriate "to our limitations (πρὸς τὰ μέτρα ἡμῶν)."[160] Didymus relates this verbal condescension to the gracious economy of the Son on two important occasions. In the former of these, Didymus writes:

> [I]n all things being brought near to us, he [namely, the Son] made use of the speech that was familiar to us, that we should understand the economy, and not be frightened away by the loftiness of the divine language. . . . It was somehow especially needful that God, in whom there is never any accusation against or rivalry with men, speak what was befitting them (ἀνθρωποπρεπῆ) and what was considerate toward them (μετριόφρονα), and do good to us without in any way bringing harm to his nature which is most serene and bestows all things. For he looks not always to his own height, but to the humility of men.[161]

The Scriptures are accommodated speech which is nevertheless truthful. Though God speaks in human language to us about divine matters, he suffers no harm to his divinity; the revelation is not compromised by the chosen vessel of God's self-communication. The Incarnation provides a loose analogy for what happens when the God who is beyond speech comes to speech. God is not made strange to himself in this act of accommodation.

Didymus draws on a similar set of ideas a short while later, this time drawing out the implications for faithful attention to the words of Christ.

> Submitting (συγκαταβάς) in all things and becoming poor in the servant's form, and remaking (μεταπλάσας) himself without change into what was common in his speech, and preserving every consequence of the Incarnation (πᾶσαν τῆς ἐνανθρωπήσεως ἀκολουθίαν), and obscuring none of the imprint of the truth, as true Wisdom he uttered what was fitting to men so that we might become like him and become perfectly conformed, according to the Apostle, doing what was

---

158. *DT* 2.17 (725BC).
159. *DT* 3.4 (837C) and 3.41.2 (985C).
160. *DT* 2.5.27 (505A).
161. *DT* 3.17 (876AB).

fitting and pleasing to him and passing from things earthly to things heavenly (αἰθέρια).¹⁶²

With these words Didymus affirms that the condescension of the Logos, who speaks to us in a manner wholly consonant with his becoming human, is no betrayal of his heavenly identity. The words he utters as one of us do not obscure "the imprint of the truth." And yet, because the purpose of this economy is to draw us heavenward, the Son performing his wonders among us "to show his eternal and all-sufficient divinity,"¹⁶³ Didymus affirms that the condescension of divinity to human language has an anagogic purpose. He became "like us" that we might become "like him."

The condescension implies that in God's communication with us, there is something beyond human apprehension, a fullness into which the human knower must grow. The "hidden sense (κρύφιος νοῦς)" of Scripture is a function of this dynamic.¹⁶⁴ Chief among his complaints against the heretics is their failure to observe the importance of this point. They are ever "making war on the words of God by the thoughts of men."¹⁶⁵ They are ever attempting to understand "the things of God" as if they were "human things."¹⁶⁶ In fact, Didymus goes so far as to say that it was on account of them that God had deliberately hidden certain meanings in the Scriptures, lest they transgress into them.¹⁶⁷

This concealed sense is occasionally hidden even from the human authors of Scripture. Didymus notes that Paul calls the Son "first-born of creation" in a sense so deep that "Paul was speaking what he did not understand, and was trusting in what he was speaking since there was a prompting (ἐπειδὴ ὑποβολὴ ἦν) of the true Wisdom and since he [Wisdom] was making all these things plain to him [Paul]."¹⁶⁸ David likewise is described as "necessarily ignorant of future things and things heavenly"; therefore, he argues, the Scriptures say that he spoke "by the Holy Spirit."¹⁶⁹ A slightly more ambiguous argument occurs later in the treatise when Didymus writes that the Holy-singer of Psalm 108 was "somehow both hiding and openly displaying [the unspeakable mystery of the Incarnation], and revealing it rather than being ignorant of it, and

---

162. *DT* 3.21 (901C).
163. *DT* 3.17 (876B).
164. *DT* 3.35 (965A).
165. *DT* 1.16.32 (336B).
166. *DT* 3.40 (981B). For similar expressions, see 1.9.43 (289A), 1.16.1-2 (332AB), 1.26.60 (392C), 1.27.7 (396BC), and 3.35 (964A and 964C).
167. The best example of this is when Didymus writes that some Scriptures are written "in a hidden way (μυστικῶς)." "Moses—or rather, the God who was inspiring him—looking at these things, did not consider them to be appropriate to the multitude" (*DT* 2.7.3.3 (565C)).
168. *DT* 3.4 (828CD).
169. *DT* 3.33 (960AB).

being ignorant of it rather than revealing it."[170] It seems best to understand Didymus' argument as allowing for the partial knowledge and ignorance of the singer. The psalmist has a partial apprehension of that which is coming, but it surpasses his ability to comprehend it utterly.

Coupled with the remarks in the last chapter about the divine use of human language in divine self-revelation, the above remarks merit a few observations. God assumes human modes of speech as a part of the divine economy in which he wills to make himself known to creatures as he is. The God who speaks with thunder and lightning on Mt Sinai adopts words that are "common" or "low-to-the-ground,"[171] lest we be frightened away. In such a situation as this, it is not surprising that human language finds itself over-burdened with the task to which it is being put. Human language is pressed into divine service and thus frequently signifies "improperly" or "approximately" (καταχρηστικῶς)."[172]

Didymus does not indicate explicitly how he would wade into the *thesis-physis* debate about the nature of human language, yet his distance from Eunomius at this point is evident. Language is put to divine use, but not because it has some innate capacity to designate and reveal essences.[173] The divine Author of Scripture uses human language parabolically, taking examples from creaturely realities and employing them in the service of conveying the truth about himself in an analogical fashion. So when human language refers to divine realities, the divine pedagogy must be duly acknowledged. Scripture intermingles the various "dispositions" of the Logos in his economy precisely to incite us to "join in the hunt for the divine sense,"[174] rather than to cast aspersions on the nature of the Logos by predicating these things of the divine essence.

For this reason, the divine use of human language to refer to God under various "conceptions" has a corollary in human attention to divine speech. The human listener must always be asking how divine being-in-action generates human attentiveness to the various aspects under which God has willed to

---

170. *DT* 3.6 (844B). Didymus cites Psalm 108:27 LXX.

171. *DT* 3.17 (876D).

172. See, e.g., *DT* 3.40 (981C–984A). "For his [namely, the Holy Spirit's] divinity is found to be beyond knowledge, so such things were said about the unspeakable Trinity improperly (καταχρηστικῶς)." Cf. *DSS* 167: "Now every human term can indicate nothing other than corporeal things, and the Trinity . . . is beyond all material substances. For these reasons, no word can be applied to him in the proper sense and thereby signify his substance. Rather, when we speak about incorporeals in general and especially about the Trinity, every thing we say is said καταχρηστικῶς, that is, in an improper sense" (DelCogliano, Radde-Gallwitz, and Ayres, *Works on the Spirit*, 194).

173. For a more thoroughgoing discussion on Eunomius' theory of language, see Richard Paul Vaggione, "Prelate," in *Eunomius of Cyzicus and the Nicene Revolution* (Oxford: Oxford University Press, 2000), 201–266.

174. *DT* 3.21 (909A).

make himself known. As in the passage on the Holy Spirit cited above, the various activities that he undertakes on behalf of the creation (sanctification) require human receptivity to and participation in the sanctifying work of the Holy Spirit if they are to be known truly. The Scriptures, which have been so ordered by God so as to bear witness to him, can only be heard aright in light of the divine pedagogy of which they are an essential part.

The Prophets and Apostles

Considering the character of the treatise, it is perhaps unsurprising that the most common category employed by Didymus to describe the authors of Scripture is that of witness. He is continually calling upon the saints of the OT and NT to corroborate his arguments,[175] arguments he expects his audience to follow, sometimes through nothing but the linking together of multiple scriptural texts. In contrast to the occasional acknowledgment, noted above, that God intends by the Scriptures more than the human authors understood, Didymus more often appeals to the human authors of the Scriptures as witnesses who see, in their spiritual vision, what God intended for them to see. Thus they are those who participate in the economy to which they testify.

Communicant with the Spirit

They are so above all by being communicant with the one of whom they speak. In the first extant sentence of the treatise, St Paul—who is "subject to the Law (ἔννομος)"—offers himself as bond for those who are unfamiliar with the Law or outside it as Gentiles. They are secure in their opinion that the worship of the Son is consistent with the teaching of the OT because Paul has made a thorough study of the OT. He does so not as a grammarian or a historian, but rather as one who "has been made wise (σεσοφισμένος) by the divine Spirit."[176] David makes his confession of the Spirit's honor and power only as one who is a "bearer of the Spirit (πνευματοφόρος)." This same Spirit keeps him pure from sin and maintains him in the ability to prophesy.[177] Elisha, the most worthy of the prophets, is worthy of knowing the Holy Spirit as God.[178] When the Son testifies to his own "goodness," he is joined by numerous other voices in the Scriptures. Didymus implicitly suggests that such people are worthy of our credence, since they are not "obscure men (ἀφανεῖς ἄνδρες)" but

---

175. Documenting this claim thoroughly is unnecessary. See, e.g., DT 1.15.11 (300B), 1.27.2 (396A), 1.32.1 (425A), 1.33.2 (432B), 2.1.14 (453AB), 2.6.18.3 (548A), 2.7.3.17 (576A), 2.8.1 (604B), 2.8.1 (613C), 2.10 (648B), 2.11 (660CD), 2.12 (672A), and 3.21 (901CD and 916C).

176. DT 1.7.1 (269A–272A), following Hönscheid's interpretation of ἔννομος as "bound by the Law (im Gesetz gebundene)" in De trinitate, Buch 1, 15. Mingarelli's rendering: "expert in the Law (peritus in lege)" (271CDn7) makes too much of the word.

177. DT 2.17 (725A).

178. DT 2.11 (653A).

those "especially conversant (σφόδρα προσομιλήσαντες) with the divine Spirit."[179]

The heretics and the "wise pagans" are useful foils for this characterization of the authors of Scripture. The former have, by virtue of their refusal to acknowledge the divinity of the Son and the Holy Spirit, renounced the very possibility of understanding the Scriptures rightly. It is "difficult to teach when the grace of the divine Spirit is not present";[180] these "heresy-warriors are not participant (οὐ μετέχουσι) in the divine Spirit."[181] This lack of communion with the Spirit has numerous consequences. Not being in the Spirit, neither are they able to affirm rightly the Lordship of the Son;[182] not confessing the divinity of the Spirit, they steer the ship of faith into the rocks.[183] Macedonius, by demeaning the Spirit's divine "substance (οὐσία)," consequently is neither a "fellow-sharer (συγκοινωνός)" in his grace nor a recipient of his "eternal gifts."[184] In understanding the divine oracles, everything depends upon the reception of divine help; without it, the proper understanding of the Scriptures is impossible.

Didymus' appeal to secular poets, philosophers, and to characters of dubious authority in Scripture (like Job's friends) rounds out the above picture somewhat. Didymus' appeal to them is often qualified by explanations that underline the supplementary, rather than primary, character of their witness. Some of the Greek poets have received a "tolerable awareness (μετρίαν... συναίσθησιν)" of the equality of the *hypostaseis*.[185] Some of their theologians have spoken worthily concerning God's relation to the universe.[186] Didymus accounts for their truthful witness once by saying that the one Wisdom who bestows all things has addressed "those outside." Yet even in this instance, their testimony tends to highlight in contrast the "great speech of the saints."[187] If they are frequently useful allies for Didymus, their work just as often suffers from a lack of clarity; they offer no very precise vision of the Trinity.[188] They speak "in proportion to their own weakness."[189]

Didymus uses both Eliud and Porphyry as examples of witnesses whose testimony is somewhat mixed. Eliud is reliable testimony to the creating and sanctifying activity of the Spirit, but when Didymus comes to explain how this

---

179. *DT* 1.18.44 (353A).
180. *DT* 2.7.8.7 (588B).
181. *DT* 2.21 (741C).
182. *DT* 2.21 (741C).
183. *DT* 2.26 (752BC).
184. *DT* 2.10 (633BC).
185. *DT* 2.27 (753A).
186. *DT* 3.2.25 (796C).
187. *DT* 3.21 (901CD).
188. *DT* 3.24 (936C–937A).
189. *DT* 3.2.9 (792A).

can be the case—since Eliud errs on other important matters—he writes: "I know not how (οὐκ οἶδα πόθεν)."[190] Didymus likewise equivocates over the value of including Porphyry in his company of witnesses to the saving Spirit's work. He confesses that though Porphyry is in most cases "not sound in mind" about divinity, in one case where he speaks well he is "raging against himself (αὐτοχολωτῶν)."[191]

Didymus does recognize the presence of wisdom outside the scriptural canon; he can only explain this by appealing to the one Wisdom who is the bestower of all wisdom.[192] He likewise recognizes that this exterior wisdom is of a very piecemeal kind. It is imprecise; with it is mixed much error; he refers to it as an "awareness (συναίσθησις)." When he attempts to explain its piecemeal quality, his equivocation stems from his insistence that there is only one Wisdom and that the wisdom among "those outside" can only be explained by his self-communication to them. It makes sense then that errors of judgment in matters theological are explained, where Didymus cares to do so, in terms of a failure of the "interior vision (τὸ ἔνδον ... διορατικόν)."[193]

Illumined

Illumination is the dimension of the sacred writers' receptivity to divine grace that is of greatest interest to Didymus in DT. The sacred writers celebrate the Son as the one who "by his own incessant light illumines the eyes of souls that do not wander and are receptive, even leading them into spiritual contemplation (περιωπῆς) and making them to see what they were not able to beforehand by themselves on account of their sins."[194] The eyes of the mind/soul are a consistent theme. The Holy Spirit teaches us by "illumining the eyes of our souls, showing us many times in different ways what will be." Didymus follows the claim with scriptural examples of the fulfillment of

---

190. DT 2.10 (632B-632C).

191. DT 2.27 (760B).

192. This point is consistent, incidentally, with Didymus' preferred interpretation of Proverbs 8:22 in DT 3.3. There is a wisdom in the world which has its basis in the divine Wisdom who is the Son of God.

193. DT 2.27 (760C-761A): ὡς τὸ ἔνδον τεθολωμένος καὶ βεβλαμμένος διορατικὸν ὁ ἐπάρατος Πορφύριος καὶ πρὸς τὴν τελεωτάτην ἀδυνατῶν θεολογίαν, ἅτε μήτε κατ' ἐπιθυμητικὴν καὶ φοιτικὴν αὐτοῦ ὁρμὴν, τὴν παροῦσαν ποιούμενος ἐξήγησιν ἀμυδρῶς τὸ ἓν καὶ σωστικὸν ἅγιον Πνεῦμα τοῦ Θεοῦ ψυχὴν προσηγόρευσεν. "Since the accursed Porphyry was disturbed and perverted in his interior vision and he was unable [to arrive] at the most perfect theology since it was not in agreement with his affective and frenzied appetite, when he made the present explanation, he referred unclearly to the one and saving Holy Spirit of God as soul." The seat of the affections, τὸ ἐπιθυμητικόν, is meant to be ordered by the highest part of the soul: the "governing faculty (τὸ ἡγεμονικόν)" or "intellect (νοῦς)," the latter of which contains the capacity for spiritual sight. But with Porphyry, so Didymus has it, the horse has become the rider. His spiritual sight has become clouded by his inconstant affections.

194. DT 1.28.1 (408C-409A).

prophecy.¹⁹⁵ Possibly including both the saints of his day with the saints of the Old and New Testaments, Didymus urges the heretics to "hold to such saints who possess mental eyes as watchful as the Cherubim."¹⁹⁶

As those who are especially conversant with the Spirit of God, the saints are the prime examples of "the spiritual," whom Didymus describes at length in Book 2, chapter 20. Among the effects of the Spirit's coming upon them, they are described as being "illumined (καταλάμπονται) by the divine light" of the Trinity, becoming like the "one who illumines (φωτίζοντι) them so far as this is possible (κατὰ δύναμιν)." When the "vision of their inner eye" becomes pure they see God as he is. They see God "as he allows" and "receive according to his desire." The nearer they come to him, "they recognize all the more the incomprehensibility of his divinity."¹⁹⁷ The passages in which the saints are credited with being full of wisdom or understanding are numerous. Didymus' epithets for the sacred writers or short descriptions of the authors' condition underline the point: Paul is "most wise (σοφώτατος)," "replete with understanding (συνέσεως πλήρης)"; Moses is "all-wise (πάνσοφος)"; Isaiah speaks "by a certain unspeakable insight (ἀπορρήτῳ ... θεωρίᾳ)," etc.¹⁹⁸

An essential aspect of the prophet's or apostle's condition therefore is his intellective disposition before divine grace. By the Trinity the authors of sacred Scripture are renewed in the mind toward an understanding of that which God wills to reveal to and through them. They are caught up in the sanctifying activity of the Trinity to which they bear witness, given an eye that is full of light. Didymus asserts that the interpreter of Scripture must be likewise transformed. Those who would interpret the OT in its fulsome Trinitarian sense must become receptive of "divine vision (θεοπτίας)."¹⁹⁹ To know the Trinity they must arrive at the "utmost point of meditation."²⁰⁰ Though they are in themselves powerless to approach the Holy Spirit worthily even by their best interpretive efforts or interior vision (θεωρίᾳ νοῦ), the Holy Spirit "mitigates (παραμυθούμενα)" their powerlessness and gives them confidence to confess his consubstantiality and entrust themselves to his sanctifying work.²⁰¹ Thus they are able to perceive "the beauty of divine truth";²⁰² thus they too, illuminated by him, come to understand the divine oracles.²⁰³

---

195. *DT* 2.7.12 (597D).
196. *DT* 2.8.1 (613C).
197. *DT* 2.20 (737AC). The question of the character of the beatific vision in the *eschaton* is raised in chapter 5.
198. *DT* 3.23 (929B), 3.16 (869B), 3.36 (968B), and 3.21 (908B).
199. *DT* 1.18.22 (348BC).
200. *DT* 1.36.1 (440A).
201. *DT* 2.3.2 (465AB).
202. *DT* 2.6.8.5 (533AB).
203. *DT* 2.19 (729B).

Morally Sanctified

Though the theme is somewhat less prominent, it is also clear that Didymus includes in this description of the apostles and prophets an emphasis on their moral disposition. In an anti-Macedonian discussion about the Father's use of the word "my" of his Spirit, Didymus notes other homonyms. God says "my" and "first-born" of Isaiah and Israel. Noting that the connotations of the word differ when used of beings of different natures, Didymus writes that the word "my" is used of humans to set them apart from others by their proximity to God. People are called "mine" by God when "they approach him by their deeds (πράξεσι)." Israel, for instance, was first "to serve (λατρεύειν)" God; he was God's son by his "disposition (διαθέσει)" and his "attentiveness" (φροντίδι)" toward him.[204] Didymus is clearly thinking here of Israel's moral disposition, of the nation's willingness to obey the commands of God. The idea recurs later when Didymus characterizes the forefathers as those who were pleasing to God before the apostles, and "marvelled at for their virtue (ἐπ' ἀρετῇ θαυμασθέντας)."[205] In the context of speaking about the passions that war against the soul, Didymus holds up St Paul as an example of an "unconquered athlete."[206]

The Scriptures attest to the fact that the saints can lie;[207] however, in the context of their witness to God in the speaking of sacred Scripture, they do not do so. Sustained by the God who co-authors Scripture with them, they are "teachers of sacred truths (ἱεροφάντες)," "God's interpreters (ὑποφῆται)," "unstained (καθαροί) by any opinion that denies the truth."[208] Utterly receptive to the work of the un-lying God, they profess what belongs to right faith.[209] So when the heretics speak in opposition to the saints, they are opposing the opinions of "men who speak as from God (θεηγόρων ἀνδρῶν)," who are receptive to the grace of God and therefore say what is "fitting (διαπρέπειν)."[210]

---

204. *DT* 2.2.32–33 (461C). Though the discussion is not related to the prophetic ministry, Didymus speaks in 1.18.40–42 (352B–353A) of distance from God in terms of a person's "relationship" (σχέσει) with and "disposition (διαθέσει)" toward God (a frequent pairing in the exegetical literature). "Opposition to the good" and "sluggishness to virtue" are expressive of relational and dispositional distance from God, who is the source of all goodness and virtue.

205. *DT* 3.29 (948BC).

206. *DT* 3.1 (777A).

207. *DT* 2.6.13 (540C).

208. *DT* 1.19.1–2 (364AB).

209. Though not explicit, it appears that Didymus accounts for this in the passage where he speaks of lying among the saints (*DT* 2.6.13 (540C)). Though they are capable of lying and do lie, the Holy Spirit communes with all, ἔτι μὴν καὶ εἰς τὸ ἀψευδεῖν. Seiler translates the phrase: "so daß wir auch nicht mehr lügen können" (*De trinitate, Buch 2*, 157).

210. *DT* 2.5.5 (492C).

If the moral transformation of the sacred writers of Scripture plays an important role in their reliability as witnesses, so likewise does it play an important role in their interpreters' proper response to their testimony. To participate in that to which they bear witness, the interpreter must become a different kind of person in the moral sense. Christ, Didymus twice asserts, renders those who partake of him sharers in his own "tranquillity (ἀπάθεια)" of soul.[211] Those who are receptive to the things of the Spirit of God are being transformed from their enslavement to the various passions to a condition in which they are able to cling to God in obedience. The "spiritual" are described "as if they somehow ascend (ἀναθρώσκοντας) by thoughts and deeds that are conspicuous." They receive divine grace "in an unhindered way (ἀνεμποδίστως)" and in consequence of this they are able to escape temptation and to "be strong (ἐρρῶσθαι) in the face of the uncertainties and vicissitudes of life."[212] As a foil to them the "worldly" are those who, because of their enslavement to the passions, become hindered in the "vision of their soul (τὸ διορατικὸν τῆς ψυχῆς)."[213] We see here what will prove an important *topos* in the *CZ*: the ethical life and theological vision are integrally linked together.

More than Human

A final theme merits attention, inasmuch as it clearly reveals the teleological import of the others. Didymus consistently avers that the saints who author Scripture are, in a sense, unlike others. He writes that they are variously—in a biblical idiom—those "of whom the world was unworthy,"[214] "men worthy and secure in their way of life (τὸν τρόπον)—who are not merely (ἁπλῶς) human,"[215] and those whose words are "beyond us."[216] Next to such affirmations, Didymus' various descriptions of St Paul seem anything but casual: he is "divine (θεσπέσιος),"[217] "most eminent among men,"[218] and "superior to humankind."[219] And in contrast to this, Didymus asserts that the heretics' teaching is "from men."[220] Such notions argue at the very least that Didymus is affirming that the Scriptures are not attributable only to the work of

---

211. *DT* 1.26.14 (384BC) and 3.12 (860C).
212. *DT* 2.20 (737AB).
213. *DT* 2.20 (740C).
214. *DT* 1.32.1 (425A), quoting Hebrews 11:38.
215. *DT* 3.28 (945B).
216. *DT* 2.8.1 (620A).
217. *DT* 1.15.3 (296B) and 2.8.2 (621B).
218. *DT* 1.27.34 (400A).
219. *DT* 2.6.4.9 (520BC). The phrase in the manuscript reads: Παῦλος . . . οὐ κρείττων ἢ κατ' ἀνθρώπους. With Mingarelli (519Dn79) and Seiler (*De trinitate, Buch 2*, 124), the οὐ—inconsistent with Didymus' other affirmations and making little sense of the argument—is to be replaced by ὁ. For my translation of the phrase, cf. Seiler's: "Paulus . . . der größer war, als es Menschensart ist" (Ibid., 125).
220. *DT* 2.3.32 (480A).

men, being the work of God. The people by whom the Scriptures are written are to be understood primarily in terms of their participation in this divine work. They are, in short, deified humans.

Describing the authors of Scripture in these terms—terms that have a consistent use in the exegetical corpus—has given rise in recent years to the suspicion that Didymus is functioning with an almost unilateral account of inspiration. Robert Hill has argued that Didymus' conception of inspiration is heavily influenced by secular models of the same. Employing diction that denotes a state of prophetic ecstasy or "divine possession," Didymus conceives of the prophetic event, argues Hill, along lines that are parallel to those of pagan "prophets (μάντεις)." Zechariah is "taken hold of by God (θεοληπτούμενος)" and is thus in a state of rapture during the course of his numerous visions.[221] Hill, in turn, links this concept of inspiration to Didymus' lack of "interest in the narrative setting."[222]

Hill's description of Didymus' understanding of the prophetic event is not without some advantages. Indeed, as we will see in chapter 6 of the study, Didymus' understanding of divine visions does tend to dislocate these visions from Zechariah's "narrative setting," which suggests an oracular bent in Didymus' thought about inspiration. However, that the prophetic event is to be understood as somehow occasional, something taken in abstraction from the life of the prophet, is a conclusion that should be avoided. As Didymus regularly affirms in DT, the prophet is understood as one who speaks 1) out of familiarity with the subject of which he is speaking. The event of inspiration is continuous with the course of the prophet's life. He has been claimed by God for relationship with him. 2) Didymus does not understand deification and humanization to be mutually exclusive processes.[223] The teleological account

---

221. For his various statements of the argument, see Robert Hill, "Introduction," in *Didymus the Blind: Commentary on Zechariah* (Washington, D.C.: Catholic University of America Press, 2006), 10 and "Zechariah in Alexandria and Antioch," 330–331. Hill has helpfully pointed out that criticisms of the Fathers as being so concerned with divine authorship that they have overlooked the human dimension of Scripture are often misguided. The Fathers frequently exhibit sensitivity to the issue of the prophet's cooperation in the writing of Scripture. See his "Psalm 45: a *locus classicus* for Patristic Thinking on Biblical Inspiration," *Studia Patristica* 25 (1993): 95–100. Didymus fares less well in his later analysis.

222. Hill, "Zechariah in Alexandria and Antioch," 332.

223. In Didymus' mind, deification and humanization are not competitive. Didymus speaks of people who are truly human as those who preserve the "image and likeness of God." See, e.g., *EcclT* 231,25–27, where Didymus contrasts those who have many different guises (πρόσωπα) with those who have the appearance of a human being. This latter appearance is praiseworthy, for it is the "principal appearance (προηγούμενον πρόσωπον)" of mankind and is "in the image and likeness of God." Humanization inheres within deification. Cf. *EcclT* 331,14–19.

of human existence that Didymus develops in *DT* suggests that the divine and the human are not in competition during the prophetic event.

Nor are these kinds of observations the province of the dogmatic literature only. In *CZ*, Didymus argues for both of these ideas. In the explication of Zechariah's words: "the angel speaking in me," Didymus argues that the angel—who is Christ—only speaks in the one who listens to him if the latter participates in Christ.[224] Zechariah is a participant in Christ already, and in continuity with this participation in the Word of God he says: "the word of the Lord came to me." The revelation he receives, in other words, is continuous with his posture of receptivity to the Word who is present to him before his coming for the purpose of inspiring Scripture.

Later Didymus takes up the prophetic formula: "the word of the Lord came (ἐγένετο) to me." Likening the Word's coming to the prophet to the learned speech that a teacher acquires only by first being filled with knowledge, Didymus argues that those who see the "mysteries of the truth and wisdom of God" first require the coming of the word of the Lord to them. He then argues that this "word" is none other than God the Word, "who comes (γίνεται) to holy men and angels . . . even while he is ever-present (ὢν ἀεί) with the Father who begot him."[225] The remark is of paramount importance for what follows. Didymus is anxious to explain the passage in such a way that the "becoming" of the Logos, whom he has identified with the Son, in no way compromises who he is.

Hill's translation of the important section that follows fails to note this basic contrast, between being and becoming, and fails to pick up consistently on the personal force of Didymus' exposition of this "word." Hill renders what follows: "It [the word] comes to Spirit-filled men without remaining, since it is there at the time it comes to them; then, in fact, then is the time they will also be gods whom he enlightens by coming."[226] Russell's rendering of the same passage is much better: "The Word is described not as *being* in men inspired by the Spirit . . . but as *coming* to them. It is not until then that it comes to be in them. For it is then that they will be "gods", when the Word of God has come to dwell in them."[227] By rendering οὐκ ἔστιν as "without remaining" and by misconstruing the word ἐπιφοιτάω, Hill takes the passage in a very different sense than Didymus intends.

If we follow Russell here, the meaning emerges more clearly. The Word of God certainly "comes" to people. The basic contrast here is between the being

---

224. *CZ* I.32.

225. *CZ* II.2–3.

226. The phrase he is rendering runs thus: Γίνεται δέ, καὶ οὐκ ἔστιν, πρὸς τοὺς πνευματοφόρους ἄνδρας, ὧν καὶ τότε πρὸς αὐτοὺς ὅταν γένηται. Τότε γὰρ τότε καὶ θεοὶ ἔσονται πρὸς οὓς ἐπεφοίτησεν καὶ γέγονεν. Hill mistakenly derives the aorist ἐπεφοίτησεν from ἐπιφωτίζω rather than frwom ἐπιφοιτάω (FC 111:115).

227. *Doctrine of Deification*, 147. Emphasis original.

of the Word, his eternal identity, and his activities undertaken in relationship to us. But he comes to "holy men" who are likened to teachers in possession of knowledge. And when he comes, he comes "to dwell in them," not departing from them again in an instant when they have served their purposes as servants of the prophetic word. Didymus will describe this state teleologically: those who are "carried along by God (θεοφορούμενοι)" are deified. They achieve the true *telos* which is the very purpose of human existence. They are made like God insofar as this is possible; as we have noted above about the preservation or attainment of the image and likeness of God, they become truly human.

When seen in this light, Didymus' remarks about divine inspiration do not negate the human role in the prophetic event, but rather highlight the place of these moments within the context of the prophet's ongoing relationship with the God who is inspiring him. Hill's analysis of Didymus' doctrine of inspiration isolates its features from their place in Didymus' understanding of the economy. When it is understood that the true end of humanity—true humanness as it were—is not competitive with but rather achieved in utter receptivity to God, the language of "divine possession" does not serve to render Didymus' account of Scripture less human. The prophet is caught up in a more particular way within the purposes of God for humanity, but this particular function that the prophet performs arises out of his fellowship with the Word; it is brought into existence in a manner continuous with his relation to the Word. The problem in Didymus' conception of inspiration is not so much his conception of the dynamics of divine-human interaction, as it is his anthropology.

Conclusion: a Scriptural Ontology

It is time to give a summary of the chapter, with a view to offering a sketch of Didymus' ontology of Scripture. Arguing that the creature is dependent upon the activity of the Trinity for divine knowledge, Didymus develops a fulsome account of that which God has done on humanity's behalf to overcome human ignorance of God. God has, at the first creation, made humanity for communion with himself by the gift of reason and a free will. These the human creature is to put to use in obedience to the divine will by faith in the goodness of God. The end of this obedience is deification: becoming like God insofar as this is possible for the creature by sharing in the gifts of the Spirit and by being conformed to the image of the Son.

With the loss of this image, the saving (or re-creative) activity of the Trinity consists above all in restoring the divine image in humanity to its former condition. To this end, the Son becomes human, taking upon himself the consequences of human sinfulness and alienation from God so that he may render their humanity like his own: obedient to the Father and fully receptive to the Spirit. Through his saving Incarnation he remakes humanity. In baptism,

Christians come to share in the saving work of the Son, being deified by the Holy Spirit and made communicant with God. They are conformed to the Son, the true image of God the Father, and are thus in receipt of the blessings of heaven. The sanctifying and deifying work of the Holy Spirit after baptism consists in fully realizing what is already effective for the Christian in baptism. The Holy Spirit sanctifies the human mind and the human will so that his creature sees and knows God insofar as this is possible to the creature, guaranteeing the continuity of human communion with God into the age to come.

The repetition of these themes in the case of the human authors of Scripture is not accidental. They participate in the saving activity of God to which they testify. The Scriptures are fundamentally, for Didymus, participating—and for this reason, faithful—testimony to the economy of the Trinity and (by this means) to the knowledge of this God. To be a human author of sacred Scripture is to be one whose life is claimed for God's purposes for all humanity: to know God truly and so become like him. Didymus conceives of the prophets and apostles' conformation to the Son chiefly in terms of their 1) illumination (or intellective sanctification) and 2) moral transformation (or moral sanctification).

Since the purposes of God for all humanity are realized in precisely these terms, it is not surprising that these are precisely at the center of the interpretive enterprise. If we would, as interpreters of the Scriptures, read in a manner consonant with what the Scriptures are and with their purpose in the economy of God, we will read them as those who desire to know God and to be transformed by this encounter. We will read, in short, as if there is nothing more decisive to our understanding of Scripture than our baptism. For in its waters, as Didymus says, our Adamic humanity—with all its disordered thoughts, affections, and acts—was put to death so that we might be raised to new life in Christ. Now we no longer live, but Christ lives in us. This being the case, the new creation is fully realized in us as interpreters when we pursue not our own mind but the mind of Christ. More needs to be said about the imperatives that this account of Scripture generates for its readers, but for the present it is the participational character of reading in the economy that is most decisive.

It would be hard to improve on the broad features of this scriptural ontology. On the one hand, it seems to eschew the problematic of needing to do justice to both the human and divine dimensions of Scripture by separating them from one another. For Didymus, these dimensions are not in competition. The "divine dimension" of Scripture has its basis in the human-loving character of the God who chooses to address humanity not in the loftiness of divine speech but rather in the words that are familiar to us. This movement is analogous to the ostensible humiliation of the Son, which is actually the full revelation of the glory of God. The "human dimension" of Scripture is caught up in the realization of the divine image in its human authors. Deified humanity is true humanity, humanity as it is meant to be in communion with God.

The human authors of Scripture participate by the saving work of the Trinity in the deifying humanity of Christ, who is the true image of God and their true end.

On the other hand, this ontology also avoids the particularly modern problematic of seeking to establish the truthfulness (or in late modernity, the meaningfulness) of Scripture within a purportedly broader context. As Didymus rightly recognizes, there is no more comprehensive context than the being and activity of the Trinity, who in Scripture reveals himself and his saving purposes to humanity. Scriptural teleology is tightly bound up with scriptural ontology. When we read the Scriptures with Didymus, we are brought into conformity with the divine intent (*skopos*) as it relates to the economy we have been describing.

Closely related to this latter point is the deeply participational character of the prophetic and apostolic witness. Faithful witnesses are not those who stand at an "objective distance" from the Subject who addresses them. Neither are faithful hearers of the Word. Didymus ties the participational experience of the prophets and the apostles closely to the imperative of faithful reading: it is only in the context of becoming different kinds of people (receptive to God's saving activity) that the Scriptures are opened to us in their true character as Sacred Scripture.

Finally, Didymus' reflections on the relation between the testaments are also quite promising. What binds the two together is, above all, the consistent activity of the three *hypostaseis* in accomplishing the divine economy of re-creation. They are related to one another in such a way that the OT speaks in a concealed way of that which the NT makes explicit. As we saw in the last chapter, Didymus gives a lively account of the activities of the Word and the Spirit throughout the OT, securing this account on the basis of the differentiated inseparability of divine activity.

Some issues are, however, raised in connection with the themes that will form the investigation in the second half of the book. The saving work of the Trinity focuses on conforming the creature to the image of the Son; this conformity has consequences for the two categories explored above: moral sanctification and illumination. Because Didymus appears to envision these in highly-realized terms in this life, the question must be asked: what is the precise scope of Didymus' "insofar as this is possible to the creature" both in the present life and in the age to come? Didymus' initial remarks about the authors of Sacred Scripture are persuasive. All are caught up to bear witness to the saving economy of the Trinity in which they are, in some sense, participant. Some, however, on a literal sense reading of the Scriptures, would appear to fit more awkwardly into the highly-realized terms in which the saving activity of the Trinity has been appropriated to them. We see Didymus trying to wrestle with this question with a character like Eliud. One wonders also what would become of someone like Solomon or Balaam.

For our purposes, then, the major questions that will be taken up in the second half of the book will revolve around two issues: 1) what is the ethical life and how fully realized can it be in the present life? 2) How does the contemplative life proceed in this age and what is its *telos* in the age to come? In order to answer these questions, we will have to turn to the CZ, where Didymus is given the freedom to explore the anagogical content of the Christian faith in more irenic circumstances.

I have argued in this chapter that the human situation, characterized at present by sinfulness and creaturely limitation, calls into question the very possibility of divine revelation. God's response to humanity's alienation from him is his self-revelation in the economy of salvation, an economy that begins with the creation of the world and continues into the *eschaton*. The economy of salvation centers on the re-creative work of the Son who refashions humanity in his own fullness as the Son, and receives the Spirit for us so that we may, by the Spirit who ever rests upon him, be conformed to our *telos* as sons and daughters of the Father. Given that this is the way in which God has willed to reveal himself, attending to God or knowing God proceeds by knowing him in this activity. One does this chiefly by participating in it in the waters of baptism.

I argued that Didymus' ontology of Scripture cannot be abstracted from Didymus' vision of the economy. By locating scriptural ontology here, we see that God has not left this activity within a void of creaturely speculation about its meaning, but has rather called to himself the "goodly fellowship of the prophets" in order to speak his own words to us about these activities in which the prophets were participants and therefore credible witnesses. In God's use of human speech, he has truly revealed himself to us in continuity with his own being, even though the endless depths of Scripture are occasioned by the dynamics of an eternal God coming to finite speech. These depths of Scripture are plumbed only as we ascend with Christ, whose condescension toward us enjoins our ascent to join him where he is.

Just as the prophets were made servants of the Word and Spirit of God by being conformed to their true end in the Son, so we too are enjoined to become like them. The baptismal life continues to norm human receptivity to God in the act of hearing the words of Scripture, for only in that life is attentiveness to the Word made possible. We take on the mind of Christ and become like him in the hearing of the Word of God, when by the grace of the Spirit our Adamic humanity is put to death and we are raised to new life with Christ.

4

THE MORAL LIFE AND ITS END

In this chapter I examine the theme of moral sanctification in *CZ*. My aim is to provide a description of how the moral life proceeds in Didymus. The argument unfolds in three sections. In the first, I provide a brief sketch of Didymus' anthropology and his teaching on the virtues. This section allows us to properly locate his treatment of the moral life within the broader matrix of his description of the human composite, and to appreciate the role that moral virtue plays in connection with contemplation.

In the second section, I explore several passages in which Didymus provides us with material suitable for developing an account of that in which the moral life consists. In this section, I argue that the moral life 1) is described chiefly in terms of the imitation of that which the Savior reveals to us about true humanity, and 2) that complete moral conformity to the Incarnate Son is conceived of by Didymus as a real possibility in the present life. The saving work of the Trinity consists specifically in the Father's will to receive adopted sons who are fashioned in the likeness of his Son. The latter reveals and enables the moral life by defeating the powers arrayed against us. Participants in the Holy Spirit reiterate the path trod by Christ in company with him.

In the final section of the chapter I relate Didymus' account of the moral life to the earliest passages of the *CZ*. I argue that his consistent assertions about the possibility of moral conformity to the Son's humanity are closely related to what is a, if not the, central theme of the *CZ*: the attainment of stability. The prophets, who are the servants of the Spirit of God, reveal the course of the soul's ascent from vice to virtue and from vicissitude to peace. Those who heed the prophets and do what they say become sharers in the nature that is beyond the possibility of change.

The sections discussed above extend Didymus' reflections in *DT* on the subject of moral sanctification. In *DT*, this sanctification proceeds specifically in being conformed by the Holy Spirit to the image of our Creator, the Son. The end of this conformation is our deification: our being made like God "insofar as this is possible." In this chapter we seek to clarify this latter point: to what extent does Didymus think this is possible in this life? The answer to this question bears significantly on the interpretation of Scripture.

Humanity and Virtue

We begin the study on moral sanctification in CZ by examining the broad outline of Didymus' teaching on the virtues. Three items in particular merit discussion: 1) the anthropological framework in which the struggle for virtue takes place, 2) the definition(s) of virtue, and 3) the relation between moral and contemplative virtue. These items are important in properly discerning the relationship between this chapter and the following one, not least because noetic sanctification (illumination) is consistently related to moral sanctification.

Anthropology: a Brief Sketch

Didymus' anthropology is basically dichotomous.[1] The living human is a "composite (σύνθετον)" of "body (σῶμα)" and "soul (ψυχή)."[2] The soul and the body are of different natures: the one is spiritual and the other material.[3] To the body are ascribed the powers of perceiving the sensible world; the soul is, on the other hand, the animating principle of the body and that which perceives the spiritual world and is (thus) the *locus* of human participation in God. The soul, not the body, is made in the image of God[4] and is therefore the means by which humanity shares in the divine life. Yet the unity achieved between the body and the soul is such that the soul shares, by the senses of the body, in the perception of the material world, while the soul renders the body "alive (ἔμψυχος)."[5] Between the two there is no absolute division; the union achieved in the composite is such that each shares to some extent in the properties of the other.

Though Didymus is not forthcoming in CZ about protological issues relating to the formation of the material body and the soul's pre-existence, there are sections of the CZ that only appear to make sense in light of Didymus' clearer affirmations of the soul's virtuous pre-existence elsewhere. We need

---

1. With Reynolds, "Man, Incarnation, and Trinity," 9. See also Gesché, *La christologie*, 130–131, and Ghattas, *Die Christologie*, 233. For the most persuasive and complete discussion of Didymus' dichotomy or trichotomy, see 'Ορφανός, *Ἡ ψυχὴ καὶ τὸ σῶμα*, 60–74. Didymus' adoption of the tripartite schema σῶμα—ψυχή—νοῦς (see CZ IV.235) is primarily a polemical move, inveighing against ontologically deficient conceptions of the humanity assumed by the Son (especially Apollinarian denial of a higher soul in Christ). Didymus thinks of the rational dimension (νοῦς) and spiritual dimension (πνεῦμα) of the human person as inhering within the ψυχή, and not as separate elements within the human composite.

2. See CZ IV.180. This is the closest Didymus comes to providing a definition of ἄνθρωπος in the Commentary.

3. See CZ III.312–314.

4. See CZ III.314.

5. CZ IV.181.

only sketch the critical features of this doctrine that other studies have identified. Didymus affirms that the soul is originally created "in the image and likeness of God" and is endowed with a spiritual body in which it dwelt for a time in paradise with God.[6] Though it is unclear whether Didymus conceives of a protological state that is entirely incorporeal, as certain remarks in the *GenT* suggest, it is certain that he associates the skin tunics of Genesis 3:21 with the soul's assumption of materially-embodied existence. The spiritually-embodied soul takes on a material body that is by nature prone to decay and change.

The "soul (ψυχή)" then, which can ordinarily be rendered in *CZ* as "the rational soul,"[7] is united to a corporeal "body (σῶμα)" whereby it is affected by "passions for things material."[8] Corporeally-embodied existence occasions the soul's struggle against the passions for life with God. Didymus provides further clarity to this dynamic psychology by adopting the Platonic tradition's use of the "rational (λογιστικόν)," "appetitive (ἐπιθυμητικόν)," and "passionate (θυμικόν)" powers of the soul.[9] The higher of the powers is the λογιστικόν—or the "intellect (νοῦς)"—which is receptive to reason and is the power by which the soul gains some apprehension of God.[10] Although the lower powers frequently arouse the passions within the soul, they are not an evil in themselves, but are to be converted so that the soul's affective capacities are directed toward their true goal. They are converted when they are ruled by the "intellect" so as to direct the course of a person's life in accordance with reason. Didymus seems to have this scenario in mind when he speaks of there being a

---

6. Didymus clearly asserts the soul's pre-existence to the *material* body. The faultline issue on Didymus' understanding of the pre-existence of the soul to material embodiedness centers on whether he asserts a two-fold or singular movement of the soul toward material corporeality. Is the soul in its pristine condition purely incorporeal, becoming embodied in a spiritual body (such as the angels possess) at some stage before the creation of the cosmos, and then becoming embodied in materiality with the sin of the protoplasts? Or is the movement singular: is some kind of body always assumed in created existence, the protoplasts thus moving from spiritual embodiedness (their pristine condition) to material embodiedness with the transgression of the divine command? For some important studies on the question, see Simonetti, "Didymiana," 129–142, and Steiger, "Theological Anthropology," 363 (who take the singular movement view), and Layton, *Didymus the Blind and His Circle*, 85–113 (whose position is more ambiguous).

7. Reynolds, 10. He notes in this connection that terms or phrases like ψυχή, νοῦς, ἔσω ἄνθρωπος, διάνοια, and καρδία are all directly ascribed with the capacity for spiritual sensation, and are more or less synonymous within the Commentary.

8. Cf. *DT* 3.1 (773BC and 777B).

9. See Ὀρφανός, 139–145. Cf. Placid Solari, "Christ as Virtue in Didymus the Blind," in *Purity of Heart in Early Ascetic and Monastic Literature* (Collegeville, MN: Liturgical Press, 1999), 77–78.

10. On the equivalence of the λογιστικόν and the νοῦς, see Ὀρφανός, 141.

throne in the soul for which two pretenders, "anger" and "reason," strive for mastery.[11]

Where the mind is not ordered by the truth, the soul is plunged into great darkness. The moral function of the soul, its "governing faculty (τὸ ἡγεμονικόν)," is paralyzed. Didymus likens those in habitual sin and those under the influence of heresy both to people who inflict wounds on others and to those who are inflicted by deadly weapons. In both instances, the cause of this distress is a "broken" ἡγεμονικόν.[12] When the lower powers of the soul gain control of the soul's governing faculty, confusion and unruly behavior are the consequence.[13]

The person's "spirit (πνεῦμα)" is rightly regarded, not as a third element within Didymus' ontologically dichotomous description of the human composite,[14] but is better understood as a description of the "soul" in a certain condition. Solari rightly attaches no ontological weight to the word "spirit," arguing that it functions primarily in a dynamic anthropology concerned with illustrating the diametric opposition between the "flesh" and the "spirit" in struggle for the soul.[15] Ὀρφανός' trajectory is similar to Solari's. He collects the various texts on the human πνεῦμα and concludes along similar lines that the word "spirit"—when used in its special sense in differentiation from "soul"—

---

11. *CZ* III.113.

12. The adulterer is like one whose ἡγεμονικόν is rent asunder by a scythe (*CZ* I.360); the "broken bows" of the heretics are their "governing faculties" (τὰ ἡγεμονικά), whence evil words issue like sharpened arrows (III.188).

13. It is beyond the scope of this study to examine whether Didymus conceives of the ἡγεμονικόν as a "part" of the soul in distinction from the νοῦς, as Ὀρφανός claims (p. 155). *CZ* offers little help in this matter, as Doutreleau recognizes (*Sur Zacharie*, 101).

14. See Reynolds, 20–23, for this argument. Reynolds takes the passage in *CZ* IV.182–184 as warrant for this move. He argues that Didymus means to distinguish πνεῦμα and λογικὴ ψυχή (or καρδία) here 1) because he is unwilling to attribute formation (πλάσις) to the uncreated (!) element in man and 2) because he means to show that the spirit is the principle of the rational soul's pedagogical formation. There are antecedents in Didymus for the second argument, where πνεῦμα is described as training the ψυχή. The first argument is suspect on several points. Reynolds defends it grammatically by suggesting that the two genitive phrases πλάσις . . . αὐτοῦ and τῆς τοῦ πνεύματος πλάσεως (IV.183–184) are to be read as subjective genitives, where the spirit is the agent rather than the object of formation. However, reading a subjective genitive at this point would demand a somewhat opaque shift in logic within Didymus' comparison: "the formation of [the spirit] is unlike the formation of the body" (IV.183). One would be required to read the first genitive as subjective and the second as objective. More importantly, earlier in the same argument (the argument starts in IV.182), Didymus uses the phrase τὸ πλαττόμενον πνεῦμα, explicitly noting that the "spirit" is formed. Whatever distinction Didymus sees between the πνεῦμα and the λογικὴ ψυχή here—he distinguishes the two in IV.182—, appealing to the "spirit" as a third element in Didymus' anthropology seems to create more problems than it solves.

15. Solari, "Christ as Virtue," 78–79.

does not designate an ontologically distinct other within the human person, but rather emphasizes the soul in a certain condition. The soul, constantly in the state of flux, is called "spirit" when it is receptive to the grace of the Holy Spirit.[16]

It follows from the above then that the human person is constantly pulled between two poles. On the one hand, there is the allure of the passions and the imitation of evil occasioned by the soul's love of material pleasures and its conjunction with the material body; on the other hand, there is the beauty of divine truth and the participation in the divine life.[17] Placing a premium on the freedom of the will against static conceptions of the human soul (Manichean perhaps), Didymus endorses the notion that the soul is constantly and independently mobile.[18] When it is oriented God-ward, the movement of the soul is unhindered; when it is oriented toward the passions, it is described as nearly immobilized.[19] The effects upon the body are inversely described: the body is skittish and wild when its rider (the soul) loses control.[20]

On Virtue

For Didymus, then, the soul is perfected and guarded from passion when it pursues the virtues. The divine pedagogy consists in revealing the virtues to the Christian and enabling participation in them. It is by the continual practice of the virtues that a person discovers peace and finds rest from the barrage of the passions that war against the soul. And for Didymus, as we have intimated in the section on the Spirit's being the source of every virtue, the virtues are conceived of both as resident without the possibility of change in God[21] and as being available to created natures only because the virtues have real existence in him.[22]

---

16. Ὀρφανός, 56–57.

17. I distinguish between "imitation" and "participation" here because, while evil may be imitated it is not something in which one can "participate." The goodness that God is, however, is that in which humans can participate, since it has 1) real existence and is 2) the substantial reality underlying all creaturely forms of goodness, as the following section will show.

18. *CZ* I.43. See Ὀρφανός, 130, for the philosophical antecedents of this idea.

19. See *CZ* III.310. Those who are lovers of pleasure and enslaved to the passions are in a condition "somewhere close to immobility (ἐγγύς που τοῦ ἀκινήτου)."

20. *CZ* III.270.

21. See Layton, *Didymus and His Circle*, 47: "Christ is the summation of the virtues, in whom righteousness does not exist as a "condition" or a "disposition"—that is, as a quality subject to *alloiōsis*—but whose existence as consubstantial with God means that he "is" righteousness. . . . Individual souls become perfect through obtaining the virtues that God's "only-begotten" possesses "without change" (*atreptos*)."

22. See Solari, 81: "Virtue, as a good which exists, has the foundation of its existence in God. This identification of virtue with God is the core of Didymus' theory of

As some important studies indicate, critical to Didymus' "theology as a whole" is his distinction between natures that are able to be partaken of and those that partake.[23] The fact that each *hypostasis* of the Trinity is, in Jerome's Latin, "capabilis (able to be partaken of)" has felicitous consequences. As Heron notes with particular clarity, the gifts of the Spirit, such as they exist among creatures, are "not simply a matter of some external operation of God upon creatures, nor the mere infusion of qualities into them. [They are] a genuine participation in God, enabled by a genuine communication of himself."[24] Where, then, virtue exists among creatures, it exists because there is a participation in God. Thus Didymus eliminates from the very outset the idea that true virtue can be had without the self-communication of God.

In light of the above, Didymus' operative definitions of the word ἀρετή in *CZ* demand some clarification. For Didymus appears to use the word quite broadly to signify two separate semantic fields: 1) the practice of virtue, and 2) the disposition or condition of the soul in separation from its practice. Likewise, he regularly distinguishes between two kinds of virtue: the practical and contemplative. What is the significance of these distinctions? For on an overly-literal reading of portions of the *CZ* one might conclude on the basis of these distinctions that Didymus conceives of a hard line drawn between the moral and contemplative life.

Didymus' frequent employment of the word ἀρετή together with phrases like: "and its practice" or "and the actions done in accordance with it," suggests that a virtue is in some sense separable, at least conceptually, from its practice. For instance, when discussing the rewards given to the virtuous person, he writes that "each virtue, and the works done in accordance with it, possesses (ἔχει) its own particular crown."[25] And not long afterward, he discusses "the particular virtues and the works they produce, the fruits of righteousness."[26] Unless he is speaking pleonastically, Didymus is using the term "virtue" to speak of a state or habit that conditions the soul, of which virtuous action is the consequence.

On other occasions, however, Didymus appears to use the term differently, referring to the activity. Interpreting a passage on justice and truth, he proposes that truth "signifies the hidden and elevated vision of the pious doctrines" whereas righteousness is "virtue of an ethical and practical charac-

---

virtue." Ibid., 83: "God is the source of virtue. Humans are virtuous not by nature but by participation."

23. Plaxco, "Metaphysics of Participation," 231. Heron, "The Holy Spirit in Origen and Didymus the Blind," 301–304.

24. Ibid., 303.

25. *CZ* II.20.

26. *CZ* II.57. For other instances of the same division, see II.139, II.248, II.347, and V.137.

ter."[27] In another, and even clearer instance, Didymus speaks of "the corrective instruction of ethics and the corresponding practical virtue" which are both prelude to the study of "the knowledge of God's mysteries."[28] Though Didymus occasionally speaks of "practical virtue" in terms that suggest the conception rather than the performance of this kind of virtue, here he clearly means its practice.

This distinction helps us interpret places where it seems that Didymus might endorse a distinction between "contemplative virtue" and the doctrines of the faith. In perhaps the clearest instance of this in the CZ, Didymus distinguishes "the various practical and contemplative (διανοητικαὶ) virtues" and the "fruitful doctrines of piety."[29] Unless the phrase is pleonastic, then the possibility arises that Didymus conceives of a set of contemplative virtues that serves as a middle term between the doctrines of the faith and the moral life. This could, in turn, be taken to be a kind of philosophical contemplation that is preparatory to spiritual vision.

But, on the basis of Didymus' usage of the term "virtue" alone, it would be difficult to build a case for this possibility for two reasons: 1) Didymus most frequently makes it clear when he is distinguishing virtue from spiritual knowledge or piety that he is using "virtue" to refer to its practice. In an example of this, Didymus contrasts two pairs of terms which are strictly supplementary to one another: "the practice of vice" and "ignorance" are contrasted with "ethical virtue" and "divine knowledge."[30] 2) On one occasion, he informs us that he means nothing other than the "knowledge of the truth" by the phrase "contemplative virtue."[31] Once this is observed, it is clear that Didymus—at least on the basis of his "virtue" vocabulary—does not draw a distinct line between spiritual knowledge and contemplation. They are, for him, one and the same.

The Contemplative and the Active Life

In keeping with his anthropology, Didymus develops the moral function of the soul in terms of the interior vision of the human person. The human "heart (καρδία)," or "spirit (πνεῦμα)," is malleable because it is receptive to the "impression of thoughts and rational images (τύπωσιν ἐννοιῶν καὶ λογικῶν φαντασιῶν)." Rightly formed or habitually trained in virtue and sanctification, the human heart is purified so as to "act and think clearly and har-

---

27. CZ II.302.
28. CZ III.252.
29. CZ V.169.
30. CZ IV.17. For the same pairing, cf. V.6.
31. See CZ I.409: "For it is [possible] to be of an erroneous opinion concerning both practical and contemplative virtue, which is nothing other than the knowledge of the truth" (Ἔστιν γὰρ ψευδοδοξεῖν καὶ περὶ τὴν πρακτικὴν ἀρετὴν καὶ τὴν διανοητικήν, οὐκ ἄλλην οὖσαν τῆς γνώσεως τῆς ἀληθείας).

moniously."[32] When the person's intellective capacity is habitually oriented toward God, the person becomes capable of right action. Conversely, the practice of virtue forms the heart so that its vision is purified.

Thus when Didymus draws up a division between "two forms of virtue," it is crucial to remember that he does not intend to suggest that some virtues are purely contemplative while others are purely practical. Every active virtue has some basis in the soul's interior vision of the truth, while every contemplative virtue gives rise to virtuous activity. This is why, for him, errors about one form always have consequences for the other.[33] The Jewish error regarding the proper practice of the Law was, for Didymus, rooted in the failure of their contemplative vision. They were devoted to the practice of the Law, but their "meditation" on the Law was futile as long as they failed to distinguish its spirit from its letter. Thus they failed to discern the true moral sense of the Scriptures, putting into effect that which the Law commanded for a time while remaining ignorant of its lasting import.[34]

The distinction between the two kinds of life—active and contemplative—is developed at greatest length near the beginning of Book 3. Didymus divides the "words of God" into two categories: the first kind concerning "virtue of a moral and practical kind" and the second kind "things mystical and meriting contemplation (τῶν γνωστικῶν καὶ ἐποπτικῶν)." The former virtues are "to be enacted (ποιεῖσθαι)"; the latter are "to be discerned through the interior vision (θεωρεῖσθαι)."[35] Didymus develops both categories at length in this section, arguing that some Scriptures are given for one purpose, others for another.[36]

That the contrast does not imply that moral and contemplative instructions are separable is, however, made clear in a paragraph near the beginning of the argument. Didymus argues that it is fitting for "ethical instructions" to be pursued in a manner consonant with each virtue's end: justice is to be pursued justly, temperance temperately. What Didymus means by this observation is explained, with Didymus twice repeating the observation that the practical virtues are to be pursued with understanding (νόησιν αὐτῶν ἔχειν . . . σὺν νοήσει). People behave virtuously only when they are conformed in their interior life to the virtues that Jesus commands. Didymus cites Jesus' words in the

---

32. *CZ* IV.183.

33. See *CZ* I.409, with Doutreleau, *Sur Zacharie*, 409. Didymus takes the two bronze mountains of Zechariah 6:1 as symbolic of obstacles raised against the knowledge of God. He devotes a separate discussion to the significance of their two-foldness and concludes: ἀσεβοῦσι γὰρ οἱ ἀπὸ τῶν αἱρέσεων περὶ ἀμφότερα τὰ εἴδη τῆς ἀρετῆς. The two obstacles against the truth, errors regarding practical and speculative virtue, occur together.

34. See *CZ* V.146-148.
35. *CZ* III.5.
36. *CZ* III.8-15.

conclusion of the Sermon on the Mount to the same effect: the life of the disciple of Christ is characterized both by hearing and acting. Only the one who approaches Jesus both by listening to him and putting into action what he says is made wise.[37]

In light of these passages, I posit that there are two aspects of Didymus' teaching on the virtues that are of significance in attempting to give an account of his teaching on the pursuit of the moral life. Moral virtue and contemplative virtue are 1) inseparably and 2) asymmetrically related. Bienert has made the former argument in his important discussion of the introduction to Book 3, noting that "the inviolable unity"[38] between the contemplative and practical life is implied in Didymus' treatment of the terms σοφία and γνῶσις. If the former is largely ethical in its import and the latter is largely spiritual, they are nevertheless related in such a way that it is "nearly impossible to draw up a division between a spiritual and a moral sense of Scripture within Didymus' exegesis."[39] True knowledge—which is above all the knowledge of God—and true virtue are a unity. The practical life is inseparable and derivative from the contemplative.

Contemplative virtue is privileged over moral.[40] In one notable instance of this, Didymus describes Christian "shepherds" as those entrusted with overseeing "the practical life" and "good works." In addition to these things they are to pass on "the faith and counsels of Christians in a non-elevated manner (οὐκ ἀνηγμένως)."[41] Far from deprecating the office, Didymus recognizes the need for Christian teachers to adapt their teaching to the dispositions of their audience; spiritual milk, not solid meat, is most needful for the infants in Christ.[42] But there is a need for infants in Christ to grow up to maturity. In another example of this superiority of the "contemplative life," Didymus implicitly argues that it reveals and directs the "active life," just as the lamp sheds light on the lamp-stand below.[43]

---

37. *CZ* III.7. Though "seeing" is Didymus' primary mode of speaking about the interior life in *CZ*, "hearing" also plays an important role. The "eyes" and the "ears" of the Body of Christ are consistently related to the contemplative dimension of the Christian life; the "hands" and "feet" are consistently related to its active dimension.

38. Bienert, *"Allegoria" und "Anagoge"*, 75. He speaks of "die unaufgebbare Einheit vom θεωρητικός und πρακτικός βίος des Menschen."

39. Ibid.: "Aus diesem Grunde ist es fast unmöglich, innerhalb der Exegese des Didymos zwischen einem geistlichen und einem moralischen Schriftsinn zu unterscheiden, obwohl Didymos den ethischen Sinn einer Textstelle gelegentlich hervorhebt."

40. Cf. Doutreleau, *Sur Zacharie*, 106: "[L]a vie théorique est plus haute."

41. *CZ* IV.51.

42. Cf. *CZ* I.32-34. The motif of infancy in spiritual matters is common in the NT. See, e.g., 1 Corinthians 3:1-2 and Hebrews 5:11-14.

43. *CZ* I.290.

Numerous other instances within the *CZ* could be produced. It is sufficient for our purposes to note that, just as the two kinds of life are inseparable in Didymus, so the moral is governed by the contemplative. And these observations have a major implication for the main theme of this chapter: the moral life being inseparable from the contemplative life, it is impossible to pursue a study of the moral life *per se*. Since the pursuit of the moral life *always* involves some level of understanding of the doctrines of piety, it is essential to articulate the doctrinal basis of Didymus' ethical instructions.

The Incarnation and the Moral Life

The doctrinal basis of Didymus' account of the moral life is the Incarnation of the Logos, as I will argue below. It is by perceiving the prophet's vision of the Incarnate Word that the Christian community is informed as to the meaning of Zechariah for the present and future life of the Church. In this section, I examine the christological turn of Didymus' exegesis particularly in relation to what it reveals about the possibilities of the sanctified life. I examine this theme in relation to several recurring motifs in the *CZ*.

Clouds and Heavens

The first motif is that of the clouds and heavens. In two discrete passages in the *CZ*, Didymus takes these images figurally, associating them primarily with Christ as the perfect embodiment of virtue and the *locus* of their availability to us. Didymus secondarily relates the images to the saints as those who mediate virtue to us, insofar as they imitate Christ. In the first of these passages, Didymus is interpreting the second chapter of Zechariah, which concludes with the Lord's promise to return and dwell in the midst of his people. The scope of the reference to God's people broadens not only to include the returned exiles but also the peoples of many nations (2:14-16). Zechariah strikes a note of imminence in the final words of the prophecy: "Let all flesh show reverence before the Lord, for he *has aroused himself* (ἐξεγήγερται) from his holy clouds" (2:17).

Given the themes under discussion: 1) the inclusion of the Gentiles in the people of God and 2) the promise of the Lord's imminent appearing, it is not surprising that Didymus gives the concluding lemma (2:17) a christological interpretation.[44] He begins by asking: what are the referents of the terms "flesh" and "holy clouds"? Surveying the various definitions of "flesh" in the Scriptures, Didymus argues that only one of these definitions makes sense of the imperative: "be reverent (εὐλαβεῖσθω)!" The flesh under discussion here must be capable of reverence for God. Therefore, he argues, the term "flesh" refers to rational humanity. In parallel development, the "holy clouds" do not

---

44. Didymus' treatment of the lemma occurs in *CZ* I.168-181.

discharge a "sensible downpour." The wording of the text—i.e. *holy* clouds—suggests to him a figural interpretation. Finding a promising parallel in Isaiah's vineyard allegory (5:6), Didymus takes Zechariah's holy clouds "in an anagogical sense (κατὰ ἀναγωγήν)"[45] as a reference to the "divine prophets." These holy clouds rain down "righteousness (δικαιοσύνη)" (Isa 45:8). They are holy because they are "inspired (κάτοχοι) by the Holy Spirit."[46]

The lemma under interpretation therefore exhorts every rational being to show reverence before the one who has come in fulfillment of the Law and the

---

45. For the best discussion of the anagogical sense of Scripture in *CZ*, see Bienert, 69-109. For his summary of the term ἀναγωγή's use in the rest of the corpus as well, see pp. 160-164. I assume Bienert's understanding of the term ἀναγωγή in what follows: the word is primarily descriptive of Scripture's spiritual sense. The anagogical sense of Scripture has a pedagogic function "by which it shows men the way to God and brings them forward on this way (indem sie dem Menschen den Weg zu Gott zeigen und ihn auf diesem Weg voranbringen)." Bienert argues that it is sometimes possible to discern a distinction between the terms ἀναγωγή and ἀλληγορία, with the latter often serving as an aid in the discovery of the spiritual sense. Didymus sees a difference between allegorical interpretation (ἀλληγορία) and the spiritual significance (ἀναγωγή) of a text (pp. 106-107), but at times the semantic ranges of the words overlap considerably.

A very different articulation of the terms is given by Tigcheler in his *Exégèse allégorique*. He prefers to see the term ἀναγωγή in *CZ* as signifying the fourth stage in Didymus' hermeneutical schema. For Tigcheler, Didymus portrays the reading of Scripture as a four-stage process in which the interpreter brings four questions to bear on every text. 1) What is the text saying as such (πρὸς ῥητόν)? 2) What transpired from the perspective of the facts or of material perception (καθ' ἱστορίαν)? 3) Is what is written intended as a figure (κατ' ἀλληγορίαν)? 4) If the answer to the third question is a "yes" what is the significance of the text (κατ' ἀναγωγήν) (pp. 154-159)? But it is difficult to escape the conclusion that Tigcheler's schema is too elegant a description of Didymus' hermeneutical practice. The argument is most forced in his discussion of allegory. To prevent the two final questions from collapsing into one another, he asserts that ἀλληγορεῖσθαι is "the simple assertion that a word or a phrase may be considered as a figure (la simple constatation qu'un mot ou une phrase peuvent être considérés comme une image)" (p. 131) but is not "an interpretation of the figural language (interprétation du langage figuré)" (p. 132). Didymus does not seem to have observed such a distinction, readily interpreting the allegory that he has identified without appealing to another hermeneutical move. And Tigcheler's thesis has met with limited success in terms of its distinction between the other moves as well. See Emanuela Prinzivalli, *Didimo il Cieco e l'interpretazione dei Salmi* (Rome: L'Aquila, 1988), 25n8, who argues that there is no tangible distinction between ἱστορία and ῥητόν in the *PsT* (pp. 23-25). For more recent assessments, see Layton, *Didymus the Blind and His Circle*, 173n68, and Steiger, 131-140. Though approving of the study as a whole for the *CZ*, Steiger nevertheless notes that Tigcheler's hermeneutical framework is not supported by *GenT*, which "appears rather to have a two part structure for the majority of individual lemmata" (p. 134). However, as I will note later, Tigcheler rightly critiques Bienert's understanding of the "literal" and "historical/sensible" levels of interpretation.

46. In summary of *CZ* I.168-173 and 175.

Prophets: the Savior. Spending some of the capital of his earlier identifications, Didymus revisits the terms "flesh" and "cloud," this time with reference to the Incarnation. Appealing to Isaiah 19:1, Didymus argues that the Son took on a "light cloud"—"flesh" with no experience of sin—when he entered into the world.[47] Jesus' soul, the rational dimension of the humanity the Son assumes in the Incarnation, is guilty of no sin but rather clings to righteousness. Didymus concludes his reflections on Jesus' assumption of "flesh" by noting that he became the "cloud" that rained down righteousness. This righteousness is productive of three kinds of benefits for others: 1) saving fruits, 2) covering from the heat of temptation, and 3) shelter from the cold of sin.[48]

Didymus concludes the section with a parenesis that recapitulates most of the elements of his interpretation. His readers are to take the text in hand "with discernment," having a fleshly heart that is obedient to God's commands. In this way they will practice the "reverence" of which the text speaks; in return God will inscribe on their fleshly hearts divine letters by his living Spirit, so that they will pass from a partial vision to the vision that is "face to face."[49] What are these commands? Didymus does not specify here, but they are clearly spelled out earlier. The Son's assumption of a complete humanity (Didymus' "rational flesh") generates certain possibilities and imperatives for the Christian life. "The understanding person (ὁ νοήμων)"—namely, the one who interprets this text with an eye discerning the significance of the Son's Incarnation in appropriate reverence—will produce beneficial fruits and be preserved from temptation and sin by the Son.

Didymus' characterization of the prophets in the passage is closely tied both to the Son's own performance of his humanity and to Didymus' parenetic turn. The prophets are, like the Incarnate Son, characterized as productive of "righteousness" in others. They embody a holiness born of participation in the Holy Spirit that Didymus commends to his audience. By practicing reverence for the Savior to whom they attest, Didymus' audience is made participant in the same Spirit who inspired the prophets. The prophets are held up as examples of those who are at the very least somewhere further along the path of being conformed to the Incarnate Son.

In a later passage in the Commentary, Didymus associates the "heaven" and "dew" of Zechariah 8:11–12 with the cooperation of the saints in the bestowal of the gifts of heaven.[50] Dealing with Zechariah's enumeration of the promised restoration of the land to God's people, a text that promises the dew of heaven to the parched land, Didymus passes quickly over the "literal sense

---

47. The connection between this passage of Isaiah and the body assumed by the Son in his appearance is repeatedly made by Eusebius of Caesarea. See, e.g., his *Dem. ev.* 6.20.2 and 8.5.4 (GCS 23:285 and 401).

48. In summary of *CZ* I.174–180.

49. *CZ* I.181.

50. *CZ* II.328–343.

(πρὸς ῥητόν)" of the passage before settling into an interpretation that treats the elements of the passage "spiritually (νοητῶς)."[51] The land, or the soul, is made spiritually fruitful at the coming of the dew from heaven.[52]

Didymus identifies "heaven" with each person who "bears the image of the heavenly man." These people are the "heavens" of Psalm 18:2 LXX, who "recount the glory of God" and rejoice together with the Savior when they are conformed to him. They are also those of whom St Paul speaks as faithfully and truly revering God, predestined to be conformed to the image of the Son, the heavenly man.[53] Didymus articulates this conformation to the Son in terms of their conspicuous attainment of "moral and contemplative virtue." They, both collectively and individually, yield their spiritual dew to others. Was not Moses, he argues, held up as an example of one whose moral and contemplative instruction descended like the dew?[54]

As in the earlier discussion of clouds, Didymus notes that this dew is "chiefly (προηγουμένως)" the gift of the "Lord of the heavens." Though those zealous in pursuit of the active and contemplative life are to look to the saints, they are primarily directed toward the one to whom the saints are conformed. Didymus concludes the reflection by giving the passage an eschatological rendering. Implying a comparison between the dead and plants, Didymus says that the dew from the Lord of the heavens (the Son) will cause those who are in the tombs to arise at the general resurrection. Didymus then makes a quantitative distinction between human reception of the dew in the present age and that in the age to come, when the partial knowledge passes away.[55]

Both the above passages reveal that Didymus' moral program is closely tied to the imitation of Christ. Didymus exalts Christ as the one by whom the

---

51. Summarizing *CZ* II.329–338. For the sense πρὸς ῥητόν Bienert is too restrictive when he speaks of this level of reading as "an immanent understanding (ein immanentes Verstehen)" of the text (p. 108). Didymus develops the πρὸς ῥητόν meaning of some texts in directions that assume a great deal of involvement from things that are not "visible" or "sensible" (see, e.g., *CZ* I.208–212). Doutreleau (*Sur Zacharie*, 51) does better when he speaks of the sense πρὸς ῥητόν as an interpretation of the text that follows from taking the words "as they sound." I take this reading to be a non-figural mode of exegesis, preferring to translate the phrase with "in the literal sense" to preserve Didymus' parlance. The presence of an intended figure was, in Didymus' mind, cause to abandon this sense in search of a more adequate mode of rendering the text's meaning. In this Didymus' vocabulary runs parallel to Origen's. See de Lubac's discussion of "proper literal sense" in *History and Spirit*, 129–130, and his *Medieval Exegesis* II:14–15: "[Origen] says that "the letter" . . . is missing, where we, to signify the very same thing, would say that the text presents a figurative or metaphorical literal sense."

52. *CZ* II.337–338. The land-soul figure is one Didymus uses regularly in the *CZ*. He is drawing from Jesus' Parable of the Sower (Matt 13:1–23).

53. Didymus cites Romans 8:29 and 1 Corinthians 15:49.

54. Summarizing *CZ* II.339–341. He cites Deuteronomy 32:2.

55. *CZ* II.342–343. Presumably Didymus goes here under pressure from Isaiah 26:19.

saints are transformed and to whom the saints are conformed. The extent of the saints' conformity to the Son is such that the saints can be said to confer their own virtues upon others. There are, however, two distinctions that are continually made between receptivity to Christ's virtues and receiving the virtues of the saints in the exegetical corpus: 1) the virtues of the saints are quantitatively inferior to those present in Christ and 2) the saints may be imitated, while only Christ may be both imitated and partaken of. Only the first of these distinctions is clearly found here, and it does not in itself rescue Didymus' christological vision from the charge of exemplarism: Christ's virtue is chief among the saints since he is the Lord of the heavens, the light cloud whose sinless flesh is without equal. Of the virtues revealed by the Son in the Incarnation, righteousness[56] is chief in the above. Didymus does not clearly define the extent to which the righteousness of Christ can be said to be realized in the saints, but he is clear that they are enjoined to pursue its realization.

Building the House of God

The restoration of the temple is a theme that figures largely in the prophet Zechariah. It is impossible to do justice to Didymus' treatment of the theme without ranging broadly through the Commentary. Didymus is keen to reveal the spiritual import of the rebuilding of the temple, giving the phrase "house of God" a number of figural interpretations. His central interpretation, however, takes the "house of God" as a figure for the humanity assumed by the Savior. Clearly dependent upon this figure are two others that Didymus regularly joins to it: the ecclesial and the individual dimensions of the divine house.

"My House Will Be Rebuilt in Her" [57]

Didymus first treats the rebuilding of the temple in Jerusalem in connection with the Lord's promise to extend his measuring line over the city (Zech 1:16). He explicitly avoids the treatment of the "measuring-line" at this juncture, because its development would prevent him from making his central interpretive identification of the "house" with the humanity assumed by the Savior.[58] This "house," he argues, was born of Mary and built by divine Wisdom.

---

56. For an important discussion of this virtue, see Solari, 82–83. Didymus elsewhere in the corpus distinguishes between particular virtues and virtue in general. "Righteousness" is occasionally treated as the summation of all the virtues (cf. *PsT* 59,3-7), but in the above passage it is perceived as a particular virtue.

57. *CZ* I.70-74.

58. In *CZ* I.71, Didymus promises to treat the "measuring-line" later in the Commentary. He fulfills his promise in I.105 when commenting on Zechariah 2:1-2. Here Didymus places the "measuring-line" in the hand of Jerusalem's divine architect, the Savior, and takes it as a figure for the "angels and holy men who are co-builders with

In his fairly brief exposition of the meaning of the phrase "house of God," Didymus hardly moves beyond three identifications and a brief scriptural defense for each. The "house" can be interpreted as 1) the Church of the living God, 2) the humanity of Jesus, and 3) each one of the faithful. In each of these God dwells. An unfortunate lacuna follows, in which Didymus provides some discussion of the terms "temple," "house," and "dwelling." This particular collection of terms suggests the possibility that Didymus says something here about the goal of the Christian life, contrasting the permanence of these structures with the tents that serve the pilgrims in their journey toward perfection.[59] Whatever the case, Didymus does not get beyond stating the three figural referents of the phrase "house of God." The second referent—the assumed humanity of the Savior—plays a significant role in the interpretation of what follows.

"Let Your Hands Be Strong"[60]

Later in Zechariah, the Lord urges the builders of the temple to be strong and to remember the words of the former prophets who foresaw the completion of the house of God: "Let your hands be strong, you who are listening in these days to these words from the mouth of the prophets, from the day when the house of the Lord Almighty was founded until the day the temple was built" (8:9). Clarifying how the text should be read,[61] Didymus isolates two important features of the text: 1) the second set of days ("from the day . . . until the day") are "former days," 2) the condition for the fulfillment of the command is to understand properly how the words of the prophets relate to the time when the house of the Lord is founded.[62]

With these determinations in mind, Didymus launches on an interpretation of the text. "Hands," he argues, are the active powers of the soul that grow strong when the moral teachings are enacted. The words of the prophets are these moral teachings. The text enjoins its hearers to enact the moral teachings of the prophets. But when, Didymus reasons, will the teachings of the prophets be zealously pursued in both a true and godly fashion? This can only happen, he notes, when the divine house is founded as in the "former days." And what is this house? If one expects a historical report at this juncture, Didymus' development is surprising. The "house of God" is the same as

---

him" by their active power (ἐν τῇ πρακτικῇ δυνάμει). Given this latter identification, Didymus cannot then associate the building of Jerusalem and the house of God within it with the humanity assumed by the Savior.

59. Cf. *CZ* V.161–164.

60. *CZ* II.307–315.

61. Didymus shows a great deal of flexibility in his procedure. See Doutreleau, *Sur Zacharie*, 64–65. But more often than not he begins his interpretation with a brief clarification of this kind, often isolating certain aspects of the text that he will develop further. Cf. pp. 50–52.

62. *CZ* II.308.

the one that Wisdom built, the body prepared by the Father for the Incarnate Lord. He provisionally concludes his first interpretation: "Once the aforementioned house with its foundations is built like a holy temple, *the hands*—that is, the active faculties—are strengthened according to the ancient illuminating insights, called *days*."[63]

As subsequent paragraphs suggest—where Didymus treats the imperative from the point-of-view of the coming of the Gospel—Didymus appears to be wrestling here with the question of how a command that assumes knowledge of the Incarnation could be kept before the time of the Incarnation, since he identifies the building of the temple precisely with the creation of the Savior's body. Zechariah's reference to "former days" is an awkward detail of the text for his christological development. Didymus could argue that the "house" is a reference to the Temple and thus avoid the problem altogether. However, instead Didymus resolves the aporia by arguing that these "former days" are "former illuminating visions" that Zechariah's audience possessed.

The solution is incomprehensible without assuming the luminous preexistence of the soul. The illuminating effects of the Incarnation could be conceived of as prior to life before the Incarnation of the Savior only if one grants that the knowledge communicated by this event was somehow present to humanity prior to materially-embodied existence.[64] The saints before the coming of the Incarnation were somehow capable of drawing on a prior memory of the glory of the Son of God.

In his interpretation of the lemma Didymus then passes on to two other interpretations of the "house of God." Both are now anticipated: the "Church of the living God" and "each of the pious." With reference to the former, Di-

---

63. *CZ* II.310 (FC 111:173, emphases original).

64. Doutreleau suggests this line of interpretation (*Sur Zacharie* 579n3): "Ces φωτεινὰς θεωρίας font difficulté. S'agit-il des contemplations antérieures à la vie présente, que les âmes pratiquaient avant d'être emprisonnées dans les corps d'ici bas?" He suggests a second interpretation which, judging by his translation, he thinks less likely: "S'agit-il seulement des « théories », des points de vue d'autrefois (c'est-à-dire de l'A.T.), des vues éclairées d'autrefois qui permettaient aux hommes de l'A.T. de marcher dans la vérité?" With Doutreleau, I think the context favors the former. Wrestling with the question of how people in the OT could have kept a command that assumed the Incarnation, Didymus appeals to the notion of a luminous pre-existence of the soul. Though not as forthcoming about his commitment to the theory of pre-existence as he is elsewhere, Didymus nevertheless appeals to the notion in CZ when he speaks of the righteous being numerous "before the present life" (III.288). For an argument supporting the reading of this text as a reference to pre-existence of souls, see Peter Bouteneff, "Placing the Christology of Didymus the Blind," *Studia Patristica* 37 (2001): 393. A comment of similar import occurs in relation to the phrase: "tents saved as from the beginning" (Zech 12:7). Taking the tents as figures for "progress," Didymus argues that people are saved "as from the beginning when they attain the perfect state and virtue" (IV.224). Attaining perfection implies restoration to a prior condition.

dymus speaks of the completion of the house taking place at the time when all who adhere to the Gospel through perfect faith and virtue "are built on the foundation of the apostles and prophets, with Jesus Christ as its cornerstone, into a holy temple in the Lord, as a dwelling-place" for the Trinity." Severally conceived, the individual dwelling-places of God are to obey the command of the passage by doing that which is commanded in the Gospel.[65]

Didymus now relates every facet of his interpretation. Standing on the far side of the Incarnation, the disciples of Christ in Didymus' day recognize the true significance of Zechariah's moral imperative to be fully-revealed in the Gospel. By attending to the Gospel, they hear the words of the prophets in relation to their true end: the revelation of Christ and the life enabled in fellowship with him. Didymus highlights in the final paragraphs of his interpretation that his audience is living in the days when the prophecy has been fulfilled; the foundations of the house that Wisdom built were laid when the Holy Spirit came upon the Virgin. For this reason, the Son of God is present in power in the Church and in the followers of Christ, enabling them to grow in the moral precepts of the Gospel and to experience victory over their spiritual enemies. The founding of the "house" that is the body of Jesus is the basis of his confidence that the other interpretations will come to fulfillment as well. The Church and its members will triumph over vice by the "supernatural power (ἰσχὺν ὑπερφυῆ)" given to them by the One who is present with them as the Lord of his Body.[66]

For the first time, all three interpretations are clearly related to one another. The Incarnation proves to be the pivotal moment in articulating an account of the moral life. The Lord reveals in his own life the possibility of triumphing over vice, and enables the triumph of his ecclesial Body and its members over the same. The Church is built on the foundation-stone of Christ when, by participation in Christ, it follows in the path of his victorious life, being built up to maturity in faith and virtue. Didymus conceives of this as taking place on the individual level when the disciples of Christ obey the Gospel imperatives.

"Come to Him, the Living Stone" [67]

Didymus contributes to the development of the motif in the Commentary by addressing it in connection with other images as well. The "house of God" is composed of "stones," spiritually conceived. Didymus treats two disparate texts (Zech 3:8-9 and 9:15-16), as occasions to further develop the significance of Christ's Incarnation and the saints' imitation of his humanity. On the first occasion, the application of the text to our theme is by no means apparent. Didymus takes the "stone with seven eyes" as an opportunity to explore the

---

65. *CZ* II.311–312.
66. *CZ* II.313–315.
67. *CZ* I.254–261 and III.215–223.

Spirit's role in the Incarnation and draws applications from this for the stones that are built upon this cornerstone to form a spiritual "temple" and "house." In his conclusion to this first passage, Didymus strikingly describes each of these stones as "becoming an expiatory sacrifice (καθάρσιον)."[68] In the second passage, Didymus offers another description of these stones as holy "on account of their lightness [κοῦφον] and weightlessness [ἐλαφρόν]."[69]

Didymus notes that the "seven eyes" of the stone in the first passage are a reference to the Incarnate Savior's nature, which is "endowed with the sevenfold faculty of sight (τὴν ἑπταδύναμον διορατικὴν)." Equating this with Isaiah's enumeration of the seven gifts of the Holy Spirit,[70] Didymus argues that the Incarnate Son possesses the Spirit in a double sense. On the one hand, the first six gifts of the Spirit in Isaiah 11:1-3 are all proper to the Son's own nature; he is not endowed, for instance, with a wisdom that he did not formerly possess. On the other hand, Didymus struggles to accommodate the final gift of the Spirit, "fear (φόβος)," with something proper to the Son's divinity. He therefore establishes the semantic domain of the word under "reverence (εὐλάβεια)," recalling that this was said of the "man who is from Mary." This one prevailed with God in prayer because of his reverence (Heb 5:7). Didymus concludes: "He does not have reverence as God (καθὸ Θεός), but insofar as he is human (καθὸ ἄνθρωπός ἐστιν)."[71]

Didymus then appears to change directions somewhat in his interpretation. He suggests a range of scriptural texts in which the Son is referred to as stone (among them Psalm 117:22 LXX). Though rejected by men, he is the cornerstone upon which the Church is built. In him Jew and Gentile are reconstituted into one new human, forming one new "building (οἰκοδομή)." Though the platform has been laid for moving to the ecclesial interpretation via St Peter's reflection on Psalm 117, Didymus does not at first connect the "cornerstone" with the stones built upon him but writes that all who believe in this "cornerstone" become expiatory sacrifices themselves. He follows this observation with another, in which 1 Peter 2:4-7 is the subtext. Those who come to the living Word (St Peter's "living stone"), are themselves made alive, and form a spiritual house and altar upon which spiritual sacrifices are rendered to God. Didymus concludes the section with an exhortation: "May we also be-

---

68. *CZ* I.260. Doutreleau, *Sur Zacharie*, 328n1, notes that later readers of the text sought to emend the text here, though the reading is preferred as a *lectio difficilior* with considerable contextual support.

69. *CZ* III.222 (FC 111:229).

70. Hill (FC 111:80n50), seems to miss the connection between the number seven and the Isaiah passage when he says that "Didymus does not proceed to develop [the number's] significance." The seven-fold capacity of sight is followed immediately by four paragraphs that reflect on the seven gifts that the Spirit gives to the Incarnate Son, as Isaiah enumerates them.

71. Summarizing *CZ* I.254-257.

come living and holy stones "rolling on the land of God," that we, "being built upon the foundation of the apostles and prophets of Christ Jesus," might complete a spiritual temple and house, in order that God might inhabit us."[72]

It is possible to over-relate these two interpretations of the stone. In the former, the pneumatological discussion dominates; in the latter the "stone" comes to have a primarily corporate significance. However, two connections emerge between the two: 1) in the former interpretation of the stone, reverence is predicated of Jesus' humanity. According to the Hebrews-citation, the reverence by which Jesus prevails with God delivers him from death. In the second interpretation of the stone, both of these themes—prevailing with God and being rendered immortal in proximity with the ever-living Word—recur. The believer becomes an "expiatory sacrifice" and offers spiritual sacrifices to God and is made alive by approaching the living Word. 2) The language of indwelling and inhabitation at the end of the second passage has antecedents in the Spirit's resting upon the Son in the first interpretation.

I propose that the structure of Didymus' thought runs as follows. Jesus' receptivity to the Spirit in the Incarnation is expressed, in his full humanity, by his reverence before the Father. By this reverence, Jesus prevails with God over death. He is the "stone" upon whom we are to be built. We, like him, are to prevail with God specifically by faith in the Son, the offering of ourselves as spiritual sacrifices acceptable in his sight. Being made alive and holy by virtue of this faith, we become more fully receptive to the indwelling of the Persons of the Trinity, receiving like Jesus the seven-fold activity of the sanctifying Spirit upon us.

Didymus later speaks of people being made into "holy stones that roll on God's land" (Zech 9:15–16), a text to which Didymus alludes in the closing parenesis of the section above.[73] These stones, writes Didymus, are able to be rolled around when their "weight" and "stoniness" is removed. Then they become both "light (κούφους)" and "easily-moved (εὐκινήτους)." Didymus articulates a progression from the early stages of this transformation to the latter ones: at the end of this progress, people become stones that are parts of the city built by God.[74] With this observation, Didymus launches into the connection with which we are concerned.

Though the text is lacunose, the broad features of argument are discernible. Such "stones," who because of their "lightness" and "weightlessness" are able to be transported to the "immovable foundation (([ἀ]μετακινήτῳ θεμελ[ίῳ]))" of Jesus Christ, are formed into a spiritual house. Scripture calls them "stones" because of their proximity to the Lord. It is difficult to conclude more from the text, although Jerome—who is here dependent upon Didymus

---

72. Summarizing *CZ* I.258–261.
73. *CZ* I.261: "May we, too, become living stones that are holy, rolling on God's land" (FC 111:81).
74. *CZ* III.222 and 221.

to the point of citing the same scriptural texts—accentuates the progressive element. For him "holy stones" are those who are "so light and upward-striving that they do not await the hand of the builders but they themselves rush headlong to be built upon the foundation of Christ."[75]

The holiness of the stones built upon the foundation stone of Christ is for Didymus contingent upon their progress in the virtues. Weighed down by sin, they are unable to rise quickly to be built upon Christ. When they are built upon Christ, Didymus conceives of them sharing to such an extent in him that they are described as taking on functions that are first associated with Christ. Having seen in him, by a pious regard for his Incarnation, the example to which their own moral striving must attain, they set out toward this goal. They become righteous to the point that their righteousness is bestowed upon others. They become holy and living stones or "expiatory sacrifices." The above passages suggest that Didymus conceives of Christ's Incarnation as a model for human striving in the virtues, implying in the process that, at the very least, sanctified humanity can proceed a long way toward the achievement of this goal in this life. But it should also be noted here that Didymus begins to reveal the other element of his thinking about the virtues: it is always in communicative, and not merely ethical, proximity with Christ that the soul progresses in the virtues.

Crowned with Many Crowns[76]

Didymus sheds more abundant light on the exact extent of this conformity to the virtues revealed by Christ in his treatment of Zechariah 6:9–11. In the text, the prophet is commanded to take gold and silver from the leading men among the people during the captivity, and to make crowns of this material for placing on the head of Joshua the high priest. These men are separated into three groups: "rulers," "useful ones," and "those familiar" with the end of the captivity.

Didymus devotes the first phase of his exposition to dwelling on the historical sense of the passage. When the exile took place, there were some who were taken away from their homeland not because of their own sins but for the benefit of those around them. Their function was to encourage the people and remind them of the Law during the exile. Likewise, among these were some who were familiar with the end of the captivity, whose function was to lead the people in rejoicing at their return to the homeland.[77]

Staying with the historical situation, Didymus lays the groundwork for his spiritual development of the text by dwelling on the significance of their ac-

---

75. *In Zach.* 2, 9:16 (CCSL 76A:836): "lapides sancti . . . qui tantum erunt leues et in sublime nitentes, ut non praestolentur aedificantium manus, sed ipsi festinent imponi super fundamentum Christi."

76. *CZ* II.6–30.

77. Summarizing *CZ* II.6–9.

quisition of possessions and of the prophet's taking of these possessions into Josiah's house.[78] Having acquired "virtues and wise thoughts (σοφὰ νοήματα)" in their duress, these men returned with them to the land and entered into Jerusalem.[79] When the prophet then takes their possessions into the house of Josiah son of Zephaniah (6:10), Didymus argues that this means that those who are "saved" (his etymological interpretation of Josiah) are granted to remain forever in God's presence (Zephaniah being interpreted to mean "Yah's tarrying").[80] The historical reference and its development are important to bear in mind in what follows. Those who acquire the virtues so as to see peace are brought into the presence of God where they are no longer under threat of exile. In his presence they make an offering of the virtues they acquired during the time of exile.

With the making of the crowns and their placement on the head of Joshua the high priest (6:11), Didymus moves firmly into his christological development of the text. Picking up on a typological link between Joshua and Jesus that he has explored earlier,[81] Didymus now takes Joshua the high priest almost solely to refer to his antitype: the Savior. The crowns of gold and silver that were fashioned out of the possessions of the exiles are placed on the head of Jesus. Given the link that Didymus has established between possessions and virtues, Didymus argues that these crowns are the rewards given out in the contests of virtue. Those involved in athletic contests for "godliness (εὐσεβείας)" struggle to attain them. They are then rewarded for their struggle by donning crowns made of the same spiritual elements. The reward for the

---

78. I differ here with Hill (FC 111:116–117n13–14) to some extent. Hill takes CZ II.10–11 as a departure from the "historical reference" of Zechariah. But in saying this he seems to anticipate too quickly the movement to the spiritual sense. Didymus is convinced that the returned exiles who were of use to the people returned with real "sensible vessels (αἰσθητὰ σκεύη)" and with virtues acquired during the exile. The possessions are both literal and figuratively conceived in reference to the historical situation facing the returned exiles. The prophet really entered into Josiah son of Zephaniah's house with articles of silver and gold (see the language in II.12). Didymus is clearly anticipating his spiritual development of these events, a development that begins in earnest in II.15 where the silver and gold are allegorically conceived, but he is convinced that these events are both historical and spiritually useful events to recount.

79. Didymus' citation of one of the Psalms of Ascents (127:5 LXX) at this juncture suggests that he may also be thinking of the spiritual significance of the term "Jerusalem." Because of their acquisition of virtue, the righteous exiles not only enter into the historical city, but likewise "see peace" of a spiritual nature. (This is Didymus' consistent etymological explanation for the name "Jerusalem" in the CZ.)

80. Summarizing CZ II.10–13.

81. In Zechariah 3, Didymus establishes a precedent of reading references to Joshua the high priest in light of their fulfillment in Christ. I deal with Zechariah 3 exclusively in Chapter 6.

contests, in other words, is nothing other than the virtues that are gained in them.[82]

Didymus notes that the text mentions not a singular crown but many crowns.[83] This is appropriate, he argues: "Since the contests are many and varied, necessarily the prizes are also. For each virtue and the deeds that are completed by it have a crown that is proper to them. Therefore not one but many crowns are fashioned." Didymus then launches into a description of the several kinds of contests that are described in Scripture and the rewards promised to those who are victorious in them. He suggests three contests: that of obedience, that of innocence (with Eucharistic development), and that of faith. The foremost contest has as its goal the prize of grace, the next the crown of delight, the lattermost the prize of righteousness.[84]

Didymus concludes the lemma with three important reflections: 1) the one head of Jesus is given many crowns. "Tempted in every way yet without sin" (Heb 4:15), Jesus was involved in all the contests of virtue. 2) The head of Jesus refers particularly to those who govern the body of Christ. These are called "head" because they best exemplify the whole Christian life: the "active and contemplative life." 3) It is possible for one head to possess all the crowns because the crowns represent particular virtues. One who possesses one of the virtues necessarily possesses the others, since the virtues are all interconnected.[85] Didymus repeats his insistence that this refers "principally (προηγουμένως)" to "the human being assumed by God the Word," and "thereafter (ἔπειτα)" to "those who imitate him (οἱ μιμηταὶ αὐτοῦ) and are themselves called "christs" because they are sharers (μέτοχοι) in the one of whom it is said: "Christ the wisdom and power of God" (1 Cor 1:24)."[86]

Didymus could hardly be clearer about the extent to which the virtues revealed in the Son's assumed humanity are imitable, and of the importance of struggling for them in the Christian life. The exiles are figurally significant in this narrative precisely because they illustrate the point that Didymus is drawing out for his audience. They struggled for piety; they won through in the contests for virtue, seeing the peace of the spiritual Jerusalem even as they

---

82. Summarizing *CZ* II.14 and 19. We revisit II.15–18 in the next chapter where we take up the allegorical significance of silver and gold for Didymus.

83. *CZ* II.20. The LXX encourages Didymus' reading here, having "crowns" (Zech 6:11).

84. Summarizing *CZ* II.20–26.

85. Didymus' endorsement of this Stoic axiom is conditioned by his conviction that all virtue is united because it is all substantially present in God and—thus—in the one who participates in God. Cf. Solari, 81–84, who notes along similar lines that Didymus' endorsement of the axiom is derivative of his conviction that "virtue [is] connected with God and Christ" (p. 82). His ethical theory is eclectic, combining originally competitive theories about virtue in an attempt to do justice to the ideas that all virtue is one in God and that degrees of virtues are present among humanity.

86. Summarizing *CZ* II.27–30.

returned to the earthly city. As recipients of God's saving work, they were granted security in the spiritual Jerusalem to which they had returned. Just as he urges his audience to imitate these spiritual athletes, he likewise urges them to see how their virtues are pre-eminent in the one who took part in all the contests so that his victory might have benefits for those who imitate him.

Didymus clearly once again asserts a difference and priority between the assumed humanity of the Son and all other humans. He is the "principal" wearer of the crowns.[87] But on this occasion, he clearly asserts another important distinction as well. Only of him is it said that we both participate in and imitate his virtue. With the saints, it is possible for us only to imitate them. They, on the other hand, imitate Christ's virtues and are described as "partaking (μέτοχοι)" of him. The distinction is critical in maintaining the distinctiveness of Christ. Only because Christ is "capable of being partaken of" is it said that there are others who are bedecked with all the crowns as well. Their sharing in all his virtues plays an important role in their pursuit of the goal to which they strive. Didymus secures the possibility of attaining the human *telos* by asserting an ontological, and not merely quantitative, distinction between Christ and the saints.

Keeping the Festival [88]

To this *telos* we now turn. In a few places in the Commentary, Didymus hints that at the end of the virtuous life there exists a "final object of all desire (ἔσχατον ὀρεκτόν)." When one arrives at this "goal (τέλος)," there is no further need for "progress (προκοπή)," because the aim of the sanctified life has been reached.[89] This is also referred to in the CZ as the "praiseworthy measure (ἐπαινετὸν μέτρον)," which is completed when "no righteous attitude or holy action is lacking."[90] Toward the close of the CZ, Didymus develops a spiritual reading of the Feast of Tabernacles in which this goal is reached, further cementing the distinct role of Christ in this process.

The apocalyptic vision of the prophet Zechariah reveals a coming day (14:9) when Jerusalem will dwell in confidence (14:11), with its enemies cut off. On that day, even the Gentiles will go up to Jerusalem to keep the Feast of Tab-

---

87. The notion of a distinction in degree between the humanity of the Savior and the humanity of others is consistently reiterated. Cf. *PsT* 3,9–16: "As many things then as are said concerning the human [assumed by the Word] may also be said both of angels and of perfect men. . . . Now many others [like him] spoke the truth when they learned it from God. But he did so more (πλειόνως); he did so more greatly (μειζόνως); he did so incomparably ([ἀ]συνκρίτως)." And in 5,27–29: "He is second to none, nor is anyone his equal in the things common [to his humanity and theirs]. I was saying that the things of the Lord's man and of holy men are common. But none is his equal, nor is he second to anyone; for this reason he is called founder (ἀρχηγός) [of salvation]."

88. *CZ* V.155–177.
89. *CZ* III.299.
90. *CZ* I.367 (FC 111:104).

ernacles (14:16). Didymus takes the description of the Feast of Tabernacles in two senses. There is a first interpretation that "concerns history and the letter (πρ[ὸ]ς ἱστορίαν καὶ ῥητὸν)."[91] The Jewish people keep the Feast in this first sense. There is a second interpretation that is "intelligible (σ[ύ]νοπτος) and allegorical (π[ρὸς ἀλληγο]ρίαν)";[92] within this second interpretation several figural senses are proposed. The literal sense is exploited as the basis of the figural senses.

Didymus focuses his attention on three elements in particular in his discussion of the letter. 1) The Jewish people left Egypt and crossed the Red Sea; there they beheld the destruction of the armies of Pharaoh, but they did not "immediately (εὐθέως)" enter the Land of promise. As a result, they were compelled to construct moveable dwellings (or tents) for themselves. The yearly construction of tents once they had entered the Promised Land was to remind them of God's goodness to them during the time of their wandering. 2) The Feast of Tabernacles was celebrated in the seventh month, on the fifteenth day of the month. 3) The people were to take ripe fruit and the branches of various trees to assist them in the celebration.[93]

As he has promised, each of these elements corresponds to something "intelligible (νοητός)," appropriate to the person who keeps the Feast by "ascending on high (ἀναβαίνω)." Just as the Jewish people lived in tents, so those keeping the Festival of Tabernacles in a spiritual sense must dwell in tents on their journey toward the house of the Lord. "Tent" is the name given to spir-

---

91. *CZ* V.156. On the meaning of ἱστορία see Doutreleau, *Sur Zacharie*, 51–52, who argues that there is a theoretical difference between this sense and the sense πρὸς ῥητόν but that the difference is rarely observed in practice. Bienert acknowledges a difference between the two senses, with ἱστορία having more to do with the text's "truthfulness, historical reliability and validity in general." In his words: "[D]ie Methode καθ' ἱστορίαν den Text auf seine Wahrscheinlichkeit, historische Zuverlässigkeit und Stichhaltigkeit im Allgemeinen untersucht" (p. 108). Tigcheler, 76–77, argues that Bienert improves on Doutreleau but that he does not go far enough. The readings πρὸς ῥητόν and καθ' ἱστορίαν are distinct: the former involving what the text says and the latter involving the facts (of a generally scientific or historical character). In this instance, Tigcheler's distinction is well-founded, though Tigcheler pushes to absolutize this division between the two where it is not always defensible to do so. He writes: the Jews "celebrate the Feast in actuality [καθ' ἱστορίαν] and as the text describes [πρὸς ῥητόν] (célèbrent la fête réellement et comme le texte la décrit)" (p. 78).

92. *CZ* V.157. Doutreleau's reason for thinking that the anagogical sense and the allegorical often overlap in *CZ* (*Sur Zacharie*, 60–61) has some support in this passage, where Didymus promises an allegorical interpretation and then delivers one that is πρὸς ἀναγωγήν (*CZ* V.161). The spiritual interpretation offered here is based on the identification of the figural referents of each significant item in the literal or factual reading.

93. Summarizing *CZ* V.158–160. For this last item, see Leviticus 23:39–40 (loosely cited by Didymus).

itual progress, which consists of growth in virtue and wisdom. Like tents, the virtues provide spiritual pilgrims with a shelter from the vicissitudes of their spiritual environment. The heat of temptation and the cold of sin are kept away by the tent, as one makes progress in the virtues. We recognize this pairing in reference to the shelter that Jesus—the "light cloud"—provides earlier in the Commentary.[94]

This progress, however, has a definite terminus. Didymus argues:

> One who is making pilgrimage to the house of God needs to have a place to set up a tent, even as he needs to make admirable progress. But when he dwells there he no longer sets up the tent, since after much progress (προκοπή) he has reached the goal (τέλος).[95]

After having striven and toiled to reach the house of God, the tents are to be replaced by a house. Or rather, those who have struggled through the pursuit of virtue toward Christ-likeness must arrive at the house whose foundations God himself has laid. Once again, Didymus alludes to something he has developed at length in the Commentary. The "house" whose foundations are laid by God is none other than the humanity assumed by Christ, upon which the Church and its members are built into a perfect temple. Didymus concludes his reflection on the journey with the words:

> For it is imperative that progress ceases, when the goal is achieved that is called "house," since it is neither possible nor appropriate to be always progressing while never arriving at the perfect state (κατάστασις) that is termed "house." In this house the true servants of God, performing spiritual acts of worship forever and ever, praise and glorify God with thanksgiving for his perfect and faultless judgments.[96]

In the perfect state (κατάστασις), the soul is no longer subject to the mutability that characterizes the journey toward God, but has been made stable.

Having explored the significance of the wilderness wandering for the spiritual meaning of the Festival, Didymus now examines the meaning of the fruitful boughs that were to assist the revelers. Each element of the Leviticus-text is explored here. The ripe fruit, Didymus argues, is derivative of wisdom, called a "tree of life." This tree brings life and safety to all who are near it and depend upon it as on the Lord (Prov 3:18); another name for this tree, in case we miss the first figural allusion to Christ, is the "true vine" (John 15:1).[97]

---

94. Summarizing *CZ* V.161–162. The motif plays a significant role in the corpus. See Layton, *Didymus the Blind and His Circle*, 36–55, for the role of the motif in the *PsT*.
95. *CZ* V.162.
96. *CZ* V.164.
97. Cf. *CZ* II.333–335.

Didymus creatively renders the next element in the Leviticus-text, the palm branches, and argues that the branches from this tree would have been employed by the woman who was cleaning her house in search of her lost coin (see Luke 15:8–10).[98] When she has swept the house clean, she finds the coin that bears the image of the "King of the Universe (παμβασιλεύς)," which coin is made according to God's image and likeness.[99] The leafy branches are taken as a reference to specific virtues of the practical and contemplative life. The final element (the willow branches) is taken as a symbol of "purity" and "incorruption."[100]

These symbols reveal that the Festival of Tabernacles was, in Didymus' mind, synonymous with speaking about the goal of the Christian life. In arriving at the foundation of the house built by God (wisdom, or Christ), the soul is defended securely. No longer bearing only the image of God, it comes to bear his likeness.[101] This implies that nothing is lacking in specific virtues; all coexist perfectly in the person who is conformed to Christ. Notably absent here is any sense that such conformation is a prospect to be awaited only after death.

Didymus then develops another interpretation, related to the one above, this time querying the relationship of the soul's stability to materially-embodied existence. The NT sometimes employs the word "tent" as a figure of substitution for the body.[102] Didymus makes an immediate application to the ascetic life. Men and women who devote themselves to the pursuit of "holiness (ἁγιότης)" in spirit and body by pursuing the ascetic life are keeping the Feast of Tabernacles in this spiritual sense. Likewise those who, while married, keep the marriage bed pure. Having explored the ascetic connection, Didymus then develops the eschatological. Though he is convinced that some can keep the Feast in the present life, he argues that it will be even better-celebrated "on high (ἄνω)" at the rising of the body in the general resurrection. Then, he says, the corruptible will rise incorruptible. The "psychic (ψυχικός)" body will

---

98. Didymus is preceded in this connection by Methodius of Olympus. See Jean Daniélou, "La Fête des Tabernacles dans l'exégèse patristique," *Studia Patristica* 1 (1957): 267.

99. Didymus sees here an inter-textual link between Matthew 22:20 and Genesis 1:27. For the same link see Origen, *Hom. Gen.* 13.4 (FC 71:192–193).

100. Summarizing *CZ* V.165–171. See Doutreleau, *Sur Zacharie*, 1064–1067n1, on the history of the notion that the flower of the willow tree, when distilled in water, makes its drinkers infertile.

101. In his treatment of the distinction between the two in *GenT* 58,25–59,5 Didymus notes that the likeness is a matter of attaining perfection, whereas the image represents approaching God in reverence. He is here speaking of "image" and "likeness" in ethical terms, not ontological ones, as he does above.

102. See 2 Peter 1:14 and 1 Corinthians 5:4.

arise "spiritual (πνευματικός)."[103] This latter remark is relatively brief. However, it serves to illustrate that Didymus is thinking in eschatological terms. The Feast of Tabernacles is to be celebrated spiritually in two ways: one arrives at the goal in this lifetime and arrives at it again in the age to come when the body is rendered incorruptible by becoming wholly spiritual.[104]

The overall structure of Didymus' interpretation is admirably clear, even if it develops over several paragraphs. Beginning with the literal sense of the passage as the Feast was celebrated in Israel's history, Didymus explores three important dimensions of the celebration of the Feast: the tents in the wilderness wandering, the branches of the Festival, and the obligation to celebrate at a particular time. Each of these dimensions corresponds to something spiritual. The first spiritual interpretation given to the Feast revolves around identifying Jesus as its *telos*. The spiritual pilgrim is to pursue Christ-likeness to the point that the virtues are so solidly established in her that they all inhere together within her person. She is to clear the rubbish from her house by the practice of the virtues, until the coin of the Sovereign is found. Only by clinging faithfully to him can she, a bride of the Word, find rest. Eschatological themes are absent. The second spiritual interpretation introduces these themes through the NT figure of the body as a "tent," although Didymus does not stay long with the eschatological interpretation. The "Jerusalem" of the final few paragraphs is predominantly a spiritual, rather than an eschatological vision.

The eschatological reality of being so united to Christ that the likeness is complete compels Didymus to encourage those committed to the virtuous life to set their hearts on high while still in the "tent" of the body. The ones who do this are those "raised with Christ Jesus" and "seated with him in the heavenly places" (Eph 2:6), no longer being burdened down by earthly deeds. They have arrived at the "beautiful city that sees peace." They have ascended to the city with "unbreakable foundations." They worship and acknowledge the Lord, neither excluding the Son from the worship of the Father nor the Father from the honor of the Son, but adoring the whole Trinity. They do now what all rational creatures will do in eternity, even as they await a coming transformation.[105]

---

103. 1 Corinthians 15:42–46. In light of Didymus' anthropology, the Pauline distinction between ψυχικός and πνευματικός carries with it the additional meaning that the soul—transformed utterly into "spirit" by the Holy Spirit—renders the body communicant with its properties.

104. Summarizing *CZ* V.172–175. Didymus is not forthcoming about what this resurrection body will be like here. We investigate this *topos* in the next chapter.

105. Summarizing *CZ* V.178–182. Didymus ends this section with a parenetic revision of Philippians 2:11.

Summary

The passages above illustrate that Didymus is concerned with establishing his account of the moral life chiefly in conversation with the doctrine of the Incarnation. The Son in the humanity assumed by him reveals the possibilities of the moral life and enables them in us by our participation in him. As others have observed, Didymus is optimistic about the possibilities of achieving utter conformity to the virtues revealed by the Son.[106] The precise character of this conformity can be articulated in a two-fold way: 1) the saints are always second to Christ in terms of their demonstration of the virtues because they participate in the virtues which are his, and 2) the perfect among the saints are able to achieve—in the present life—the state in which their virtues are so conformed to Christ that they are not lacking in any of them. Though they anticipate a condition in the age to come in which the body is rendered spiritual, by the practices of abstinence and purity they partake in some way in the incorruptible eschatological condition in the present.[107]

Divine Constancy and Human Mutability

The importance of the above to Didymus' account of the sanctified life is best demonstrated in relation to what I take to be the organizing theme of the *CZ*. Zechariah's prophetic burden is the pursuit of stability, figurally correlated to the theme of Israel's return from exile. This burden is announced at the

---

106. There was some discussion about this point in relation to the *EcclT*, the editors of which have gathered testimony to two different conceptualizations of "progress" in Didymus' corpus. That on display in *CZ* is typically one of "linear development (lineare Entwicklung)." Frequently in *EcclT*, another conceptualization occurs: one of "interaction (Wechselwirkung)," in which each "goal" is also the "beginning" of a new pursuit of virtue. See Gerhard Binder and Leo Liesenborghs, eds., *Didymos der Blinde: Kommentar zum Ecclesiastes*, vol. 6 (Bonn: Habelt, 1969), 41n4-15. Simonetti, in conversation with Binder and Liesenborghs, supports the conclusion from the rest of the exegetical corpus that the two frameworks can be harmonized. Though the pursuit of "progress" demands the pursuit of one goal after another, there is a final goal which represents the terminus for which each of the prior "goals" was pursued. See his "Didymiana," 146-151. More recently Layton in his *Didymus the Blind and His Circle*, 47-48, notes a competitive tension between seeking (as perfection) and arrival at the goal. He rightly identifies this latter "goal" with deification, and writes: "the *telos* of deification anticipates a state that sets a limit to the possibility of qualitative change.... Didymus anticipates that being "changed to the goal" consummates a process beyond which no advance is possible." Layton carefully balances the tension between these two competing themes, and rightly points out that, having defined human perfection in terms of being in continual "quest for God," Didymus seems to compromise this "aspect of being human" by asserting that one can arrive at the goal of "immutable wisdom."

107. Didymus calls this "serenity" in *DT*; in *CZ* he frequently uses synonyms of "peace" like "rest" or "security."

beginning of the *CZ*. In this final section of the chapter, I locate Didymus' affirmation of human moral perfection in the likeness of the "man of heaven" in relation to the central theme of the *CZ*: the attainment of stability, the state in which human mutability no longer threatens the relationship between God and humanity.

The Earliest Vision[108]

The first lengthy exposition of this theme occurs near the beginning of the *CZ*. It unfolds in three basic stages: 1) a summary of the prophetic message of repentance in relation to the ontological stability of God, 2) an introduction to the identity of the man on the red horse and his significance, and 3) a description of the goal of the human life as the attainment of stability by reverence before this man. I follow the argument of the *CZ* through these sections, relating each of the sections to the one that precedes it.

"Return to Me, and I Will Return to You"

The first six verses of the Zechariah-text situate the numerous prophetic visions that follow. God is provoked to anger by Israel's refusal to listen to the warnings of the prophets. His punishment (exile) overtook former generations, and now he urges the current generation to return to him. When they do so, he will return to them (1:3). After some brief introductory remarks about Zechariah's parentage and his historical setting, Didymus slows down somewhat at v. 3.

Didymus first addresses the language of divine returning and human repentance. It is necessary to establish the metaphysical principles that determine how the language of divine anger and returning is to be understood. Since God is "unchangeable (ἄτρεπτος)" and "immutable (ἀναλλοίωτος)," he only seems to turn away and to return to us though his disposition toward us remains constant. In reality, those who are far from God have the cause of his remoteness in themselves. The language of God's returning is phenomenological, argues Didymus, appealing to the impression people have of the land moving away from them when they embark on a ship. Didymus therefore takes this language as descriptive of the "attitude" (σχέσις) and "disposition" (διάθεσις) of the soul.[109] Those who turn to God do so in the disposition of the inner person. God's disposition toward them, however, remains constant. They may experience him in his censure or in his comfort, but both are indicative of his unfailing goodness toward them.[110]

---

108. *CZ* I.10–54.

109. The phrase reads only: σχέσει δὲ καὶ διαθέσει, ἀλλ' οὐ τόπῳ γίνονται αἱ λεγόμεν[α]ι ἐξαναχωρήσεις καὶ ἐγγύτητες. But given what Didymus has said earlier about the phenomenology of God's returning, Doutreleau is surely right to specify in his translation that the language of disposition and attitude is predicated only of the soul, and not of God. See Doutreleau, *Sur Zacharie*, 197.

110. Summarizing *CZ* I.9–14.

Concluding his interpretation of this lemma, Didymus contrasts the false prophets and those led astray by them with the prophets who set before the people the councils of the Holy Spirit. On the one hand, the false prophets and those deceived by them are no more.[111] But on the other, the Holy Spirit has proposed divine and salutary "pursuits (ἐπιτηδεύματα)" to the people of God by the mouth of the prophets.[112]

Two basic themes are introduced here to which Didymus returns in subsequent lemmata: 1) the contrast between divine constancy and human changeability introduces a dilemma, the resolution of which requires that human changeability no longer pose a barrier to divine-human relationships, and 2) the prophets declare the divine and salutary pursuits that are involved in overcoming this barrier. The prophet Zechariah is to be heard as one whose burden is to reveal the course of the soul's journey toward God and to aid it in its journey.

The Man on the Red Horse

Zechariah situates his prophecy within the reign of Darius (1:7) before proceeding to give an account of his first vision. A man seated on a red horse appears between two shadow-covered mountains; behind his horse are several other horses of various descriptions (1:8). Didymus recounts the various features of the scene: the man on the red horse is the Incarnate Savior, the mountains are the Two Testaments, and the other horses are all those prophets, apostles, and angels who served as emissaries and witnesses of the Son before and during the time of his Incarnation.[113]

At the center of the Two Testaments of Scripture is the Incarnate Savior. Didymus describes the Testaments as "bearing fruit and providing shade because of the density of their thoughts and the abundance of their words about [the Savior's] divinity (θεολογίας) and Incarnation (ἐνανθρωπήσεως)."[114] Their obscurity and depth is signified by the adjective "shadowy." Didymus

---

111. Didymus takes v. 5's remark: "Your fathers, where are they now? And the prophets, will they live forever?" as a sign that Zechariah has false prophets in his sights. The language of them "being no more" is clarified by later comments in the *CZ*, wherein Didymus reveals that it is impossible for them to cease to exist as rational beings. They only cease to exist as beings perverted by evil; their "underlying substrate (ὑποκείμενον)" is not destroyed but re-directed toward its proper *telos* (cf. *CZ* III.97, III.207–208, and IV.240–242).

112. *CZ* I.14–15.

113. *CZ* I.22–24.

114. There is some ambiguity about whether θεολογία should be taken as a reference to Christ's divinity (his eternal identity as the divine Logos) or to the doctrine of the Godhead (i.e. the Trinity). Here it seems probable that Didymus has the former in mind, as Hill rightly notes (FC 111:233n8). See a similar and less ambiguous formula in *CZ* III.251.

leads us to expect that the Savior is the key to its understanding.[115] Didymus turns to the horses. These horses that follow behind him, Didymus argues, come "after him"—i.e. after his divinity. The various colors of the horses are indicative of the kind of message proclaimed by each: some hand over "the human matters of the Word who came down and became flesh," others speak of matters that are both "sensible and spiritual," while others hand over "divine matters that are separate from all matter." It is important to note here that Didymus sets up a distinction that he will develop in his account of the contemplative life. The Incarnation and the human matters of the Word are contrasted with the divinity and the divine matters that are separable from materiality.[116]

Didymus then adopts a different interpretation of the middle horses, arguing that they are those who adapt their message to the "dispositions" (ἕξεις) of those whom they instruct. Paul, Isaiah, and David are held up as examples of those who take on various modes of discourse in order to instruct their audience. It is highly significant for Didymus' argument that precisely at this point he turns to address the text that speaks of the angel who speaks in the prophet (Zech 1:9). After raising the possibility that this is an angel who "presides over prophecy" Didymus turns to an identification that he will make consistently throughout the Commentary. This is the "angel of great counsel" (Isa 9:5), the Logos. As such, he is pre-eminent among the teachers of the human race. For it is only true of divinity that others can be taught by him through participation.[117] Christ speaks both in and to the hearer. He gives others a share of that which he is in himself by nature; he conforms others to his teachings in this way.[118]

---

115. Didymus makes this point explicitly with a nearly-identical image in CZ V.57–58. In this latter quotation the mountains are the prophets. In their midst is the deep valley that stands for the depth of their obscurity (ἀσαφεία). He who came to fulfill both Law and Prophets fills in the valley so that they may be rightly understood. The difference here is the contrast between the Testaments (above) and the Law and the Prophets.

116. Summarizing CZ I.22–25. Didymus regularly distinguishes these two modes of knowing the Savior, assigning the latter to a more advanced stage of knowledge. Investigating the precise character of this assertion and its ramifications is the burden of the next chapter.

117. See CZ I.32: Λαλεῖ δὲ ἐν τῷ ἀκροατῇ ὁ διδάσκαλος ὅτε μετέχεται ὑπ' αὐτοῦ ἢ κατὰ διάθεσίν ἐστιν ἐν αὐτῷ. Didymus talks about effective teaching as obtaining either when the student participates in the teacher or when the teacher is in the student "by disposition (κατὰ διάθεσιν)." Consonant with his claims that only divinity can be participated in (DSS 54–56 and DT 2.6.7 (529A)), Didymus holds up four examples of the student's participation in the teacher: all of them refer to divinity. Didymus' example of dispositional instruction appeals to the Hebrew priesthood (CZ I.33).

118. Summarizing CZ I.26–34.

Didymus' exposition of these two lemmata (1:8 and 1:9) seems to stand ambiguously beside the earlier themes that he has introduced. The introductory matter (1:1–6) orients the reader to the dilemma facing the human race: namely mutability. In this first section, Didymus invites the reader to attend to the Spirit's revelation of the path toward proximity with God, in which this problem is overcome. The first lesson (1:7) in the Spirit's curriculum, however, orients the hearers of the prophecy to the broad landscape of the Scriptures: finding their unity in the Incarnation of the Word, they are filled with various kinds of discourse on this central subject. Some, like John the Theologian, communicate the pre-cosmic identity of the Word with utmost clarity. Others are content to focus more on the human matters in which the Word revealed his glory. These differences between the divinely-inspired heralds illustrate what Didymus considers to be a central pedagogical tenet: the best teachers are those who attend to the limitations of their audience and adapt their speech to their benefit. Of these, none is superior to Christ himself; he speaks in the hearer. It is not until the third stage of the interpretation that these observations about the Incarnate Son and his witnesses are brought to bear on the issue of mediation between divine constancy and human mutability.

The Earth Is at Peace

The prophet Zechariah reports that in his vision the angels return to the Rider on the Horse after having surveyed the earth. They report: "The earth (γῆ) is inhabited and at peace" (1:11). Didymus' subsequent comment is somewhat surprising:

> Since the rational soul (λογικῆς ψυχῆς) of itself has the power of independent and constant movement, it is at peace and unaffected by any disorderly turmoil when it moves properly and in a blessed manner, and it is from reverence for the divine (θείας εὐλαβείας) that it attains this stability (εὐστάθειαν).[119]

Relying on an established allegorical identification,[120] Didymus takes "earth (γῆ)" to refer to the rational soul. The soul—which is independently and constantly mobile—is calm and at rest when it moves rightly and blessedly. It attains "stability (εὐστάθεια)" when it is reverent towards God. Didymus produces as counter-examples the prohibited movement of Cain (Gen 4:7) who turns away from God to sin and the adulterous woman of the Proverbs who restlessly wanders (Prov 7:11), instead of abiding with her true spouse: God the Word.[121]

---

119. *CZ* I.43 (FC 111:37).

120. See, e.g., *GenT* 30,6–13, and *PsT* 67,27–38. Cf. Origen, *In Prov.* 3:19 (PG 13:29C) and *Hom. Ezek.* 4.1.8 (ACW 62:69).

121. Summarizing *CZ* I.43–45.

In the final two lemmata, the "angel of the Lord" inquires of the Lord Almighty when such a peaceful condition will obtain among the inhabitants of Judah and Jerusalem, and he is answered with words of consolation (1:12–13). Taking Jerusalem and Judah severally as figures for the soul or the Church in various degrees of progress toward their goal,[122] Didymus concludes the section, drawing his various threads together in two concise parenetic sections.

> Since these divine verses describe who is the discerning soul, termed Jerusalem, and who are the ones that confess, being the cities of Judah—for Judah is translated "confessor"—let them learn from Jesus, "for he is gentle and humble in heart, in order that they may find the rest (ἀνάπαυσιν)" (Matt 11:29) that comes to pure souls, when the seventieth year is completed due to the cyclical motion of the "sun of righteousness" (Mal 4:2) who encircles pure and transparent hearts (καθαρὰς καὶ διαυγεῖς διανοίας).[123]

The parenetic remark is followed closely by another one in the next paragraph, in which the theme of rejoicing at God's comforting presence figures predominantly.[124] He writes: "May the Lord Almighty reply in fine words also to us through his Angel of great counsel in order that we, obtaining all that is praiseworthy, might be perfectly consoled by his perfect words, entering into a life that is free and blessed."[125] The intent of both parenetic remarks is clear: those who confess Jesus and learn from his humility will attain rest when they come to share in the benefits of his saving economy.

In the third section Didymus brings to coherence the themes introduced in the first two. Two preliminary themes are introduced: 1) rest, peace, and stability are the goal of the soul. 2) They are attained by heeding the prophetic curriculum. The first section problematizes the acquisition of this stability on the basis of a distinction between divine and human nature. The manner of the acquisition of stability by the soul is determined first of all by the soul's reverence before God, who is not subject to change. In the second section the content of the prophetic curriculum is further developed: human and angelic teachers in every age proclaim the Son in his divinity and in the Incarnation. Of these teachers, none is superior to Christ, the "Angel of great counsel," who speaks in the one who hears by giving the other a share in himself. In the third section, Didymus reveals above all the importance placed on the imitation of

---

122. *CZ* I.48–49.

123. *CZ* I.52.

124. Significantly, Doutreleau notes that of the 110 identifiable sections in the *CZ*, only sixteen of these reveal the presence of an audience (*Sur Zacharie*, 43–44). The presence of an audience here is almost certain, and it occasions the highly unusual inclusion of two separate parenetic conclusions in quick succession.

125. *CZ* I.54.

Jesus' gentleness and humility in properly attending to the words of the prophets. To the soul that submits to the gentle yoke of Christ comes the promise of perfect consolation and the blessed life. Reverence before God thus takes the form of submission to that which the Incarnation reveals about the imperatives of the Christian life. Rest is attained through obedience to and imitation of Christ, by attaining "all that is praiseworthy."

The section supports the idea developed above that Didymus conceives of the Incarnation as the "doctrine of piety" *par excellence* for developing an account of the moral life. The gentleness and humility of the Savior in the Incarnation are the basis of Didymus' first moral imperative. By attending to the "human matters" of the Logos, one becomes illumined as to the path of the moral life. One pursues this path in the hope of attaining to the security that "resides in" God as a matter of his nature.

Watchtowers Ensuring Salvation

The theme of attaining to stability is ubiquitous throughout the *CZ*. These passages likewise fill out the background against which the pursuit of moral virtue takes place, illustrating the idea that the soul is constantly being contested. Didymus argues that the soul must, given the conditions in which the state of stability is pursued, consistently be seeking out the place of strength and be vigilant in spying out enemies as they advance from afar.

Ashkelon: the Praiseworthy Stronghold [126]

Didymus speaks of the enemies of the people of God becoming claimed for their true end: fellowship with God. The judgment-language of the prophet is to be understood as purgative. By being subject to its cleansing power, the enemies of Israel will be rendered a "remnant for our God" (9:7).

Didymus takes each of the foreign cities enumerated by Zechariah in this passage as descriptive of a spiritual condition that obtains to those who are in bondage to evil. Briefly treating the literal sense, Didymus turns to "the things of the elevated interpretation (τὰ πρὸς ἀνηγμένην ἀπόδοσιν)," arguing that repentance directs the soul away from vice to a more praiseworthy state. The passage is worth quoting in full:

> Ashkelon, being highly esteemed because it is precious and well-founded when it takes up watchful understanding (σκοπητικὸν νοῦν), will see, no longer blinded by the lowest pleasure and other passions, when it adopts reverence so as to be numbered among those who possess this virtue, concerning which people the oracle from Proverbs speaks about Wisdom and its [his?] Father: "He will guard the way of those

---

126. *CZ* III.99–103.

who revere him" (Prov 2:8).[127] The prophet under discussion summons—or rather the Word in him summons—all people to enter into this praiseworthy state when he says: "Let all flesh be reverent at the presence of the Lord" (Zech 2:17) Almighty.

Once again, as in the programmatic introduction, reverence is particularly defined in relation to the appearance of the Son, a connection made clear not only by Didymus' citation of the Proverbs-text but also by a passage in Zechariah that he has already discussed in reference to the Incarnation (2:17). Reverence guards the soul from the allurement of the passions; the soul in this condition receives the promise of God's protection. On this occasion, Didymus argues that reverence becomes a guarantee of God's future benefits. He goes on to cite passages that speak of the plenitude of gifts given to those who fear the Lord.[128]

The Church as Fortress

Didymus proceeds to discuss the "stronghold" of reverence later in the same chapter.[129] Zechariah speaks of Jerusalem's deliverance from the "waterless pit" as a result of the blood of the covenant (9:11). The prisoners are enabled to return to their stronghold (9:12). Didymus reads the "fortress" to which they return as symbolic of the reality of the Church and the virtues proper to living in it, "reverence (εὐλάβεια)" being the first mentioned. He argues in the early section of the interpretation that the blood of the covenant here is the blood of Christ that delivered those who died before his descent from the bonds of their captivity.[130]

More importantly for our theme, at the end of the lacunae Didymus also speaks of the significance of the deliverance for those who are presently alive. Souls who profit from the blood shed for them are taken captive by the Church. They are given "security (ἀσφάλεια)" and "repose (καθεδοῦνται διαναπαυόμενοι)" after their deliverance from the waterless pit. They are secure because they have reached the city whose "watchtowers ensure salvation."[131] Unlike the culpable cities of Tyre and Nineveh whose strongholds

---

127. Didymus is alluding to Proverbs 2:6: "The Lord gives wisdom." The Father gives Wisdom—the Son—and guards the way of the one who reveres the Son.

128. See Sirach 25:11 and Psalm 33:10–11 LXX.

129. *CZ* III.160–176.

130. There are numerous *lacunae* from *CZ* III.164 to 171. I have leaned on Koenen ("Ein theologischer Papyrus," 65) for the reconstruction of the text from III.165-8 on one occasion. For the purposes of my reading here, he differs significantly from Doutreleau's text only in III.168. See Doutreleau, *Sur Zacharie*, 699n2. Koenen takes the illegible letter as an ι instead of a ν (which allows him to read "blood" (αἷμα) into the text). The upshot of his reconstruction is that the dead are released from the "waterless pit" of Hades when the blood of the Savior is shed on their behalf.

131. *CZ* III.173 (FC 111:219).

were built for the confinement of their prisoners and in conceit against God,¹³² those who enter the Church are guarded from all that seeks their harm.

Didymus then speaks of the praiseworthy strongholds of the city of rest:

> In the divine text of Proverbs reverence is called a stronghold for those who practice holiness and righteousness: "The fear (φόβος) of the Lord is the stronghold of the holy one" (Prov 10:29). The one who is sheltered by the fear of God and ascends beyond this protection (ὑπεραναβάς), praying to be guarded by God himself, says to him in prayer: "Be for me God the protector, to deliver me into a strong place" (Ps 70:3), and again in the Thirty-first Palm: "You are my refuge from the affliction that surrounds me; O my joy, ransom me from those who pursue me" (Ps 31:7). . . . What is more, he who fights the good fight and finishes the good course, and keeps the faith is himself kept by it (αὐτῆς); he shows that it is built securely (ἀσφαλῶς) and is impregnable when he shouts in thanksgiving along with those who resemble him: "Behold, the strong city, even our salvation! He will erect its inner and outer walls" (Isa 26:1).¹³³

Drawing heavily from the wisdom literature of the OT, Didymus observes that the fear of the Lord is the guarantee of God's presence. The comments about reverence being the guarantee of future benefits from God—in the passage about Ashkelon—are further clarified here. Reverence guarantees receptivity to the benefits of God because God himself takes up his habitation in those who fear him. Where God is, there nothing good is lacking. Where one recognizes that God is to be obeyed in reverent fear, there God is.¹³⁴ The two passages above share a common interest in describing the spiritual life in terms of a progress from the fear of the Lord (i.e. reverence) to the possession of God himself. Images of captivity give way to those of rest and rejoicing in the protective company of God.

Completing the Tower

A final kind of passage concludes our treatment of the theme. Given that the pursuit of the virtuous life does not take place in a vacuum, Didymus recognizes that it is sustained only through constant vigilance: the person who pursues it is constantly on the lookout for the commands of God *and* constant-

---

132. Cf. *CZ* III.86–88, 92–93.

133. *CZ* III.175–176.

134. The same point is given a pneumatological application in *CZ* II.131. The person who by the active practice of the commands of God seeks to enjoy spiritual fertility is given a "spring of life welling up to eternal life" (John 4:14) by the Savior. Cf. John 7:37–39.

ly aware of the advances made by the enemies of the soul. Keeping a close watch on the desires of the heart, the perfect is able to resist temptation when it comes. Didymus' treatment of Zion illustrates the former kind of attentiveness:

> Zion is translated "watchtower for the performance of a command," and Jerusalem "vision of peace." Zion at the anagogical level is that which attends not to temporal things but to eternal ones, in the performance of the commands given to it. The clarity and tranquility of those who practice these things follows upon this state.[135]

Obedience to God's commands, spiritually interpreted, is the prelude to the experience of God's peace. The watchful life is a life of obedience to God's commands.

Another kind of watchfulness is directed toward the enemies of the soul. In the final chapter of Zechariah, Didymus comments on the tower of Hananel (Zech 14:10), exploring the parabolic significance of the tower in connection with Jesus' story of the man who built a tower without counting the cost (Luke 14:28–30). How could the one who builds this tower not finish the work that is begun? Establishing the foundation securely, he must go on to erect its summit so that he may stand upon it "to keep a lookout for the enemies who hasten toward him from afar."[136]

Reverence toward God in the present life implies vigilance. Although it is possible to speak of attaining a certain kind of security in the present life for Didymus (when no virtue is lacking the soul is able to resist all kinds of temptation), this security is always under threat as long as one is in the "tent." It is maintained only as the soul is defended by attentiveness to the commands of God. So Didymus enjoins his students to complete their progress in virtue with due zeal and haste.[137] They are to make an offering of their virtue in obedient response to the Son's gracious decision to receive the virtue "found among human beings."[138]

Summary and Critique

This chapter has treated the question: to what extent is the moral life revealed by Christ realizable in the present age? Didymus answers that it is pos-

---

135. Σιὼν μὲν γὰρ ἑρμηνεύεται σκοπευτήριον ἐντολῇ πεποιημένη, Ἰερουσαλὴμ δὲ ὅρασις εἰρήνης· Σιὼν κατ' ἀναγωγὴν καλεῖται ἡ μὴ τὰ πρόσκαιρα ἀλλὰ τὰ αἰώνια σκοποῦσα τῷ ποιεῖν τὰς δοθείσας ἐντολάς. Ἕπεται δὲ τῇ τοιαύτῃ καταστάσει τὸ ἀσύγχυτον καὶ ἀτάραχον τῶν κατορθουμένων (CZ I.64–65).
136. CZ V.113.
137. CZ V.186.
138. CZ II.63 (FC 111:128).

sible for the zealous to be fully conformed to this life. However, Didymus is always insistent, even when he is speaking about the perfect, that the virtues of Christ are the grounds of those that exist in the saints. They are virtuous only by participation in him, and the virtue that he possesses as an ontologically and morally perfect human being is superior to that possessed by the saints. This superiority is explained in one instance—the crowns of Joshua—in light of the fact that the saints receive his virtue by sharing in him.

Didymus' teaching about moral virtue also reveals at every point its codependence on contemplative virtue. The gravitational center, so to speak, of Didymus' understanding of moral virtue is the proper contemplation of the Incarnation. This contemplation involves proper reverence before the Son, and directs the active life of obedience to his commands, since it is not fitting to enact the commands of God without understanding. It is in light of the asymmetrical character of Didymus' anthropology and (thus) his prioritizing of the contemplative life that his statements about the superiority of contemplation over action are to be understood. A fuller account of the content of the contemplative life is provided in the next chapter.

The pursuit of stability takes place in the context of struggle for mastery of the soul. Didymus appeals on one or two occasions to a protology that assumes that things were not always as they are at present: in the luminous preexistence of the soul, it was filled with virtue and with the knowledge of God. The recovery of stability involves a return to a former state of proximity with God that existed before the soul's exile. The exilic motifs of the book of Zechariah are thus grist to the mill of Didymus' spiritual pedagogy. Given Didymus' protological commitments to the pre-existence of the soul before its descent into material embodiedness, Didymus' emphasis on attaining absolute likeness to the Son as a means of guaranteeing stability is understandable. It is only by being completely attuned to him that the soul is guarded from a return to vice. Yet, as Didymus himself appears to have recognized, even utter conformity to the Son in the present life is still an insecure "utter": the soul in its perfect state has the power to resist evil, but also has the possibility of not doing so if it becomes inattentive. Didymus implies in his two-fold account of keeping the Festival of Tabernacles that the resurrection of the spiritual body is key in guaranteeing eschatological stability, in which the possibility of lapsing into vice again is no more.

On the contemplative dimensions of Didymus' eschatology, we will have more to say in the following chapter. For the present, however, it is fitting to register two observations: one that guards against a misunderstanding of Didymus' account of the moral life and one that offers a criticism of it. Didymus is clearly optimistic about the possibilities of being conformed to the virtues revealed by the Son in the Incarnation. The accent of his pedagogical exegesis falls heavily on the identification of these virtues and on pointing his students toward the manner of their acquisition by the soul.

Consequently, Didymus' Christology has a heavily exemplarist accent. Yet it would be far too facile to argue that Didymus' exemplarism is proto-Pelagian.[139] On at least three very significant counts, Didymus' theology is on much firmer ground: 1) Didymus understands the experience of sin to have had distortive consequences on the moral faculty of the human soul, such that it is impossible for the human to pursue virtue without the help of God. If he is sometimes unclear about the priorities of the life of obedience—does God's help precede or follow after human repentance?—he is quite clear that the Christian life is pursued only in dependence upon God.[140] 2) Didymus secures this point most persuasively in his account of the human acquisition of virtue, which is always a matter of both imitation *and* participation. Christ is the example *par excellence* of perfect humanity, but is not merely this, since as the eternal Logos of the Father he is the one in whom all others are made perfect. Hence Didymus makes a crucial distinction between Christ, the possessor of all the virtues and the best of all teachers, and all other athletes for piety and teachers of virtue. Others come to possess that which he himself is by participation in him, and not merely by imitation of him. 3) As the divine Son of God, Christ accomplishes certain things that humanity cannot imitate, things which are proper to himself alone. Just as in the *DT*, Didymus draws our attention to these things in the *CZ*: the blood of his covenant is what releases the dead from Hades. His victory over sin and death is something that takes place for us and on our behalf, without which our "striving would be losing."

If Didymus is as optimistic as Pelagius purportedly is with respect to the possibility of attaining to conformity to the virtues of Christ in this lifetime, he describes the process far more adequately. However, Didymus' optimism is not inconsequential. In subsequent chapters, we will have cause to examine the ramifications of Didymus' doctrine of perfection for his interpretation of Scripture. For the present, it is sufficient to say that this dimension of Didymus' thinking is overly-realized. He will have difficulty defending it by

---

139. I refer to the characterization of Pelagius' teaching as understood by the later tradition.

140. See Heron, "The Holy Spirit in Origen and Didymus," 304: "There is a certain vagueness . . . as to whether the gift of the Spirit or the turning away from faults comes first, and that vagueness is characteristic of Didymus. He can speak sometimes as if the mortification of the flesh or the overcoming of mental "perturbations" are preconditions for the gift of the Spirit; but he can also ascribe mortification or the conquering of perturbation to the Spirit himself. Nor is clarity greatly increased when he comments that "those who have often received the benefits of God know that they have achieved them more by his grace and mercy than by their own efforts"! But Didymus is not in fact concerned with the issue which would only arise sharply with Pelagius; he is describing the dynamic of an ongoing interaction rather than the priorities in its beginnings." Cf. Prinzivalli, *Didimo il Cieco*, 21, who notes that Didymus is optimistic about the possibility of not sinning, but that this progress takes place "with the help of God (con l'aiuto di Dio)."

appealing to the plain sense of certain scriptural texts, and on more than one occasion his appeal to the examples of the saints in the OT and the NT will beg the question. We note also that it is this aspect of his teaching about the spiritual life that raises the most puzzling question for the broader exegetical corpus: namely, what to make of the literal sense of Scripture when it clearly predicates moral imperfections of the saints or of the authors of the Scriptures?[141]

Secondly, and more critically, it must likewise be asked if Didymus can really secure an adequate notion of security/stability by pursuing his account of salvation in this direction. Even if the Christian can succeed in being utterly conformed to the goal of all progress, described as the "house of God," there is still the possibility of lapsing again into vice as long as the Christian remains subject to temptation. There are few reasons to suppose that well-formed habits or dispositions—even perfectly formed ones—will secure for her the peace and the rest that she desires, since it was precisely in such a pristine condition that the soul (whether it was purely incorporeal or spiritually embodied in its pre-existence) turned away from God toward materiality. If salvation consists in large measure in the realization of the virtues of Christ in us, and these virtues were ours "before the present life"—as Didymus asserts—then there is cause to wonder whether eschatological security will be attained merely by recovering that which we formerly possessed. Clearly this is where Didymus invests his greatest capital when he argues that the Feast of Tabernacles will be observed more perfectly on high when the body rises spiritual and incorruptible. It would be anticipating our conclusions in chapter 5 to discuss here how Didymus deals with this theme. For the present, we note only that the question of stability is not secured for Didymus by insisting on absolute conformity to Christ in the present life. The resolution of the aporia, if there is one, awaits his treatment of the *eschaton*.

---

141. Cf. Layton, *Didymus the Blind and His Circle*, 72. Layton's compelling reading of Didymus' *HiT* highlights the significance of Didymus' conviction that Job is a model of virtue. The doctrine of pre-existence serves to rescue Job from the charge of capitulating to "contempt" or "disapproval (ὀλιγωρία)" of God's plan when he curses the day of his birth. He is not abandoning his courage or speaking idle words, but rather agreeing with God's judgment of the evil choice by which the soul sinned in its pre-existent state and (thus for Didymus) became embodied. The interpreter may not threaten "the coherence of the narrative by introducing unacceptable inconsistency into the character of Job. . . . As God has judged the servant to be righteous, so also the interpreter is under the obligation to delineate the virtue in *every* action of the hero." A similar conviction with respect to the inspired authors of Scripture causes Didymus to equivocate over passages where "sin" and "restoration" are predicated of them, as occurs frequently in the Psalms.

5

THE CONTEMPLATIVE LIFE AND ESCHATOLOGICAL KNOWLEDGE

We turn to the investigation of Didymus' account of illumination, or as he more commonly calls it in the *CZ*: the pursuit of the "contemplative (θεωρητικός) life" or "intellective (διανοητικός) virtue."[1] That there is a privileging of the contemplative over the moral life in *CZ* is evident on a casual reading of the text. I have argued that this priority is in part a function of Didymus' anthropology, in which the soul's interior vision is determinative of the moral conduct of the human person. I have also noted, with others, that the division between ethics and contemplation by no means implies that one can pursue one without the other: both moralism and a morally fruitless contemplation are false polarities that must be avoided in the pursuit of Christlikeness.

In Didymus' account of illumination, there are three stages that are described in the *CZ*: 1) the proper regard for the world in light of God's "providential care (πρόνοια)" for it, 2) the doctrine of the Son's Incarnation, and 3) the interior vision of the divinity of the Only-begotten, which is also the beatific vision of the Trinity. Of these, deference is shown to the final stage, a feature that is consistent throughout the Commentary. In this chapter, we shall query the significance of Didymus' subordination of the doctrine of the Incarnation to the doctrine of the eternal identity of the Son. Is this merely an assertion of the *ordo cognoscendi*? Or are there reasons to suppose that Didymus conceives of the knowledge of the Son in the Incarnation as provisional, an accommodation to human modes of knowing before full knowledge is possible?

I get at the answer to this question in three ways: 1) by examining the passages in *CZ* in which the two are juxtaposed, 2) by examining Didymus' statements about the *eschaton* and the knowledge of God, and 3) by appealing to Didymus' discussion of the role of Christ's humanity in the *eschaton* in the broader corpus.[2] I conclude the chapter by offering a composite sketch of

---

1. For the former, see *CZ* I.229, I.266, II.29, and V.112. For the latter, see I.409, II.341, and V.169.

2. My selections are drawn from *PsT*. On the dating of the Commentary, see Gesché, *La christologie*, 400–409, who suggests that the work is composed sometime between 370 and 385. Sympathetic with a date in the 380s are Bouteneff, "Placing the Christology," 395, and Simonetti, "Lettera e allegoria," 386–387n147. Although the data

Didymus' doctrine of Scripture and a summary of the ramifications of his understanding of the sanctified life for his exegesis. The final chapter takes these reflections and illustrates them concretely in reference to Didymus' interpretation of Zechariah 3.

Zechariah: from Word to Vision

The genre of the book under discussion plays an important role in Didymus' development of the themes of the contemplative life. As scholars have recognized, Didymus is sensitive to the various requirements of the books he is interpreting and their location in the curriculum of the Holy Spirit.[3] Zechariah, whose visions provide ready material to the allegorist, is regularly described by Didymus in the CZ as one who is receptive to visions that are beyond the visible and material order. As one who receives the Word of God, he is rendered receptive to divine "speech." As such, his visions demand the application of the "mental eye."

This emphasis on the priority of intellective vision is especially notable 1) in the introductions that Didymus gives to some of his books within the commentary and 2) in his comments on Zechariah's introductory formulae. In the formal Prologue, for instance, Didymus establishes that Zechariah is both "illumined in the eye of his mind (ὄμμα διανοίας)" and "divinized (θεοποιηθείς)" by the Word who has come to him to deliver the prophetic word. The emphasis on intellective sight continues throughout the Prologue. Zechariah "saw great visions (ὀπτασίας)." By the divinizing Word, he was made capable of proclaiming these visions "under many figures and images."[4] The demands placed upon the interpreter of Zechariah and upon those gathered to

---

is too general to assign a precise date to the *PsT*, the Commentary is likely written within the same decade as the *CZ*. Didymus is more explicit in the *PsT* than in the *CZ* on the theme under discussion. Didymus does not seem to vary greatly between *CZ* and *PsT* on his Christology, save that in the *PsT* he tends to be more forthcoming on the various christological *topoi*.

3. See Simonetti, "Lettera e allegoria," 386–389. See also his discussion of *EcclT* in which Simonetti locates Didymus' treatment of Ecclesiastes within the curriculum expressed by Origen: Ecclesiastes is suitable reading for those who are prepared to investigate a philosophy of nature. It deals chiefly with what is visible and sensible (p. 375). Simonetti notes that Didymus does not wholly observe the limitations of this identification, but appeals less often to allegory and the spiritual sense than he does in *CZ* and *PsT*. Cf. also Stefaniw's discussion of Origen's curriculum—with some comparisons to Didymus'—in *Mind, Text, and Commentary*, 276–289.

4. *CZ* I.1. With Bienert, 73, who takes the words πολυτρόπως and πολυειδῶς to imply that the prophetic word is proclaimed "in ever new ways and in ever new figures (in immer neuer Weise und in immer neuen Bildern)."

hear him expound the Scriptures are two-fold: 1) they must pray to receive the Word[5] and 2) prepare themselves to understand the text "inwardly."[6]

In his introduction to the Fourth Book, with one eye turned toward the difficulties of interpreting Zechariah 11:1, Didymus appeals to the unique character of that which the prophet is describing.[7] The "riddles" of Scripture demand that the interpreter be "wise according to God (κατὰ Θεόν)." The one who is made wise by God possesses "understanding that is articulated and made wholly exact" to comprehend what is said in a figure. In all of the formal introductions in CZ, two emphases continually re-appear: 1) the interpreter needs divine help in interpretation and 2) this divine help comes in the form of the gift of illumination. In each of these instances, divine assistance is sought so that the mind of the interpreter might be so reformed that he is made participant in the same reality to which Zechariah attests.

As the above suggests, and as we have already noted with respect to DT, the participatory character of the prophetic utterance is central to Didymus' account of the experience of the prophet. No passage better illustrates this than the opening to Book Two, which we have already briefly discussed in chapter 3. Interpreting the meaning of the phrase: "the word of the Lord came (ἐγένετο) to me (Zech 6:9)," Didymus notes that

> when the word of the Lord comes to such a person [as the prophet], it gives him sight (ὀμματοῖ) and illumines him to behold (θεάσασθαι) the beauties and mysteries of the truth and wisdom of God. This word that comes (γίνεται) to the prophet is none other than God the Word, who comes to holy men, angels, powers, authorities, thrones, and lordships, while he is always (ὢν ἀεί) with the Father who begot him.[8]

Didymus, as he does earlier in the Prologue, affirms the relationship between the reception of the divine Logos and the inwardly visual character of this reception. The implications of these formal introductions are spelled out further in Didymus' treatment of items within the text.

Didymus appeals to the genre of "vision" in accord with the above, articulating the superiority of this mode of apprehension over all others. In the most notable instance, Didymus argues that the "house" of Zechariah 4:9 is not a

---

5. Didymus expands on the theme of the Prologue in CZ III.1–3 (the introduction to Book Three) when he clarifies that the word of which he is speaking is the "word of wisdom and knowledge." This "word" is nothing other than the gift of the Holy Spirit, and (necessarily) signifies nothing other than the interpreter's receptivity to all the Persons of the Trinity. The one who has this "word" is "thrice-blessed (τρισμακάριος) because the God of the Universe is his instructor."

6. Bienert, 73.

7. CZ IV.2.

8. CZ II.2–3.

"sensible building," but rather that it is revealed to the prophet Zechariah "in the mode of a vision (ὀπτασίας τρόπῳ)." Stressing the advantage of this mode of communication, Didymus writes that God communicates by revelations to those who "are contemplative in the inner man." The divine "speaks" by visions rather than by words that require the proper articulation of the tongue, passage of sound through the air, and the proper function of the ear. God the Word communicates directly to those who possess the Spirit of adoption. "Being the true light, he illumines the mind (διάνοιαν) of those whom he wishes to receive his divine speeches (ὁμιλίας); he speaks by vision (ὁράσει) rather than to the ears (ἐν ὠσί)."[9] Divine speech in its purest form is for Didymus nothing other than the conveyance of truth directly to the mind. Didymus accordingly observes that Zechariah was one such as could see these visions "luminously (φωτεινῶς)."[10]

The expository remarks on Zechariah's introductory formulae contain the same emphasis on illumination. The prophetic formula: "I lifted my eyes" (Zech 2:1, 2:5, 5:1, 5:9, and 6:1) is treated on several occasions, Didymus arguing in a representative example that "a person lifts the eyes of the inner man (τοῦ ἔσω ἀνθρώπου) to contemplate the visions (θεαμάτων) that concern him."[11] Didymus uses the observation in this case to argue that the rebuilding of Jerusalem is chiefly concerned with the anagogical meaning of the city's name; one applies the "vision" to the soul, the Church, and the eschatological City of God. Elsewhere, he notes that the lifting of the eyes implies that the scriptural passage intends to reveal "what is not plain from what is manifest, . . . intelligible things (νοούμενα) from things sensible (αἰσθητῶν)."[12] The vision concludes with an exhortation to revile the "wings of a stork" in favor of bearing the wings of the Holy Spirit, by which a person ascends to the regions above heaven.[13]

The primacy of the visual sense of the soul is affirmed in the CZ in various other ways as well. Didymus privileges thought over speech in his allegorical treatment of certain pairings. Taking Zechariah 6:11 ("Take from them silver and gold") as an opportunity to introduce a distinction of this kind, Didymus

---

9. *CZ* I.314–318.

10. *CZ* I.416.

11. *CZ* I.102. Cf. I.82–86. Unfortunately lacunose, this latter discussion majors on the importance of divine illumination, the first sentence contrasting one set of eyes with "[eyes?] illumined." Didymus then appears to contrast within this latter category two kinds of vision: the vision of God himself and the vision "of that which comes from him." In the case of Zechariah's vision of the four horns, he is illumined by "the true light," the Son. These eyes are therefore the eyes of his διάνοια, beholding the powers of evil with divine help so that he may put on the panoply of God. See also I.345 (the eyes of the διάνοια), I.386, and I.404 (in which he takes the phrase "I lifted up my eyes" to mean that the prophet is "turning to yet another revelation (ἀποκάλυψιν)").

12. *CZ* I.345 and 354.

13. *CZ* I.401.

interprets silver as "speech (λόγος)" and gold as "understanding (νοῦς)." Citing a passage from the Canticle (1:11-12) in which gold figurines are engraved with silver markings, Didymus argues that gold is specifically a reference to the "teachings (παιδεύματα)" of the OT that testify to the good things to come. These teachings have diverse forms because of the various "words" in which they are couched. Linking the observation back to Zechariah, he argues that the "athletes of piety" who are crowned in silver and gold crowns are to put these treasures to good use. Didymus is arguing in abbreviated fashion that the athletic contests of virtue are engaged in properly when the contestant discerns the meaning ("gold") of Scripture by properly handling the words ("silver") in which this meaning resides.[14]

The priority of intellective vision over speech is likewise highlighted in Didymus' comments on Zechariah 9:9 ("Rejoice greatly, daughter of Zion; proclaim, daughter of Jerusalem"). Didymus takes the "daughter of Zion" as the soul adept in the moral life, attentive to the commands of God. The "daughter of Jerusalem" is the soul that sees peace, or the contemplative soul. The daughter of Jerusalem is given precedence over that of Zion because "the one who only performs the practical life is able to rejoice, whereas in addition to rejoicing the one that possesses vision (θεωρίαν) proclaims, because [that soul] possesses the supernatural gift of the Holy Spirit, the word of wisdom and knowledge."[15] To this passage we can fruitfully link those places in which Didymus calls the prophets those who "possess the Spirit of truth and are made ready by him to declare [the truth]."[16] Versed in all the doctrines of true religion, they are capable of adapting their discourse to those under their instruction.[17] Vision precedes truthful speech.[18]

The prophets are not only filled with the knowledge that they commend to others, but they are so endowed with understanding by the Spirit and the Word of the Father so as to speak in a manner befitting their divine Subject. Because the apprehension of divine things demands a mode beyond that asso-

---

14. *CZ* II.14-19. With Bienert, 94: "in a spiritual sense [silver and gold] become ... figures for the word and the sense of Spirit-inspired Scripture (im geistlichen Sinn [Silber und Gold] werden ... zu Bildern für Wort und Sinngehalt der geistgewirkten Schrift)."

15. *CZ* III.135-137.

16. *CZ* I.15.

17. *CZ* I.26, 32-34.

18. Though infrequent, Didymus' appeals to the concept of the "expressed word (προφορικὸς λόγος)" are of similar import. Divine "speech" to spiritual beings, like the devil in *CZ* I.198, is immediate. It does not require the use of human words or organs. Didymus implicitly privileges the "mind" or the "understanding" (νοῦς) over the "proffered word (προφορικὸς λόγος)" in *CZ* I.289, where the former is the "light" and the latter the "lamp-stand." He is not denigrating speech, since the wise teacher will and must make use of it so that the student is brought into the same knowledge that he possesses. However, he is acknowledging its mediating function or provisional role.

ciated with the five physical senses, the prophets commend their discourse to those who are likewise committed to moving beyond the materially visible order in their apprehension of God. For this, they require the purification of their interior vision, this being the most immediate mode of receiving divine revelation.

Such an account of Scripture is consistent with the mode in which Didymus discusses the relation of human language to divine reality in DT, though here Didymus gives freer rein to the provisional character of human language. God's being, beyond the order of the mind, must necessarily be beyond the order of human language as well. Because human language is best suited to the definition and circumscription of that which belongs to the corporeal order, it takes on an increasingly imagistic character when pressed into the service of revealing that which is beyond this order. For the higher beings, Didymus insists that thought is capable of apprehending what language cannot. But in the case of God, we stand in the difficult position of maintaining that One beyond the order of human thought has consented to reveal himself through spoken words. How can such revelation be received in a manner appropriate to such a One? Didymus' account of the progressive stages of the contemplative life contains his answer to the question.

The Stages of the Contemplative Life

Didymus avails himself of several opportunities to discourse upon the stages of the contemplative life. Of these, one passage in particular deserves lengthy treatment: Didymus' interpretation of the lamp-stand in Zechariah 4. The section serves to provide an outline of what, in particular, Didymus means by the content of the contemplative life. What, in particular, are the doctrines of piety that are to serve as the objects of spiritual contemplation? And how are they related to one another?

The Vision of the Lamp-Stand [19]

Didymus is most forthcoming about the various stages of the contemplative life in his reflections on Zechariah 4. In the vision, Zechariah beholds a golden "lamp-stand (λυχνία)"; at its top rest a "lamp (λαμπάδιον)" and seven "lights (λύχνοι)." Above the lamp are two olive trees, bearing fruit that nourishes the light by the oil that runs, via oil-conduits, from the trees to the lamp (4:1–3). Zechariah returns a second time to discuss the meaning of the olive trees at the end of the vision (4:11–14). My exposition of Didymus focuses on these sections of Zechariah 4, which correspond to the initial and final lemmata of the vision. Comparison of the two is warranted insofar as Didymus

---

19. *CZ* I.271–343.

speaks of the two lemmata as appropriate to the novice and the advanced stages of contemplation.[20]

The First Treatment of the Vision

Didymus loses little time in reinforcing the notion that Zechariah 4 is a vision that concerns intelligible realities. The angel asks: "What do you see?" Zechariah answers that he sees a lamp-stand of pure gold. The "spiritual (νοερά)" and "incorporeal (ἀσώματος)" character of the vision is indicated by this first identification, argues Didymus. Gold is employed in Scripture as a figure for spiritual realities;[21] the mode of "apprehension (ἀντίληψις)" appropriate to such a vision is the sight that is enabled by the "illumined eyes of the heart (καρδίας)." What follows is spiritually perceived.[22]

The summit of pure spiritual vision is the "luminous doctrine [λόγος] of the Trinity,"[23] the lamp that is set atop the lamp-stand, shedding its radiant light on all else. This is the very lamp from which the five wise virgins lit their lamps in order to meet the Bridegroom (Matt 25:1-7). They are wise for no other reason than that they share in divine knowledge by participation in God (the Father), the True Light (the Son), and the Holy Spirit. Didymus then notes that the seven lights appear, like the lamp, on top of the lamp-stand. This unexpected detail of the text—one anticipates the lights atop the lamp rather than the lamp-stand—is not incidental to the meaning of the vision for our exegete. Taking these lights as a "seven-fold illumination (ἑπτάφωτος ἐπίλαμψις)" or a "perfectly luminous understanding (τελεία φωτεινὴ νόησις)," he implicitly associates the lamp with the lights. The Trinity (the lamp) stands in the same place as perfect illumination (the seven lights) because the one who knows the Trinity is perfectly illumined.[24]

This first move contextualizes all that follows. Didymus proceeds to develop an identification of the lamp-stand, which he has avoided until this point. No longer functioning strictly within the limitations of the first figural mode,[25] Didymus takes the lamp-stand to refer to the "soul and flesh that the

---

20. See *CZ* I.336.

21. Didymus grants counter-examples to this claim in *CZ* I.278, but the concession does not affect the trajectory of his interpretation.

22. Summarizing *CZ* I.277–278.

23. FC 111:85. On the use of λόγος, see Doutreleau, *Sur Zacharie*, 342n1, who notes the priority of θεωρία over λόγος, describing the former as "an immediate illumination of the mind (une illumination ... directe de l'esprit)" and the latter as "the discursive process of the mind (la démarche discursive de l'esprit)." With Doutreleau, who notes that λόγος is "the daughter of contemplation (fille de la contemplation)" in *CZ* I.340, the superiority of θεωρία should not imply here a kind of subordinate status to the λόγος of the Trinity, since accurate λόγος assumes authentic θεωρία.

24. Summarizing *CZ* I.279–280.

25. *CZ* I.280. He introduces the shift from the discussion of the lamp and its lights to the lamp-stand with the phrase "in a different figure (καθ' ἕτερον τρόπον)." The

Savior assumed in his descent." Just as its golden quality is indicative of Christ's moral purity, likewise Christ's soul "undergirds" the seven-fold illumination spoken of above. He is, as one receptive to the Holy Spirit, perfectly illumined in this assumed humanity. The significance of this identification is left un-developed, save that Didymus, passing quickly onto the manner in which he and his audience are to likewise seek for perfect illumination, holds up the humanity of Christ as the primary instance of divine contemplation and knowledge.[26]

How is this divine knowledge attained? Seven oil-conduits bring oil from two olive trees to nourish the lights on the lamp-stand. Didymus singles out the oil and the olive trees for comment. The "oil" signifies "meditation on the knowledge of the truth." The olive trees represent two kinds of meditation: "the oil obtained from the olive tree on the right means meditation [μελέτη] on the intelligible realities [τῶν νοητῶν] and the gifts of the Holy Spirit" and "oil pressed from the olive tree on the left means meditation on the world, its composition, and God's providence for it."[27] Didymus commends to his audience the benefits of both kinds of meditation, noting that "from meditation we derive the profits of memory (μνήμην) and a more robust contemplation (θεωρίαν)."[28] He finishes the exposition of the lemma 1) by introducing interpretive alternatives—some of which he will revisit in his second treatment of the olive trees—and 2) by developing an applicative sense of the text to Christian teaching.[29] We will return to #1, but for the present these alternatives need not concern us.

The above represents Didymus' initial foray into the meaning of a text that is, from the outset, meant to be understood in a purely inward way.[30] Several items within his interpretation deserve comment. 1) Didymus establishes that the doctrine of the Trinity is the summit of all knowledge in the intelligi-

---

phrase contrasts with the earlier "in the same figure (ὅνπερ ... τρόπον)." Didymus does not mean to imply by this that he has abandoned the first line of interpretation—its kinship with what he has already said is evident—but rather acknowledges that he is making a coherent interpretation by appealing to multiple figural modes of reference. Namely, given that the "gold" of the lamp-stand serves primarily as a reminder of the spiritual character of the vision, it has a secondary function to play within Didymus' account of illumination as a reference to the moral purity of Christ's humanity. The golden lamp-stand serves two functions within the same interpretive scheme.

26. Summarizing *CZ* I.280–282.
27. *CZ* I.284 (FC 111:86–87).
28. *CZ* I.283–284. See Doutreleau, *Sur Zacharie*, 341.
29. *CZ* I.285–290.
30. It is noteworthy that Didymus is unable to live up to the genre identification he provides earlier. The purely intelligible quality of the vision is compromised by Didymus' inclusion of features like the "flesh" assumed by the Savior and the world with its composition. However, there is a clear emphasis on the priority of the intelligible throughout.

ble order. The one who knows the Trinity is necessarily participant in this God whom she knows, as Didymus' use of the parable of the virgins illustrates. 2) The fulsome knowledge of the Trinity to which the zealous aspire is illustrated chiefly by the morally and contemplatively perfect life of the Savior in the humanity that he assumes. 3) Didymus commends meditation to his audience as the means whereby they become, like the Savior in his humanity, more fully luminous with the radiant doctrine of the Trinity. In this meditation, they ponder intelligible realities and the spiritual gifts as well as the world in light of God's providence for it.

We note that the major themes of the contemplative life are all present and outlined in clarity for the first time: the Trinity, the Incarnation, and the providential ordering of the world.[31] The doctrine of the Trinity is given priority of place; under it, in the spatial matrix of the vision and in Didymus' use of it, is the doctrine of the Incarnation. In the right-left contrast between the olive trees we see also a priority established between meditation on spiritual realities and meditation on the world in light of God's providential ordering of it. Though this second kind of meditation stands in the lowest place, it is contributory to the brightness of the light that is the mind illumined by the Trinity. We see here a kind of reflexivity in Didymus' thinking. Partaking of the Trinity and sharing in divine wisdom is that which allows a person to know all other things rightly. The converse also holds true: meditation on that which is truly the case about the material and intelligible orders gives rise to a more accurate contemplation of the Trinity. Meditation bears fruit when it considers God and all things in God.

The Second Treatment of the Vision

Didymus returns to a consideration of the two olive trees in the final lemma of the vision. Anticipating his treatment of the final element of the vision, Didymus had noted earlier that in the later stages of illumination, the spiritual days illuminated by the Sun of Righteousness become longer.[32] The saints are to become like the "all-holy cherubim," who gaze with seven eyes upon the things of God.[33] Accordingly, Didymus describes the matter of the final lemma as a movement from an earlier stage of contemplation to one that is more advanced. Didymus notes that the prophet's repetitive questioning of his exegetical helper indicates his advancement from a lower to a higher way of knowing. The appropriate stage of illumination is pre-requisite to the understanding of certain visions.

---

31. The possible exception to this is Didymus' earlier articulation of the same three stages in *CZ* I.23–25, where Didymus articulates a distinction between 1) that which is behind the "back" of the man on the red horse, namely creation, 2) the human actions of the Logos, and 3) the things pertaining to his divinity, things wholly removed from the material order. This first distinction is, however, not as clear as in the above.

32. See *CZ* I.327–329.

33. *CZ* I.332.

The angel's silence in response to Zechariah's first question ("What are these olive trees?" (4:11)) prompts him to ask a less ambitious one. He ventures: "What are the two branches of the olive trees" (4:12)? Didymus refers us back to his earlier interpretation of the olive trees, which he had identified with "divine meditation." It is by means of this process of meditation that one arrives at the answer to later questions. The prophet reveals this process to us when he asks what the parts of the trees are. "[H]is hope is to benefit from these parts of the trees so as to succeed eventually in knowing what the olive trees are."[34] Given that the former identification of the trees belongs to an earlier stage of knowledge—Didymus cites portions of 1 Corinthians 13:9-12 in this connection—the prophet reveals to us how to pass into a more immediate vision of them.[35]

Didymus then retrieves an earlier interpretation that he had raised as a possibility for the olive trees in his first treatment of the vision. The olive trees are in this higher way of knowing the Son and the Holy Spirit. It is impossible to comprehend these two divine "trees" directly, but their "branches" are the means by which they are made known to us. In the case of the Son, "a branch would be the Word's becoming flesh"; in the case of the Holy Spirit, the branch is "initial insight [εἰσαγωγικὴ θεωρία] into him."[36]

By making these identifications, Didymus anticipates the angel's answer: these olive trees, the angel tells Zechariah, are the "sons of plenty who stand by the Lord of the whole earth" (4:14). Didymus' treatment of this verse is somewhat unclear,[37] but it is possible to articulate his main thrust: the doctrine of the Father is "plenty" and "its sons" are the doctrines of the Son and the Holy Spirit. He concludes the lemma by proposing several other alternative interpretations, but it is clear that the above is primary. Didymus' final words in relation to the lattermost stage of contemplative vision reveal that he is keen to maintain St Paul's distinction between knowing in part in this life and the knowledge that is "face to face." The knowledge of the Trinity and our contemplation of the Persons are in this life partial. Hence Didymus issues the caveat about this final stage of interior vision: "insofar as it is possible for one who is still in a body to know."[38]

On the basis of the above, we conclude that Didymus envisions three interrelated, but distinguishable, moments in the contemplative life. At the earliest stage of meditation, the contemplative is to discern the relation of the doctrine of the Trinity to the cosmos: namely, how the world's composition

---

34. *CZ* I.336 (FC 111:98).

35. Summarizing *CZ* I.336-337.

36. *CZ* I.338 (FC 111:98).

37. See Doutreleau, *Sur Zacharie*, 374-375n1. Cf. Hill (FC 111:98n40). The ancient readers of the text were likewise puzzled by Didymus' assertion that he had formerly identified the Father with the tree "on the right" (*CZ* I.340).

38. *CZ* I.340: ὡς ἐνδέχεται γνῶναι τὸν ἔτι ἐν σώματι ὄντα. Cf. *PsT* 131,16-18.

and sustenance is the result of the Trinity's providential care for it. In the next stage, he is to move toward the contemplation of the Trinity. Unable to accomplish this movement without the priority of divine action, the contemplative is to focus his thoughts on the Incarnation of the Logos and the "pledge (ἀρραβών)" of the Holy Spirit. It is possible to identify this stage with Didymus' discussion of the gifts of the Holy Spirit in the first vision; the "pledge" of the Spirit is the guarantee of good things to come for the contemplative, the participation in which he becomes wise with spiritual wisdom. Likewise, we are given an example of the branch of the Son in the first lemma, where Didymus treats the Incarnation of the Son—in flesh and soul—as instructive in our pursuit of the moral life. With these stages completed the contemplative is finally to pass into the contemplation of Persons of the Trinity in a direct sense, though Didymus gives the final stage an eschatologically-realized dimension. The above passage is the most significant in the CZ on the relationship between the various stages of the contemplative life in their relationship to one another.

The Inner and Outer Walls[39]

A second passage reinforces the notion that these stages have a certain solidity in Didymus' mind. Zechariah, in a passage that describes the coming restoration of the Messianic age, informs the exiles that they will be set free to return to their stronghold (9:12). Our exegete links the passage in Zechariah to Isaiah 26:1, in which the prophet speaks of God erecting the "wall (τεῖχος)" and "outer wall (περίτειχος)" of the city of salvation. Four pairs of contrasts between these walls emerge, all of them related to the "strong city" whose walls they are: the Church. Didymus contrasts 1) the inner fortification of the spiritual and elevated contemplation of Scripture with the outer fortification of its literal and historical sense. 2) There is also the inner fortification of faith in the Trinity and the only-begotten Son of God, whose outer fortification is the doctrine of the Incarnation and the Virgin Birth.[40] 3) The godly thoughts of the Church are prioritized over its ethical instructions. 4) And finally, the contemplation of spiritual and incorporeal things has precedence over the knowledge of the "sensible world, its parts, and the divine providence (προνοίας) that governs it."[41]

The second pairing adds to that which we observed in Didymus' treatment of the Vision of the Golden Lamp-Stand. For here the theologian clears up an ambiguity: faith in the Trinity and faith in the Only-begotten Son of God, "who

---

39. *CZ* III.176–179.

40. *CZ* III.177. As we noted in *DT*, Didymus is consistent in arguing that the Virgin birth of the Son is an iconically-related reiteration in time of the Son's begetting from the Father. The Virgin remains a virgin as an image of the Father's eternal identity as Father of the Son.

41. *CZ* III.179.

is God the Word," are correlated at the same level of contemplation. Believing in and knowing the Son as the Only-begotten is tantamount to faith in the whole Trinity, for it is in knowing the Son in this way that one attains to the knowledge of the Father and his Spirit. This is an important move, for it reveals the basically pro-Nicene character of Didymus' spiritual theology at work in his reflections about the contemplative life. There is no sense that the knowledge of the Son must give way to a more advanced knowledge of the Father (cf. chapter 3). The same priority of spiritual contemplation over the contemplation of the world is once again present; notably, once again, there is no such thing in Didymus' mind as a contemplation of the world *in se*. It is always a matter of contemplating the world *sub specie divinitatis*.

The Former and the Latter Rains[42]

The pairing of former and latter rain in Zechariah 10:1 occasions similar reflections. Once again, Didymus proposes four readings (not all repeated here). All of these readings hinge on an earlier decision to take rain as "God-given teaching." The "ground" upon which this rain falls is the soul that is to bear fruit by receiving the sowing of Jesus.[43] Divine instruction and the soul are the fixed points of Didymus' interpretive framework, around which he gathers several insights. The first of these is a comment about Scripture: only those who drink from the early and the late rains of Scripture bear fruit. Those of the circumcision drank from the former but not of the Gospel; the "heterodox" drank of the New but not of the Old Testament. The apostolic church bears fruit that is sweet and edible from both rains.[44]

Following this first rendering, Didymus brings up an earlier distinction: the early rain is the doctrine of the "Inhumanation" of the Logos; following it is that which concerns "his divinity."[45] He also provides some commentary on this point, allowing us to grasp the significance of the claim for him more fully. The apostles John and Paul are examples of those who received both kinds of rain from the Lord. Did not the former confess that the Incarnate Word was also the Father's Only-begotten? The Theologian confessed that this Word became flesh in order that we might "see his glory" (John 1:14). The Apostle of the divine economy likewise affirmed that though he once knew the Christ

---

42. *CZ* III.249–253.

43. The Parable features largely in Didymus' explanation of the appearing of the dry "land (γῆ)" in the Creation account (see *GenT* 30,10–13), at which point he also draws the connection "at the allegorical level" (*GenT* 30,6) between "land" and "soul." Cf. *CZ* I.43 (discussed in chapter 4), in which Didymus makes the move from "earth (γῆ)" to "rational soul (λογικὴ ψυχή)."

44. Summarizing *CZ* III.249–250.

45. Cf. the more ambiguous wording in *CZ* I.22. Here the inclusion of the pronoun "his (αὐτοῦ)" qualifies θεολογία.

"according to the flesh" (κατὰ σάρκα), he knows him thus no longer (2 Cor 5:16).[46]

Didymus had earlier connected these passages to the same effect.[47] In both cases, Didymus understands the Pauline sentence to be making a declaration about the believer's acknowledgment of Jesus' full humanity. The adverbial phrase κατὰ σάρκα is taken as a reference to this humanity, rather than to a mode of knowing that is inherently this-worldly: i.e. bound up with sin and death. Locating the acknowledgment of Jesus' humanity, as Didymus does, within the realm of "God-given teaching" would seem to exclude taking κατὰ σάρκα in a pejorative sense. It is precisely the failure to see Christ κατὰ σάρκα that characterizes certain heresies: doubtless because of his expansive understanding of σάρξ (inclusive of rational humanity, and not just the material aspect of humanity) Didymus would include not only docetist christologies here but also Arian and Apollinarian ones as well. Didymus is therefore surely arguing that the recognition of Jesus' assumption of a complete humanity is an essential doctrine of the Christian faith. And yet its glory is meant to lead us beyond itself in some sense to the prior glory of the eternal Word of God.

Didymus then brings his two identifications of the "rains"—the two Testaments and the two ways of seeing the Son—into conversation with one another.[48] The Pauline sentence that he quotes (Rom 1:1–4) intertwines them both. Paul's "new" Gospel was announced by the prophets long ago; this Gospel concerns the one who came from David "in the flesh (κατὰ σάρκα)" and was declared to be the Son of God "by the Spirit of holiness." The passage is well-chosen. Just as the OT recounts the history of the chosen people with a special focus on the human lineage of the son of David, the NT reveals that the son of David is the Son of God. With this knowledge, the one who reads the Old may now read it as that which bears witness to the divine activity of the Logos in the Old. Thus the early rain of the Old Covenant, as it were, becomes infused with the latter rain of the New.[49]

The third rendering of the "rains" can be briefly mentioned here. There is a limit to what can be known in this life; in the world to come the raised will

---

46. *CZ* III.251.

47. The earlier passage (*CZ* I.141–2) connects Moses' vision of God's back (Exod 33:19) with the two passages mentioned above. Here Didymus refers to the two "glories" of the Son: the first is the glory of the Son "in which he is the Only-begotten God the Word" and the second glory is the "visible (ἐμφάνιος)" glory of the Incarnation. The prior glory is the more important of the two for him. The contrast between these two aspects of Christ's person is shared by other theologians as well. For Gregory of Nyssa's employment of the distinction, see John Behr, *The Formation of Christian Theology 2: The Nicene Faith, Part 2: One of the Holy Trinity* (Crestwood, NY: St Vladimir's Seminary Press, 2004), 450–451.

48. He refers to one explicitly; the other is included within the quotation.

49. *CZ* I.251.

see "face to face."⁵⁰ Didymus makes a similar remark in the passage on the olive trees; some things are impossible to know "while a person is still in a body." Resurrected existence implies a way of knowing that is fuller and more immediate.

Summary

At the beginning of the contemplative life, one takes in the light of the Sun of Righteousness in a mediated way. Perceiving the world in light of God's "providential care (πρόνοια)" for it, the contemplative rises above an immanent perception of the material world. Didymus cannot countenance such a perception of the material order as a truly contemplative moment. Even in the earliest stages of the contemplative life, the end—the Trinity—is assumed. It is always in the light of the creating and redeeming activity of the Trinity that the world is rightly understood. At the culmination of this stage, one perceives the ultimate expression of God's governance in the Incarnation of the Logos.⁵¹

This second stage of the contemplative life, as long as the stages are understood to bleed into one another, stands at the gravitational center of the Commentary. Didymus' moral sense is utterly dependent upon it, as we noted in the last chapter. For with the proper perception of the Incarnation of the Logos inheres Didymus' whole teaching about the moral sense of the OT. It is by reading the OT spiritually—i.e. reading it as that which bears witness to the presence of the Logos as he intimates his coming incarnate presence to us—that one discerns the pattern of Christian action enjoined therein. Proper contemplation at this stage gives rise to proper ethical action. It is as the contemplative is conformed to the image of the "man of heaven" that his contemplative vision is purified to discern the divinity of the Incarnate Son of God.

This final stage is nothing other than the discernment of the Son's prior and eternal glory as the Only-Begotten Son of the Father. It is also nothing other than the interior vision of the Father, Son, and Holy Spirit in their one divine being. Didymus contends that there is a certain measure of knowing God in this manner in the present life. When the intellect becomes purified from its attachment to materiality, it sees God clearly. At this stage, however, Didymus also notes that there is an eschatological climax to be awaited. Material embodiedness presents an obstacle to complete receptivity of this lattermost vision of God.

In short, the stages concern the contemplation 1) of God's provision for creation. This provision includes 2) the Incarnation of the Logos which stands as its ultimate expression and climax. The Word becomes a creature, while remaining the Word. Hereby the Logos accommodates himself to our ways of

---

50. See 1 Corinthians 13:9, 12.

51. See *CZ* I.140, in which Didymus explicitly ties the "Inhumanation (ἐνανθρώπησις)" and "descent (ἐπιδημία)" of the Logos to God's "administration (διοίκησις)" of the created order.

knowing. 3) The descent of the Logos enables an ascent of the mind from things earthly to things heavenly: the knowledge of the Son (or the Trinity) *in se*. In this account of the *ordo cognoscendi* there is primacy given to the final stage.[52] To know the Trinity *in se* is the goal of human knowing, and—in contrast to the imitation and (thus) requisite knowledge of Christ's humanity—is in some sense a state to be awaited in the age to come.

We proceed to ask, on the basis of the latter two stages in particular, what is the significance 1) of Didymus' claim that embodiedness constitutes an obstacle to divine knowledge and 2) of his citation of 2 Corinthians 5:16 ("Once we knew Christ according to the flesh, now we know him thus no longer.") in connection with the movement from the second to the third stage of contemplation. In short, Didymus' understanding of the role of Christ's assumed humanity in the *eschaton* is critical in knowing precisely *how* the former stages of the contemplative life are subordinate to the final stage. Is the subordination of the knowledge of the Son in the Incarnation to his eternal identity merely a recognition that one comes to the knowledge of the eternal Son through his Incarnation?[53] Is this subordination of the economy of the flesh merely an indication that Didymus' primary concern is to guard against subordinationist accounts of the Son's generation?[54] Or are there reasons to suppose that the subordination is better explained in Didymus by recognizing that, in the perfection of knowledge that we await in the age to come, the assumed humanity of the Son plays a less significant role?

Eschatological Vision

In this section, I examine the claims that Didymus makes about the *eschaton* in CZ. But before doing so, I must make the observation that Didymus' eschatological teaching in CZ is minimal. Due caution is required in interpret-

---

52. Cf. *CZ* IV.146.

53. So Reynolds, 82–83: "Didymus is quite consistent in relegating the knowledge of the Incarnation to a lower and more elementary level than that of the Trinity, as that which is accessible to those who know in part. . . . It does not, however, indicate that the Incarnation was unimportant for Didymus, or even that it was unimportant in comparison with the Trinity; on the contrary, it indicates that knowledge of the Trinity is posterior to and dependent upon knowledge of the Incarnation."

54. Doutreleau appears to take this position (*Sur Zacharie*, 309n3). Commenting on this phenomenon of the subjection the Incarnation to the Trinity in CZ he writes: "For Didymus, the study of the Trinity comes before that of the Incarnation and that of redemption. This [tendency] certainly characterizes his age. The problems of Arianism at that time compelled [them] to give priority to the Trinity within theological studies and within the liturgy. (Pour Didyme, l'étude de la Trinité passe avant celle de l'Incarnation et de la Rédemption. Cela marque bien son époque. Les problèmes de l'arianisme obligeaient alors à donner le prépondérance à la Trinité, dans les études théologiques et dans la liturgie)."

ing his thought on the *eschaton*, in light of the fact that he often plays on the polysemy of eschatologically significant phrases like "that day" and "the heavenly Jerusalem." To illustrate, the former functions in the *CZ* 1) as a reference to the "day" accomplished by the Sun of Righteousness in the Incarnation,[55] 2) as a reference to a "spiritual day" in which the recipients of divine light become illumined,[56] and 3) as a reference to the "last day."[57] Without clear contextual markers, it is difficult to conclude from such phrases that Didymus has the *eschaton* in mind. This suggests that it is wise to limit the scope of the investigation to those passages in which Didymus' reference to the *eschaton* is unequivocal. The following represent the more significant of a handful of such passages.

"The Lord Will Be One, and His Name One"[58]

Didymus' contemplative vision of the Trinity remains tied to his vision of the Trinity in the *eschaton*, a point that secures the non-provisional character of the Son's revelation of the Father both now and in the age to come. To know the Son as he is is to know the Trinity. Didymus interprets Zechariah 14:9 in light of the second coming of the one expected, whom he identifies as "the only-begotten Son of God" and as the "Sun of Righteousness." After affirming that the prophecy relates to the universal confession of divine unity in opposition to idolatry and the worship of the creation, Didymus notes that God "will be referred to by one name [ἑνὶ ὀνόματ[ι]]."[59]

Didymus appears to recognize that his language is in danger of being construed improperly. So he plants a hedge around it: "When we hear that God is one, [we do not recognize] the Trinity so as to consider that the signification ([σ]ημασίαν) concerns the Father but not the Son and the Holy Spirit. For the divinity of the Father, Son, and Holy Spirit is one."[60] Wholly consistent with what is said in *DT* and with what is affirmed throughout the *CZ*, the passage reveals Didymus' sensitivity to two issues: 1) the name "God" is used in a hypostatically specific sense to refer to the Father and in a general sense as the designation of the Trinity. It is this latter sense that is meant here. 2) The Persons of the Trinity are eschatologically one in the same sense in which they are presently one. This affirmation avoids the Sabellian and (later) Marcellan tendency toward regarding the eschatological vision of the Trinity—in which hypostatic differentiation no longer obtains—as expressive of a truer mode of

---

55. See *CZ* IV.109.
56. This is certainly the most common use of the phrase. See *CZ* I.325–329, II.244–255, IV.230–233, and V.103–104.
57. See *CZ* V.72–78.
58. *CZ* V.91–99.
59. *CZ* V.96 (FC 111:336).
60. *CZ* V.99. For discussions on the various *lacunae* in this section, see Doutreleau, *Sur Zacharie*, 1024–1026n2.

being for God. The hypostastically differentiated being of the Trinity has eternal consequences for our knowledge of the Trinity. The one name to be confessed into eternity, "God," is forever elucidated to us by a name that is its exact equivalent and exposition: "Father, Son, and Holy Spirit."

Forming a Single Man[61]

In a significant lemma (Zech 8:10), the prophet affirms the Lord's desire to restore the exiles to their land, so that they will be as numerous as they were before. He sowed them like seed among the peoples, where they had children and raised them; the Lord will now return them all to Gilead and Lebanon. In his interpretation of the passage, Didymus takes the promised restoration christologically, largely on the basis of a *defectus litterae* with respect to the promise of children,[62] framing the vision in terms of the cosmic exile of souls from original righteousness in the divine Presence and the economic function of the prophets and apostles in bearing spiritual children. Didymus envisions the end of the lemma as containing a prophecy of divinization and eschatological union with God for all rational beings.

The influence of Origen is seldom, if ever, more apparent in CZ than in this lemma. We have had cause to mention Didymus' assertion of pre-existence in connection with the idea that the righteous were "numerous even before the present life,"[63] an idea that occurs to him early in the interpretation of this passage. Correspondingly, at the end of it, the doctrine of the *apokatastasis* looms large, with Didymus asserting that the enemies from which God redeems his people will no longer "remain." Quick to explain himself, he argues that these enemies remain in existence "since it is impossible for a rational essence to return to non-being (εἰς τὸ μὴ ὄν)."[64] It is their enmity toward God that is done away with. We are interested here in the terms in which this restoration is envisaged.

With Didymus already tipping his hand in the eschatological direction, he launches into a full-blown eschatology in the subsequent paragraph: "This will occur especially when "God becomes all in all" (1 Cor 15:28)." Didymus cites several passages in quick succession. With the first, Ephesians 4:13, Didymus associates this divine becoming "all," with the growth of all to perfect maturity, Christ being held up as the one already filled with God in this sense. From this citation, Didymus proceeds to gather testimony to eschatological "unity." In the maturity envisioned, all will share the "same mind" and be granted the

---

61. CZ III.280–308.
62. See CZ III.288. For this consistent feature of allegorical exegesis more generally, see Jean Pépin, "A propos de l'histoire de l'exégèse allégorique: l'absurdité, signe de l'allégorie," *Studia Patristica* 1 (1957): 395–413.
63. CZ III.288 (FC 111:244).
64. CZ III.307.

"oneness" in the Father and the Son for which Christ prays as high priest in the Upper Room (John 17:21). Didymus concludes the reflection:

> Clearly, when all receive the fullness [πλήρωμα] of divinity, there is no one left who is cut off from this unity [ἑνώσεως], outside and alone [καθ' ἑαυτόν]; then all "grief, pain, and groaning will disappear," and likewise in place of great numbers all will be combined in one single man [εἰς ἕνα ἄνδρα].[65]

Minimally, the language demands to be understood as a christological account of eschatological union with God in which the members of Christ are assimilated to him to such a degree that they are, like the humanity the Son assumed, utterly receptive to the divine life. Their deification implies their arrival at the place in which they no longer know "in part" but know God fully.[66]

Didymus' assertion that plurality will give way to singularity is also tantalizing. However, given the paucity of his exposition on the theme, it would be dangerous to press the language too far in pursuit of his meaning: singularity need not imply a total loss of creaturely differentiation from God, but only—as Didymus actually asserts—that creatures share so utterly in the mind and will of Christ so as to attain union with God. What is clear from the above, however, is that Didymus' eschatological commitments are patient of several interpretations. Assimilation to Christ proceeds to such an extent that rational beings, in the age to come, attain to the measure of knowledge that Christ himself possesses. Are we here in the presence of an idea that envisions a *telos* to contemplative progress, just as we observed such a limit with respect to the moral life in the last chapter?

Lights Illumining Themselves[67]

The dynamics of contemplative assimilation to Christ are most clearly spelled out in the *CZ* in Didymus' reflections on Zechariah 14:5-7: "And the Lord my God will come and all the saints with him. And in that day there will be no more light." Didymus proposes that the text can be taken in reference to the "second and glorious appearance (παρουσίαν) of the Savior," and in this context he takes the phrase "holy ones" as a reference to both "men and angels," whose role it is to "shine (ἐπιλάμπειν) together with him."[68]

Didymus explores the significance of the "light" and "day" language. Staying with his first identification of the "day" as a reference to the second coming, he notes that there will no longer be any "sensible (αἰσθητόν) light." In its place the true and everlasting light will provide "perfect illumination (τελείου

---

65. *CZ* III.308 (FC 111:248).
66. Cf. Didymus' treatment of "Gilead" in *CZ* III.302, which is assumed in the conclusion quoted above.
67. *CZ* V.68-78.
68. Summarizing *CZ* V.69-70.

φωτισμοῦ).""[69] These early moves in the interpretation of the lemma set the stage for the remarks that follow. Didymus clearly wishes to explore the significance of the second coming in terms of the epistemic dimensions of life in the age to come.

The importance of the remarks that follow merit full citation:

> The following must also be said. Those who are not light are in need of that which shines upon them, though they do not require this (any longer) when they themselves become light. Since then in the coming age, allegorically referred to as "day," "the righteous will shine like the sun in the kingdom of their Father" (Matt 13:43), being proclaimed to be light because they illumine themselves (φῶς ἀναδειχθέντες ἑαυτοὺς καταλάμποντες), they live in the day without need of the light that is external (οὐ τοῦ ἔξωθεν φωτὸς δεόμενοι). Even in this life, for example, those who illuminate themselves with the light of knowledge so as to hear from the Savior: "You are the light of the world" (Matt 5:14), live in a luminous condition (λαμπρᾷ κατ[αστάσε]ι) not from another source (οὐκ [ἄλ]λοθεν) but from being light and day itself, concerning which the chorus of the saints resounds: "Let the splendor of the Lord our God be upon us" (Ps 89:17 LXX).[70]

With the above passage we contrast Didymus' earlier use of similar language. He speaks of those who "illumine themselves with the light of knowledge" or of one "who sheds the light of knowledge upon himself."[71] In this former instance, Didymus speaks of this in terms of the virgins sharing in "God's light." We recall that this passage is situated in Didymus' primary interpretation of the lamp-stand, suited to those who are beginning the contemplative life. In it there is a marked emphasis on the participatory character of divine knowledge.[72] Participation is—in the lengthy quotation above—implicit within the early stages of illumination as well: "those who are not light are in

---

69. CZ V.71. Here Hill (FC 111:330) proves less reliable. He fails to distinguish between φῶς and φωτισμός in his rendering, obscuring somewhat the epistemic character of the beginning of the vision (a feature of the vision he recovers on in V.72 (p. 331)).

70. CZ V.72.

71. CZ I.279 and I.290.

72. With Doutreleau, *Sur Zacharie*, 105–106, who writes about the theme generally: "It should be noted that this knowledge is not purely intellectual, for Didymus is very careful to distinguish speculative knowledge from knowledge with participation. . . . It is this latter that is proper to the gnostic. (Il est à remarquer que cette connaissance n'est pas purement intellectuelle, car Didyme a bien soin de distinguer la connaissance spéculative de la connaissance avec participation. . . . C'est cette dernière qui est le propre du gnostique)."

need of what illumines them." However, the notion of growth in illumination by receptivity is notably absent in the age to come, just as was the case in Didymus' account of the pursuit of moral virtue. Didymus asserts, quite explicitly, that the perfectly illumined in the age to come are only termed so if there is no longer any need for further receiving of the divine light.

There are two ways of understanding what is being affirmed. Either Didymus is happy to envision a time 1) when the soul becomes so luminous that it no longer requires participation in the radiant light of the Son of God, or 2) when it is so completely participant in the radiant light of the Son that this light can no longer be considered in any way external to the soul. If one countenances the first interpretation, one of two infelicitous consequences is implied. Since the Son is identified as the provider of illumination in this context[73] and this illumination must come to an end, Didymus either envisions the illumination of the Son as preparatory to further illumination by the Father or he envisions a time when relational participation in the Son is no longer necessary. Neither coheres with Didymus' remarks elsewhere. We have already noted Didymus' persistent correlation of the knowledge of the Son with the knowledge of the whole Trinity. To know the Son fully is to know the Father and the Spirit with equal fullness. The one divinity that continues to govern the course of the contemplative life in the *eschaton* is that shared by the three Persons; thus, to know the Son is to know the Trinity. Nor does it seem likely that the perfectly luminous soul could in Didymus' mind be rendered autonomous, since the source of all beatitude is God.

The second interpretation seems more consistent with Didymus' assertions elsewhere. As with growth in virtue, so with illumination: reaching perfection requires a cessation of pursuit in the contemplative life after perfect contemplation is achieved. This is surely what Didymus means to affirm, but this interpretation presents us with some difficulties of its own. 1) Given that light is here taken to mean "perfect illumination" or "knowledge"—which is nothing other than the participatory knowledge of the Trinity—it is unclear how this can ever be said to be completely interior without implying that creatures can know God exhaustively. Didymus is quite explicit in this passage that receptivity and interiority are inversely proportional: one can receive only that which is external to the self. 2) Given that the source of light in the age to come is taken to be the Son and that Didymus' account of eschatological illumination assumes utter conformity to the highest stage of the contemplation of him, any notion of eschatological mediation seems to be rendered unnecessary. Didymus' willingness to find instances of such a degree of illumination among the apostles during the course of their earthly life only heightens this tension.[74]

---

73. See *CZ* V.71: "On the day the Lord God will come . . . the true and eternal light will provide the daylight" (FC 111:330).

74. See *CZ* V.72.

This passage should be set within the context of the broader argument of the CZ. Given that the pursuit of stability is the course that Didymus wishes to elucidate for his students, affirmations of complete assimilation to the moral and contemplative virtues revealed by Christ play an important role in securing this stability. It is only as one who knows God fully and who is obedient to all the commandments of God that one is guarded from the vagaries of one's own will. In the above instance, Didymus' intent may be to affirm the fulsome character of creaturely knowledge of God in order to secure his readers' confidence in their own attainment of stability in the "luminous condition" of the apostles. But he does so in this place at the cost of casting a long shadow over the question of 1) human growth in participatory knowledge in the *eschaton*[75] and 2) (hence) the continual character of Christ's mediation of divine knowledge.

The testimony of CZ is highly suggestive. Didymus instructively conceives of the contemplative life in light of the realities of the *eschaton*. We are to strive in the present life toward the fulsome participatory knowledge of the Trinity that will be ours in the age to come. Didymus again is instructively unwilling to conceive of any goal beyond this goal, but the train appears to come off the tracks when he suggests that this knowledge reaches a definite terminus. It is possible to be so fully alight with divine radiance that growth in illumination is no longer necessary or possible. Having attained to maturity in receiving the fullness of Christ's (human) knowledge of the Trinity, and being no longer in need of receiving more light from the Sun of Righteousness, any sense that Christ's humanity continues to mediate the knowledge of the Trinity to us appears to be excluded as a possibility.

The Humanity of Christ in the Psalms

In this section of the chapter, I turn to two passages in the broader corpus to interpret Didymus' thinking on the *eschaton*, particularly as they relate to the question of the role of the Son's humanity. In the first instance, Didymus discusses Christ's role as Savior and Teacher, suggesting that these roles come to an end in the age to come, when the goal is reached for which he took up these roles in his humanity. Didymus' reflection on the doubly referential character of language that is predicated of the Son clearly illustrates that Didymus conceives of certain aspects of Christ's incarnate ministry coming to an end. The second passage contains Didymus' reflections on the post-resurrection appearance of the Savior, particularly in the ascension. This passage reveals more clearly that it is the Son's material embodiedness after the resurrection with which Didymus is uncomfortable.

---

75. Nor is this the only place in the corpus where this is the case. My critique here extends the observation offered by Layton, *Didymus the Blind and His Circle*, 47–48.

He Hands over the Kingdom of His Humanity

The opening discussion in *PsT* contains two ideas in particular that provide greater clarity about Didymus' vision of the economy: 1) the Son's "becoming human (ἄνθρ[ωπος] γενέσθ[αι])" has an "explanation" or "cause (διά τι)," rooted in the accomplishment of salvation. 2) Certain aspects of this saving work—including the instruction that he undertakes in his "condescension (συνκατά[βα]σιν)"—are *necessarily* set aside. Didymus develops both of these notions in conversation with Neo-Arian accounts of the Son's identity and Marcellan interpretations of the Son's handing over of his kingdom to the Father.

Didymus' concern in the Prologue of his interpretation of Psalm 20 is to demarcate some principles of his exegesis. 1) The Scriptures must be read by bearing in mind that words are best understood in relation to the matters of which they speak.[76] Targeting anthropomorphic interpretations of divine sitting or rising, Didymus argues that the Scriptures only lead to what is beneficial to us when they are understood properly; language is subordinate to "reality (πρᾶγμα)." 2) The most important instance of the need to discern the matters under discussion in Scripture occurs in the naming of that which is proper to the Savior's divinity and that which is proper to his humanity.[77] 3) The recognition that there is an "explanation (διά τι)" for the humanity assumed by the Savior and the deeds done in the Son's humanity is crucial in moving from recognizing the meaning of the text to doing what is enjoined by it. Namely, what is done in the Son's humanity is meant to be imitated. What is done in his divinity is inimitable.[78]

Didymus provides several examples of things that are proper to the Son's divinity and his humanity, and in the course of this enumeration appears to become sidetracked by the phrase: "speaking the truth." He has placed this item in the human category since Jesus calls himself "a man who speaks the truth that [he] heard from God" (John 8:40).[79] In the course of this apparent digression Didymus notes that the Savior says: "I am the truth" in a manner that no creature can affirm in reference to itself. "Truth" is therefore doubly referential: appropriate to human receptivity of divine truth and to divine being as truth. The discussion leads in due course to the treatment of the first

---

76. *PsT* 1,8–12.

77. *PsT* 2,3–5.

78. *PsT* 3,4–7. We see here greater clarity than Didymus expresses on the question of imitation of Christ in the *CZ*.

79. *PsT* 3,13–4,7. Didymus cites a heretical objection to the notion that humans spoke the truth before the coming of Christ, articulating several articles of this rival confession that are consistent with Valentinian Gnosticism. See Doutreleau, Gesché, and Gronewald, eds., *Didymos der Blinde: Psalmenkommentar*, vol. 1 (Bonn: Rudolf Habelt, 1969), 13na. Didymus' fundamental counter-objection is that such a confession "divides (διακόπτειν)" both the Scriptures and the Godhead (*PsT* 3,23–24 and 28).

verse of the Psalm ("Lord, by your power the king will be made glad" (Ps 20:2)). The purpose of the foregoing discussion becomes evident in Didymus' two-fold treatment of the word "king."

Didymus discerns two "kingdoms" appropriate to the Logos. The first of these kingdoms was neither "assumed (ἀναλημπτή)" nor can it be "abdicated (ἀπο[βληθ]ῆ[ν]αι)." Since the Logos is the king of this realm as one who possesses it by virtue of his eternal identity as "King from King" and "God from God,"[80] it belongs to him in an absolute sense. The second of these kingdoms is "acquired (ἐπίκτητον)" in the Son's descent. As is the case with the humanity assumed by the Son (above) there is a definite purpose behind the Word's acquisition of this kingdom: "to put down the enemies of the race of men and to lead them into the care of his rule (νομ[ίμη]ν ἐ[π]ιστασίαν)." Didymus cites Psalm 2:6 in defense of the notion that the Son becomes a king in this second sense.[81]

A final element remains before the application to our theme becomes evident. Didymus takes "kingdom" in both of the above senses as a reference to "instruction (διδασκαλ[ί]α)." The instruction of the Logos pre-exists the Incarnation. Divine truth is revealed in the OT. If this is the case, and the truth is one, then the Son was leading the people of Israel to himself throughout all the Scriptures.[82] On the other hand, the instruction that he takes up in the "descent (ἐπιδημία)" has "a beginning and an end."[83] In the descent, the Savior ruled from "the time that he was appointed (ἐκ χειροτονίας)" until the purpose of his rule was achieved. Didymus then plays on the contrast: the absolute kingdom of the Word—granted any number of ages to come—remains forever. It is "without end (ἀτελεύτητος)." The kingdom that he has "in the condescension (κατὰ συνκατά[βα]σιν)" is brought to an end at some point in time even as it had a beginning in time. "For it has a cause (διά τι γάρ ἐστιν)," Didymus argues, "because of the salvation of the world, for the sake of the removal "of the sin of the world.""[84]

There is an analogy to this in the work of the doctor and the teacher. One becomes a doctor or a teacher when one takes up the craft: acquiring the skill of healing or knowledge. One becomes a doctor or a teacher for someone else's benefit when one exercises the skill on the other's behalf. A person ceases being doctor to another when the other is brought to health; he is no longer the teacher of another when the other is "perfected according to his teaching." The latter idea is of some significance for Didymus; it would be a poor teacher

---

80. *PsT* 4,8–12.
81. *PsT* 4,12–16.
82. This theological argument is of enduring importance in Didymus' disagreement with Theodore of Mopsuestia on the issue of human knowledge of the Trinity in the OT. We take this up in the final chapter.
83. *PsT* 4,16–18.
84. *PsT* 4,30–5,2.

who always remained so in reference to the same student, since this would imply a lack of progress in the student. The student must be ushered into the same knowledge that the teacher possesses.[85]

Didymus concludes the idea:

> When (you) hear such passages in the Scriptures, do not understand them in this manner (οὕτω). For example: "When he hands over the kingdom to God the Father" (1 Cor 15:24), he no longer rules *in this way*. For (it does not imply) that he no longer rules in an absolute sense (καθάπαξ), but that he rules no longer *in this way* (οὕτως).[86]

Didymus has already hinted that this text from Corinthians is in the back of his mind by introducing the notion of the Son's "endless kingdom." Critical here in rightly evaluating Didymus is recognizing his attempt to steer wide of the Marcellan problem.[87] On the one hand, because he does not embrace an eschatological vision of the Word's re-assimilation into the Father, Didymus is not calling into question the continued existence of the Son's humanity. For Didymus the functions of the humanity, not the humanity itself, are "abdicated" in the age to come. This latter kingdom—the one assumed—is abdicated when the purposes for its existence are fulfilled. What are these purposes? The education of the human race and its salvation. And Didymus casts this in what follows in terms of the saints' imitation of Christ in his humanity, who themselves become "kings" in the sense that they rule over themselves and bring others under the rule of the spiritual law.[88] Didymus is now free to interpret the psalm in light of two different frames of reference: 1) what the Psalm reveals about the Son's divinity and 2) what it reveals about his humanity and the moral life.

With the broad structure of Didymus' argument in place, we are in a position to evaluate its import. Didymus conceives of a distinction between that which the Son does as the eternally existent Logos and that which he does in the humanity he assumes. He articulates this distinction chiefly in terms of causality or explanation (διά τι). The Son has the cause of his divine activities

---

85. *PsT* 5,2–9.

86. *PsT* 5,10–12, emphases mine. This is a good instance of the oral character of the *PsT*. Didymus tells his students not to understand the text from Corinthians and similar texts "in this manner." If Didymus is referring to what follows, he seems to forget that his introductory phrase: "Do not understand the text thus," leads his audience to expect a rejected interpretation. Instead, he introduces the reading he accepts, briefly noting that the text does not "absolutely (καθάπαξ)" preclude the notion of the Son's rule. His overall point is, however, quite clear.

87. See Khaled Anatolios, *Retrieving Nicaea: The Development and Meaning of Trinitarian Doctrine* (Grand Rapids, MI: Baker, 2011), 90–91.

88. See *PsT* 5,30–6,21.

in himself, in his ontological relation with the Father. He has the cause of his human actions "in us." That which he does as man is done because of our subjection to sin. The teaching undertaken in the human actions of the Logos befits its *necessarily* temporally-circumscribed character: its ἀρχή is the Word's temporal election to kingship (occasioned by human disobedience and enslavement to the cosmic powers) and its τέλος consists in human return to fellowship with God.

Troubling in this account is how Didymus dissociates what the Logos takes on in his humanity from any eternal paideutic function. What the Incarnate Logos teaches us in and about his true humanity is a provision for human ignorance and moral weakness until the time when this ignorance and weakness is done away with. There is little to suggest here (once again) that the Logos' assumption of humanity has an eternal role to play in the revelation of his divinity. Didymus' response to Eunomian and Marcellan interpretations of the Son's kingship is effective. In the former case, the Son's temporal election as king is an event that must be construed in light of the Incarnation: it cannot be read as descriptive of the Son's mode of generation from the Father. In the latter case, a robust account of the Son's eternal activity as king guards against the notion that the Son gives up this role and (likewise) his hypostatic differentiation from the Father in the age to come (as Marcellan eschatology would all but guarantee). But Didymus' solution—the Son hands over his human kingdom to the Father—runs afoul of the criticism that the Son's Incarnation has only a temporary function to play in God's self-revelation.

Not That He Has Wounds[89]

Later in the same Commentary, Didymus provides an interpretation of Psalm 23 LXX, a text frequently taken by the Fathers as a description of the Ascension of Christ.[90] The logic of the psalm supports the interpretation: only the guiltless person enters into the sanctuary of the Lord (vv. 3–6). The one described in the second half of the psalm as entering into the sanctuary is the "king of glory," the Lord himself (vv.7–10). He ascends the mountain of God after a great victory (vv. 7–8). Didymus refers these verses to Christ, who enters the heavenly city after dealing defeat to the powers of darkness. To two groups of angels Didymus gives the antiphons: "Lift up the gates . . . and the King of glory will enter in!" and "Who is this King of glory?"

Early elements of the interpretation anticipate Didymus' christological development. The superscription of the Psalm: "on the first day of the Sabbath (τῆς μιᾶς σαββάτων)" is taken as an indication that the psalmist will discourse

---

89. *PsT* 70,22–72,4. For the English translation of the text, see Albert-Kees Geljon, "Didymus the Blind: Commentary on Psalm 24 (23 LXX): Introduction, Translation and Commentary," *VC* 65 (2011): 50–73.

90. See, for example, Gregory of Nyssa's *Asc. Chr*. For the enumeration of a much longer list of interpreters see Geljon, "Commentary on Psalm 24," 70n49.

on the theme of the "eighth day." The eighth day signifies the Gospel's fulfillment of the Law, just as the one who holds to the "Church's opinion" sees beyond the seven days of creation.[91] The superscription suggests that the first two cosmological verses will yield to descriptions of what Christ accomplishes in the Gospel. Didymus therefore delays his interpretation of the cosmological elements until he has established that the psalmist is concerned primarily with describing the one who ascends to the hill of the Lord (v.3).[92] Thus the foundation of the "earth" upon the "seas" becomes a figure for the soul that bears the fruit of the Spirit in the midst of the perils of life.[93] After stating this idea, Didymus returns to a theme with which we are familiar from CZ. The one who is of clean hands and a pure heart pursues the perfection of the Heavenly Father until arriving at the final "limit (πέρας)" of perfection.[94] After progressing through each of the initial stages, this person "ascends the mountain" of the Lord and takes up his stand, no longer requiring any further advancement in the virtues since these are attained. At length Didymus arrives at verse 6, where the psalmist argues that the "one" who ascends is expanded to include the "generation" that seeks God, since it "is not one person who is able to acquire virtue."[95]

The christological turn of Didymus' interpretation gains traction in the second half of the verse: "(This is the generation) of those who seek the face of the God of Jacob." To seek God's face is to seek his "appearance."[96] Didymus refers his readers back to the psalm's superscription—with the eighth day signalling the resurrection—as justification for his decision to relate the appearance of God to the coming of the Savior. The significance of this move in Didymus' narrative of ascent is apparent: the Savior comes "supplanting vice, in order that we may learn from him to tread down our adversaries, who are workers of vice, and "him who is at work among the sons of disobedience" (Eph 2:2)."[97]

Didymus then turns to consider the ascension of the Savior, since the appearance of God is followed by the King's glorious ascent to the holy hill of God (v.7). For our purposes, this section describing the ascension of the Savior into

---

91. *PsT* 65,10-21.

92. Hence, after the development of vv. 3-4 (where the progressive or spiritual application of the text is more obvious), Didymus returns to give the earliest verses of the psalm a "spiritual (πρὸς ἀναγωγήν)" reading. Cf. Geljon, 56-57n22-23.

93. For a similar passage, see Didymus' treatment of the Parable of the Net in *CZ* III.309-314. Both are given a pneumatological interpretation.

94. *PsT* 68,21.

95. *PsT* 70,11-12 (Geljon, 60).

96. *PsT* 70,22.

97. *PsT* 71,2-24. Didymus' play on the meaning of Jacob's name—the supplanter—capitalizes on a grammatical ambiguity within the lemma: is God called Jacob or is Jacob in the genitive case? The move allows him to associate God with the one who supplants vice: namely, Christ. Cf. Geljon, 69.

the heavenly city is of paramount importance. The angels' hesitation in raising the immortal gates of heaven is occasioned by their temporary failure to recognize the Savior. Didymus links their question: "Who is this king of glory?" to the question raised in Isaiah 63:1-2: "Who is this coming from Edom, with red garments from Bozra? Why are your garments red?" They do not recognize the body of the Savior, newly-risen from the dead, because it appears to have "the properties (τὰ ἰδιώματα)" of a fleshly body.[98]

Didymus makes much of this point. The fleshly appearance of the body of the Son is a concession to the temporary failure of the angels to recognize that the one ascending is the Son who became incarnate. The appearance of this body is gratuitous, meant to assure them of the identity of the ascended Lord. In reality, however, the body he now possesses is "spiritual (πνευματικόν)"; "traces (ἴχνη)" of the fleshly body of Christ, now "transformed (μεταβεβληκός)," remain so that those heavenly gatekeepers may know "whence (πόθεν)" he comes.[99]

Didymus seeks to establish the interpretation by appealing to the Lord's manifestation of the nail-wounds to the disciples. Once again the importance of the event, Didymus argues, does not consist in the fact that the resurrected body of the Savior possesses wounds but in the fact that he shows them to the disciples. He showed them these wounds "to establish (βεβαιῶσαι)" them in the opinion that the same body that had rested in the tomb was now raised. The showing was not to instruct them about the character of this resurrected body. Didymus is quite clear about this:

> He showed them the marks of the nails and he showed them the wounds, not that that body has any wounds—for only a hard and resistent [sic] body can receive wounds—but in order to prove that it is he himself who has risen. After that, he went in, after the doors were closed [John 20:19] lest they understand the resurrection wrongly based on the sign of the proof of the resurrection, namely that they believe that after the resurrection the risen body bears the same marks [τὰ ἰδιώματα] again as a destructible body.[100]

Didymus' defense of this interpretation of the resurrected and ascended body of the Savior takes the form of proving the unclear by the clear. To posit that the Savior ascends with a body of flesh implies that this body possesses the "properties" of our fleshly bodies. If this is the case, Jesus' body would be subject to being wounded again (and no one wants to affirm this). The body that ascends must be a body possessing the "properties" appropriate to spiritual existence, not materially corporeal existence. Didymus cites examples

---

98. See *PsT* 71,17-20.
99. *PsT* 71,19.
100. *PsT* 71,21-26 (Geljon, 61).

from the resurrection narrative that he feels support his case. If he had a solid corporeal body after the resurrection, how did he pass through a closed door? Are Didymus' opponents willing to assert that the eating of Christ has a revelatory function to play in terms of his mode of existence (and ours) in the age to come?[101] Didymus concludes the argument by insisting that not all of the things shown by Jesus after the resurrection remain.[102]

Didymus is clearly guarded in this passage. The reason for his defensiveness is not difficult to identify. The discussion of the "properties" of Christ's spiritual body—namely, whether it is "hard (σκληρόν)," "rigid (ἀντίτυπον)," and capable of eating—suggests that Didymus is responding to anti-Origenist polemic. These characteristics of Christ's resurrected body, taken together with the passage under discussion, were the subject of much scrutiny by those who felt that Origen's account of the resurrection of the Savior was inadequate.

Epiphanius' *Panarion* draws attention to the passage in Luke 20 with which Didymus is concerned above, and investigates the question of the character of this body. Epiphanius writes:

> For Christ displayed even the mark of the nails and the mark of the lance, and left those very wounds [αὐτὰς τὰς οὐλάς] in his body even though he had joined his body to a single spiritual oneness. Thus he could have wiped the wounds away [ἀπαλείφει] too, but to refute you, you madman, he does not.[103]

Not long after, Epiphanius raises the issue of the closed doors and of the character of Christ's spiritual body. Though Epiphanius will affirm that this body is "spiritual" and not "material [ὑλικόν]," his subsequent exposition reveals that he means that it is not *merely* material:[104]

> Why, then, did he enter where the doors were barred? Why but to prove that the thing they saw was a body, not a spirit— but a spiritual body, not a material one, even though it was

---

101. *PsT* 72,1–2.
102. *PsT* 71,27–72,1: οὐδὲ ἐκεῖνα ἃ ἔδειξεν ... ἔμεινεν αὐτὰ ἔχων.
103. Cf. Epiphanius, *Pan.* 64.64.6–7 (GCS 31:504; trans. Williams, 198).
104. Epiphanius and the Origenist tradition both use the word "immaterial" in a sense that may be easily misunderstood by the contemporary reader. On the surface, the terms in which the argument is conducted are somewhat confusing. Epiphanius appears—to a modern reader—to concede the critical point in confessing the resurrected body's immateriality. However, as Epiphanius makes clear, he conceives of the body of the Savior in physical terms; that is, the body of the Savior remains within the sensible order. It is immaterial in the sense that it is no longer prone to decay; though physical, yet it transcends and transforms the conditions in which the physical world, as we experience it and understand it, operates.

accompanied by its soul, Godhead, and entire incarnate humanity. It was the same body, but spiritual; the same body, once gross, now fine; the same body, once crucified . . . the same body, once conquered, now unconquerable. It was united and commingled with his divine nature and never again to be destroyed, but forever abiding, never again to die.[105]

The ontologically-material character of the body is sustained as such in the body's unity with the Son's divinity, where by virtue of this union it is never again to die.

There is a degree of caricaturizing on both sides of the argument. Didymus is unfair to suggest that anti-Origenists like Epiphanius envision a situation in which the resurrected body of the Savior—composed of parts though it is—is subject to corruption. Clearly, however, he feels that this is at stake if the body of the Savior is a material one. Neither do committed Origenists like Didymus want to propose that another body—other than Jesus' physical or material body—was the one that was raised, although Epiphanius suggests in a polemically unfair (and unhelpful) moment that this might be the case.[106] The question at stake is whether or not the physical body that is raised remains truly material, or whether its spiritual transformation eliminates its materiality.

Didymus' position on the resurrected body of Christ asserts its spiritual character at the expense of its material character. He could hardly be clearer. Certain of the properties of Christ's resurrected body are docetic. He only appears to have a body of flesh; he only seems to have wounds. In reality they are manifestations that serve the purpose of securing his disciples' confidence that it is really his material body that was raised. The intention of the claim is to argue against any sense that the eschatological condition of humanity will be under threat of corruption. Materiality and corruptibility are inseparable. The intention is admirable, but critically he can only secure it by explicitly denying that the resurrected body of the Savior has any of the properties associated with materially-embodied existence. The material appearance of the Savior's body is a ruse for a benign purpose.

Epiphanius is, for all his feistiness, on much firmer ground in affirming that the spiritual character of Jesus' body is not compromised by its ontological materiality. The crucial note that he sounds here is not to describe more adequately the properties of Christ's risen body. (If the debate is carried on at this level, then Epiphanius' categories of spiritual "fineness" and "thickness"

---

105. Epiphanius, *Pan* 64.64.8–9 (GCS 31:504; trans. Williams, 198).
106. Epiphanius, *Pan.* 64.64.3 (GCS 31:503; trans. Williams, 197–198): "And you see that the ensouled body is the same as the spiritual body, just as our Lord arose from the dead, not by raising a different body, but his own body and not different from his own. But he had changed his own actual body to spiritual fineness [λεπτότητα] and united a spiritual whole, and he entered where doors were barred."

are clumsier than the categories used by Didymus.) The properties of the body of Christ *per se* are not what secure the incorruptibility of his flesh. Rather, it is in his refusal to isolate the body as the *locus* of theological reflection about the resurrection that he is decisive. The body of Christ is incorruptible because it is "united and commingled with [Christ's] divine nature."[107] The incorruptibility of Christ's flesh is secured in this union, and not in the denial of its material corporeality. For Epiphanius, the material dimensions of Christ's humanity do not compromise its utterly spiritual character.

Summary and Critique

With the help of the supplementary material from *PsT*, it is possible to speak more clearly about the suggestive remarks in the *CZ*. Certain roles taken up by the Son in his humanity no longer remain necessary in the age to come. The extreme example of this is the Son's assumption of a material body, which is not only denied a significant function in the age to come, but is a necessarily docetic feature of Christ's mode of existence in the ascension. A less extreme example, but one that is just as significant to our argument, is the teaching function of the Son's assumed humanity. The Son becomes human in order to reveal the path of the virtues and to teach humans how to tread the enemy of the soul underfoot.

In the age to come, these functions of the Son's humanity are no longer necessary. Material embodiedness—which plays such a precise and important role in Didymus' protology as the result of human sin and departure from its paradisiacal condition—is the problematic element of the post-resurrection appearances of the Savior. The existence of the soul in a materially-embodied state in the age to come could only serve to cloud the interior vision of the soul. Though some kind of corporeality may always be a part of the soul's existence, it passes beyond a dependence upon material things. The point is also related to the cessation of the Son's human instruction; the humanity assumed by the Savior serves its role in human recovery of the likeness of the divine Son. Once the assumed humanity of the Son has fulfilled this function, there is little reason why, in Didymus' understanding of the divine economy, it should continue to mediate the knowledge of God and the way of virtue to us. Such a situation could only imply for Didymus that the Incarnation had failed to achieve its goal.[108]

---

107. Ibid. 64.64.9 (GCS 31:504; trans. Williams, 198).

108. Didymus' contemplative vision is in this respect like Origen's, where it is difficult to conceive of the Incarnation as having more than a provisional role. For this argument, see Andrew Louth, *The Origins of the Christian Mystical Tradition: From Plato to Denys*, 2nd ed. (New York: Oxford University Press, 2007), 60–68. Louth describes Origen's mystical theology as primarily Word-centered rather than Christ-centered. "[T]he soul, it seems, passes beyond faith in the Incarnation in its ascent to God. The

There are therefore sound reasons for thinking that Didymus privileges the final stage of contemplation—the immaterial vision of the Trinity—in a manner that eclipses the earlier stages of contemplation. Didymus' contemplative vision is tied to an eschatology in which the Son restores the soul to its former splendor by his Incarnation. When this restorative purpose is fulfilled, the Incarnation ceases to play an identifiable role in our knowledge of God. It should be noted here: Didymus neither denies the continuation of Christ's humanity nor even the continuation of some manner of spiritual embodiedness for the Son into the age to come. Rather, he fails to conceive of the role of the assumed humanity of the Son in the mediation of divine knowledge. The Son reveals himself to us "in the flesh" so that we might progress to the point of knowing him in his former and eternal glory. There is little sense in Didymus that the Son's assumption of material flesh might continue to reveal the mode of the Trinity's self-disclosure to us in the age to come.

We are now in a position to offer a critique of this latter point before concluding the chapter with a composite sketch of Didymus' understanding of the location of Scripture within the divine economy to which it bears witness. Didymus, in spite of some helpful concessions (or clarifications) to Origen's critics, does not finally evade the problematic of the soul's pre-existence and the ramifications that this doctrine has for eschatology. By insisting as he does in *GenT* that embodiedness of some kind is ever a feature of created existence, he avoids one Methodian critique of Origen: that the soul, coming to sin before coming to embodiedness, is in fact the cause of sin's entry into human experience. As Methodius pointed out, an eschatological vision of disembodiedness does not secure the soul's stability, since it was precisely in this condition that the soul turned away from God.[109] Didymus affirms that some kind of body is always present with the soul, and thus evades, at least formally, the Methodian critique of the Origenist position.

However, what Didymus' eschatological vision does not evade is a more basic issue, raised in its most incisive form by Maximus the Confessor and Didymus' contemporary Gregory of Nyssa.[110] The protological schema of original

---

Incarnation is only a stage. . . . We might conclude by saying that Origen's mysticism centred on Christ is ultimately transcended by a mysticism centred on the eternal Word" (p. 64).

109. For this critique, see Methodius of Olympus, *Res.*, in Epiphanius, *Pan.* 64.21 (GCS 31:433–435). Gregory of Nyssa repeats the same critique of the notion of incorporeal pre-existence, as Brian Daley argues: "Such a theory . . . implies that even a life of heavenly contemplation is not secure from sin, so that the prospect of an endless cycle of falls and restorations cannot be ruled out" (*The Hope of the Early Church: A Handbook of Patristic Eschatology* (Cambridge: Cambridge University Press, 1991), 86).

110. Maximus the Confessor, *Amb.* 7 (PG 91:1068D–1101C). I am indebted to Adam Cooper for directing me to Maximus' argument in his keynote paper at the St Andrew's Greek Patristic Symposium (Sydney, 2012). The paper is published as "The Gift of Receptivity: St Athanasius on the Security of Salvation," *Phronema* 28, no. 2 (2013): 1–20.

rest giving way to movement away from God raises the question: on what basis is eschatological rest secure? Maximus calls attention to a problematic of preexistence which is rooted in the idea that the soul could come to a place of "satiety" in the knowledge of God in its luminous pre-incarnate life.[111] If this were possible, then there would surely be a sense in which the soul could be said to reach a definite terminus in its knowledge of God, beyond which it was neither possible nor desirable to progress. God would not be able to satisfy utterly because his plenitude would be either withheld (in which case God would be envious) or because it would be exhausted. If this was the case in the pre-existence of the soul, then the eschatological security of the soul is under threat, whatever else one wants to affirm about the nature of the kind of body it possesses in the age to come. Whoever Gregory and Maximus' specific targets are (Evagrian Origenists?), the shoe fits for Didymus' protology[112] just as well as for his eschatology.

Didymus, in securing an account of eschatological security, runs headlong into the difficulty that 1) rest in the age to come can be secured only as the soul comes to participate fulsomely—i.e. without possibility of further participation—in the divine. To make this claim, however, is to attempt to secure stability at the cost of an aspect of creatureliness: limitation.[113] 2) What is also

---

111. On this see Paul Blowers, "Maximus the Confessor, Gregory of Nyssa, and the Concept of "Perpetual Progress"," *VC* 46 (1992): 152-154.

112. With the original creation of humanity (i.e., the soul's creation), there is only a conceptual distinction between the "image" and the "likeness"; both are possessed simultaneously. See *GenT* 58,22–59,5. This implies for Didymus that the human soul was created not in a state of distance from God to strive toward him in virtue, but rather in a state of graced union with God. It was not on the way, as it were, to fullness of communion that the race was side-tracked, but at the very height of communion that it was drawn away.

113. Gregory of Nyssa is on firmer ground in maintaining the idea that perfection is infinite, since no limit to perfection can be defined. As he writes: "always desiring to have more of the good, [this] is the perfection of human nature" (*Vit. Mos.* 1.8 and 1.10 (SC 1:50)). That human progress toward the knowledge of God is inexhaustible because God is so is affirmed throughout the writing. I lean on Philip Kariatlis, ""Dazzling Darkness": The Mystical or Theophanic Theology of St Gregory of Nyssa," *Phronema* 27, no. 2 (2012): 99–123, for a distillation of these themes in Gregory. It should be noted here that both Didymus and Gregory are dealing with an issue that Origen leaves somewhat open-ended. Tantalizingly, Origen articulates the notion of persistent progress in the knowledge of God in relation to the motif of "tents" and "houses" that we see Didymus employ to opposite effect in his account of the Feast of Tabernacles. See Origen's *Hom. Num.* 17.4 (von Balthasar, 25–26). He affirms the position again in *Prin.* 4.3.14 (Butterworth, 310–312). However, Origen, unlike Didymus and his Cappadocian contemporary, asserts that God is not by nature incomprehensible. On this, see Frances Young, "The God of the Greeks and the Nature of Religious Language," in *Early Christian Literature and the Classical Intellectual Tradition: in honorem Robert M. Grant* (Paris: Beauchesne, 1979), 56-57. Didymus' clear assertions of divine incomprehensibility and limitlessness—which

clear from this eschatological schema is that the material embodiedness of the Second Person of the Trinity, for all its necessity, can play no role in continually revealing to us the knowledge of God, since its role is provisional, its function exhausted when the soul is returned to the immaterial contemplation of the Trinity. The hermeneutical consequences of the above observations are unhappy ones. To these we turn.

A Composite Sketch of the Dogmatic and the Exegetical

The prophets and the apostles are, by and large in Didymus, the zealous or the perfect in contemplative and practical virtue. Rare indeed are those passages where Didymus suggests a measure of immaturity in them. Two examples from Zechariah 4 suggest that the prophet is being inaugurated into a mystery that is too great for him. He is awakened from sleep.[114] He requires the use of a second question.[115] In both instances, the prophet's purported ignorance is somewhat relativized. First of all, the matter before him in both passages is the doctrine of the Trinity: the knowledge of the Persons in their prior and eternal glory. This is the final stage of the contemplative life, the one for which materially embodied existence (usually) presents an obstacle to pure spiritual vision. What is more, in the first passage Didymus likens the prophet's being awakened to the rising of Christ from the dead; the prophet's sleep is of benefit for others. In the second case, his ignorance occasions the instruction of those who would learn the meaning of the mystery of the olive trees from him.

But these are exceptional to the usual flow of Didymus' thinking on the subject of prophetic identity. The prophet is illumined and divinized by the Word of God; being made wise by God, the prophet speaks as he does in a

---

arise in the dogmatic as well as the exegetical literature, often in anti-Eunomian contexts—are held together with a vision of eschatological contemplation in which human knowledge of God reaches an end-point. For this to occur, Didymus must clearly adopt an account of deification in which creaturely limitations no longer obtain. Though I cannot defend this idea here, I think it possible to account for Didymus' position as a response to Methodian polemic which calls into question the notion of eschatological stability. Didymus pushes beyond merely asserting the return to an original and luminous pre-existence, and asserts creaturely union with God that to some degree eliminates key distinctions between creating and creaturely natures. I am sympathetic to Steiger's assertion ("Theological Anthropology," 379) that Didymus conceives of the age to come along lines that raise the bar on the protoplastic condition in Paradise. It is not simply a return to the pre-existent state that he envisions. However, Didymus' indications about what this "more" entails are not defensible.

114. *CZ* I.274–277.
115. *CZ* I.335–338.

manner appropriate to that which he knows and to the instruction of others. The riddling character of Scripture reflects this two-fold character of prophetic speech: the decoding of the figure—which assumes the help of the Spirit of God—draws the reader into more adequate knowledge of the Truth who impresses himself upon the mind of the prophet. For this reason the prophets are like rain-bearing clouds that water the earth: producing in others a harvest of righteousness. They are "God's eyes," perceptive of "divine visions."[116] They are like the mountains, set apart from others "for their characteristic loftiness of knowledge and wisdom . . . [and] for the superiority of their life in practice."[117] They are everlasting because they look toward that which is eternal: "illumination about the Trinity" came from them.[118] Like Noah, Moses, Elijah, and Paul they are "souls" in Christ, "men of God," who are so near to the Savior so as to share "in the same holiness and virtue."[119]

The Prophets and the Trinitarian Economy

Didymus places a great deal of emphasis upon the conformity of the servants of the Word of God to Christ. The emphasis on the (near-)perfection of the prophet's imitation of Christ's morally and contemplatively perfect human life plays an important role in Didymus' vision of ascent. The prophets are conformed by the Spirit of God to the image and likeness of God the Father in the Son. They are deified by this conformation to the goal of all human desire to the extent that their speech, in the writing of Scripture, can be described as divine. The goal of divine address to us through them, the purpose of Scripture within the divine economy of salvation, is our moral and contemplative conformation to the Son so that we attain the goal for which we were made: deification. It is therefore imperative in Didymus' mind that the prophets know about the things of which they speak in a highly realized sense. They participate in the reality to which they testify. They are far-advanced in the contests of virtue, seeing the peace of Jerusalem. They behold the Trinity in the interior vision of the "inner man," insofar as this is possible in the present life.

It would be hard to over-state the role that imitation plays in proper attentiveness to the prophetic message. If we would benefit from their discourse, we must learn from their virtues. We must submit ourselves, like them, to the "easy yoke" of the one who says to us through them: "Learn from me." If we would understand them rightly, we must like them have our vision purified by the Sun of Righteousness. Fleeing from the confusion of Babylon, we will take our rest in the city whose watchtowers ensure salvation; going beyond the Scriptures in the introductory senses (the literal and historical), we will ascend to the spiritual meaning of the Law.

---

116. *CZ* III.130.
117. *CZ* V.57 (FC 111:327).
118. Ibid.
119. *CZ* IV.93. (Ibid., 270.)

The saints of the Zechariah narrative play the same role in the exile of Israel that they play in the cosmic exile of souls from God. Sowed among the rest of humankind for the sake of God's economy, the saints remember the Trinity in their exile from direct communion with the divine, bearing the fruits of the virtuous life during the time of duress. They set out in "boats" (materially-embodied existence) and brave the "seas" of this life to wrest souls from the grasp of the serpent that dwells in its depths.[120] It is useful to recall to mind here also that Didymus is at times explicit about the saints' own innocence in their pre-existent condition. In some instances they are, in imitation of Jesus, scattered in the world to serve the saving purposes of God and not at all for any fault of their own.[121] Remembering the true Canaan, they compel others to return there with them.

By reading Scripture in the way that Didymus does, he and his students become willing participants in the economy of the Trinity so understood. They are conformed to the virtues of the true humanity that the Son reveals and enacts; they are made wise with the knowledge of the Trinity: first in relation to the providential care of God over the world, next in the Incarnation of the Son of God, and finally by the direct vision of the Trinity which is the goal of human life and the end of all knowledge. They become the "sons of the prophets," the spiritual children of the saints, gathered by them to enter into the spiritual Jerusalem on high.[122] To this end, Didymus prays when he opens the Scriptures that God would "grant [him] a word in the opening of [his] mouth" (Eph 6:19).[123] Such great things are spoken of there; so much is at stake.

An Instructive Account of Scripture?

It is fitting at this stage to offer an evaluative critique of Didymus' understanding of Scripture, now that its salient features are more abundantly delineated. The remarks offered here anticipate the aspects of Didymus' interpretive practice that I commend and critique in a more textually specific way in the final chapter of the study. As I comprehend them, the basic features of Didymus' understanding of Scripture may be described in the following terms. 1) The human authors of Scripture are servants of the One who makes them eloquent with his Word and inspires them by his Spirit. There is a basic asymmetry or priority of action in the inspiration of Scripture: the words of the prophets are primarily God's words. 2) The words of Scripture are primarily concerned with the self-revelation of the Trinity in the activity of creation and salvation. The saving and recreating work of the Trinity, as it concerns humanity, has as its end the restoration of human fellowship with God. For this

---

120. *CZ* III.313–314.

121. See *HiT* 56,28–29. Cf. Albert Henrichs, *Didymos der Blinde: Kommentar zu* Hiob, vol. 1, PTA 1 (Bonn: Habelt, 1968), 174–175n93.

122. See *CZ* IV.209–210.

123. See *CZ* I.1, I.343, III.3, and III.325.

saving and recreating work of the Trinity as it relates to the human race, the baptismal event is paradigmatic, both in relation to the prophets and to us. 3) The human character of Scripture is understood properly only in light of the above two realities: a truly human word is sounded only under the deifying influence of the Word, who brings humanity to its true end in him insofar as this humanity is receptive to his saving work and made ready by him to declare it. 4) Just as the saving work of the Trinity centers on the Incarnation of the Word, so the central theme of the Scriptures—functioning as they do within this Trinitarian economy of salvation—is the Incarnation.

Each of these points may be developed further. The first point has several implications. First of all, that God is the author of Scripture has as its consequence that Scripture is a unity. The diverse historical and cultural locations of the servants of the Word do not give rise to a piecemeal account of the central narrative of Scripture because the eloquent Father is always speaking by the Word and the Spirit whom he sends. A second implication of the above is that the OT is one with the NT in the sense envisioned by Didymus only if it too is understood as part-and-parcel of the outworking of the missions of the Son and the Holy Spirit toward the end of reconciling estranged humanity with God.[124] We are not surprised, therefore, to see Didymus interpreting the OT narrative in such a way that the missions of the Son and the Spirit therein serve as a unitive principle of his exegesis.

The second point concerns the subject matter of the Scriptures, and (hence) the primary orientation of the reader of Scripture. Scripture has, as a second principle of its unity, the saving and recreating activity of the Trinity to which it bears witness. This activity points toward and finds fulfillment in the Incarnation of the Son. Didymus' account of the economy provides the unitive framework in which to view each stage of the scriptural narrative. An important hermeneutical implication of this point is that the interpreter knows in broad outline what constraints bear upon his interpretation of the Sacred Page. It is not primarily as a grammarian or a historian that he comes to the text (though such tasks are bound up with the work of the interpreter), but as one called to participate in the saving work there described. In short, one comes to the text of Scripture to die and to be made alive again with the life of Christ. Baptism is both paradigmatic and hermeneutically-significant. In this saving work of the Trinity, Didymus is quite clear that the interpretive moment, the moment in which the community attends to the Word of God in prayer, is itself a moment within the divine economy. Bienert is right to highlight the importance of Didymus' sense that he and his hearers are not simply

---

124. Just as in *DT*, Didymus is insistent on this point throughout the corpus. See *PsT* 2,14–21, especially: ἐπιδημίαν δὲ οὐ πάντως λέγω τὴν κατὰ σάρκα· πο[λλὰς γὰ]ρ [ἠθ]έλησ‹εν›· ἀ‹ε›ὶ ἐπιδημεῖ. "[When I speak of the Savior's visitation] I do not at all mean the visitation in the flesh, for he willed to have many visitations: he is always visiting."

confronted by the prophetic writing "as text, but as living word."[125] The reading of Scripture is also an event within the divine economy of God's re-creating speech to creatures.

The third point above is where Didymus' account becomes somewhat difficult to sustain. Instructively, the human dimension of the text is done justice to insofar as the reader of Scripture recognizes humanity to be properly described only in light of its participation in the saving work of God. Properly articulated, deification need not imply that the human dimension of Scripture is under-appreciated. It is only as the human servant of God is understood to become truly human under the influence of the divine Word that a non-competitive account of the divine and human agents may proceed. The anthropological problem arises, however, in Didymus' insistence that the prophets are fully or nearly conformed to the humanity revealed by the Son. Didymus' doctrine of moral perfection and his vision of contemplative perfection give rise to readings of Scripture in which claims are made for the prophets and apostles that are difficult to sustain from a plain reading of the text.

Didymus could, I think, have rescued the instructive elements of his theological anthropology with respect to the prophets by building on the notion in *DT* that the baptismal event—which he treats as paradigmatic of God's dealings with humanity—continues to inform their speech. The prophetic burden to speak or write is continuous with the Christian life understood more fulsomely. The indwelling Spirit of Christ both mortifies and vivifies. Voices like Jonah and Solomon, who serve as witnesses to God's saving economy, are no less reliable than Isaiah and Daniel in doing so, for what is decisive about them is not so much their ethical or contemplative achievement as their receptivity to the Spirit and the Word of God, who in the inspiration of Scripture mortify human sinfulness and vivify the prophet's affective and noetic powers toward the single aim of communicating to others the central fact of the economy identified above: the mystery of Christ.

This leads to the fourth and final point. Didymus instructively determines to do with Scripture what he does with Christ. He is, finally, its proper interpretation, insofar as God's economy is summed up in him. This aspect of Didymus' thinking about Scripture is at once its saving grace and its most glaring problem. For it is Didymus' thoughts about the economy and its relationship to God's eternal identity that are finally problematic. In *DT* and *DSS*, Didymus eschews the protological and eschatological dimensions of his thinking that are most problematic. But the exegetical corpus reveals a basic rupture between divine being as such and the economy with respect to Christ's assumption of the material conditions of God's creation. Because this is largely a provisional measure and because Christ's ascended humanity reveals the mode of creaturely existence in the *eschaton*, the enduring value of sense perception in the contemplation of God is radically undermined.

---

125. Bienert, 73.

The Results of the Christological Problem

Two distinct problems emerge from Didymus' Christology for his hermeneutics. Both are directly related to the ideas—so crucial in his account of salvation—that the humanity of the Son is imitable in the present age and that this humanity ceases to play any role in the mediation of divine knowledge to us in the age to come. We note here for the first time that these two ideas are, strictly speaking, two sides of the same coin. The perfect imitation of Christ's humanity, from a noetic standpoint, assumes that the saint becomes filled with the same knowledge proper to the humanity assumed by the Son. Given the provisional function that this assumed humanity plays in Didymus' economy, its teaching function must necessarily be set aside when those under instruction become mature with the knowledge of the Son of God.

The results of these determinations for the interpretation of Scripture are unhappy ones. Given that Didymus understands creaturely language to be appropriate to the description of corporeals, and given that the re-created cosmos is not secured in its spiritual materiality by the enduring material dimensions of the humanity assumed by the Son, 1) the corporeal senses (i.e. those that have to do with the literal or historical account of the narrative) are frequently given only a provisional status within the overall scheme of Didymus' interpretation. The words of Scripture, which often refer to corporeal things or matters subject to time, are preparatory for a higher sense that moves the student beyond the contemplation of such things into the vision of things that are super-sensible. But in the process, it is often difficult to see how the preliminary senses remain in view even as the interpreter develops the higher spiritual senses. This is not to claim, as Bienert does,[126] that these preliminary senses are purely immanent modes of interpretation. Attending to Didymus' account of the contemplative life should guard against such a conclusion. The content of the literal senses is sometimes surprisingly "spiritual"; however, its status is frequently provisional.

2) Nor, as I hope to show in the next chapter, are the preliminary senses the only ones to suffer. The anagogical sense in Didymus, especially when he concerns himself with moving to the highest stage of contemplation, is improperly governed christologically. For he assumes that the highest way of knowing God is made possible by the Incarnation, but refuses the Incarnation itself any lasting function in divine self-revelation. The highest anagogical sense is insufficiently grounded in the realization that the Son assumes our humanity in a manner that is irrevocably and eternally revelatory of who he is. Given that Didymus is fundamentally concerned with articulating the mystery of Christ as the central theme of the divine economy in Scripture, we should expect that aspects of this mystery are lost in conceiving of the Son's humanity in the way he does.

---

126. Ibid., 108.

6

"CULLING THE FLOWERS"

In this final chapter, I bring my prior observations about Scripture's place in the divine economy into conversation with Didymus' interpretation of Zechariah 3. His interpretation of the vision serves as a case study in which to illustrate the interpretive tendencies that result from his account of the life in fellowship with the Trinity. His interpretation will be looked at from two vantage points. 1) I investigate the specific hermeneutical moves that he makes as an interpreter in light of his commitments to and descriptions of moral and contemplative perfection. Of special interest here is the relationship between the senses of Scripture. 2) I attempt to give an overall valuation of the relationship between his scriptural ontology and the exegetical practices that this ontology generates.

On the one hand, I propose here that late moderns have much to gain from engaging with Didymus the Blind's exegetical work in a theologically-invested way. There are two respects in particular in which Didymus' work is promising. 1) The blind exegete is committed to working out the consequences of functioning within a unitive account of Scripture. The principle of this unity is the inseparable activity of the Trinity in the accomplishment of the economy of salvation, as this activity enables and draws us into fellowship with Christ. Every scriptural episode illuminates another dimension of the mystery of Christ and draws us into this mystery. 2) Didymus reminds us that all the tasks of scriptural exegesis are to give testimony to the irreducibly baptismal character of the Christian life. To see Christ in his merciful Incarnation is to be reminded that our vision of him is purified only by repentance and the pursuit of likeness to him by participating in the perfections of the Persons of the Trinity. This is no less true of Didymus' treatment of the literal sense than it is of his treatment of the higher senses.

On the other hand, I propose here that a recovery of his exegetical *praxis* must be critical because of Didymus' theological deficiencies. In what follows I argue that Didymus' doctrine of attainable perfection has a distortive influence on his reading of the literal sense. Wishing to vindicate Joshua the high priest from any complicity in Israel's guilt, Didymus re-frames the scene in a manner that obscures an aspect of Christ's priestly function. I also argue that, because of Didymus' vision of the *eschaton*, the latter stages of the contemplative life are misleadingly described. The promising trajectory of Didymus' interpretation of Zechariah 3 in light of its fulfillment in the Gospel is compromised by his playing down of the role of Christ's embodied humanity in revealing the age to come.

Didymus on Zechariah 3[1]

Zechariah opens the vision of the third chapter with a description of Joshua the high priest standing opposite the angel of the Lord. He is accused by Satan, who stands at his right hand. The accusation, however, does not prevail; the Lord rebukes the devil and divests the high priest of the filthy garments that occasioned the accusation. The Lord promises to Joshua that he will be pre-eminent in the Lord's house, judging it and living in the midst of its attendants. He and his companions are promised the appearance of the Lord's servant: the Dawn. At his rising the Lord will put down all unrighteousness and usher in an era of prosperity and peace. The vision serves as a case study in which to illustrate Didymus' interpretive *skopos* and the hermeneutical tendencies that play an important role in his exegesis.

Establishing the Interpretive Frame

In the first two lemmata (3:1 and 3:2), Didymus accomplishes several goals: 1) he brings his identification of the genre of the section to bear on the question of its primary subject matter: Jesus Christ the high priest. 2) He illustrates the significance of the vision in terms of the modalities of spiritual warfare. 3) He establishes how Satan functions in the divine pedagogy, as one who reveals the virtues and vices of those tempted by him and thereby is an unwitting agent in their purification.

Matters neither Sensible nor Human

In the first part of his interpretation,[2] Didymus frames the arguments that follow. The passage provides a description of the spiritual conflict in which the saints, or the "athletes for piety," are engaged. They are tempted by the devil,

---

1. *CZ* I.182–270. Some justification is required for my decision to isolate this particular section, which contains six lemmata. 1) Immediately preceding Didymus' citation of Zechariah 3:1, Didymus offers a parenetic conclusion (*CZ* I.181). 2) Didymus takes the verb ἔδειξεν (3:1) to indicate a shift in genre (I.183). We are now involved in an interpretation of something that God himself shows. Though the earlier identification of the angel with the Angel of Great Counsel would seem to relativize the point somewhat, Didymus seems to hold fairly consistently to this notion throughout the six lemmata. In his opening remarks to Zechariah 4:1, for example, Didymus remarks that the angel "turned from one revelation (ἀποκαλύψεως) to another vision (θεωρίαν)" (I.272). 3) Didymus' attentiveness to the theme of spiritual warfare throughout the section—a theme that is largely absent in his treatment of the vision in Zechariah 4—suggests that he is developing a continual interpretive aim. My exposition of the interpretation will make this interpretive aim explicit.

2. *CZ* I.182–206.

but in their presence stands the One who has been victorious in all the spiritual contests, to whom they look both for instruction and salvation. The adversity of the devil is the occasion in which God proves the worth of his saints. The literal account of the text is momentarily eschewed for the sake of establishing the principles by which it should be read.

Appealing at the beginning of his interpretation to the fact that Zechariah names the Lord as the revealer of his vision, Didymus argues that what follows must be "great and supernatural, neither sensible nor human."[3] The observation allows Didymus to isolate the word "standing (ἑστῶτα)." Given that this is not a vision that concerns sensible realities, "standing" indicates steadfastness; the one standing in the vision is "unshaken (ἀκλόνητος)" and "steadfastly established (βεβαίως ἱδρύμενος)" in the moral sense. On the basis of the common office held by Joshua and Jesus and the latter's primacy with respect to this kind of "standing," Didymus loses little time in arguing that the text is applicable primarily to Jesus. In the Gospels, he is described as standing in such a way that the thirsty who come to him drink; they drink because he stands "with constancy (παραμόνως)."[4]

The purpose of these observations is to recast the interpretive frame of the passage from its judicial setting into a frame in which it becomes morally instructive. This move has several follow-on consequences, one of which is that Didymus seems to be excluding the possibility that the vision is speaking of the moral failure of Israel's high priest. Didymus argues instead that Jesus is the fixed point of the moral universe. Since he stands immovably, those who approach him and have him near become like him, imbibing his virtue and his serenity in the face of temptation. Of significance for the arguments to come is Didymus' insistence that this passage is *primarily* about Jesus, but not exclusively about him. Although he is presently unconcerned with the historical situation facing Joshua the son of Jehozadak, he returns to him presently.

The Dynamics of Spiritual Struggle

Didymus' next move is to illustrate, from various NT texts, the dynamics of spiritual warfare for those whose struggle against the powers of darkness places them between Christ and the devil. Passing quickly over the description of Jesus' standing before the "Angel of great counsel,"[5] Didymus notes that the

---

3. With Doutreleau, *Sur Zacharie*, 289. *Contra* Hill (FC 111:66), who renders the phrase: "beyond human powers to perceive." Didymus thinks the vision is not a "sensible (αἰσθητός)" vision; the power appropriate to its perception is in the νοῦς, and is therefore susceptive to human perception.

4. Summarizing *CZ* I.183-184.

5. The image of the Angel of Great Counsel—whom Didymus has already identified with the Son—standing opposite Jesus is possibly suggestive of a dichotomous perception of Christ's person. However, a judgment of this kind should be suspended in light of the fact that Didymus is hardly beholden to a kind of allegorizing such that each element in the sensible order must correspond to something different in the spiritual.

devil stands in opposition to him "at his right hand." Employing an interpretive move we have already seen in the description of the builders of the heavenly Jerusalem, Didymus takes this "right hand" to refer people who stand beside Jesus, and hence (implicitly) do what he commands. Those who stand at Jesus' right hand are helped by him. On the contrary, when Satan takes up the right hand he does so to bring an accusation against someone; when that person yields to his temptation, the sinner takes up the devil's place.[6]

Yielding ground before the devil is disastrous to the soul, Didymus argues, because the person who does so takes on the characteristics of the devil and shares in the devil's name. By doing that which the devil proposes to the soul, the person becomes "energized" by the devil for the doing of his will. Such was Judas: by betraying the one who was "both excellent teacher and Savior"[7] Judas became like the one whose companionship he had accepted, sharing even in his name. Others, like St Peter, were the objects of the devil's attack, Didymus recounts. However, because the saint was supported in his faith by the Savior who prayed "that [his] faith would not fail" (Luke 22:31), he stood firm. Didymus assures his audience that those who continue to hope in God during temptation are themselves "unharmed (ἄβλητος)" and "unshaken (ἀκλόνητος)." They become secure against the wiles of the devil.[8]

In the final example of those tempted by the devil, Didymus turns to Jesus himself, "insofar as he became human when he assumed a human soul and body."[9] Both elements of Christ's humanity are significant here. Didymus gives

---

The principle that the same spiritual referent can be indicated by two diverse sensible symbols is articulated in *CZ* V.195-197. The vision indicates nothing more than that the prophet is revealing the Son under two different aspects: he is both the one who assists those accused by the devil (as Angel of the Lord) and is like the accused insofar as he too is subject to temptation (as the human high priest). This is Jerome's interpretation of Didymus' argument in his *In Zach.* 1, 3:1-5 (CCSL 76A:771). The ecclesiastical writers, he observes, take both figures as a reference to the Son "not because he is one and also another, or that we should admit two persons in the Son. Yet because he is one and the same, he is both shown to be shabbily dressed as a man, and is said to appear as an angel: the mediator between men and God (non quod alter et alter sit, ut duas personas recipiamus in Filio, sed quod idem atque unus, et quasi homo sordidatus ostenditur, et quasi angelus mediator hominum et Dei apparere dicatur)." The duality is aspectual.

6. Summarizing *CZ* I.185-187.

7. FC 111:67.

8. Summarizing *CZ* I.187-193.

9. *CZ* I.193. Apollinaris of Laodicea is the likely target of the "complete man" claim here, given Didymus' bipartite anthropology in which the νοῦς inheres within the ψυχή. See Apollinaris' *Kat. Pist.* 30 (Lietzmann, 178): "For when God became flesh (σαρκωθείς) in human flesh (σαρκί) he preserved his own activity, being a spirit (νοῦς) unbeaten by psychic and fleshly passions and leading the flesh and the fleshly motions both divinely and without sin; not only was it unconquered by death, but it even loosed death." There is no human "spirit" present in the Incarnate Christ for Apollinaris.

more than notional assent to Christ's full humanity in recounting the fasting of Christ—in which Christ's bodily appetites occasion his temptation—and in grouping together the latter temptations, in which Satan appeals "deceitfully (δολερῶς)" to Jesus' putative desire for power and glory. These temptations, of a more spiritual nature, would appeal directly to Jesus' soul. Didymus insists that the outcome of this contest is decisive in two respects. 1) Jesus renders the devil a vanquished competitor.[10] 2) The reality of Jesus' temptation indicates that he is truly human. In this entire section[11] Didymus has studiously avoided any references to the deity of the Savior.[12] His moral stability as the eternal Logos is re-iterated in terms of his faithful human life, a life that is truly subject to temptation because Christ's soul is consubstantial with our own. Christ's life is both morally instructive and vicariously significant only insofar as it possesses the actual possibility of giving in to temptation. Only if he is truly human does his victory over the devil become significant for the rest of Adam's race.[13]

---

10. Paul's boasting in Christ is approximated here by Didymus' swaggering description of the wrestling match between Jesus and Satan. Satan the ἔξαθλος has been taken out of the game altogether, and is now nothing more than an "also-ran." Didymus describes the saints as "God's athletes" (CZ I.39) or as those who "compete for piety" (II.19).

11. CZ I.182–195 seems to be bracketed off from what follows by the prayer in I.195.

12. Cf. HiT 63,30–64,4. ο[ὐ γ]ὰρ ἥρμοζε γυμνῇ θεότητι κα[τ]αργῆσαι τὸν διάβολον, ἀλλὰ διὰ [το]ύτου ναοῦ τοῦ λόγου γεγενημένου, ὃς ἐκ σπέρματος τοῦ ἀπα<τη>θέντος καὶ β[λαβ]έντος ὑπὸ διαβόλου γεγένη[ται]. καύχημα γὰρ αὐτῷ ἦν εἰ γ[υ]μ[νῇ] θεότητι χειρωσάμενος α[ὐ]τ[ὸν ὑ]πῆρχεν. "For it did not befit bare divinity to overthrow the devil, except by this one who became the temple of the Word, who came from the seed that was deceived and harmed by the devil. Otherwise it would have been a source of boasting to him if God had subdued him by means of bare divinity."

13. Summarizing CZ I.193–194. For lengthier reflections on this theme in the PsT, see Gesché, "La nature de l'âme humaine de Jésus," La christologie, 124–211. With Reynolds, 60–68, the reflections on the mode of Jesus' engagement with the passions (e.g., the doctrine of the "fore-passion") is limited in the CZ, but there is no reason to doubt that the assumption of the soul is not instrumental in overcoming Satan (p. 67). For a summary of Didymus' response to Apollinaris and the importance of the doctrine of the pre-existence of Christ's soul, see Ghattas, Die Christologie, 157: "Die Lehre von der Präexistenz der Seele hat große Bedeutung in der Anthropologie des Didymus. . . . Die Verbindung der Seele mit dem Körper ist ein Resultat des Sündenfalls. Darum ist die Seele veränderlich. . . . Die Seele des Heilands ist ὁμοούσιος mit uns. Dies betrifft auch die Lehre von der Präexistenz der Seele Christi. Ihre Verbindung mit dem Leib ist nicht ein Resultat des Sündenfalls wie bei dem normalen Menschen, denn sie ist sündlos und hat sich die schöpfungsmäßige Gottebenbildlichkeit bewahrt und ist darum Vorbild. (The doctrine of the pre-existence of the soul has great significance in Didymus' anthropology. . . . The union of the soul with the body is a result of the Fall. Therefore the soul is mutable. . . . The soul of the Savior is ὁμοούσιος (consubstantial) with ours. This relates even to the doctrine of the pre-existence of Christ's soul. Its union with the

Satan as Instrument in the Divine Pedagogy[14]

Zechariah recounts the Lord's response to the devil. The Lord rebukes him in the name of the "Lord who has chosen Jerusalem." As if in explanation of the rebuke, the Lord adds: "See! Is not this one (τοῦτο) like a brand snatched from the fire?" (3:2) Didymus reflects that the Lord's speaking about the Lord should be taken to refer to the Father's speech about the Son. It is because the Son has chosen to redeem that the Father rebukes the devil. Didymus then focuses his energy on explaining the mode of the rebuke. The rebuke is delivered in a manner appropriate to the discourse of an incorporeal and "spiritual being." The observation serves to cement the earliest interpretive decision that this is a divine vision and must be treated accordingly.[15]

It is Didymus' interpretation of the rebuke and the burning brand that is of greater significance for what follows, however. The LXX contains at this point the grammatically ambiguous phrase: ἐπιτιμήσαι Κύριος ἐν σοί, διάβολε. The phrase ἐν σοί being patient of two interpretations, Didymus obliges with both. With the discussion about Judas and the "sons of disobedience" in the background, Didymus first interprets the rebuke as a sign that God intends to use the devil as a "vessel of wrath ... by whom and through whom" God punishes those who act "wickedly (φαύλως)." The devil, in spite of his own malicious will, is God's instrument. Didymus' second interpretation of the phrase takes the prepositional phrase as denoting the object of the verb. The Lord not only rebukes "by the devil" but also rebukes the devil himself, when he sees the evil hidden within him and punishes him for it.[16]

Significantly, it is this first interpretation of the phrase—in which Satan serves as God's instrument despite himself—that governs what follows. Didymus does not take the "burning brand" as a reference to Joshua but to the devil. He is, like a burning brand, no longer capable of bearing fruit. However, he is useful to other ends, argues Didymus. The exegete concludes his treatment of the burning brand with the observation that a burnt piece of wood is useful for the formation of "silver and golden vessels," since these must be "smelted and beaten" while they are hot.[17] From this fire the captive Israel was delivered when the Lord led the nation back to its homeland. The interpretation is, at this juncture, slightly confusing. Having identified the "brand" with the devil, Didymus proceeds to develop the significance of his being

---

body is not a result of the Fall as is the case with the typical human being, because it is sinless and has preserved the created image of God and is therefore a model.)"

14. *CZ* I.196-206.
15. Summarizing *CZ* I.197-198.
16. *CZ* I.199-201.
17. The textual issue—whether καλου should be accented on the ultima or the penult—does not bear overmuch on the interpretation of the passage. Hill translates πρὸς καλοῦ (FC 111:70); Doutreleau translates πρὸς κάλου, but admits that the translation remains doubtful (*Sur Zacharie*, 300-301n1).

burned. But when he interprets the phrase "snatched from the fire," it is no longer of this brand that he is thinking, in spite of the fact that Zechariah says that the brand is what is snatched from the fire. Didymus takes the nation Israel or the captive soul as the entity being delivered from the burning fire when the Redeemer brings it out of its enemies' sphere of influence.[18]

Summary

In this first section, Didymus establishes several precedents for his interpretation. 1) A divine vision demands a reading consonant with its mode of apprehension, since what is spoken of in such a vision is unable to be apprehended by the physical senses. 2) This vision is framed within the modalities of spiritual warfare: the contestant has before him the Angel of the Lord his helper and the example of Christ his teacher as he resists the tempter. He may be formed to Christ-likeness, or may take on the quality of the devil. Should he cling to the Lord in obedience, he is promised protection from his enemy; he becomes, like the morally incorruptible High Priest, immovable. 3) Consonant, in Didymus' mind, with the divine quality of the vision is his studious avoidance of any suggestion that the devil's accusation might be due to a real failure on the part of the accused. Taking the "standing" (3:1) as a sign of moral incorruptibility and the "burning brand" (3:2) as a reference—not to Joshua—but to Satan, Didymus suggests that he is unwilling to concede that the accusation against the high priest has some credibility. Zechariah's court-room scene is, for Didymus, chiefly about temptation rather than conviction or acquittal.

Sketching the Interpretive Skopos

There follows Zechariah's description of Joshua the High Priest, clothed in soiled garments and standing before the angel. The angel orders those around Joshua to divest him of these garments and place upon him a full-length robe. Interpreting these actions, the angel says to him: "See I have taken away your sins (ἀνομίας)" (3:3–5). Didymus' interpretation of the above passage draws together much of what preceded. 1) Returning to Joshua the high priest, Didymus interprets the historical narrative of Zechariah's time in light of its fulfillment in Jesus Christ. 2) Didymus articulates an account of the Son's assumption of the priesthood in which his pre-incarnate ministry plays an important role in Didymus' conception of the OT. These latter moves are critical in revealing how Didymus' theology of the missions of the Son influences his reading of an exceedingly important christological theme.

The Joshua of the Exile

Didymus interprets the passage first at the "literal level (πρὸς ῥητόν)."[19] Asserting that the Joshua of the exile serves as a figure for Jesus, the true and faithful high priest, the interpreter launches into a description of the elements

---

18. Summarizing *CZ* I.203–206.
19. *CZ* I.208.

of the narrative. What follows can only be described as a theologically-oriented reading of the narrative under the pressure of what Didymus had earlier established about the spiritual "standing" of Jesus. Though Didymus moves to the literal level and the priest of the exile, he is still convinced that the narrative bespeaks Jesus "iconically."[20] Consonant with this conviction, most of what he says at the literal level either recapitulates what he had earlier said about Jesus or introduces new themes that he will take up with respect to Jesus later in the interpretation. The theological argument underpinning this move is critical. As Didymus argues later on when he moves into "things of the spiritual sense (τὰ πρὸς διάνοιαν)," the priestly function of Christ is associated with the pre-Incarnate activity of the Son, which includes the period of Joshua's activity in the exile.[21] Didymus' understanding of the OT priesthood assumes that the mediating ministry of the Son of God (his priestly service) was operative before the Incarnation.

With the above in mind, we may better understand what follows. The Joshua of the exile is described as he is—namely, as clothed in filthy garments—because the saints are "full of charity (ἀγαπητικοί)." They "have compassion (συμπαθοῦσιν)" with those in a state of misfortune. This Joshua, who for Didymus was pictured by the prophet as ensconced in Babylon,[22] has compassion with Israel while it remains in a state of exile. The compassionate association of Joshua with Israel's grief echoes Didymus' earlier treatment of Jesus' prayer for St Peter and is re-echoed again by Jesus' association with human sinfulness.[23]

Didymus interprets the symbol of the filthy garments in conjunction with the angel's interpretation of them in Zechariah 3:4. The filthy garments are the actions accomplished "without regard for the law (ἄνευ νόμου)." Yet there is nothing in Didymus' interpretation to suggest that these actions are Joshua's. Joshua is a saint. His investment in the garments of lawlessness is occasioned by his office and his compassionate and charitable exercise of this office. The guilt he bears is purely a function of his priestly representation of the people before God. Therefore, explains Didymus, the angel commands these filthy garments to be taken from him by those "who by sinning became the causes of his being clothed in such clothing."[24] Each of the above moves are important, insofar as they continue to distance Joshua from participation in the sins of which he stands accused. The earlier tendency to distance Joshua from any language suggesting guilt is brought to full realization here. And the reasons for this are obvious; Didymus is about to move to the one pre-figured by Joshua: the Christ who knew no sin.

---

20. See *CZ* I.214.
21. *CZ* I.223 and I.239–244 feature prominently.
22. See *CZ* I.214.
23. Ibid.
24. See *CZ* I.212.

Didymus offers a third parallel between the historical narrative and that which comes after. When Jerusalem is restored, and those who were formerly captive in Babylon are brought back, their representative "suffers grief no longer (τὸ μηκέτι πενθεῖν)" and instead "rejoices (ἀγαλλιᾶν)" and "exults (εὐφραίνεσθαι)."[25] Important here again is the way in which the priest continues to function as representative. Since his guilt does not implicate him personally, so his joy is expressed not for himself alone but rather on the people's behalf. This theme parallels Didymus' description of Jesus' cessation of "being made sin" when we "become the righteousness of God in him" (2 Cor 5:21).[26] As representative, he suffers; as representative, he is vindicated.

More can be said of the connections between the two priests. "The figural (εἰκονικός) Joshua who lives in Babylon with the exiles bears a type" of Jesus the High Priest. The icon was exiled to Babylon with the captives of Israel for no fault of his own; implicitly, the one pre-figured accepted the consequence of human exile from God and lived among sinners, though he himself committed no sin.[27] The one anticipated was invested in sin when he "became sin" for us by ascending the cross. Of note here is the extent to which Didymus establishes connections between Jesus and Joshua in such a way that his reading of the "literal sense" is brought into conversation with its figural significance. This is so much the case that the "literal sense" is transfigured by the conversation.

This feature of Didymus' reading of Zechariah 3 must be judged in relation to his account of the Son's activity in the OT. It is sufficient for the present, however, to note that it is impossible to understand Didymus' reading of the "literal sense" in isolation from the higher senses that he develops prior to and subsequent to it. Tigcheler is therefore justified in drawing attention to the inadequacy of Bienert's claim that the πρὸς ῥητόν reading of the text of Scripture is "an immanent understanding of each text."[28] Didymus' interests in the "literal sense" here are hardly "immanent" ones. His account of Joshua's exercise of the priesthood is mostly determined by considerations developed in the spiritual sense of the passage. The two senses are exceedingly conver-

---

25. *CZ* I.211.
26. *CZ* I.220.
27. *CZ* I.214.
28. Bienert, 108. For Tigcheler's critique, see *Exégèse allégorique*, 76–77. Tigcheler is overly zealous in pursuing an absolute distinction between πρὸς ῥητόν and καθ' ἱστορίαν, but correctly draws attention to Bienert's unsatisfactory definition of ἱστορικά realities as those things "that are accessible to the human mind without spiritual help, are scientifically verifiable, or historically determinable (die dem menschlichen Verstand ohne geistliche Hilfe zugänglich, wissenschaftlich überprüfbar oder geschichtlich fixierbar sind)" (p. 76). Bienert is perhaps drawn to this conclusion because his study focuses mainly on the higher senses. He also emphasizes the fact that Didymus identifies the impossibility of the literal sense as the means *par excellence* of justifying the shift between the senses. See pp. 78–80.

sant with one another. Consistent with the stages of contemplation that Didymus identifies in CZ, there can be no such thing as a truly immanent account of the narrative or historical senses.

The Vestments of Jesus, the Great High Priest

Having mined the "literal sense" to his satisfaction, the exegete now brings the athletic motif (signifying spiritual combat) into further focus in the light of Jesus' investiture in the "filthy garments" of human sin. Here Didymus also offers some hints as to why he has developed the literal sense in the manner that he did. The higher sense of the passage contains three basic moves, each of which serves to triangulate Didymus' basic point: that Jesus' triumph over sin is to be re-iterated in the Christian life of conformation to him. 1) Jesus, who is like Joshua in the respects indicated above, put on the filth of sin "without sinning himself or experiencing sin."[29] 2) He did this for a definite purpose: that we might "live by his righteousness" (1 Pet 2:24). 3) This "righteousness" is conceived of here in terms of being conformed to the ethical and contemplative virtues taught by Christ, the good teacher. It is a "righteousness" that is contested by the spiritual forces of evil. The latter point serves to connect Didymus' treatment of this lemma (Zech 3:3–5) with the earlier two (3:1–2a and 3:2b). Just as in his treatment of the "right hand" of Satan, so here. One may either be animated by evil powers by "putting them on" or one may "put on Christ" (Gal 3:27).[30]

Each of the above points is repeated again with greater specificity. 1) Jesus identifies with our state in such a way that it is clear that he is invested with garments that are not "woven" by him. He puts them on to transform the conditions in which human life proceeds thereafter. Jesus' investiture in human sin was for the fulfillment of divine beneficence; "tasting death" (Heb 2:9), the Incarnate Lord delivered the human race. At this point, Didymus makes a brief and striking remark: "At any rate, even while clad in the filthy attire, he [namely, the high priest] stood before the angel, not keeping his distance from him."[31] Given that Didymus' portrait of the "high priest" in the spiritual sense has focused on the human actions of the Incarnate One, especially in his susceptibility to temptation, the "angel" here is the Son under the aspect of his divinity. The remark is meant to ward off any suggestion that one can conceive of the death of the Savior as though it is without consequence for the Savior's whole person. Without the sophistication of later generations, Didymus is alive to the threat posed by conceiving of the death of Christ as something that takes place only with consequences for the humanity that the Word assumes.

---

29. *CZ* I.214 (FC 111:72). The allusion to 2 Corinthians 5:21 is apparent, and is later made explicit in *CZ* I.220.

30. *CZ* I.217.

31. *CZ* I.218 (FC 111:73).

These observations then lead into a re-iteration of the second theme: he does these things so that we might put on his righteousness. 2) The angel—or the Son in his divinity—now commands us to take off the "defiled garments" of Jesus. Didymus has transformed the imperative of Zechariah 3:4, with Israel as its addressee, into an imperative for his audience. We remove the garments from him, he says, by repenting of our sin. Didymus then adduces several texts that speak of the reciprocity involved between Jesus and us on whose behalf he serves as priest. When he became sin, we became God's righteousness (2 Cor 5:21). When he became a curse, we gained a blessing. When we repent, he is divested of sin.[32]

But what is the specific form that this repentance must take? 3) Didymus concludes this pivotal section with a reflection on the three articles of priestly clothing in which Jesus is invested *by us*: the "garment (ἱμάτιον),"[33] the "long robe (ποδήρης)," and the "turban (κίδαρις)." It is the latter phrase—"by us"— that determines the figural referent of each: the "garment (ἱμάτιον)" is the body that he assumes in the Incarnation. Didymus argues: "since we became the causes of his making use of such a garment, we clothed him in it."[34] The "long robe" designates our "discernment (θεωρία)" of Jesus' Incarnation and the "turban" designates our attainment to the "summit of the divine doctrine about Christ (τὸ κεφάλαιον τῆς περὶ Χριστοῦ θεολογίας)." This "turban" covers the "mind (νοῦς)" of the high priest.[35]

The passage brings up several elements of Didymus' thinking with which we are already familiar. The economy of salvation, in which the Son assumes a material body, is occasioned by our sin. As in his explication of Psalm 23 LXX, the cause of the humanity of the Son is "in us." Secondly, we see again a distinction between the preliminary doctrine of the Incarnation and that which must follow after it: the doctrine of the divinity of the Son, which is also the intellective vision of the Trinity. Didymus here expresses the goal of attaining to righteousness in terms of our faithful response to precisely these imperatives: repent in recognition of the Son's Incarnation, and raise your interior vision beyond all that is "material (ὑλικόν)" or "defiled (ῥυποῦν)" to the contemplation of the Son's anterior divinity.

A final element, bracketed out above, is also introduced here. As was noted earlier, the phrase "by us" constrains Didymus' interpretation above: he speaks of our investiture of Christ and thus of the "body" of the Son and of our ascription of Incarnation and divinity to the Son. The notion of ascription is crucial to the latter item, since he cannot speak of our being the cause of the Son's divinity without a serious lapse in doctrine. Out of nowhere, however, Didymus introduces a fourth article—a "priestly tunic (ἱερατικὸν χιτῶνα)"—

---

32. Summarizing *CZ* I.219–221.
33. The item is plural in Zechariah 3:5; Didymus takes it singularly here.
34. *CZ* I.222.
35. Summarizing *CZ* I.222–224.

into his interpretation. Didymus' treatment of this article is so monumental and so basic to the underlying presuppositions of his interpretation that the passage must be quoted in full:

> Yet even if he is invested with the afore-mentioned garment while saying to God, "A body you have formed for me," he continues as high priest to wear the priestly tunic, that long tunic upon which the weavers modelled the sensible one, when they were filled with a spirit of wisdom.[36]

Didymus hints at the fact that the priestly role of the Son is in some sense in play before his Incarnation; the Spirit-filled fashioners of the vestiture of the priesthood were looking upon the mystery of Christ's incarnate ministry in the theophany of Sinai (see Exodus 26:3).

The point is further defended later on in Didymus' development of the theme of Jesus' priesthood, which he explicitly connects with these earlier reflections on the priestly office of the Son.[37] In a sustained polemic against those who argue from Hebrews 3:1–2 that the Son is "made" rather than "appointed" to the office of priesthood, Didymus argues that the Son of God's appointment to the office stems from the time "when they came to be to whom he was sent and for whom he acts as priest."[38] Somewhat surprisingly, given the context, Didymus argues that the commencement of the Son's high priestly service is associated with the coming into existence of the human race. Though it achieves its ultimate expression in the Incarnation or ἡ δεῦρο κάθοδος of the Son, it is in some way carried out in the pre-Incarnate activity of the Son of God, and is thus operative during the time of Joshua the high priest.

Summary

Before moving onto the final section of Didymus' interpretation, I summarize what has gone before and highlight some of the advantages of Didymus' reading of the text thus far. Picking up on an earlier motif, Didymus rehearses the point that the student is to be conformed in obedience to the thoughts and actions of the good teacher: the Son. But now these thoughts are concretely identified both negatively and positively. Negatively, the student is enjoined to repentance from conformity to the thought-patterns suggested by the ones against whom they direct their struggle. Positively, the hearer of the Word is

---

36. CZ I.223 (FC 111:73). The text reads: Πλὴν εἰ καὶ περιβέβληται τὸ λεχθὲν ἱμάτιον τῷ Θεῷ λέγων· « Σῶμα δὲ κατηρτίσω μοι », ἀλλ᾽ οὖν μένει πάλιν ἱερεὺς μέγας περικείμενος τὸν ἱερατικὸν χιτῶνα, τὸν ποδήρη ἐκεῖνον πρὸς ὃν τὸν αἰσθητὸν κατεσκεύασαν πνεύματος σοφίας πεπληρωμένοι ὑφάνται.

37. See CZ I.239: "In what went before, Joshua the high priest represents the one who serves as priest in the order of Melchizedek" (FC 111:76).

38. CZ I.242 (FC 111:77; with Doutreleau, *Sur Zacharie*, 319). The text reads: ἀφ᾽ οὗ ὑπάρχουσιν οἱ πρὸς οὕς ἀποστέλλεται καὶ ὑπὲρ ὧν ἱερᾶται.

to perceive the moral life revealed by the Son's Incarnation and so respond in reverence to it that he comes to possess the vision of the Son's divinity.

For this course of training, both Joshua the high priest and the one revealed by him are paradigmatic. The saint is so conformed to the virtues of the Incarnate Son that Didymus' accounts of both run parallel. The "literal sense" bends under pressure from the "mind (διάνοια)" of the passage. I have suggested that there is an implicit explanation for this porous conception of the senses in terms of the Son's exercise of his priestly office in the OT. Joshua is an imitator of Christ precisely because he is, as one who possesses the office of the priest, conversant with the Son who precedes him (!) in the office and sustains him in the proper exercise thereof. The pre-Incarnate missions of the Son, continually defended by Didymus, are essential to the proper understanding of the "literal sense" of Zechariah 3:3–5.[39]

Perfect Holiness, Perfect Vision

Three lemmata conclude the revelation (ἀποκάλυψις).[40] In the first of these (3:6–7), the Lord promises Joshua that he will be given the role of judging God's house and will be given those who live therein if he walks in God's ways. In the second, the angel of the Lord assures the priest and his intimates—who are described by the LXX as "seers of wonders (τερατοσκόποι)"—that the Lord will bring forth his servant "Dawn," relating his appearance to a seven-eyed stone (3:8–9a). In the final lemma, the Lord promises to do away with all "unrighteousness" in "one day"; on that day the beneficiaries of the promise will invite their neighbors under their "vine" and "fig tree" (3:9b–10). Didymus continues to develop the sense of the passage in light of his earliest frame—spiritual struggle—linking the first of these three lemmata to the discipline of celibacy. The second lemma focuses on the "seer" and the "stone" as images related to the attainment of seven-fold illumination. The final lemma draws together the moral and contemplative aspects of the imitation of Christ under the images of the "fig tree" and the "vine."

"Established in Holiness"

Though the promise of pre-eminence over the divine household is given to Joshua, Didymus first appears to take the promise generically. A saint learns the ways of God by divine instruction in the virtues and thereby receives the role of judging the divine house.[41] The grip on the Joshua of the exile, developed somewhat above, appears tenuous from this point onward. Christ dominates the development, and through him Didymus makes his application to his

---

39. I offer a mixed assessment of this passage with respect to Didymus' understanding of the relationship between the senses (in conversation with Eusebius of Caesarea, Theodore, Jerome, Cyril of Alexandria, and Theodoret).

40. See *CZ* I.272.

41. *CZ* I.226.

audience. The house of God is the "assembly" of God's people, and the one who judges this house is Jesus, who appoints for the Church the various offices so that the saints may be made perfect (Eph 4:11). The ecclesial interpretation of "house" leads Didymus to enumerate the members of Christ's "body," in which the charismatic dimension of the Church is developed.[42]

Jesus, the judge of God's house, is then given the reward consonant with his labor; the reward of Jesus' perfect obedience to the Father is to receive "those firmly established in holiness (οἱ βεβαίως κατὰ ἁγιότητα ἱδρύμενοι)." Didymus derives the point from the language of "standing" (3:7), a verb that he has already lengthily developed in terms of moral stability. These are the ones who are given to Jesus by God. They are, like those who make contest for the crowns, described as growing stable in faith and love. Didymus summarizes the argument:

> Among such people, who are truly in the image *and likeness* of God, lived Jesus, who received them [namely, the people] from the Father, and who "appeared on earth to live among them," bestowing a type and example for those who choose to imitate him.[43]

The emphasis on "likeness" here indicates that Didymus is conceiving not only of those who are far advanced in the virtues, but of those who have obtained to absolute conformity to the Son.

Didymus completes the development of the lemma by examining another dimension of the word "standing." The angels are those who stand by, singing the praises of the Savior and never leaving his company in their divine liturgy. Didymus sounds an eschatological note: this is to be our lot in the age to come when "after the resurrection" we become "like angels." Didymus isolates two aspects of the angelic condition: they are unmarried and incorruptible. The two are associated insofar as marriage is a provision for the present age in which death makes necessary the birth of children. But Didymus urges his hearers to live the heavenly life in the present age. Devote yourselves to celibacy and to purity of both body and soul. Do not be parted from the divine Bridegroom for a moment.

In this vein he concludes the interpretation of the lemma. In the exegetical literature, the inclusion of the "likeness" language here implies much the same that the language of the "final goal" does. As in other places in the *CZ*, there is no sense that such conformity is a condition only to be awaited. Those who are faithful to the image and likeness are established in holiness in the present life. They are so by imitation of Jesus in the Incarnation, and their life is in some way like that of the angels.

---

42. Summarizing *CZ* I.226–231.
43. *CZ* I.233. Emphasis mine.

"Seers"

The subsequent lemma majors on the illuminative dimension of this conformation. Since I have treated the text on the "seven eyes" of the stone and the lengthy digression on the meaning of Jesus' "faithful" priesthood, I will only briefly discuss the significance of these passages in the interpretation of the lemma. Of greatest significance for our purposes is Didymus' treatment of the LXX's affirmation that those who are "nearby" Jesus are called "observers of signs (τερατοσκόποι)" or "seers."

Didymus sees an important parallel between those "nearby" Jesus and those in Hebrews 3:1 who consider Jesus' priesthood rightly and are thus "partakers of a heavenly calling." To interpret the language of the Son's being "appointed" as an indication of his creaturely status is to overthrow the entire course of the spiritual life, argues Didymus. Only the mature discern the significance of the Son's assumption of the priestly office; it is not rooted in the Son's subordinate status, but rather takes place "for and because of" those who require his priestly service. Again, Didymus returns to the idea that the Son serves as priest during the time in which Zechariah is writing.

Returning from Hebrews to the Zechariah text, Didymus describes those "near" Joshua—now the emphasis being on contemplative knowledge—with those who are "priests in a spiritual sense." Didymus proposes groups who fit this description: those who are chaste, those reborn after the general resurrection, and the apostles. It is this latter group that Didymus singles out for special comment. The apostles who are near to Jesus are neither infants nor children but rather "are mature men arriving at the state of being a man perfect in the fullness of the knowledge of the Son of God."[44] Again, Didymus is thinking of perfect illumination, and he describes the consequences of such vision.

Such people, called "seers" by the Scriptures, were men like Moses and Aaron. They possessed not only the "vision of wonders and signs, but the very words by which these things were accomplished."[45] We have already visited this idea above; the perfect contemplative is a master of his speech as well, becoming capable of communicating all that is seen in the vision. Didymus then provides us with several examples of what the apostles and contemporary "seers" might see as they look into the Gospel narratives. Taking the events of John 9:1-7 and Matthew 9:20-22 as miracles that have a signifying

---

44. With Doutreleau, *Sur Zacharie*, 321. *Contra* Hill, (FC 111:78): "mature men, face to face with a man who is mature with the fullness of the knowledge of the Son of God." The disputed phrase is ἄνδρες τέλειοι καταντήσαντες εἰς ἄνδρα τέλειον τοῦ πληρώματος κ.τ.λ. (CZ I.247). Doutreleau's rendering is preferable, more closely tied as it is to the definition of καταντάω + εἰς, which has the sense of "attaining to" an object. The maturity—or perfection—to which they attain is fullness of knowledge of the Son. Hill's rendering sounds dangerously dichotomous as an articulation of the relation between the Son and the humanity he assumes.

45. *CZ* I.248.

function, Didymus takes the man born blind as a symbol of the conversion of the Gentiles and the purification of the Gentile Church. Those who peer into the higher meaning of the Scriptures, he argues, see these things in the Gospel narrative. Those who are mature in knowledge and not beginners in being conformed to the humanity revealed by the Incarnation are capable of looking into the mysteries that are revealed in the *phenomena* of the miracles of Jesus.

The final element of the lemma—the seven-eyed stone—is interpreted as the seven-fold gift of the Spirit who endows the one who partakes of him with complete illumination. We have dealt with this passage in a previous chapter in which I argued that the Son's receptivity to the Spirit norms the possibilities of human receptivity to the Spirit of God. The "holy stones" that we are to become are made so by full participation in the Spirit.

Vine and Fig Tree

Didymus concludes the interpretation with a reflection on the "one day" in which God will put down iniquity. Eschewing a purely eschatological interpretation, he argues that the day of which Zechariah is speaking is the "time of our Savior's sojourn (ἐπιδημίας)."[46] On this day the Lord inaugurated a period of "profound peace (εἰρήνη . . . βαθεῖα)."[47] The blind theologian is thinking here of the consequences obtaining from Jesus' victory over sin as it is being realized fully among the nations. The prophecy is for his time. As the victory of Jesus works like leaven through the nations, each enemy will be put down until there is no longer any cause for fear. When this is so, all wars will cease.

The international scope of Didymus' vision is dependent upon the outworking of this victory in the lives of his students and others like them. So Didymus concludes his reflections with an implicit invitation for his students to cultivate the "vine" and the "fig tree" for the benefit of their neighbors. Taking the reference to these plants as a scriptural riddle and defending the move on the basis of a *defectus litterae*,[48] Didymus argues that the fig tree signifies the active life. It is "bitter" and "harsh" because the practical virtues are

---

46. *CZ* I.264.

47. *CZ* I.264–265.

48. Didymus writes: "What do the aforementioned plants—namely the vine and fig tree—suggest by way of riddling (αἰνίττονται) other than the contemplative and active life?" (*CZ* I.266) He defends the point by using Proverbs 27:18 as a scriptural passage that interprets the "fig tree" here: "The one who plants a fig tree eats its fruits." Pointing out that there are counter-examples to the factual claim made here (some people die before they eat the fruit of a tree they plant), Didymus therefore gives the passage in Zechariah only a spiritual interpretation (cf. I.267). Given that Didymus himself has described the scenario in Zechariah as obtaining only when abundant peace fills the earth and all the enemies of God are put down, the objection to the ἱστορία (an objection that applies better to the Proverbs 27:18 text) seems somewhat contrived. With Hill, *Commentary on Zechariah*, 83n56.

acquired only with great pain and sweat.⁴⁹ The vine on the other hand signifies the contemplative life.

How should the hearers of Zechariah respond to this revelation? Didymus holds up one final vision of the perfect person, formed according to both kinds of virtues.

> Finally, when you see the gnostic (γνωστικὸν) man desiring to lead his neighbors under the sage vision of God and the doctrines and thoughts that concern him, you are seeing how he invited his neighbors, whom he loves as he loves himself, under his own vine so that they might feast and rejoice together. Likewise, the doer of good works leads those he loves under the fig-tree he planted—namely, practical virtue—that they may be at rest (ῥᾳστωνεύσωσιν) together, when they enter into the joy of their Master.⁵⁰

The end of the struggle to attain the virtues revealed by the Incarnate Son is described by images dear to Didymus: the pain and sweat of the acquisition of the virtues gives way to rejoicing and rest in the company of the saints. The goal of the Christian life is attained when someone becomes so attuned to the virtues that he is able, like holy Joshua and the One he represents iconically, not only to provide an image of the virtues for others but also to love his neighbors with such compassion that their joy in attaining virtue becomes his own.

Summary

In these final three lemmata, Didymus concludes his sketch of the struggle for virtue. Those who "stand firm" in holiness and stay near the Lord offer perpetual service to the Lord. This is not a condition to be awaited, but for Didymus and his audience is one that is to be attained specifically through the disciplines of abstinence, purity, and contemplation. By such purification, they are to pass into the heights of the contemplative vision of God, becoming "seers" like the apostles. In this condition, the perfect becomes capable of reading the Scriptures in their highest sense and communicating to others the deepest meaning thereof. At the conclusion of the revelation, Didymus then offers a picture of the perfect sage, who invites his fellows into the joy and rest of his Master by loving them as himself. Thus they become "Joshuas." In this way they fulfill their priestly office in a spiritual sense, drawing others out of the bonds of servitude to destructive oppressors and into the joy of life in the heavenly Jerusalem even while the present age endures.

We may offer here a summary of the interpretation as a whole. Didymus frames the vision within the genre of divine speech. Its central subject is spiri-

---

49. *CZ* I.266.
50. *CZ* I.269–270.

tual warfare: resisting temptation and staying near to Christ the students learn from their divine Teacher what is required for the growth in virtue. Above all, for Didymus, this requires the recognition that Christ is the embodiment of all virtue and the place where this virtue is available to us. Specifically, Christ calls us to the active life of love for the neighbor (demonstrated by Joshua) and into the contemplative life of moving from the recognition of Christ's incarnation to his anterior divinity. In this way we become firmly established in the active virtues, seers like the apostles who understand Scripture in the highest sense and who receive the abundance of the Holy Spirit which Christ's own reception of the Spirit makes possible, and cultivators of the active and contemplative life to such a degree that the fruits of our life give benefit to others.

Retrieving Didymus the Blind

I want to now offer a critique of Didymus' reading of Zechariah 3 under three headings. In the first of these I examine the content of the literal sense in relation to the treatments given the same by Didymus' (near) contemporaries. In the second, I examine the content of the spiritual sense and look reflexively at its basis in the literal sense. In the third, I take on a final issue, one which is of ultimate importance in commending Didymus to current readership. Now that we are in a position to relate Didymus' interpretive *skopos* to his account of how the Scriptures function in the Trinitarian economy of salvation, we may ask how well his interpretive *praxis* coheres with his account of what God intends to do, or better, of what God is doing with Scripture. In short, is Didymus' interpretive *skopos* in harmony with the divine *skopos*?

On the Content of the Literal Sense

In this section, I take a look at the theologically-motivated link between the senses that Didymus establishes in his exegesis of Zechariah 3 and the challenges that he presents to the theologically-deficient proposals of Eusebius of Caesarea and Theodore of Mopsuestia. I then examine the questions raised by Jerome, Cyril, and Theodoret about Didymus' way of accounting for the historical dimensions of the narrative. In light of these discussions, I offer an evaluation of Didymus' literal sense, with a view to its impact on the christological sense(s) that he develops in reference to it.

Israel's High Priest

Didymus' indebtedness to Eusebius of Caesarea's reading of Zechariah 3 in the *Demonstratio Evangelica* cannot be established here, but the kinship between their treatments is striking.[51] For our purposes, however, the most significant feature of Eusebius' argument with respect to the priesthood of the Son is the theological underpinning that he develops elsewhere in the same

---

51. Eusebius treats the passage in *Dem. ev.* 4.17.9–23 (GCS 23:197–200).

book. As Joseph Lécuyer points out, Eusebius is keen to secure the hypostatic integrity of the Son against certain forms of modalism, and so predicates the priestly ministry to the Son as an aspect of his eternal identity.[52]

> Standing midway between God the ingenerate and the things that came into being after him (τῶν μετ' αὐτὸν γενητῶν) and taking upon himself the care of the universe and serving as priest to the Father on behalf of all the obedient, and by himself rendering him [namely, the Father] well-disposed and compassionate to all, he is called eternal high priest and indeed Christ of the Father.[53]

As the example illustrates, Eusebius' conception of the priesthood of the Son locates the mediation in the Son's pre-existence, and explicitly ties this mediation to the Son's relative ontological proximity to the created order. The Son is priest because he is "midway between God the ingenerate and the things that came into being after him."

The problem raised by Eusebius could be avoided by speaking of the mediation purely in terms of the Son's assumption of humanity. The Son becomes high priest when he becomes human.[54] The mediation is a function of his Incarnation. Didymus' position on the question is, as we have seen, somewhat more complex. For him, the Son is not priest by virtue of any subordinate status in relation to the Father, but rather takes up the priestly function as soon as the creation comes into existence. That this priestly service achieves a certain kind of prominence in the Incarnation is affirmed, but the priestly work of the Son starts with the beginning of the economy, conceived in its broadest sense. So tightly woven together are the narratives of creation and re-creation in *DT* that the Incarnation is a continuation of that which the Trinity had begun when the Father said to the other two *hypostaseis*: "Let us make a man in our image." The Son, as the true image of the Father, is the focal point of human relationship with the Trinity. The priestly function that the Son takes up in the Incarnation is thus, as Didymus rightly notes, the outworking of something that is nascent in the creation of the race of Adam and in the Son's continual presence to the people of Israel.

The advantages of this formulation of things are especially seen in Didymus' linking together of the senses. The literal and spiritual senses are typi-

---

52. For a brief, but very lucid discussion of the basic elements of his treatment in its theological context, see Joseph Lécuyer, "Jésus, fils de Josédec, et le Sacerdoce du Christ," *RSR* 43 (1955): 92–95.

53. *Dem. ev.* 4.10.16 (GCS 23:167–168).

54. This is Cyril of Alexandria's tendency. For a sample of this, see his *Glaph.Gen.* 2.3.4 and 2.3.7 (PG 69:88B and 100A). Cf. Gerald O'Collins and Michael K. Jones, *Jesus our Priest: A Christian Approach to the Priesthood of Christ* (Oxford: Oxford University Press, 2010), 99, who note that the tendency is prominent in Cyril's later literature as well.

cally linked because they are economically linked. The priestly ministry of the Son in the OT provides the appropriate theological framework in which to read the "literal sense." Thus Joshua the high priest not only anticipates Christ but participates in the Son who through the OT priestly line indicates his own coming. Didymus makes the connection to the Son's ministration of the priesthood an integral aspect of the right interpretation of the narrative.

Theodore of Mopsuestia has little patience for arguments of this kind, as he reveals quite early in his commentary on the same prophet. After introducing his readers to the principle that some of the things revealed by the prophet are "emblems (γνωρίσματα)" of other "realities (πραγμάτων),"[55] he rejects the notion that the man on the red horse (Zech 1:8) should be regarded as a reference to the Son of God. Theodore's principle objection to this interpretation—aside from the fact that it is full of "deceit," "foolishness," and "impiety"—is that

> before the coming (παρουσίας) of Christ the Lord no one (οὐθείς) knew the Father and the Son, nor that God the Father was the Father of God the Son, nor that God the Son was the Son of God the Father, though this is what the Father is, since he [i.e. the Son] is also from him.

After acknowledging that the names "Father" and "Son" had a less hypostatically specific role to play in the OT, Theodore re-iterates the point: "as I was saying earlier, of those who lived at that time absolutely no one (καθάπαξ οὐδείς) knew [these things]."[56]

Theodore's defense of this claim deserves special consideration. He first adduces the argument that Jewish piety during the time of the OT was characterized by the knowledge of God and the creation only. For this reason, it took the "blessed apostles" a long time to come to the recognition that Jesus' claim to divine Sonship was something more than a mere claim to close "affinity (οἰκείωσις)" with God, as the term "son" had been used in the OT. Theodore supports the point in light of Philip's desire for Jesus to show the disciples the Father (John 14:8), trading on the idea of the Father's invisibility. He taught them of his Sonship when they learned to see him with their eyes opened to his divinity. They see the Son properly when they know him as "God from God in essence (κατ' οὐσίαν)." If the apostles knew neither the Son nor the Spirit until they learned of them in the NT, neither could the prophets have known, Theodore concludes. Let angels be angels, as the writers of the NT called them to distinguish them from the Persons of the Godhead. Thus Theodore defends his interpretation that the vision of the man on the horse signified an angel in the form of a man.[57]

---

55. *In Zach.* 1: 8b–11 (Sprenger, 324.16–17).
56. *In Zach.* 1: 8b–11 (Sprenger, 325.1–11).
57. *In Zach.* 1: 8b–11 (Sprenger, 325.11–328.27).

His application of this historical *ordo cognoscendi* clarifies some ambiguities. He is not here denying the OT a prophetic or foreshadowing function. Zechariah 9:9–10 really prophesies the coming of the Lord Christ, even as the authors of the NT recognized.[58] But he does appear to be fairly consistent in denying the Son and the Holy Spirit any *recognized* role in the history of Israel. As we noted in the first chapter, coming across the pneumatologically explicit language of Zechariah 4:6, Theodore passes by the reference to the Spirit of the Lord in silence.[59] Two important moves are made here: 1) the authors of the OT did not know the Son or the Spirit. 2) On this basis we should not identify the Son and the Spirit as protagonists in the narrative of the OT.

Both claims are dubious. 1) The authors of the NT attest to the knowledge of the Son among the authors of the OT. Isaiah sees the glory of the Son and speaks of him (John 12:41). David acknowledges two Lords, one of whom Jesus identifies with himself (Ps 109:1; cf. Luke 20:42). Elihu speaks of the creative activity of the Spirit (Job 33:4), Moses of the Spirit of the Lord whom he longs to see poured out on all Israel (Num 11:29). 2) And are there not numerous instances when the writers of the NT identify the agency of the Son and the Spirit of God in the OT, even if the issue of the people's knowledge thereof is left ambiguous? Jesus (!) saved his people from the land of Egypt (Jude 5). The people "drank from the spiritual Rock that followed them, and the Rock was Christ" (1 Cor 10:4). If they inquired into the mystery of Christ by the Spirit of Christ who was in them (1 Pet 1:11), should we who read by the apostolic counsel be less eager to join them in this discovery?

Theodore's argument also raises a serious difficulty for the doctrine of God. If the knowledge of God revealed in the NT is an utter *novum*, then does this not imply that God discloses himself in the OT in a manner that is at the very least opaque to the hypostatic identities of the Persons? The divine freedom for self-disclosure is a freedom defined in abstraction from the hypostatically differentiated being of God. In consequence, the saving and self-revealing economy of the Trinity becomes bifurcated into two economies. And in the former economy, the doctrine of the Trinity is of no material significance, except perhaps as a distant *telos* toward which this former economy of Israel is directed. Didymus, even if his application of the principle of the christological meaning of Scripture is at times too exuberant,[60] is on far firmer ground. God the Trinity had, from the very beginning of the economy, moved toward his creatures in the knowledge-creating fellowship of the three *hypostaseis*. In con-

---

58. *In Zach.* 9:9–10a (Sprenger, 367.24–368.7).

59. *In Zach.* 4:4–6 (Sprenger, 345.22–346.5).

60. One thinks of Jerome's uncharacteristically restrained rebuke of Didymus for departing from the traditional interpretation of the "mountain" of Zechariah 4:7. "Some" interpreters had, "with no small degree of indiscretion," made the mistake of "referring to Christ what was manifestly said of the devil" (*In Zach.* 1, 4:2–7 (CCSL 76A:780)).

tinuity with that which he would do in the Incarnation, the Son of God took up the office of the priesthood. The pre-incarnate Son of God is the true high priest of Israel during the ministration of the son of Jehozadak.

On the Inordinate Pressure of the "Useful"

Didymus' theological grounding of the "literal sense" of Zechariah 3:3-5 in the Son's exercise of the priesthood in the OT is warranted. But it does not go far enough and it is applied with too little critique of his doctrine of perfection. I argue here that the "literal sense" reading of Joshua, the exilic high priest, is deficient on two accounts: 1) Didymus' reading suggests that a "literal sense" reading of Zechariah 3 cannot be sustained consistently. 2) His application of the doctrine of perfection to the literal sense undermines the fulsome christological potential of the higher senses.

The first objection is not merely a contemporary one. In a different passage of his *Commentary on the Twelve Minor Prophets*, Theodore complains about exegetes who divide the text in an atomistic way between Zerubbabel and Christ. Such readings, he argues, pull "against the grain (ἀλλόκοτον)" of the prophecy. Let the "obvious (πρόχειρος)" meaning refer to Zerubbabel, and the "truth (ἀλήθεια)" be fulfilled in Christ.[61]

Jerome also shows a greater sensitivity to the need for narrative coherence, even if his standards are not quite up to the level that Theodore would have preferred. Though individual moments of his interpretation are heavily dependent upon Didymus, his interpretative structure is more easily discerned. Reporting on the Jewish exegesis of Zechariah 3:1-5, Jerome argues: given the magnitude of the scenario envisioned, it would not be "appopriate (appositum)" to identify the Joshua in this vision with the post-exilic priest.[62] This must refer to Jesus. Hence, he develops a christological reading of the text until the lemma of Zechariah 3:8-9. Here the burden of explaining why Jesus is promised a vision of himself as "the Dawn" becomes too difficult to carry, so Jerome drops it and switches tacks. Here, he argues, the Jewish exegetes have the advantage of their ecclesiastical counterparts in taking Joshua as a reference to the son of Jehozadak.[63]

Jerome's reading raises Theodore's question afresh, and because Jerome remains so closely tied to Didymus, the question may be heard in the latter's register. We have seen Jerome follow Didymus in identifying several "characters" in the same vision with different "aspects" of Christ. But by Zechariah 3:8-9, this procedure becomes dizzying in Didymus' interpretation. The Son has been introduced under several aspects and is now promised, the prophet

---

61. Theodore, *In Zach.* 9:9-10a (Sprenger, 367.24-369.26).

62. Jerome, *In Zach.* 1, 3:1-5 (CCSL 76A:771).

63. Jerome, *In Zach.* 1, 3: 8-9 (CCSL 76A:774). Here Jerome points out that the Jewish interpreters of the passage are on firmer ground in referring the discussion to Joshua the son of Jehozadak.

tells us, a further vision of himself under yet another aspect. He will come as the Dawn (3:9). Didymus assimilates the text to his earlier procedure, dwelling on the illuminative dimension of Christ's ministry and his receptivity to the Holy Spirit. The development can no longer proceed, as it did earlier, parallel to the "literal sense" that was introduced in Zechariah 3:3–5, for Didymus would then be faced with the awkward question of how Joshua's promised vision (of the Son who would surpass him) corresponds to something in the life of Christ. Jerome here resolves the tension by abandoning any meaningful connection between the senses: in the first part of the chapter we have a text that is purely about Christ (functioning without any meaningful connection to the historical dimension of Zechariah 3) and on the other hand we have a text about Joshua (functioning historically with a prophetic, but no typological, link to Christ). The historical character of the vision and its obvious resonances with events in the life of Christ seem to press both Didymus and Jerome to take up the historical narrative in places where it suits their interpretive *skopos*. But in neither of them is there a sustained development of this sense.

On the question raised by Theodore, Cyril and Theodoret both take up instructive positions. Cyril wrestles explicitly with the genre question, just as Didymus did earlier. But his conclusions are quite different:

> The narrative (διήγημα) is a vision (ὅρασις), but has an historical explanation (λόγον), suggesting (some things) through riddles, and again delineating Jesus beforehand (προδιαγραφόμενον) as though by an image.[64] And understand that since the things in the visions have come to pass at last, the prophet fashions his discourse concerning them and never speaks aimlessly nor indeed follows the events and accumulates a pile of countless stories for us. Rather, as I was saying in the beginning, what things he saw before they came to pass, these he also conveys as of great value in rendering Israel wise and secure.

Thus Cyril carves out an interpretive framework for himself. His concerns are two-fold: 1) to connect the vision to an historical event while 2) avoiding an account of the vision as though it contained nothing more than a narrative of

---

64. Hill takes Ἰησοῦ here as a reference to Joshua son of Jehozadak (FC 124:116). It seems more likely, however, that Cyril is referring to Jesus since 1) Joshua has not yet made an appearance in Zechariah, 2) the referent is described as being delineated beforehand (Hill does not translate the prefix προ-), and 3) Cyril's self-citation—ὡς ἔφην ἐν ἀρχαῖς—refers to the introductory matter in which Cyril explains that Zechariah "in every part (πανταχῇ)" gives indications of the "redemption that would come through Christ" and reveals this mystery "through many figures" (*In Zach.* 1:1 (Pusey, 284.9–11)).

historical events. Zechariah's message is just as much "for us" as it was for Israel.[65]

Parting company with a traditional move, Cyril does not take the exilic Joshua as a pre-figuration for Christ here, though he is willing to do so on other occasions in his *Commentary on the Twelve*.[66] Consonant with the concerns expressed in his introduction, Cyril takes all the references to Joshua in the whole of chapter 3 as denoting the exilic Joshua. He avoids falling under his own censure (about the vision being not *merely* historical), however, by noting that there is an "image and type of Christ" in the Angel of the Lord[67] and by taking the "Dawn" as a predictive reference to the coming of the Only-begotten.[68]

The concessions to Theodore's point-of-view are not insignificant, but Cyril rigorously maintains the theological aspect of the narrative that Theodore so studiously avoids. He does so chiefly by highlighting Didymus' point about the Son's involvement in the priestly ministry of Israel, albeit through a different image. The role of the Son in Cyril's interpretation is not limited purely to the future dimensions of Zechariah's prophecy. Cyril observes that Joshua's priesthood "according to the Law" necessarily proceeded in the presence of the Son, who as the "stone with seven eyes" gazed upon the OT priesthood and oversaw it. The Son's supervisory care over the priesthood likewise called forth in Joshua and his fellow "seers" an appropriate response. They were to keep Christ constantly before their eyes.[69] In the time between the restoration of the priesthood enumerated here and the coming of the Great High Priest, the Son occupies a supervisory role over the OT priesthood. As the stone, the Son is an integral part of the narrative even while he stands as the *telos* to which the narrative points. Cyril's interpretation is an improvement on Didymus' in one respect: he secures the continuity of the referents of the vision throughout the whole chapter. But likewise it recovers what is central to

---

65. The implicit critique of Theodore's *modus operandi* is evident. Theodore traverses the entire chapter without once mentioning the Son, except in introducing the Lord's testimony about angelic "standing" before God (citing Matt 18:10 in *In Zach.* 3:1–5a (Sprenger 341.11–15)).

66. He rejects the type explicitly in *In Zach.* 3:6–7 (Pusey, 317.23–318.9). His reasoning is that the Son would not be told to walk in the ways of the Father, nor would he be promised that he *would* judge God's house if he did so. "For such things would not be said of Christ, since he himself is the way, he is the just decrees of God the Father, he himself *judged* his house, exercising his authority as Son."

67. Cyril, *In Zach.* 3:1–2 (Pusey, 314.3–4). This is not the same as Didymus' *identification* of the Angel with the Son.

68. Cyril, *In Zach.* 3:8–9 (Pusey, 321.18–24).

69. Ibid. (Pusey, 322.13–22). On Cyril's treatment of the Son's priestly role in the OT, see my "St Cyril on the Priesthood of Christ and the Old Testament," *Phronema* 30, no. 1 (2015): 91–113.

Didymus' argument over against Theodore: this vision can only be fully understood in light of the Son's administrative presence in the OT.

Theodoret's contribution to the current discussion runs parallel to Cyril's in this respect. He is, however, more keen on recovering the sense in which the character of Joshua himself foreshadows Jesus. Satan opposes Joshua for offering prayers of intercession, just as he will come to oppose Jesus for taking away the sin of the world. The rebuke offered to Satan here is given by Joshua's "Lord (δεσπότης)," just as this same Lord rebukes Satan in the Gospels.[70] For Theodoret, it was the Lord—the second Person of the Trinity—who rescued Joshua from the devil.[71] With Cyril, Theodoret likewise sees in the stone a "type" of Christ, though his focus in the interpretation is on Zerubbabel.[72]

We see in the two latter interpreters a new development. Narrative continuity is maintained throughout Zechariah 3 at the same level of reading while still maintaining what is basic to Didymus' interpretation: the narrative is properly understood only in light of the priestly service of the Son, a service that culminates in the Incarnation though it is in some sense already begun in the OT. The pre-incarnate activity of the Son becomes an essential element of the narrative. Joshua—for Cyril—takes up his priestly function faithfully only by the supervisory activity of the Son. For Theodoret, the Son is present during the court-room scene, vindicating the accused Joshua from the accusations of his enemy. As with Didymus, the Trinitarian economy must be brought into conversation with the plain sense of the text. These latter interpreters have the advantage of Didymus insofar as they appear sensitive to Theodore's critique as well: in locating the narrative within this economy, it is not necessary to appeal only occasionally to the literal sense.

The Sinfulness of Joshua Reconsidered

The angel interprets the symbolic removal of the filthy garments with the remark: "I have taken away your iniquity from you" (Zech 3:4). We have seen that by casting the narrative frame in terms of the exigencies of spiritual struggle and resistance to temptation, Didymus distances himself from the possibility that Joshua is guilty of personal iniquity. His interpretation of the guilt as representational or vicarious, while partially accurate—the priest is never *merely* personally guilty but represents the people before God—appears

---

70. Theodoret, *In Zach.* 3:1-2 (PG 81:1892C). There is not enough evidence here to argue that Theodoret regards the rebuke as an intra-Trinitarian dialogue between the Father and the Son, as is the case with Jerome in *In Zach.* 1, 3:1-5 (CCSL 76A:772) and Didymus (CZ I.197). Theodoret's language is ambiguous. The phrase οἷα δὴ ὑπὸ τοῦ Θεοῦ καὶ Δεσπότου probably serves only to affirm the divine identity of the Son, not the plurality of divine Persons involved.

71. Theodoret, *In Zach.* 3:1-2 (PG 81:1892D).

72. Theodoret, *In Zach.* 3:8-9 (PG 81:1896A).

in relief to Theodoret's more measured remarks on the subject. Referring to Joshua, he writes:

> While it was likely that even he as man had some faults [πλημμελήματα], I believe that in his role of chief priest he made his own the people's lawlessness [παρανομίαν], and offered prayers as a fellow sinner [συνημαρτηκώς] of theirs; this is the reason that he receives the forgiveness of the people's lawlessness as his own forgiveness.[73]

Theodoret is sensitive to two issues here, which he highlights by the phrases: "as man (ὡς ἄνθρωπον)" and "in his role of chief priest (οἷα ... ἀρχιερεύς)." Admirably, Theodoret distinguishes the two but refuses to suggest that only one of them obtains. Though he is not forthcoming about what Joshua's transgressions are,[74] Theodoret is convinced that Joshua offered prayers as a "fellow-sinner."[75] Equally, however, as chief priest he took on the lawlessness of his people vicariously. His forgiveness and the forgiveness of his people are closely bound up together insofar as he, as a sinner, serves as their representative before God.

Theodoret's position reflects quite clearly the teaching of the *Epistle to the Hebrews*. The weakness of the high priest has a beneficial function to play in terms of his ability to "deal gently with the ignorant and wayward." His own sinfulness—asserted univocally of all the priests in the OT—occasions the need to offer sacrifice on his own behalf (5:1–3). Jesus' priesthood is in one sense happily continuous with the Levitical priesthood insofar as he is sympathetic with our weakness. Contrary to sinful human expectations, however, Jesus is

---

73. Theodoret, *In Zach.* 3:4 (PG 81:1893A). Trans. Robert Hill, *Theodoret of Cyrus: Commentaries on the Prophets 3: Commentary on the Twelve Prophets* (Brookline, MA: Holy Cross Orthodox Press, 2006), 240.

74. Jerome is the only one who discusses the issue with any specificity. Reporting on the Jewish exegesis of the text, he notes that the devil is "appropriately" said to stand "at [Joshua's] right hand—and not at his left—because the accusation was founded (vera)" (*In Zach.* 1, 3:1–5 (CCSL 76A:770)). Finding grounds to implicate Joshua in the charge of marrying a foreign woman (citing the inconclusive textual evidence of 2 Esdras 10:18 and Malachi 2), the Jewish interpreters take the "sordid garments" as a reference to a potentially three-fold indictment. Joshua is personally guilty of an illicit marriage, vicariously guilty of the sins of the populace, or shamed by the squalor of exile. (Our contemporary shame-guilt dichotomy was not so defined by Jerome and his Jewish contemporaries.) The investment in the new garments indicates that the Lord is uniting him to an Israelite wife and restoring the dignity of the priesthood after the uncleanness of its sins is taken away (CCSL 76A:770–771).

75. There is slender, but possible, support for Theodoret's ascription of guilt to Joshua in Theodore, who writes of Joshua that "during the exile it was not possible for him to perform (ἐπὶ τῆς αἰχμαλωσίας οἷόν τε ἦν)" his function as priest (Theodore, *In Zach.* 3:1–5a (Sprenger, 341.21)).

all the more compassionate precisely because, unlike the priests of old, he was tempted in every way yet did not sin (4:15). "Separated from sinners," and having no need to make daily sacrifice for his own sins and those of his people, the Son surpasses the Old priesthood in the exercise of his office. His self-offering is perfect (7:26–28).

Didymus' reading of the first few verses sits awkwardly against this background. Though the character of Satan's opposition to Joshua is highlighted in similar terms by some of the other interpreters—Satan obstructs the virtuous actions of those he opposes[76]—they do not make the motif an organizing principle of their exegesis the way Didymus does. Without exception, these interpreters take the "burning brand" either as a reference to Joshua or to the nation of Israel newly ransomed from exile.[77] Didymus alone is consistent in ruling out altogether the possibility that Joshua is complicit in the sins of Israel.

Reasons for Didymus' Limitation of the Literal Sense

For what reason does he do so? Didymus' particular mode of developing mimetic readings of OT characters is based, in part, on his commitment to working out the consequences of his doctrine of moral perfection. Joshua *per se* is instructive in this regard only insofar as he enacts the virtuous life and serves as a model of ascent for others. The paradigm of perfection in virtue that he enacts is revealed by the Son's assumed humanity: Jesus is resistant to every form of evil, steadfast in holiness, perfect in his contemplation of the Father by his complete receptivity to the illumination of the Holy Spirit. Jesus displays all of this in his self-giving love that draws others into the holiness, contemplation, and beatitude that he enjoys.

Joshua's development in the "literal sense" is parallel, though abbreviated and not as extensively realized. But, critically, he is not guilty of the sins of Israel. He is exemplary in the same way—if not to the same degree—that Jesus is, rejoicing with the people when they are no longer afflicted out of the fullness of his sacrificial love. The "spiritual priesthood" that he reveals is the calling to which Didymus summons his audience. Didymus therefore appears to introduce the "literal sense" reading of the passage only when Joshua presents us with a useful paradigm for pursuing the virtues. If in *DT* Didymus raises, as a polemically useful point, the idea that the saints are sinful, the theme plays a very meager role in his anagogical exegesis. The impression that one gets from the exegetical corpus as a whole is rather that accounts of human sinfulness are of little use to us.

---

76. Cf. Jerome, *In Zach.* 1, 3:1–5 (CCSL 76A:772) and Cyril, *In Zach.* 3:1–2 (Pusey, 314.27–315.3).

77. See Theodore, *In Zach.* 3:1–5a (Sprenger, 341.26–31); Jerome, *In Zach.* 1, 3:1–5 (CCSL 76A:772); Cyril, *In Zach.* 3:1–2 (Pusey, 315.15–19); Theodoret, *In Zach.* 3:2b (PG 81:1892D).

This constitutes an over-application of the criterion of "usefulness (ὠφέλεια),"[78] the corollary of which is the idea that Scripture must always be interpreted "worthily of God (θεοπρεπῶς)." It is improper for the divine Author of Scripture to introduce subjects for us that do not conform to the criterion set forth in Paul's summative description of Scripture: "All Scripture is God-breathed and useful (ὠφέλιμος)" (2 Tim 3:16). Mark Sheridan is right to register the need for a more thoroughgoing critique of the criterion's "presuppositions and implications"[79] in the Fathers, though the scope of his examination of the question does not range into texts where the criterion is misapplied. I argue here that where Didymus is dealing with subjects like the above—where the saints are described as guilty of sin—the application of the principle becomes suspect.

I have two reasons for making this claim. Didymus is not alone in reading the text as a description of moral struggle for virtue. But the reading tugs hard "against the grain" of the passage. Near-contemporaries like Theodore, Jerome's Jewish sources, Theodoret, and Augustine[80] recognize that the narrative sense of the passage suggests moral failure of some kind, even if the priest's representative guilt is also in play. An interpretive frame of warranted accusation-vindication makes better sense of the whole vision. And Didymus is, as we have seen, inconsistent in referring to the literal sense throughout.

Secondly, the example that he gives of those who are preserved from temptation is hardly encouraging, which raises the question of whether Didymus can establish his doctrine of moral perfection on the basis of a plausible reading of the NT passage to which he appeals. St Peter is, he says, preserved from temptation by the Lord who prays that his faith will not fail (Luke 22:32). But even a casual reading of this Gospel reveals that the Lord's prayer on the saint's behalf sustains him in the faith in spite of the fact that there is a real failure of faith (Luke 22:54–62). The sin is a serious one. The Lord had warned that a person's denial of him before others merited the denial of that person before the angels of God (Luke 12:9; cf. Luke 9:26). However, it is the Lord's priestly ministry, exercised for St Peter and in a certain sense in spite of him as well, that sustains the saint. The Lord's priestly ministry—of which the prayer on St Peter's behalf is an expression—dramatically illustrates a very different dynamic than that envisioned by Didymus. The Lord's perfect obedience to the Father is offered in Peter's place. The saints, at times, draw attention to the perfection of the Son's obedience more by failure than by imitation.

---

78. On the importance of the criterion for Didymus, see Simonetti, "Lettera e allegoria," 356.

79. Mark Sheridan, "The Concept of the "Useful" as an Exegetical Tool in Patristic Exegesis," in *From the Nile to the Rhone and Beyond: Studies in Early Monastic Literature and Scriptural Interpretation* (Rome: Studia Anselmiana, 2012), 177.

80. Augustine, *De nup.* 2.51 (CSEL 42:307.7–14).

It is this aspect of Didymus' treatment of the "literal sense" that is most disappointing. The usefulness of the account could be honored by drawing attention to what divine mercy accomplishes in spite of human sin. Those who strive after the imitation of Christ by participation in the divine *hypostaseis* are upheld when they fail to attain this end by the Son who offers his obedience to the Father on their behalf. They are re-assured of their security in the saving purposes of God on their behalf because of their union with Christ who has irrevocably taken hold of it and who has made them "his own" (Phil 3:12). My criticism need not imply a reorientation of Didymus' moral program—the Christian life, as St Paul reminds us, is utterly consonant with the kind of striving to imitate Christ that Didymus describes. But a caveat is in order. The author of the *Second Epistle to Timothy* is still awaiting the "crown of righteousness" that will be given to him on the Day of the Lord's appearing (2 Tim 4:8). It is useful for us to be reminded of the one perfect priesthood upon which all ecclesial and spiritual priesthood depends: the priestly service of the Incarnate Son.

Summary

I have argued that Didymus' "literal sense" is both instructive and problematic. On the one hand, he reminds us that any Christian reading of the OT must wrestle seriously with the question of how the Trinity was active in self-revelation during the one economy that Scripture describes. Though Didymus does not put all the pieces together for us, his discussion asserts that the Son was active in the priestly ministry during the time of Joshua (with Cyril and Theodoret). This line of interpretation could be developed at greater length to include Didymus' discussion—outlined in the higher sense—that the Lord's rebuke of the devil is an intra-Trinitarian moment in which the Son rebukes Satan (*à la* Theodoret) on the basis of the Father's election of Jerusalem. The accusation against Joshua is founded but is ultimately of no consequence; the Father chooses to deal with the high priest and with the nation of Israel on the basis of his unrelenting purpose to fulfill the priestly ministration through the true Priest of Israel. In working out the consequences of this election, the Son comes among us as the Dawn. He will have the Spirit resting upon him and will give the Spirit (*à la* Didymus) to others, rendering them participant in the saving and recreating activity of the Trinity and ushering them into the rest of the age to come.

The problematic aspect of Didymus' treatment of the literal sense is his application of a questionable account of human perfection to it. The literal sense, one feels, would be abandoned altogether (not denied as a vision with relation to historical happenstance, but eschewed as anagogically useful)[81] if

---

81. Cf. Elizabeth A. Dively Lauro, *The Soul and Spirit of Scripture within Origen's Exegesis* (Boston; Leiden: Brill, 2005), 201, who discusses the somatic sense as "*edifying* literal ... sense" in Origen's interpretation of the Canticles. The situation is the same

Didymus could not provide a case for rescuing Joshua from culpability. He is a saint, a morally exemplary type of Christ, who is at the real center of Didymus' exegetical program. For Didymus, affirming the moral purity of Joshua in the literal sense of the passage is essential in maintaining the link between the literal and the higher sense. As Layton has recognized, there is a similar tendency toward ascribing moral perfection to the saints across the exegetical corpus, which is also linked with contesting a different interpretation of the "literal sense."[82] Didymus is willing to entertain the literal sense for a few verses not only because 1) he is more interested in the higher senses generally, 2) but also because the literal sense presents something of an aporia to the interpretive frame he has selected.

On the "Mind" of Zechariah 3

Didymus' concern to prioritize the "mind" or higher sense of the passage is apparent from the first lines of the interpretation. The vision has a historical basis, but this basis is not of fundamental importance to its interpretation.[83] The primacy of Jesus in establishing the significance of Zechariah 3 is asserted from the beginning. But what of the content of this higher spiritual sense that Didymus develops? I begin by drawing out the key moves that Didymus makes in his interpretation of the spiritual sense and conclude each section with an appraisal of Didymus' exegesis.

Sharing in Christ's Victory over Satan

In the broadest sense, Didymus' discussion of the christological center of the text focuses on the theme of overcoming Satan. The interpreter and his audience begin with a description of the Son, who in his ontologically complete humanity (*contra* Apollinaris and docetist christologies) engaged in warfare with the evil one. He did this by his assumption of a human body that was

---

here. Didymus' lack of development of a sense πρὸς ῥητόν should not be taken to imply that he sees only a slender historical basis for the vision, but that he can draw little by way of edifying meaning from it.

82. See his argument on Job in Layton, *Didymus the Blind and His Circle*, 72. More recently, however, Layton has convincingly developed the above argument even further by claiming that in Didymus' argument with the *philistores* Didymus raised the issue of divergent interpretations precisely on the grounds of what constitutes the *sensus litteralis*. He was not arguing for the appropriateness of allegorical reading over against the refusal to allegorize, but rather was contesting his opponents' understanding of the "literal" or "historical" sense. See his "Didymus the Blind and the *Philistores*," 245.

83. Hill's remark: "Didymus does not allow . . . a historical basis for the vision" (FC 111:66n1) is potentially misleading. It would be better to say that there is no *identified* historical basis for the *lemma*, since Hill recognizes the historicity of a later lemma that takes place within the same vision (cf. ibid., 71n20). The "vision" encompasses the whole chapter; and as I have argued above, Joshua's exemplary priestly service is the historical basis of Didymus' remarks on Zechariah 3:3–5.

prone to hunger and a human soul that was ontologically capable of moral failure. The Lord does not overcome our enemy except under the conditions of our humanity. The significance of Jesus' victory over the evil one is far-reaching precisely because it renders Satan a vanquished competitor in the struggle against *our* humanity.

Developing the theme further, Didymus draws his audience into the heart of the mysteries of Christ's assumption of our humanity. The true High Priest put on the "filthy garments" of our sin and divested himself of them at the cross, where at the same stroke he vanquished the rulers and authorities of evil that warred against us. Christ's priesthood is exalted above Joshua's because of its glory and its scope. At the suggestion of the text, Didymus explores the significance of the "filthy garments" at length: though Christ is wholly obedient to the Father, he so identified with humanity that he "became sin" for us. The consequence of this "becoming" sin for us is his death, which is also a death *for us*. These are mysteries before which Didymus is rightly at a loss for words. How can the Incarnate Son of God be said to "become sin" and to "taste death"? Didymus is not sure how this can be the case, but he insists that in the whole course of the Incarnate Son's passion, the "angel" and the "priest"—Christ under the aspects of his divinity and his humanity—"stood" near one another, with no distance between the two.

But Didymus, admirably, does not stop here. Before this mysterious identification of the Son of God with human sin and death, there is only one possible response for those who read as participants in the divine economy. "You," he says, "divest Christ of the filthy garments that he put on for your sake!" Recognize, Didymus argues, that you are the "principal wearers" of them, and that he put them on by the lavish grace of God for you! Didymus' audience is identified here: they are participants in the narrative Zechariah is describing. They are the new Israel on whose behalf the true High Priest serves. Called into the exercise of their "spiritual priesthood," they are yet responsible for investing Christ in the garments of their sin. As such, their response can only take one form: repentance. Their estrangement with God has been overcome in their baptism, but the victory is yet to be fully appropriated. Didymus identifies himself with his audience here: "we invested (Christ)" in this clothing.

Didymus' treatment of the above theme is significant. First, it reveals that Didymus, for all his confidence that complete conformity to the virtues revealed in the Incarnation is possible in the present life, nevertheless says of himself: "not that I have already obtained it" (Phil 3:12). Consonant with his numerous confessions in the dogmatic and exegetical works that he has not uttered the final word on a given subject or that he has spoken according to certain limitations,[84] so it is here. In his journey toward the house whose foundation Wisdom laid, he is still making use of a tent. Even if Joshua is a more perfect model of imitation, he—like his students—still has need of con-

---

84. See, e.g., *CZ* I.343 and *DSS* 277.

fession. Second, it shows that Didymus is not content merely with describing the mysteries contained in Scripture, but sees the interpreter's role as one of pointing toward participation in them. Christ's investment in sin is understood only if it is comprehended with imperatival force: become the righteousness of God!

We pause here. Key to our appreciation of Didymus' exegesis is our ability to appraise him at this juncture. We may (properly) register our concern with his treatment of the "literal sense" and yet also appreciate what he offers us here only if we are willing to allow Didymus to challenge certain interpretive presuppositions. Theodore's critique of Didymus would doubtless focus on 1) his loss of a plausible reconstruction of Zechariah's epistemological possibilities, based on 2) on anachronistic distortion of earlier elements of Scripture by later ones. We have challenged both of these objections above as theologically deficient.

A more sympathetic critique might take the form of allowing Didymus' treatment of these christological themes a place within the interpretive enterprise, but only as *applicatio* or *sensus plenior* (where this sense is construed as an optional addendum to the primary meaning of the text). Perhaps Didymus is here not so much concerned with the meaning of Zechariah 3 as he is with the Christian application of it. Such a critique would allow the reader of Didymus to appreciate the confessional location of the Alexandrian and the role that this location plays in developing applications of the text while remaining noncommittal on the question of whether or not he has accurately construed the text's meaning(s).

But there is no question at all of what Didymus himself would have thought of this critique. To entertain such a notion of Scripture is to keep the Word who speaks through it at arm's length. If the Scriptures really are taken up in the divine economy of self-revelation, and if the goal of this revelation is the re-creation of humanity after the image of the Son, then it follows that the diverse voices within Scripture are referred to their πρᾶγμα only when the Word addresses and enjoins us to participate in this salvation. And for this we need to "see Jesus" (John 12:21). Through Zechariah's words, through the image of Joshua, the Trinity speaks of Christ and draws us toward him. Moreover, to hear Scripture aright is to be told who and what one is in the presence of the Incarnate Son of God. The Christian meaning of Scripture, therefore, is not exhausted even where one has rightly recognized how a certain episode in the life of Israel was what it was only in light of the re-creating activity of the Trinity. The Christian reading of Scripture insists that the divine meaning must be given greater scope. For the same Word who testified to himself through Zechariah remains living and active, testifying through the words of the prophet to us. The fulsome meaning of Scripture is never exhausted, but is rightly attended to in all its scope when we by grace respond in repentance and obedience to Christ.

Didymus is not alone in making these kinds of claims for scriptural meaning. Thus Henri de Lubac, summing up a whole traditional notion of the letter in Scripture, could write: "The men who believed that [the Word of God speaks to us still and reveals himself] could not reduce the Bible to a mere historical document, even of divine history. . . . They knew that "all these things have been written so that they might believe that Jesus is the Christ and the Son of God.""[85] The letter points beyond itself to the mystery of Christ for which it is the necessary and chosen vehicle.[86]

And we see in Didymus' movement from the literal sense to the sense that discourses on the true High Priest a discontentment merely with noting that the letter gestures toward Christ. The student of the Word of God is compelled to gaze at the profound mystery of his priesthood in order to plumb the depths of the divine vision. This is done properly only when he finds himself called into conformity with the dynamics of the baptismal life. "Have you seen Christ?" Didymus is saying. "Good, now put him on." Though Didymus' terminology differs somewhat from the language that the Tradition, according to de Lubac, would later standardize, his basic movement does not. The transfer from the revealed mystery to our participation in that same mystery is a movement that takes place "within the mystery."[87] The applicative remarks are just as inseparable from the exposition of the spiritual significance of this Scripture as the spiritual significance of it is from its literal sense.

The Problem with the Spiritual Sense

This is not to argue that Didymus' spiritual sense can be endorsed in its entirety. In our consideration of it, we paused precisely at that point where Didymus' eschatological doctrine begins to work some mischief. The putting off of our garments of sin is contemporaneous with our spiritual investment of the Son in the clothing that is proper to him. Didymus, we saw, spoke of these two final items of the priest's garments, prioritizing the doctrine of the Son's divinity over that of his Incarnation. The Son takes on a body for us, but we are to ascend beyond the vision of his Incarnation to perceive him under the aspect of his divinity. And in this latter perception, Didymus links "materiality" with "defilement." The link suggests, once again, that Didymus wishes to conceive of the beatific vision in terms that marginalize the significance of the Son's Incarnation.

The note sounded here becomes more sonorous as Didymus progresses from addressing the "new Israel"—guilty of investing Jesus in sin—to giving them a portrait of the state toward which they are headed. You are to become

---

85. de Lubac, *Medieval Exegesis* II:81.

86. Ibid., 26: "The spiritual sense is . . . necessary for the completion of the literal sense, which latter is indispensable for founding it. . . . "*Christus in littera continetur.* The spirit is not outside the history." They are given together, inseparably, through the fact of a single inspiration."

87. Ibid., 127.

"intimates" of the eternal high priest, Didymus argues, as he moves into a discussion of Zechariah 3:8-9. These "intimates" are the same as the "partners" of Hebrews 3:1-2, who see Jesus with their eyes open to the true light. Didymus is here concerned with inveighing against those who do not rightly recognize the ministry of Jesus' priesthood properly because they locate the exercise of this ministry in the Son's subordination to the Father. Again he rehearses the idea that the Incarnation is meant to lead us to the divinity, but this time through a different set of images: those who are faithful witnesses of the Incarnation see Jesus with the eyes of their heart opened to "the true light."

In this digression, Didymus is not clear about precisely when the Son takes up the priestly office in relation to his protological schema. The Son becomes priest when the creation comes into existence. But is Didymus thinking here of the creation of souls before their Fall into material embodiedness or of the creation of the material order? He is not clear. We might speculate that—given Didymus' distance from Eusebius outlined above—an assertion of the priesthood of Christ before the Fall of souls would raise the subordinationist question afresh, unless Didymus is thinking of the priesthood as involving more than the overcoming of human sinfulness. In any case the priesthood, though coming into existence *before* the time of the Incarnation, culminates in the descent of the Son. Didymus re-asserts a line we saw elsewhere: the Incarnation, as the ultimate expression of this priesthood, takes place "for us . . . and because of us." Human distance from God occasions the Incarnation.

There is no denying the effectiveness of the schema in combating subordinationist accounts of the Son's οὐσία while maintaining a grasp on a move that is basic to Trinitarian interpretations of the OT. A different problem presents itself, however. Given Didymus' protology and eschatology, it is difficult to conceive of a way in which the Incarnation is not being understood as divine response. It is foreknown, but foreknown as divine response to an exigency arising because of human sin and embodiedness. There is nothing here to prevent the conclusion that for Didymus the priesthood that culminates in the Incarnation, like the teaching of the human Jesus, is a stage on the way to a higher vision of the Trinity. The irrevocable character of the Incarnation as God's means of self-revelation is called into question. It serves to overcome sin. It is therefore continuous with what the Son was about in his pre-Incarnate ministry among the people of Israel. But with sin overcome, it is difficult to conceive of a possible function for the priesthood that Jesus takes up in the Incarnation.

In continuity with this tendency in Didymus' thought, there is an overemphasis on the invisible dimensions of Christ's earthly ministry at the expense of the visible dimensions of it. Near the climax of Didymus' outline of the spiritual journey that he and his audience are to take in the pursuit of the divine image, Didymus presents the apostles, Moses, and Aaron as "seers." A seer in our day, he argues, understands the Gospel narratives to be revelatory of hidden realities. The one who reads them with maturity looks beyond the visible to the "archetype (πρωτότυπος)." The seer takes the story of the man born blind and the woman with a flow of blood as references to the Church of the Gentiles. Like the man born blind, this Church requires the Incarnation for its godlessness and ignorance to be removed; like the woman with the flow of blood, this Church must be purified from the nations.

The conclusions that Didymus draws are relatively innocuous in themselves. There is nothing wrong with the "archetype" that Didymus identifies in each of these instances. However, the application of this principle to the Gospel narratives tends to play down the significance of these moments for what they reveal about Jesus' concern to reclaim humanity in the totality of its existence: material embodiedness included. The deeper sense that Didymus identifies here is consistent with his eschatological vision, but obscures what these moments reveal about the new creation that the Son is inaugurating in the Incarnation. Because of Didymus' eschatological commitments, these events can have only a provisional or subservient function in revealing a truer reality that lies beyond them. They are not fully integrated within the eschatological reality that the Son's Incarnation, death, resurrection, and ascension reveals.

If then, we part company with Didymus in our reading of Scripture, we ought to do so here most of all. The eschatological vision is not so much overly-realized as it is falsely identified with attaining to the state in which the humanity of the Savior—firmly a part of the economic life of the Trinity in the present age—nonetheless serves no further function in the age to come. Economy and Trinitarian being are jarringly separated most of all in relation to Didymus' vision of the *eschaton*. The eschatological vision so described serves to distort the spiritual sense, especially when Didymus is describing the advanced stages of the contemplative life. It also serves to marginalize the importance of the literal sense, since the vision of sensible realities can finally only serve a preparatory function in the progress of the soul from things earthly to things heavenly.

Conclusion: Divine Economy, Interpretive *Skopos*

The final commendation of a person's exegetical practice must focus on its serviceability to God's purposes for Scripture in the divine economy of salvation. Didymus understands the reading of Scripture as an activity that takes place under particular promises and imperatives. His practice is largely generated from this understanding. In this final section, I inquire as to the transparency of Didymus' *praxis* to God's *skopos* for Scripture, as it is revealed to us through the saving missions of the Son and the Holy Spirit.

The divine *skopos* for Scripture is derivative from Scripture's location within the Trinitarian economy of re-creation. Humanity is created in the divine image for fellowship with God. This fellowship is characterized by Didymus as including, inseparably, a noetic and a moral dimension. And these dimensions are revealed to us specifically in the life of the Incarnate Son, whose mind and will are utterly accordant with the mind and will of the Father and his Spirit. Hence, for Didymus, the purpose of creation is realized first of all in the Son and through him it is realized for the rest of the cosmos. For materially-embodied, rational creatures, God's purposes are fulfilled when they share in the knowledge of and obedience to God in a manner continuous with what is revealed in and enabled by the humanity assumed by his Son.

Here, we would wish to add a caveat. The knowledge of God is not merely "revealed in and enabled by" the humanity assumed by the Son. The knowledge of God is inseparably and eternally bound up with knowing the Son of God in this way: as the One who eternally willed to unite material or sensible creatureliness to himself in the Incarnation as an expression of the fullness of his identity as the Son of the Father. To know God as he is in eternity is forevermore bound up with the mystery of the *Incarnate* Son.

We continue. God the Father, in the missions of the Word and the Spirit to the prophets and apostles, claims them for their true end as participants in the re-creative activity of the Trinity. He does so for the purpose of making them witnesses to this activity, so that others, by hearing their faithful testimony in the obedience of faith, may be brought into fellowship with God. The specific *locus* of this saving activity is therefore the Church, in which God speaks and is heard. She hears insofar as she and her members are marked by the sign of their participation in the saving work of the Trinity: their baptism, in which they share both in the death of the Son and in his resurrection. Put to death by the Spirit, they arise to new life in Christ, putting him on: namely, putting on his life of obedience to and knowledge of his Father by that same Spirit. They experience the Lord's address to them as a call to re-iterate in each moment of their lives what Christ has given them in baptism. Henceforth, they live only for Christ by the power of his risen life, ever changing from glory to glory in the pursuit of the divine likeness.

Measured against this *skopos*, it is remarkable to observe how many of these notes are sounded in Didymus' reading of the prophet Zechariah. As we have been told from the beginning of the prophet, God addresses Zechariah by making him a participant in the Logos whom he sends. It is in the dynamics of this relational address that Zechariah is said to be illumined and divinized so that what he utters are the words of this Word. The prophetic situation reveals what is at stake in the opening of the Scriptures amidst Didymus' small community of faith. "Pray for me," he says. He will open his mouth to speak in confidence that the Lord will grant them the request for divine illumination. They must become like Zechariah.

The manner of his movement to the christological interpretation creates problems of a hermeneutical and theological character. However, that he moves from Joshua to Christ and refuses to leave his side until he has gazed long at the majesty of the one who identifies even with the sin and death of sinners is a move that the divine *skopos* of Scripture fully justifies. Moreover, this move is anticipated by a plain sense reading of Zechariah 3, in which the Israelite priesthood is once again re-instated after the Exile, not because of its own particular splendor, but because God's election of Jerusalem in the Son is irrevocable. In fact, a more serious consideration of the letter here opens up Didymus' point about this OT service of the Son of God in quite dramatic fashion. It is on the basis of the Son's Incarnation that OT saints like Joshua are surprisingly vindicated, because the Father has chosen to deal with Abraham's descendants on the basis of the covenant that he has made with his Son.[88] Nevertheless, whether disjunctively (with Theodoret) or with greater continuity (in Didymus' case), through Joshua the divine Son speaks of that to which his present priestly ministry points: his saving self-offering to the Father which is the mystery in which that OT moment takes part.

Didymus admirably explores this mystery in highly participatory terms. The phrases he isolates and expounds are chosen largely with the intent of making clear to his audience that the only way to hear this Word properly is to hear it as those who are once again confronted with the meaning of their baptism. He and his students are the ones standing around the "true Joshua," being commanded by the angel to divest him of sin. They were responsible in investing Jesus in these garments. They are called to follow him by walking in the ways of the virtues. Their hope is that, by standing firm in holiness and by continually receiving the illumination of the same Spirit who ever rests upon the Son of God, they might become seers, advancing to the place of spiritual peace in which they will invite others into the joy of their Master by feasting on the fruits of the vine and the fig.

Didymus' *praxis* mirrors what we have identified as several key themes in his scriptural ontology: 1) the Trinitarian missions of the Word and the Spirit as providing the widest context of the scriptural narrative, 2) the christological center of Scripture as the singular moment to which all other moments point and in which they participate, and 3) the baptismal character of divine dealing with humanity, inclusive of the prophets and ourselves. Each of these themes has clear ramifications for Didymus' interpretation of Zechariah 3. And what emerges from this reading of Zechariah 3 is what de Lubac terms a "total exegesis."[89] Didymus' anagogical exegesis, properly understood, is at once thoroughly theological and thoroughly participational or mystical. For him and his students, there could be no firm division between exegesis and homiletics: between the discernment of textual meaning and the applicative sense of this meaning. In other words, there could be no moment—even in dealing

---

88. I take this to be the meaning of that strangest of theophanies in Genesis 15:17, when God passes through the divided carcasses on Abram's behalf.

89. Of the exegesis in the Middle Ages and the Fathers, de Lubac writes: "[E]xcept in certain rather rare cases, the exegesis that we are studying was not yet a specialized exegesis; it was at once less and much more: it was a total exegesis; it was not an auxiliary science of theology: it was theology itself" (*Medieval Exegesis* II:77).

with the literal sense—in which the interpreter and the audience occupied some territory outside of that space which had been carved out for them in their baptism. In his *praxis* are several of the elements that are critical to the recovery of a thoroughly unitive exegesis.

EPILOGUE

In this study, I have re-visited the question of Didymus' authorship of *DT*, concluding that the evidence in favor of the attribution significantly outweighs the arguments opposing it. On this basis, I have provisionally concluded that *DT* was written by Didymus during the last fifteen years of his life, and that it is therefore the most proximate dogmatic source for comparison with Didymus' *CZ*. By using *DT* as a source for further understanding Didymus' doctrine of Scripture, we have seen how Didymus points us toward locating the inspiration and reading of Scripture within the re-creative economy of the Trinity. He likewise grounds this economy in the hypostatic identities of the Persons of the Trinity. The Son and the Holy Spirit act *ad extra* in a manner that accords with the particularity of their identities as the Only-begotten and the Only-proceeding from the Father. The whole economy of Scripture is imbued by the Son's sustaining of creation in existence and the Spirit's perfection of the creative work of the Trinity. The economy culminates in the Incarnation of the Son, wherein he becomes—without suffering change—a creature: receiving the perfecting Spirit under the conditions of our humanity and therefore for us. The sacrament of participation in this economy is baptism, which is paradigmatic for the whole of the Christian life and thus for the epistemic and moral posture of the prophets and apostles and their hearers.

The study has pointed to two separate, but closely-related, areas in which Didymus the Blind proves instructive: his doctrine of Scripture and his interpretive practices. By examining his account of the economy and Scripture's location within this economy, we have been able to define more clearly what he would have identified as the divine *skopos* of Scripture. And in this light, we have been able to evaluate his interpretive practices and his application of certain criteria to the reading of Scripture.

It would require a much lengthier book to bring what has been unearthed in this study into conversation with widely-held assumptions about the task of reading Scripture today. In what follows, I identify three areas where Didymus the Blind's understanding of Scripture and his practice of reading it cut against the grain of some contemporary bibliology and hermeneutics. I also identify an area where—in the current climate of patristic recovery—sympathy with Didymus may be misplaced. But it is better to begin with the latter.

Some schools of thought in post-modern hermeneutics see in patristic interpretation of the Bible a helpful ally in exposing the long-held assumption in modernity that a biblical passage has but one meaning. The observation that the Fathers operated with a less determinate hermeneutical method than many eighteenth- or nineteenth-century interpreters is a fair and important one to make. At times, however, proponents of hermeneutical indeterminacy have sought to garner support for an indeterminate hermeneutic among the Fathers. Perhaps nowhere is such a move more tempting for the post-modern reader than in engaging with the anagogical exegesis of the Alexandrians. But such a conclusion should be resisted. For one thing, the discovery of an eclectic *method*—such as we find in Didymus' writings—is too slender a basis from which to argue for hermeneutical indeterminacy. If my argument has proven successful at all, it will be evident at this point that the determinate principle of Didymus' interpretive acts is God himself, as he is revealed to us in the missions of the Persons throughout the grand narrative of the Scriptures. That is, there is a predictable content to Didymus' exegesis, wherein every subject taken up in his discussions about textual meaning and every hermeneutical movement is subordinate to the singular aim of rendering his students morally and noetically sanctified participants in the economy of the consubstantial Trinity. In this economy, Didymus and his students have a part precisely because they have been baptized into the Second Person of the Trinity, and are henceforth enjoined to "put him on." There is a Trinitarian and christological particularity here that sits uncomfortably beside certain post-modern attempts to locate a patristic dynamic of interpretive indeterminacy.

A more subtle, but related, danger consists in an uncritical appropriation of Didymus' anagogical exegesis (and hence, vision). Here the student of the Fathers may grasp what is a critical point that is missed in the above—true hearing of the Scriptures is a participational enterprise—but may miss another: proper participation is at every point dependent upon a proper vision of Christ. And here Didymus is to be read cautiously because of what is ultimately a deficient Christology. By overplaying the saints' degree of conformity to Christ in the present age and perhaps more crucially by painting a false picture of the *eschaton* in which 1) there is no longer any need for creaturely growth in divine knowledge and 2) (thus) no longer any need for the mediation of that knowledge by the Incarnate Christ, Didymus at times undermines the fulsome spiritual potential of the scriptural text. Because Didymus rightly regards eschatological considerations as consequential for true contemplation of God in the present, the problems with his eschatological schema are not confined to eschatology.

1) These considerations undermine Didymus' confidence in the abiding value of the literal/historical senses, since these senses are concerned with language's ability to gesture toward material corporeals. And it is precisely material corporeality which has little or no place in Didymus' eschatology. Understandably then, there are a few places where Didymus' appeal to allegory can no longer be justified merely as transforming the letter. In several places, the letter is rendered defunct. 2) They occasionally undermine Didymus' anagogical vision in the highest senses as well. The importance of this latter point cannot be over-stated, especially in a climate where the mystical theology of the Fathers is enjoying a renaissance. To argue that Didymus' occasional failure to establish a convincing account of the literal sense is incon-

sequential for his account of the anagogical significance of the text is to lose confidence in precisely that which Didymus wants to affirm: that the Spirit of God has hidden the mystery of Christ in every text of Scripture. If the mystery really is contained in the letter and is not something extrinsic to it, as de Lubac has so eloquently argued, then it follows that we deprive ourselves of the full vision of that mystery where the anagogy is not established by the letter. Christ's irreversible assumption of our whole humanity has, as a happy corollary, the abiding value of human language about sensible realities in attesting to the mystery of Christ. Particularity and mystagogy are not enemies.

Happily, however, what the Church stands to gain from a serious engagement with Didymus largely off-sets the above deficiencies. First of all, as we have seen, Didymus furnishes us with numerous elements that are foundational in the recovery of a proper ontology of the Scriptures. 1) For him, Scripture is primarily to be understood as a consequence of the missions of the Son and the Holy Spirit. His doctrine of God informs his doctrine of Scripture, such that scriptural ontology and teleology are bound up inseparably together. Scripture is not an inert depository of truthful statements about God, but is rather a living word replete with the promise of divine, re-creative encounter because of the Word of Truth who speaks through this chosen instrument. 2) In another crucial point, Didymus avers that the Father, in these missions whereby the Son and the Spirit address humanity through the words of the prophets, re-creates the filial identity of humanity by this communication. The prophets and the apostles who participate in this self-communication of God receive the charism of inspiration for the purpose of attesting faithfully to the very same God in whose economy they are participant. Because the divine economy of re-creation is summed up paradigmatically by the baptismal event, the prophetic and apostolic experience of this charism has a baptismal character.

This latter point is once again critical in recovering a proper ontology of Scripture. Within it are the seeds of a genuinely non-competitive account of inspiration. Where the functional anthropology is one of estrangement, the truthfulness of prophetic speech is called into question on the basis of humanity's participation in the writing of Scripture. But, on Didymus' account, such an account of humanity is deficient largely because it assumes that becoming like God and becoming more human are competitive processes. The deifying presence of the Word of God to the prophets renders them most truly human in the act of bearing joyful witness to this Word and their own wondrous fellowship with Him. We are not therefore—in the reading of Scripture—to be sifting the divine words from the human ones (as if we are competent to judge in these matters), but rather to profess the wondrous truth that "men spoke from God." This truth pervades the entire economy: human fellowship with God is really made possible in God's self-giving to humanity.

Didymus would do greater justice to his important point about the baptismal character of human fellowship with God (a dynamic that extends to the inspiration of Scripture as well) by acknowledging more robustly that the baptismal event is equally a mortifying one. Didymus' exemplarist accent builds rather one-sidedly on this important point. The apostles and prophets are, largely, those who have "put on Christ" to such an extent that their moral and contemplative virtues are nearly conformed to his own. The claim is unconvincing when extended too broadly, and can only be sustained in many places in an interpretive schema that sets too-strict limits on the "usefulness" of the literal account. However, if we follow the logic of the argument about the prophetic and apostolic experience of inspiration to include a more heavy emphasis on the mortifying work of the Spirit, we would do well. He who puts our Adamic humanity to death so that we may share in the new humanity of the new Adam likewise renders the prophets' and apostles' sinfulness and ignorance of God dead so that they are alive to Christ. The experience of inspiration is not abstracted from the conditions of the economy itself.

There are at least three advantages of conceiving of prophetic inspiration in this way. 1) It accords well with more of the prophetic testimony about the event of inspiration. Jeremiah speaks of the incredible weariness of being the servant of this Word, of a fiery consumption in his bones (Jer 20:9). Malachi speaks of the Word as a burden (Mal 1:1). For Jonah, the prophetic mission is one from which his whole person recoils (Jonah 1:3); it is the Presence from which no escape can be found (cf. Jonah 1:9–10). If the Psalmist can describe the oracles of the Lord as "sweeter than honey" (Ps 118:103), the apostle John can describe this same sweetness as turning to bitterness in his stomach (Rev 10:10). There is, in short, a truly mortifying element to the charism which is coincident with its joy.

2) It is a proportionate account of inspiration, duly recognizing the unique character of the event—the prophets and apostles do not always speak and write Holy Scripture—while situating this event firmly within the dynamics of divine and human relationships such as they are revealed in the economy. The mortifying and vivifying activity of the Spirit on behalf of the prophets and the apostles in inspiration is continuous with their own personal history. Inspiration is not an interruption of this personal history, a taking of the prophet out of the conditions of his humanity, but rather a moment in which the teleological aspect of this humanity is rendered utterly transparent. In speaking the Word of God, the prophet is never more truly himself, just as the baptized person is never more truly herself in being stripped bare and clothed with Christ, the incorruptible stole.

3) It secures the irreducibly participational character of attendance upon the Word of God insofar as the relational element of the speaking/writing of Scripture inheres within the confession of what Scripture is. In a dictation model of inspiration or a noncommittally agnostic or disinterested one, it is precisely this aspect of the prophetic moment and (by ramification) the interpretive moment that is marginalized. The imitative imperative, to which Didymus' account of Scripture is so closely bound, can be secured once the more

fulsome aspects of his participational ontology of Scripture are spelled out. We, the readers, must become like the prophets and the apostles if we are to hear the words of *Holy* Scripture. That is, a baptismal ontology of Scripture is transparent to a rightly-ordered interpretive *praxis*.

This ontology, which is largely implicit in Didymus' writings, bears upon two issues for OT interpretation that are present to the mind of almost every Christian interpreter, but especially to the preacher. 1) To what extent should a Trinitarian reading of the OT proceed in a Christian interpretation thereof? Contemporary readers of Didymus likely ask some form of Theodore's question: is it proper to rehearse the doctrine of the Trinity so explicitly, and to such great effect, in the reading of the OT, when such understanding was largely unavailable to the writer? The charge of anachronism looms large.

But the charge is oddly myopic. The historical context, even where it is more fulsomely conceived to include a divine element, is not nearly comprehensive enough. For—if Didymus is right that the Father always enters into the work of the other two *hypostaseis* by their missions to the created order—then the whole history of Israel and the prophetic event itself are sustained precisely in communion with the Word, from whom the Spirit is never separate. The Word who speaks to the prophets is a subsistent Word. The Word is a He. To speak of the pre-incarnate Son's activity among the people of Israel, or of the Holy Spirit's pre-Pentecostal descent upon Moses or one of the prophets, is not to speak anachronistically about the OT period, but rather to recognize the hidden meaning of that period within the most comprehensive context available to us by the grace of the Trinity. Trinitarian readings of the OT are therefore not only a permissible area of exploration for the Christian interpreter; the confession of the Nicene faith demands that such readings proceed. If a text is included in the Christian canon, it is by definition a moment in the Trinitarian economy in which the Father addresses us by his Son and his Spirit, calling forth the recognition of this same God in the hearing of the text.

2) Didymus' *praxis* of reading addresses another important question as well. For the Christian preacher, questions of meaning and application are of paramount importance. The preacher recognizes that Scripture is not only to be interpreted, but proclaimed. But the question that frequently arrests him in the study occurs to him in trying to articulate the proper relationship between scriptural meaning and application. How is the meaning of the text to be applied to the congregation? And he often has the feeling that he leaves the truly scientific character of his work behind in passing from one task to the other. The Christian application of the text is something other than its interpretation.

As I have argued in the last chapter, Didymus would have viewed this particular predicament with bewilderment. On the basis of the arguments above, I think he would challenge above all the idea that the interpretive task was one in which one could bracket aside however briefly one's own involvement in the narrative of Scripture. To separate the questions of meaning and application is to misconceive their relationship. It is to behave as if the testimony of the prophets only concerned the people of God today by some indirect route, in which only the ingenuity of the preacher salvages the message for some issue of contemporary relevance.

For this particular dilemma, only the christological center of Scripture provides an answer. We come to see how Zechariah addresses us only insofar as we see how Zechariah speaks about his contemporary situation in light of the coming of the Dawn. In Christ, I too am included in Israel's Scriptures. In Christ, I hear both God's word of address to me and see the obedient response of the only fully human person: the Incarnate Son of God. For Didymus, the question about the relation between meaning and application could never arise because the deepest meaning of every text of Scripture was Christ himself. Every Scripture pointed to him and therefore included within its purview the Body in which Didymus found himself addressed in his particular time and place. We see here the closest possible link between the Trinitarian and the christological. To equivocate about the missions of the Son and the Spirit in the OT is to pull apart the fabric in which the whole narrative of Scripture is held together. It is to see Christ only as some distant *telos* to which it all points, instead of seeing the OT (as the apostles saw it) as giving eloquent testimony to the one they had heard, seen, and touched, that one who was also "from the beginning" (1 John 1:1). To discover Christ at the center of the Scriptures is to find oneself at the joyful place where true spirituality, theology, and exegesis meet.

BIBLIOGRAPHY

Texts and Translations: Ancient Authors

Aetius, *Short Treatise*. Text and ET: Wickham, Lionel. "The *Syntagmation* of Aetius the Anomean." *JTS*, n.s., 19 (1968): 544–549.

Apollinaris of Laodicea, *Exposition of Faith*. In Lietzmann, Hans, ed. *Apollinaris von Laodicea und seine Schule: Texte und Untersuchungen*. Tübingen: Mohr (Siebeck), 1904.

Aristotle, *Metaphysics*. In Jaeger, Werner, ed. *Aristotelis Metaphysica*. Oxford: Clarendon Press, 1957.

Arius, *The Banquet*. In Athanasius, *De Synodis* 15. ET: Williams, Rowan. *Arius: Heresy and Tradition*, rev. ed., 101–103. Grand Rapids, MI: Eerdmans, 2002.

Athanasius, *Letters to Serapion*. In Savvidis, Kyriakos, and Dietmar Wyrwa, eds. *Athanasius Werke* I, Teil 1. Berlin: de Gruyter, 2010.

Athanasius, *Orations against the Arians*. In Metzler, Karin, and Kyriakos Savvidis, eds. *Athanasius Werke* I, Teil 1. Berlin: de Gruyter, 1998.

Augustine, *On Marriage and Sexual Desire*. In Urba, Carol, and Joseph Zycha, eds. CSEL 42, 211–319. Vienna: Tempsky, 1902.

Basil of Caesarea, *Against Eunomius*. ET: In DelCogliano, Mark, and Andrew Radde-Gallwitz, trans. *St Basil of Caesarea: Against Eunomius*. FC 122. Washington, D.C.: Catholic University of America Press, 2011.

Basil of Caesarea, *Letters*. In Courtonne, Yves, ed. and trans. *Sainte Basile, Lettres*, vol. 3, 47–55. Collection Budé. Paris: Les Belles Lettres, 1966.

Cyril of Alexandria, *Against Julian*. Book 1 in Buguière, Paul, and Pierre Évieux, ed. and trans. *Cyrille d'Alexandrie: Contre Julien*, vol. 1. SC 322. Paris: Éditions du Cerf, 1985. Book 8 in PG 76: 885–944.

Cyril of Alexandria, *Commentary on Habakkuk*. In Pusey, P. Edward, ed. *S. p. n. Cyrilli archiepiscopi Alexandrini in xii prophetas*, vol. 2. Oxford: Clarendon Press, 1868.

Cyril of Alexandria, *Commentary on Isaiah*. PG 70: 9–1449.

Cyril of Alexandria, *Commentary on Zechariah*. In Pusey, P. Edward, ed. *S. p. n. Cyrilli archiepiscopi Alexandrini in xii prophetas*, vol. 2. Oxford: Clarendon Press, 1868. ET: Hill, Robert, trans. *St Cyril of Alexandria: Commentary on the Twelve Prophets*, vol. 3. FC 124. Washington, D.C.: Catholic University of America Press, 2012.

Cyril of Alexandria, *Dialogues on the Trinity*. PG 75: 660–1124.

Cyril of Alexandria, *Elegant Sayings on Exodus*. PG 69: 383–537.

Cyril of Alexandria, *Elegant Sayings on Genesis*. PG 69: 13–383.

Cyril of Alexandria, *Treasury on the Holy, Consubstantial Trinity*. PG 75: 9–656.

Didymus the Blind, *Against the Manichaeans*. PG 39: 1085–1109.

Didymus the Blind, *Commentary on 2 Corinthians* (fragments). PG 39: 1680–1732.

Didymus the Blind, *Commentary on Ecclesiastes*. In Gronewald, Michael, ed. and trans. *Didymos der Blinde: Kommentar zum Ecclesiastes*, vol. 2. PTA 22. Bonn: Habelt, 1977. In Kramer, Johannes, ed. and trans. *Didymos der Blinde: Kommentar zum Ecclesiastes*, vol. 3. PTA 13. Bonn: Habelt, 1970. In Kramer, Johannes and Bärbel Krebber, ed. and trans. *Didymos der Blinde: Kommentar zum Ecclesiastes*, vol. 4. PTA 16. Bonn: Habelt, 1972. In Gronewald, Michael, ed. and trans. *Didymos der Blinde: Kommentar zum Ecclesiastes*, vol. 5. PTA 24. Bonn: Habelt, 1979. In Binder, Gerhard, and Leo Liesenborghs, ed. and trans. *Didymos der Blinde: Kommentar zum Ecclesiastes*, vol. 6. PTA 9. Bonn: Habelt, 1969.

Didymus the Blind, *Commentary on Genesis*. In Nautin, Pierre, ed. and trans. *Didyme l'Aveugle: Sur la Genèse*, 2 vols. SC 233, 244. Paris: Éditions du Cerf, 1976, 1978.

Didymus the Blind, *Commentary on Job*. In Henrichs, Albert, ed. and trans. *Didymos der Blinde: Kommentar zu Hiob*, vols. 1, 2. PTA 1, 2. Bonn: Habelt, 1968. In Hagedorn, Ursula, Dieter Hagedorn, and Ludwig Koenen, ed. and trans. *Didymos der Blinde: Kommentar zu Hiob*, vol. 3. PTA 3. Bonn: Habelt, 1968.

Didymus the Blind, *Commentary on the Psalms* (from the catena). In Mühlenberg, Ekkehard, ed. *Psalmenkommentare aus der Katenenüberlieferung*, vol. 2. Patristische Texte und Studien 16. Berlin: de Gruyter, 1977.

Didymus the Blind, *Commentary on the Psalms* (from the Tura papyri). In Doutreleau, Louis, Adolphe Gesché, and Michael Gronewald, ed. and trans. *Didymos der Blinde: Psalmenkommentar*, vol. 1. PTA 7. Bonn: Habelt, 1969. In Gronewald, Michael, ed. and trans. *Didymos der Blinde: Psalmenkommentar*, vols. 2–5. PTA 4, 6, 8, 12. Bonn: Habelt, 1968–1970.

Didymus the Blind, *Commentary on Zechariah*. In Doutreleau, Louis, ed. and trans. *Didyme l'Aveugle: Sur Zacharie*, 3 vols. SC 83–85. Paris: Éditions du Cerf, 1962. ET: Hill, Robert, trans. *Didymus the Blind: Commentary on Zechariah*. FC 111. Washington, D.C.: Catholic University of America Press, 2006.

Didymus the Blind, *On the Holy Spirit*. In Doutreleau, Louis, ed. and trans. *Didyme l'Aveugle: Traité du Saint-Esprit*. SC 386. Paris: Éditions du Cerf, 1992. ET: DelCogliano, Mark, Andrew Radde-Gallwitz, and Lewis Ayres, trans. *Works on the Spirit: Athanasius and Didymus*. Popular Patristics 43. Crestwood, NY: St Vladimir's Seminary Press, 2011.

Didymus the Blind, *On the Trinity*. In Mingarelli, J.A., trans. and ed. *Didymi Alexandrini De Trinitate Libri Tres*. PG 39: 269–992. Book 1 in Hönscheid, Jürgen, trans. and ed. *Didymus der Blinde: De trinitate, Buch 1*. Beiträge zur Klassischen Philologie 44. Meisenheim: Anton Hain, 1975. Book 2, chs. 1–7 in Seiler, Ingrid, trans. and ed. *Didymus der Blinde: De trinitate, Buch 2, Kapitel 1–7*. Beiträge zur Klassischen Philologie 52. Meisenheim: Anton Hain, 1975.

Epiphanius of Salamis, *Anchored*. In Holl, Karl, ed. *Epiphanius I: Ancoratus und Panarion haer. 1–33*, 2nd rev. ed. Marc Bergermann and Christian-Friedrich Collatz. GCS, n.F., 10. Berlin: Akademie-Verlag, 2013.

Epiphanius of Salamis, *Medicine Chest*. In Holl, Karl, ed. *Epiphanius I: Ancoratus und Panarion haer. 1-33*, 2nd rev. ed. Marc Bergermann and Christian-Friedrich Collatz. GCS, n.F., 10. Berlin: Akademie-Verlag, 2013. In Holl, Karl, ed. *Epiphanius II: Panarion haer. 34-64*, rev. ed. Jürgen Dummer. GCS 31. Berlin: Akademie-Verlag, 1980. In Holl, Karl, ed. *Epiphanius III: Panarion haer. 65-80, De Fide*, rev. ed. Jürgen Dummer. GCS 37. Berlin: Akademie-Verlag, 1985. ET: Williams, Frank, trans. *The Panarion of Epiphanius of Salamis: Books II and III. De Fide*. 2nd rev. ed. Nag Hammadi and Manichaean Studies 79. Leiden: Brill, 2013.

Eunomius of Cyzicus, *Apology*. In Vaggione, Richard Paul, ed. *Eunomius: The Extant Works*. OECT. 1987; reprint, Oxford: Oxford University Press, 2002.

Eunomius of Cyzicus, *Apology for the Apology*. In Vaggione, Richard Paul, ed. *Eunomius: The Extant Works*. OECT. 1987; reprint, Oxford: Oxford University Press, 2002.

Eusebius of Caesarea, *Demonstration of the Gospel*. In Heikel, Ivar A., ed. *Eusebius Werke 6*. GCS 23. Leipzig: Hinrichs, 1913.

Eusebius of Caesarea, *Ecclesiastical History*. In Oulton, J.E.L, trans. *Eusebius: The Ecclesiastical History*, vol. 2. LCL 265. 1932; reprint, Cambridge, MA: Harvard University Press, 2000.

Gregory of Nazianzus, *Letters*. In Gallay, Paul, ed. *Sainte Grégoire de Nazianze, Lettres*, vol. 2. Paris: Les Belles Lettres, 1967.

Gregory of Nazianzus, *Orations*. In Mossay, Justin, ed. and trans. *Grégoire de Nazianze: Discours 24-26*. SC 284. Paris: Éditions du Cerf, 1981. ET: Norris, Frederick, ed. *Faith Gives Fullness to Reasoning: the Five Theological Orations of Gregory Nazianzen*. Trans. by Lionel Wickham and Frederick Williams. Supplements to VC 13. Leiden: Brill, 1991.

Gregory of Nyssa, *Against Eunomius*. Book 1 in Jaeger, Werner, ed. *Contra Eunomium libri I et II. GNO* 1. Leiden: Brill, 1960. Book 3 in Jaeger, Werner, ed. *Contra Eunomium liber III. GNO* 2. Leiden: Brill, 2002.

Gregory of Nyssa, *Controversial Work against Apollinaris*. In Mueller, Frederick, ed. *GNO* 3, 131-233. Leiden: Brill, 1958.

Gregory of Nyssa, *Life of Saint Macrina*. In Maraval, Pierre, ed. *Grégoire de Nysse. Vie de sainte Macrine*. SC 178. Paris: Éditions du Cerf, 1971.

Gregory of Nyssa, *On the Life of Moses*. In Daniélou, Jean, ed. *Grégoire de Nysse. La vie de Moïse*, 3rd ed. SC 1. Paris: Éditions du Cerf, 2007.

Gregory of Nyssa, *On the Making of Man*. PG 44:125-256.

Gregory of Nyssa, *Oration on the Ascension of Christ*. In Gebhardt, Ernestus, ed. *GNO* 9, 323-327. Leiden: Brill, 1992.

Jerome, *Against John of Jerusalem*. In Feiertag, Jean-Louis., ed. *Hieronymus: Contra Iohannem*. CCSL 79A. Turnhout: Brepols, 1999.

Jerome, *Commentary on Zechariah*. In Adriaen, Marc, ed. *Hieronymus: Commentarii in prophetas minores*. CCSL 76A. Turnhout: Brepols, 1970.

Jerome, *On Illustrious Men*. In Richardson, Ernest C., ed. *Hieroynmus Liber de Viris Inlustribus*. TU 14, pt. 1. Leipzig: Hinrichs, 1896.

John Malalas, *Chronicle*. In Thurn, Ioannes, ed. *Ioannis Malalae Chronographia*. Corpus Fontium Historiae Byzantinae. Series Berolinensis 35. Berlin: de Gruyter, 2000.

Leontius of Jerusalem, *Treatise against the Nestorians*. PG 86: 1400–1768.

Maximus the Confessor, *Difficulties*. For *Ambiguum 7*, see PG 91: 1068D–1101C. ET: Blowers, Paul, and Robert L. Wilken, trans. *St Maximus the Confessor: On the Cosmic Mystery of Jesus Christ*. Popular Patristics Series. Crestwood, NY: St Vladimir's Seminary Press, 2003.

Methodius of Olympus, *On the Resurrection*. In Epiphanius, *Panarion* 64.12–62.

Nestorius, *Sermons*. In Loofs, Friedrich, ed. *Nestoriana: die Fragmente des Nestorius*. Halle: Niemeyer, 1905.

Origen, *Commentary on John*. ET: Heine, Ronald E. *Origen: Commentary on the Gospel according to John*. FC 80 and 89. Washington, D.C.: Catholic University of America Press, 1989 and 1993.

Origen, *Commentary on Proverbs* (fragments). PG 13: 17–33.

Origen, *Homilies on Ezekiel*. ET: Scheck, Thomas P. *Origen: Homilies 1–14 on Ezekiel*. ACW 62. New York: Paulist Press, 2010.

Origen, *Homilies on Genesis*. ET: Heine, Ronald E. *Origen: Homilies on Genesis and Exodus*. FC 71. Washington, D.C.: Catholic University of America Press, 1982.

Origen, *Homilies on Numbers*. ET: The cited section in *Homily 17* is from Balthasar, Hans Urs von, ed. *Origen: Spirit and Fire: A Thematic Anthology of His Writings*, trans. Robert J. Daly. Washington, D.C.: Catholic University of America Press, 1984.

Origen, *On First Principles*. ET: Butterworth, G.W., trans. *Origen: On First Principles: Being Koetschau's Text of the* De Principiis. Gloucester, MA: Peter Smith, 1973.

Pseudo-Athanasius, *Dialogue II on the Trinity*. PG 28: 1157–1201.

Pseudo-Basil, *Against Eunomius, Books 4–5*. PG 29: 672–768 (columns 768B.12ff. are not original).

Pseudo-Marcellus, *On the Incarnation and against the Arians*. PG 26: 984–1028.

Socrates Scholasticus, *Ecclesiastical History*. In Maraval, Pierre, and Pierre Périchon, trans. *Socrate de Constantinople: Histoire ecclésiastique, IV–VI*. SC 505. Paris: Éditions du Cerf, 2006.

Tertullian, *On Baptism*. ET: Evans, Ernest, ed. and trans. *Tertullian's Homily on Baptism*. London: S.P.C.K., 1964.

Theodore of Mopsuestia, *Commentary on Zechariah*. In Sprenger, Hans Norbert, ed. *Theodori Mopsuesteni commentarius in XII prophetas*. Göttinger Orientsforschungen 5, vol. 1. Wiesbaden: Harrassowitz, 1977.

Theodoret of Cyrus, *Commentary on Zechariah*. PG 81: 1873–1960. ET: Hill, Robert, trans. *Theodoret of Cyrus: Commentaries on the Prophets*, vol. 3. Brookline, MA: Holy Cross Orthodox Press, 2006.

Secondary Sources

Altaner, Berthold. "Augustinus und Didymus der Blinde: eine quellenkritische Untersuchung." *VC* 5 (1951): 116–120.

Anatolios, Khaled. *Retrieving Nicaea: The Development and Meaning of Trinitarian Doctrine*. Grand Rapids, MI: Baker, 2011.

Ayres, Lewis. "The Holy Spirit as the "Undiminished Giver": Didymus the Blind's *De spiritu sancto* and the Development of Nicene Pneumatology." In *The Holy Spirit in the Fathers of the Church*, edited by D. Vincent Twomey and Janet Rutherford, 57–72. Dublin: Four Courts Press, 2010.

Bardy, Gustave. "Apatheia." In *Dictionnaire de Spiritualité* 1, cols. 727–746. Paris: Beauchesne, 1937.

Bardy, Gustave. *Didyme l'Aveugle*. Études de Théologie Historique 1. Paris: Beauchesne, 1910.

Beeley, Christopher. *Gregory of Nazianzus on the Trinity and the Knowledge of God: In Your Light We Shall See Light*. Oxford Studies in Historical Theology. Oxford: Oxford University Press, 2008.

Behr, John. *The Formation of Christian Theology 2: The Nicene Faith, Part 2: One of the Holy Trinity*. Crestwood, NY: St Vladimir's Seminary Press, 2004.

Béranger, Louis. "L'âme humaine de Jésus dans la christologie du *De Trinitate* attribué à Didyme l'Aveugle." *RevScRel* 36 (1962): 1–47.

Béranger, Louis. "Etudes sur la Christologie du *De Trinitate* attribué à Didyme l'Aveugle." PhD diss., Lyon, 1960.

Béranger, Louis. "Sur deux énigmes du *De Trinitate* de Didyme l'Aveugle." *RSR* 51 (1963): 255–267.

Bienert, Wolfgang A. *"Allegoria" und "Anagoge" bei Didymos dem Blinden von Alexandria*. Patristische Texte und Studien 13. Berlin: de Gruyter, 1972.

Billings, J. Todd. *The Word of God for the People of God: An Entryway to the Theological Interpretation of Scripture*. Grand Rapids, MI: Eerdmans, 2010.

Bizer, Christoph. "Studien zu pseudoathanasianischen Dialogen der Orthodoxos und Aëtios." PhD diss., Bonn, 1970.

Blowers, Paul. "Maximus the Confessor, Gregory of Nyssa, and the Concept of "Perpetual Progress"." *VC* 46 (1992): 151–171.

Bouteneff, Peter. "Placing the Christology of Didymus the Blind." *Studia Patristica* 37 (2001): 389–395.

Clark, Elizabeth. *The Origenist Controversy: the Cultural Construction of an Early Christian Debate*. Princeton: Princeton University Press, 1992.

Cooper, Adam. "The Gift of Receptivity: St Athanasius on the Security of Salvation." *Phronema* 28, no. 2 (2013): 1–20.

Daley, Brian. "The Fullness of the Saving God: Cyril of Alexandria on the Holy Spirit." In *The Theology of St Cyril of Alexandria: a Critical Appreciation*, edited by Thomas Weinandy and Daniel Keating, 113-148. London: T&T Clark, 2003.

Daley, Brian. *The Hope of the Early Church: A Handbook of Patristic Eschatology*. Cambridge: Cambridge University Press, 1991.

Daley, Brian. "Is Patristic Exegesis still Usable? Reflections on Early Christian Interpretation of the Psalms." *Communio: International Catholic Review* 29 (2002): 185-216.

Daley, Brian. "Leontius of Byzantium: A Critical Edition of His Works, with Prolegomena." PhD diss., Oxford, 1978.

Daniélou, Jean. "La Fête des Tabernacles dans l'exégèse patristique." *Studia Patristica* 1 (1957): 262-279.

DelCogliano, Mark. "Basil of Caesarea, Didymus the Blind, and the Anti-Pneumatomachian Exegesis of Amos 4:13 and John 1:3." *JTS*, n.s., 61 (2010): 644-658.

DelCogliano, Mark. "The Influence of Athanasius and the Homoiousians on Basil of Caesarea's Decentralization of "Unbegotten"." *JECS* 19 (2011): 197-223.

Doutreleau, Louis. "Le 'De trinitate' est-il l'œuvre de Didyme l'Aveugle?" *RSR* 45 (1957): 514-557.

Doutreleau, Louis. "Vie et survie de Didyme l'Aveugle du IVe siècle à nos jours." *Le Mardis de Dar El-Salam 1956-1957* (1959): 33-92.

Ehrman, Bart D. *Didymus the Blind and the Text of the Gospels*. The New Testament in the Greek Fathers 1. Atlanta: Scholars, 1986.

Funk, Franz Xaver. "Die zwei letzten Bücher der Schrift Basilius d. Gr. gegen Eunomius." In *Kirchengeschichtliche Abhandlungen und Untersuchungen*, vol. 2, 291-329. Paderborn: Schöningh, 1899.

Funk, Franz Xaver. "Die zwei letzten Bücher der Schrift Basilius d. Gr. gegen Eunomius." In *Kirchengeschichtliche Abhandlungen und Untersuchungen*, vol. 3, 311-323. Paderborn: Schöningh, 1907.

Geljon, Albert-Kees. "Didymus the Blind: Commentary on Psalm 24 (23 LXX): Introduction, Translation, and Commentary." *VC* 65 (2011): 50-73.

Gesché, Adolphe. "L'âme humaine de Jésus dans la christologie du IVe s. Le témoignage du Commentaire sur les Psaumes découvert à Toura," *Revue d'histoire ecclesiastique* 54 (1959): 385-425.

Gesché, Adolphe. *La christologie du 'Commentaire sur les Psaumes' découvert à Toura*. Gembloux: Duculot, 1962.

Gesché, Adolphe. "Un document nouveau sur la christologie du IVe s.: le Commentaire sur les Psaumes découvert à Toura." *Studia Patristica* 3 (1961): 205-213.

Ghattas, Michael. *Die Christologie Didymos' des Blinden von Alexandria in den Schriften von Tura: zur Entwicklung der alexandrinischen Theologie des 4. Jahrhunderts*. Studien zur Orientalischen Kirchengeschichte 7. Münster: Lit, 2002.

Grant, Robert M. "Greek Literature in the Treatise *De Trinitate* and Cyril *Contra Julianum.*" *JTS*, n.s., 15 (1964): 265-279.

Gray, Patrick. *Leontius of Jerusalem: Against the Monophysites: Testimonies of the Saints and Aporiae*. Oxford Early Christian Texts. Oxford: Oxford University Press, 2006.

Greer, Rowan. *The Captain of our Salvation: A Study in the Patristic Exegesis of Hebrews*. Beiträge zur Geschichte der Biblischen Exegese 15. Tübingen: Mohr (Siebeck), 1973.

Heron, Alasdair. "The Holy Spirit in Origen and Didymus the Blind: A Shift in Perspective from the Third to the Fourth Century." In *Kerygma und Logos. Beiträge zu den geistegeschichtlichen Beziehungen zwischen Antike und Christentum*, edited by Adolf Ritter, 298-310. Göttingen: Vandenhoeck and Ruprecht, 1979.

Heron, Alasdair. "Some Sources Used in the *De Trinitate* Ascribed to Didymus the Blind." In *The Making of Orthodoxy: Essays in Honour of Henry Chadwick*, edited by Rowan Williams, 173-181. Cambridge: Cambridge University Press, 1989.

Heron, Alasdair. "Studies in the Trinitarian Writings of Didymus the Blind: His Authorship of the Adversus Eunomium IV-V and the De Trinitate." PhD diss., Tübingen, 1972.

Heron, Alasdair. "The Two Pseudo-Athanasian Dialogues against the Anomoeans." *JTS*, n.s., 24 (1973): 101-122.

Heston, Edward Louis. "The Spiritual Life and the Role of the Holy Ghost in the Sanctification of the Soul, as Described in the Works of Didymus of Alexandria." PhD diss., Notre Dame, 1938.

Hicks, Jonathan Douglas. "St Cyril on the Priesthood of Christ and the Old Testament." *Phronema* 30, no. 1 (2015): 91-113.

Hill, Robert. "Psalm 45: a *locus classicus* for Patristic Thinking on Biblical Inspiration." *Studia Patristica* 25 (1993): 95-100.

Hill, Robert. "Zechariah in Alexandria and Antioch." *Augustinianum* 48 (2008): 323-343.

Kariatlis, Philip. ""Dazzling Darkness": The Mystical or Theophanic Theology of St Gregory of Nyssa." *Phronema* 27, no. 2 (2012): 99-123.

Kerrigan, Alexander. *St Cyril of Alexandria: Interpreter of the Old Testament*. Analecta Biblica 2. Rome: Pontifical Biblical Institute, 1952.

Koenen, Ludwig. "Ein theologischer Papyrus der Kölner Sammlung: Kommentar Didymos' des Blinden zu Zach. 9,11 u. 16." *Archiv für Papyrusforschung* 17 (1960): 61-105.

Koenen, Ludwig, and Wolfgang Müller-Wiener. "Zu den Papyri aus dem Arsenioskloster bei Ṭurā." *Zeitschrift für Papyrologie und Epigraphik* 2 (1968): 41-63.

Kramer, Bärbel. "Didymos von Alexandrien." In *Theologische Realenzyklopädie*, vol. 8, 741-746. Berlin: de Gruyter, 1981.

Krausmüller, Dirk. "Leontius of Jerusalem, a Theologian of the 7th Century." *JTS* 52 (2001): 637-657.

Lampe, G.W.H., ed. *A Patristic Greek Lexicon*. Oxford: Clarendon Press, 1961.

Lauro, Elizabeth Ann Dively. *The Soul and Spirit of Scripture within Origen's Exegesis*. The Bible in Ancient Christianity 3. Boston; Leiden: Brill, 2005.

Layton, Richard. *Didymus the Blind and His Circle in Late-Antique Alexandria: Virtue and Narrative in Biblical Scholarship*. Urbana, IL: University of Illinois, 2004.

Layton, Richard. "Didymus the Blind and the *Philistores*: A Contest over *Historia* in Early Christian Exegetical Argument." In *New Approaches to the Study of Biblical Interpretation in Judaism of the Second Temple Period and in Early Christianity*, edited by Gary Anderson, Ruth Clements, and David Satran, 243–267. Boston; Leiden: Brill, 2013.

Lebon, Joseph. "Le Pseudo-Basile (*Adv. Eunom.*, IV–V) est bien Didyme d'Alexandrie." *Le Muséon* 50 (1937): 61–83.

Lécuyer, Joseph. "Jésus, fils de Josédec, et le Sacerdoce du Christ." *RSR* 43 (1955): 82–103.

Leipoldt, Johannes. *Didymus der Blinde von Alexandria*. TU, n.F., 14, pt. 3. Leipzig: Hinrichs, 1905.

Liébaert, Jacques. *La doctrine christologique de Saint Cyrille d'Alexandrie avant la querelle Nestorienne*. Mémoires et Travaux 58. Lille: Facultés Catholiques, 1951.

Loofs, Friedrich. *Nestoriana: die Fragmente des Nestorius*. Halle: Niemeyer, 1905.

Louth, Andrew. *The Origins of the Christian Mystical Tradition: From Plato to Denys*, 2nd ed. New York: Oxford University Press, 2007.

Lubac, Henri de. *History and Spirit: the Understanding of Scripture according to Origen*. Translated by Anne Englund Nash. San Francisco: Ignatius, 2007.

Lubac, Henri de. *Medieval Exegesis: the Four Senses of Scripture*, vol. 1. Translated by Mark Sebanc. Grand Rapids, MI: Eerdmans, 1998.

Lubac, Henri de. *Medieval Exegesis: the Four Senses of Scripture*, vol. 2. Translated by Edward M. Macierowski. Grand Rapids, MI: Eerdmans, 2000.

Martens, Peter W. "Why Does Origen Introduce the Trinitarian Authorship of Scripture in Book 4 of Peri Archon?" *VC* 60 (2006): 1–8.

Mingarelli, Joannes Aloysius. *De Didymo Commentarius*. PG 39: 139–216.

Moller, Philip. "What Should They Be Saying about Biblical Inspiration? A Note on the State of the Question." *Theological Studies* 74 (2013): 605–631.

Nelson, Anne Browning. "The Classroom of Didymus the Blind." PhD diss., University of Michigan, 1995.

O'Collins, Gerald, and Michael K. Jones. *Jesus our Priest: A Christian Approach to the Priesthood of Christ*. Oxford: Oxford University Press, 2010.

O'Keefe, John J., and Russell R. Reno. *Sanctified Vision: An Introduction to Early Christian Interpretation of the Bible*. Baltimore, MD: Johns Hopkins University Press, 2005.

ΟΡΦΑΝΟΣ, Μάρκος. Ἡ ψυχὴ καὶ τὸ σῶμα τοῦ ἀνθρώπου κατὰ Δίδυμον Ἀλεξανδρέα (τὸν τυφλόν). Ἀνάλεκτα Βλατάδων 21. Thessaloniki: Patriarchal Institute of Patristic Studies, 1974.

Pelikan, Jaroslav. *The Christian Tradition: A History of the Development of Doctrine 1: The Emergence of the Catholic Tradition (100–600)*. Chicago: University of Chicago Press, 1971.

Pépin, Jean. "A propos de l'histoire de l'exégèse allégorique: l'absurdité, signe de l'allégorie." *Studia Patristica* 1 (1957): 395–413.

Perczel, István. "The Pseudo-Didymian *De trinitate* and Pseudo-Dionysius the Areopagite: A Preliminary Study." *Studia Patristica* 58 (2013): 83–108.

Plaxco, Kellen. "Didymus the Blind and the Metaphysics of Participation." *Studia Patristica* 67 (2013): 227–237.

Prinzivalli, Emanuela. *Didimo il Cieco e l'interpretazione dei Salmi*. Quaderni di Studi e Materiali di Storia delle Religioni 9, no. 2. Rome: L'Aquila, 1988.

Reuling, Hanneke. *After Eden: Church Fathers and Rabbis on Genesis 3:16–21*. Jewish and Christian Perspectives 10. Leiden: Brill, 2006.

Reynolds, Stephen Craigie. "Man, Incarnation, and Trinity in the *Commentary on Zechariah* of Didymus the Blind of Alexandria." PhD diss., Harvard, 1966.

Risch, Franz Xaver. "Einleitung." In *Pseudo-Basilius, Adversus Eunomium IV-V: Einleitung, Übersetzung und Kommentar*, 3–48. Supplements to VC 16. Leiden: Brill, 1992.

Rousseau, Philip. "Appendix 3: The Date of Basil's Death and of the *Hexaemeron*." In *Basil of Caesarea*, 360–363. The Transformation of the Classical Heritage 20. Berkeley: University of California Press, 1994.

Russell, Norman. *The Doctrine of Deification in the Greek Patristic Tradition*. Oxford Early Christian Studies. Oxford: Oxford University Press, 2004.

Schermann, Theodor. "Didymus der Blinde: de Trinitate ll. III und de Spiritu sancto." In *Die griechischen Quellen des hl. Ambrosius in ll. III de Spir. s.*, 70–87. Veröffentlichungen aus dem Kirchenhistorischen Seminar München 10. Munich: Lentner, 1902.

Sheridan, Mark. "The Concept of the "Useful" as an Exegetical Tool in Patristic Exegesis." *Studia Patristica* 39 (2006): 253–257.

Sheridan, Mark. *From the Nile to the Rhone and Beyond: Studies in Early Monastic Literature and Scriptural Interpretation*. Rome: Studia Anselmiana, 2012.

Silvas, Anna M. *Gregory of Nyssa: The Letters: Introduction, Translation and Commentary*. Supplements to VC 83. Leiden: Brill, 2007.

Simonetti, Manlio. "Ancora sulla paternità Didymiana de *De Trinitate*." *Augustinianum* 36 (1996): 377–387.

Simonetti, Manlio. "Didymiana." *Vetera Christianorum* 21 (1984): 129–155.

Simonetti, Manlio. "Lettera e allegoria nell'esegesi veterotestamentaria di Didimo." *Vetera Christianorum* 20 (1983): 341–389.

Solari, Placid. "Christ as Virtue in Didymus the Blind." In *Purity of Heart in Early Ascetic and Monastic Literature: Essays in Honor of Juana Raasch, O.S.B.*, edited by Harriet Luckman and Linda Kulzer, 67–88. Collegeville, MN: Liturgical Press, 1999.

Stefaniw, Blossom. *Mind, Text, and Commentary: Noetic Exegesis in Origen of Alexandria, Didymus the Blind, and Evagrius Ponticus*. Early Christianity in the Context of Antiquity 6. Frankfurt: Peter Lang, 2010.

Steiger, Peter. "Theological Anthropology in the *Commentary On Genesis* by Didymus the Blind." PhD diss., Catholic University of America, 2006.

Swete, Henry Barclay. *On the History of the Doctrine of the Procession of the Holy Spirit, From the Apostolic Age to the Death of Charlemagne*. 1876. Reprint, Eugene, OR: Wipf and Stock, 2004.

Tigcheler, Jo. *Didyme l'Aveugle et l'exégèse allégorique: Étude sémantique de quelques termes exégétiques importants de son commentaire sur Zacharie*. Translated by Denise van Weelderen-Bakelants. Graecitas Christianorum Primaeva 6. Nijmegen: Dekker and Van de Vegt, 1977.

Torrance, Thomas F. *Divine Meaning: Studies in Patristic Hermeneutics*. Edinburgh: T&T Clark, 1995.

Torrance, Thomas F. *The Trinitarian Faith: the Evangelical Theology of the Ancient Catholic Church*. Edinburgh: T&T Clark, 1993.

Treier, Daniel J. *Introducing Theological Interpretation of Scripture: Recovering a Christian Practice*. Grand Rapids, MI: Baker, 2008.

Turcescu, Lucian. *Gregory of Nyssa and the Concept of Divine Persons*. American Academy of Religion Academy Series. Oxford: Oxford University Press, 2005.

Tzamalikos, Panayiotis. *A Newly Discovered Greek Father: Cassian the Sabaite Eclipsed by John Cassian of Marseilles*. Supplements to VC 111. Leiden: Brill, 2012.

Vaggione, Richard Paul. *Eunomius of Cyzicus and the Nicene Revolution*. Oxford Early Christian Studies. Oxford: Oxford University Press, 2000.

Vogt, Hermann Josef. *Coetus Sanctorum: Der Kirchenbegriff des Novatian und die Geschichte seiner Sonderkirche*. Theophaneia 20. Bonn: Hanstein, 1968.

Webster, John. *Holy Scripture: A Dogmatic Sketch*. Cambridge: Cambridge University Press, 2003.

Webster, John. "T.F. Torrance on Scripture." *SJT* 65 (2012): 34–63.

Widdecombe, Peter. *The Fatherhood of God from Origen to Athanasius*, rev. ed. Oxford Theological Monographs. Oxford: Clarendon Press, 2000.

Williams, Rowan. *Arius: Heresy and Tradition*, rev. ed. Grand Rapids, MI: Eerdmans, 2002.

Young, Frances. *Biblical Exegesis and the Formation of Christian Culture*. Cambridge: Cambridge University Press, 1997.

Young, Frances. *From Nicaea to Chalcedon: A Guide to the Literature and its Background*, 2nd ed. Grand Rapids, MI: Baker, 2010.

Young, Frances. "The God of the Greeks and the Nature of Religious Language." In *Early Christian Literature and the Classical Intellectual Tradition: in honorem Robert M. Grant*, edited by William Schoedel and Robert L. Wilken, 45–74. Théologie Historique 53. Paris: Beauchesne, 1979.

Young, Frances. "The Rhetorical Schools and Their Influence on Patristic Exegesis." In *The Making of Orthodoxy: Essays in Honour of Henry Chadwick*, edited by Rowan Williams, 182–199. Cambridge: Cambridge University Press, 1989.

AUTHOR AND SUBJECT INDEX

Aaron 18, 139, 249, 268
Abra(h)am 96, 97, 271
accommodation 7, 76, 94, 142–4, 154, 156, 187, 188, 197, 201, 210
active life (see moral life)
Adam 16, 125, 129, 133, 134, 137
adoption (see filiation)
"adulterous woman" 188
Aetius 72, 77
age to come 17, 109, 155, 156, 169, 182–4, 197, 211, 212, 216, 263, 269, 274
Alexandria(n) 20, 43, 44, 47–9, 51, 52, 62
allegory (*allēgoria*) 3, 6, 13, 49, 167, 180
Altaner, Berthold 36
"altars/sacrifices" 174, 176
Amphilochius 24
anagogy (*anagōgē*) 6, 12, 13, 49, 167, 180, 222, 275
analogy 107, 108, 120, 128, 144
    Adam and Eve—Seth 76, 85
    archetype—image 80, 127, 139
    archetype—image—seal 95
    Eternal Father—Ever-virgin Mary 77, 207
    human father—son 35, 76
    Incarnation—divine use of human language 142, 143, 154
    light—radiance 77, 79, 80, 86
    mind—speech—utterance 94
    oil—unction 83, 84
    person—spirit 83, 84
    root—branch 88
    root—fruit (of Eden's trees) 79, 80
    spring—river 35, 82, 84
    word—breath 95
Anatolios, Khaled 220
Angel of the Lord/of great counsel 96, 97, 187, 237, 241, 244, 245, 247, 258, 265
angels 254
    activities of 40, 187, 189, 248
    bodies of 76, 114, 159
    divine knowledge possessed by 24, 76, 114, 115, 148, 205, 223
    divine participation of 136
Anomoean(s) (see Heterousian(s))

anthropomorphism 218
Antioch(ene) 47–9, 51
Antony of Egypt 20
apokatastasis 213
Apollinaris/-arian(ism) 1, 27, 30, 64–6, 158, 209, 238, 239, 264
apophatic(ism) 14, 15, 36, 80, 83, 88, 107, 109, 120
aporia 55, 127, 172, 196, 264
Apostles 11, 12, 16, 140–2, 149, 216, 229, 249, 252, 276, 278
Aristotle 67, 87
Arius/Arians 3, 27, 30, 44, 62, 63, 65, 66, 74, 89, 93, 108, 112, 209, 211
ascent 63, 143, 150, 156, 200, 211, 222, 230, 261
Asclepius 38
"Ashkelon" 190
Asterius of Antioch 48
atemporality 36, 73, 75, 76, 81, 84, 86, 89
Athanasius 3, 8, 9, 20, 28, 29, 48, 52, 55, 71, 109
athletes for piety 149, 177, 179, 195, 236, 239, 244
Augustine 262
authorial intent 9, 11, 143–5
authors of Scripture (human)
    communicant with God or participant in his economy 9–11, 13, 16, 18, 98, 141, 145, 146, 148, 151–6, 186, 189, 199, 231, 255, 270
    conformed to Christ (baptismally-formed) 9, 11, 17, 232, 233, 271, 275, 276
    deification of the 16, 150–153, 155, 156, 198, 229, 275, 276
    illumination of the 16, 98, 144, 145, 147, 148, 152–4, 198, 201, 229, 230, 233
    partial ignorance of 143, 144, 229, 255
    sanctification of the 16, 17, 149, 153, 154, 196, 229, 230, 233
    witnesses 11, 16, 141, 145, 154, 156, 270
Ayres, Lewis 6, 14, 30, 66, 135, 144

"Babylon" (as confusion) 230

Balaam 155
Baptism 15, 16, 25, 95, 117, 120, 123, 124, 132, 134, 135, 137-140, 154, 156
Bardy, Gustave 14, 15, 25, 37, 42, 52-4, 71-4, 76, 84, 85, 99, 120-5, 129, 131
Basil of Caesarea 23-6, 29, 66, 85, 86, 109
Basil of Seleucia 31
Beeley, Christopher 109
Behr, John 209
Béranger, Louis 14, 24, 26, 28, 56-9, 63-5, 71, 78, 91, 132
Bienert, Wolfgang 6, 7, 13, 66, 165, 167, 169, 180, 198, 199, 201, 232-4, 243
Billings, J. Todd 10
Binder, Gerhard 184
Bizer, Christoph 47, 51
blood of the covenant 191, 195
Blowers, Paul 228
body
   Christ's ascended 17, 217, 223, 224, 226, 233
   Christ's incarnate 172, 173, 203, 204, 207, 209, 238, 239, 245, 246, 264, 265, 267
   material 17, 158, 159, 161, 182, 194, 206, 210, 211, 217, 223-6, 229, 268, 269
   spiritual 114, 159, 172, 182-4, 194, 196, 210, 223-6
"Book on the Spirit, the" 54-7
Bouteneff, Peter 172, 197
"branches" 181-3
Buguière, Paul 37
"burning brand" 240, 241, 261
Butterworth, G.W. 68
Byzantine 119

Caesarius of Antioch 47
Cain 188
Cappadocia(n/s) 44, 51-3
cataphatic(ism) 14, 15, 80, 108, 120
Catechetical School of Alexandria 20
causality
   as intra-Trinitarian category 14, 15, 23, 85-7, 108, 109
   between orders of being 35, 87, 99
   in economic functions of Christ 18, 218-221, 226, 227, 229, 234, 245, 246, 249, 268

Chalcedonian Definition 32-4
Church 1, 3, 108, 166, 189, 270, 275
   Body of Christ 173, 248
   "fortress" 191, 192
   "house of God" 171-3, 248
Clark, Elizabeth 43
"clouds/dew/heavens" 166-170, 181, 230
"coin" 182
conceptual distinction 28, 30, 84, 85, 87, 109
condescension (see accommodation)
constancy (see immutability)
Constantinople 25
contemplation 251
   as theological knowledge 163
   of the gifts/pledge of the Holy Spirit 204, 206, 207
   of the immaterial Trinity 17, 187, 197, 205-210, 216, 227, 229, 245, 247, 252, 267-9
   of the Incarnation/Virgin Birth 16, 166, 187, 190, 194, 197, 205-211, 245, 247, 252, 267
   of the world and Providence 17, 197, 204-8, 210
   stages of 17, 197, 202, 203, 205-7, 210, 211, 227, 244, 267, 269
contemplative life 16, 17, 156, 164, 178, 251
Cooper, Adam 227
correlative/non-correlative 14, 35, 79, 109
corruptibility (see mutability)
Council of Constantinople (381) 25
"crowns" 176-9
Cyril of Alexandria 18, 30-1, 33, 36-8, 48, 52, 247, 252, 253, 257-9, 261, 263

Daley, Brian 3, 30, 108, 227
Daniel 233
Daniélou, Jean 182
David 48, 136, 143, 145, 187, 255
"Dawn, the" 236, 247, 256-8, 263, 278
death 131, 132, 140, 175, 195, 244
"defect in the literal sense" (*defectus litterae*) 213, 243, 250
deification 7, 100, 120, 124, 125, 135, 137-9, 150-4, 157, 184, 214, 230, 275

Author and Subject Index

DelCogliano, Mark 6, 14, 30, 55, 66, 109, 144
devil(s) 132, 135, 173, 190, 193, 213, 222, 236–241, 244, 255, 259, 261, 265
De Trinitate
    communal setting of 41–6, 53, 68
    date of 14, 21, 23–37, 39, 68
    occasion of 21, 39–44, 53, 63, 68
    provenance of 21, 44–53, 68
    reception history of 21, 27, 36–8
    sources of 53, 57, 58, 63, 66–8
    style of 54, 58–63, 68
Didymus the Blind
    circle of 6, 43, 44, 62, 68, 220
    dependence on Origen 3, 68, 169, 213
    dogmatic corpus of 5, 14, 20, 21, 39, 54, 56–61, 63, 66–9, 152, 229, 233, 261, 265, 273
    exegetical corpus of 5, 6, 14, 21, 49, 59–65, 67, 69, 151, 170, 184, 196, 197, 220, 229, 233, 248, 261, 264, 265
    interpretive skopos of 1, 3, 6, 11, 194, 231, 233, 235, 236, 252, 257, 261, 264, 266, 270, 273
    interpretive practices of 18, 231, 235, 252, 265, 266, 269–272, 277
    life of 20, 22, 39, 44, 68
Diodore of Tarsus 3
docetic
    Christology 209, 264
    elements of Christ's risen body 225, 226
doctrines of piety 162, 163, 190, 202, 204, 208, 209, 229, 251
Doutreleau, Louis 20, 21, 26, 43, 47, 49, 50, 54–63, 88, 160, 165, 169, 171, 172, 174, 180, 185, 189, 191, 203, 204, 211, 212, 215, 218, 237, 240, 246, 249
dyophysite Christology 33, 34

Economy
    of creation 15, 16, 70, 96, 98, 102, 103, 106, 121, 122, 124–6, 129, 133, 137, 156, 210, 253
    of re-creation/salvation 6, 7, 15, 16, 70, 94, 96, 98, 120–4, 130–140, 144, 148, 153–6, 210, 213, 218, 221, 230, 231, 253, 263, 269, 273

oikonomia as synonym for Incarnation 27, 34, 61, 95, 98, 128, 132
    relation to theologia 139, 140, 269
    unity of the 15, 96, 97, 255, 256, 268, 269
"eighth day" 222
Egypt/Egyptian 44–6, 53, 68, 96
Ehrman, Bart 66
Elijah 230
Elisha 145
Eliud/Elihu 146, 147, 155, 255
emanation 35
Epiphanius of Salamis 25, 34, 43, 44, 66, 224–7
eschaton (see age to come)
ethical life/ethics (see moral life)
Eucharist 117, 178
Eunomius/-ians 1, 27–9, 32, 71, 74, 85–7, 93, 104, 105, 108, 113, 119, 221
Eusebius of Caesarea 26, 48, 168, 247, 252, 253, 268
Evagrius of Pontus/Evagrian 4, 228
Eve 129, 137
Évieux, Pierre 37
exegesis
    anagogical 11, 261, 271, 274
    Jewish 164, 180, 256, 260, 262
    methods of 2–4, 274
    noetic 3, 4
    normative 4, 262
    total/unitive 271, 272, 278
    worthy of God (theoprepōs) 5, 252
exile(s) 176–9, 184, 194, 213, 231

faith 126–8, 135, 153, 173, 248
Father, the
    activity of 70, 71, 74, 89, 93, 96, 98, 102–5, 109, 110, 119, 134
    divinity/essence (ousia)/nature (physis) of 70, 78, 84
    identity of 14, 53, 70, 74, 78, 79, 83, 84, 87–9, 108, 109
    knowledge possessed by 24, 44, 90, 92, 109, 112, 113, 115, 116
    name(s) of 71, 74, 83, 84, 108, 138, 212, 254
    priority of 15, 102, 103, 108–110
    unbegotten in essence? 77, 85

unbegotten in hypostasis? 85–7, 108, 109
will of 24, 70, 74, 90, 91, 103, 104, 108, 137
worship of 71
fear of God (*phobos*; see reverence)
"Feast of Tabernacles" 179–183
filiation 1, 7, 15, 16, 95, 96, 111, 120, 121, 124, 125, 128, 130, 131, 134, 135, 137–140, 153, 157, 200
First Origenist Controversy 43, 44, 68
"flesh" 166, 168, 170
forepassion (*propatheia*) 64–6
"former and latter rain" 208, 209
freedom
  angelic 91, 114
  divine 90, 91
  human 15, 90, 91, 114, 123, 125–8, 137, 140, 161
Funk, F.X. 21, 54

Gabriel, the archangel 32, 40
Geljon, Albert-Kees 221–3
Gesché, Adolphe 64, 65, 158, 197, 218, 239
Ghattas, Michael 26, 64, 158, 239, 240
"gold and/or silver" 201, 203, 204
Grant, Robert 36, 37
Gray, Patrick 30
Greer, Rowan 2
Gregory of Nazianzus 23, 48, 52, 75, 85, 86, 109
Gregory of Nyssa 23, 29, 34, 48, 85, 209, 221, 227, 228
Gronewald, Michael 67, 218

henadic gods 35, 36
Henrichs, Albert 231
hermeneutical indeterminacy 12, 273, 274
Hermes Tresmegistus 37, 38, 67
Heron, Alasdair 6, 51, 57, 58, 63, 65, 66, 100, 101, 113, 136, 162, 195
Heston, Edward Louis 15, 99—101, 120, 121
Heterousian(s) 44, 62, 76, 85, 87, 89, 104, 117, 119
Hicks, Jonathan D. 258
Hill, Robert 49, 151–3, 174, 175, 177, 179, 186, 188, 191, 193, 203, 204, 213–6, 230, 237, 238, 240, 244, 246, 249, 250, 257, 260, 264
history/inquiry (*historia*) 3, 13, 18, 167, 180, 243, 250
Holy Scripture
  accommodative character/depths of 142–4, 156, 186, 199, 230, 232, 275
  Christic center of 10, 12, 16, 18, 173, 187–9, 232–5, 266, 271, 278
  divine inspiration of 8, 10, 11, 111, 140, 141, 151, 152, 231, 275, 276
  faithfulness/truthfulness of 154, 156, 275
  "mind"/divine skopos *of* 5, 6, 12, 16, 28, 143, 145, 154, 155, 186, 230, 231, 247, 252, 266, 269, 270, 273
  necessity of 67, 118
  ontology of 1, 7, 9, 10, 11, 13, 111, 140, 141, 144, 153–6, 231, 232, 235, 266, 269, 271, 273, 275
  Trinitarian missions and 15, 16, 18, 89, 97, 98, 152, 155, 209, 231, 232, 235, 241–3, 247, 253–6, 258, 259, 263, 269, 271, 275, 277, 278
  unity of 10–12, 218, 232, 235
  usefulness of (ōpheleia) 5, 261–3, 276
Holy Spirit, the
  activity of 15, 70, 71, 84, 90, 100, 102, 105, 111, 118, 120, 122–4, 126, 133, 134, 137, 138, 154, 174
  departure of 129, 133, 134
  divine procession of 34–6, 71, 73, 80–4
  divinity/essence (ousia)/*nature* (physis) *of* 32, 34, 38, 40, 70, 73, 80, 81, 83, 102, 115
  gifts of 50, 102, 125, 140
  identity of 70, 82, 87–9
  inspiring/interpreting Scripture 11, 40, 97, 111, 141–3, 145, 152, 167, 186, 188, 233, 275
  knowledge possessed by 44, 90–2, 113, 115, 116
  mission(s) of 10, 89, 93, 94, 96
  name(s) of 66, 67, 71, 74, 80, 83, 84, 104, 118, 119
  numerical unity of 12, 75, 80

    Pentecostal mission of 92, 123, 124, 130, 133, 140
    worship of 39, 71
homiletics 18, 271, 277, 278
homonymy 90, 149
Homoousian 77, 104, 111, 119
Hönscheid, Jürgen 22, 25, 60, 76, 77, 79, 88, 106, 118, 122, 145
"horses" 186, 187
"house/temple/tent/building" 170–5, 180–3, 193, 228, 265
humanity
    definition of 157, 158, 160
    telos of 8, 15, 116, 120, 124, 125, 127, 129, 135, 139, 140, 151–4, 156, 179
humanization 9, 129, 151, 152, 154, 232, 275
Hypostas(e)is
    actual subsistence 73, 74
    equivalent to idiotēs 52
    equivalent to ousia 51, 60
    in formulae for generation and procession 71–4
    of Trinitarian Persons 14, 52, 53, 72–4, 84, 101, 106, 116
    of Incarnate Savior 31
        personality 73

identity (*idiotēs*) 52, 53
illumination 15, 17, 111, 118, 137, 147, 148, 152, 154, 197, 199, 200, 203, 204, 214, 249
image of God
    in humanity 7, 120, 124–9, 134, 135, 137, 139, 140, 151, 153, 159, 182
    loss/ruin of 124, 126, 129, 136, 140
    soul as locus of 158, 159
    the Son as 7, 80, 110, 124, 125, 127, 128, 139
imitation
    of Christ 16, 18, 157, 169, 170, 176, 178, 179, 181, 184, 189, 190, 195, 211, 218, 220, 230, 241, 244, 247, 248, 251, 252, 262, 263
    of evil/evil powers 161, 241, 244
    of the saints 17, 18, 168–170, 179, 230, 247, 251, 252, 261, 264, 265
immateriality 89

immediacy 77–9, 82
immutability (divine) 28–30, 32–4, 77, 78, 119, 185, 186, 188, 189, 237
impassibility (divine) 77, 79
improper signification (*catechrestic*; see Holy Scripture, accommodative character/depths of)
incomprehensibility (divine) 8, 87, 107, 113, 114, 116, 117–9, 148, 228
individuating marks (see identity)
ineffability (divine) 32, 142
"inner and outer walls" 207
inseparability
    of activity 82, 89, 92–5, 99–101, 104–7, 110, 121–3, 128
    of divine missions 94–6, 98, 110, 122
    of nature 77, 81–4, 88, 89, 93, 94
intellect (*nous*) 17, 111, 137, 147, 159, 237
interpreters
    as participants in the divine economy/dependent on divine help 6, 7, 10, 13, 111, 140, 145, 148, 150, 154, 155, 168, 199, 230–3, 235, 255, 265–7, 270, 271, 276, 277
    baptismal formation of 18, 140, 154, 156, 232, 235, 267, 270–2, 276
    contemplative disposition of 111, 145, 148, 154, 199, 202, 230
    moral disposition of 111, 150, 154, 199, 231
    practices of 3, 12, 18, 199, 231, 232, 252, 270
(in)visibility
    angelic 114
    divine 44, 114, 117, 142
    of the soul 114
Isaac 96
Isaiah 97, 148, 149, 187, 233, 255
Israel 10, 96, 97, 149, 183, 184, 253, 255, 258, 261, 278

Jacob/"Jacob" 96, 97, 222
Jerome 18, 20, 39, 43, 44, 51, 54, 62, 67, 162, 175, 176, 238, 247, 252, 255–7, 260–2
"Jerusalem" 177, 179, 183, 189, 193, 200, 201, 230
John, the apostle 188, 208
John of Jerusalem 43, 44

John Malalas 37
Jonah 233
Jones, Michael K. 253
Joshua son of Jehozadak 18, 50, 177, 235–7, 240–2, 246, 247, 256, 258–262, 264
Josiah son of Zephaniah 177
joy/rejoicing 192, 243, 251, 261
"Judah" 189
Judas 102, 136, 137, 238
Jude 96
Kariatlis, Philip 228
Kerrigan, Alexander 31
kingdom(s) of Christ 17, 19, 218–220
knowledge of God
    as vision 113, 116, 117, 147, 148, 198, 199, 201, 204
    eschatological 212–7, 221, 226, 227, 236, 270
    heretical 146, 150
    human 8, 80, 84, 85, 87, 111, 113, 115–120, 153, 206, 216
    Jewish 98, 105, 164, 254
    possessed by saints 146, 148, 149
    possessed by saints in the OT 97, 98, 145, 148, 254, 255, 266
    participatory/relational/sacramental 17, 111, 117, 120, 136, 140, 205, 215
    secular/Greek/philosophic 37, 38, 66–8, 105, 113, 114, 117, 118, 146, 147
Koenen, Ludwig 41–3, 46, 59, 61, 62, 191
Kramer, Bärbel 59
Krausmüller, Dirk 30

"lamp/lamp-stand/lights" 47, 50, 165, 202, 203, 205, 207, 215
Lampe, G.W.H. 105
"land" (as soul) 169, 188, 208, 222
language (human; see speech, human)
"last day" 23, 24
Lauro, Elizabeth A.D. 263
Layton, Richard 1, 5, 67, 159, 161, 167, 181, 184, 196, 217, 264
Lebon, Joseph 21
Lécuyer, Joseph 253
Leipoldt, Johannes 15, 25, 54, 61, 71–4, 120, 121, 123, 125–7
Leontius of Byzantium 30

Leontius of Jerusalem 30, 31
letter (*rhēton*) 13, 167, 169, 180, 241, 243
Liébaert, Jacques 26, 36
Liesenborghs, Leo 184
likeness of God 17, 125, 126, 129, 134, 135, 137, 151, 153, 159, 182, 183, 185, 194, 226, 248
limitatation/limitlessness 7, 76, 80, 84, 86, 107, 114, 115, 117, 119, 142, 156, 184, 228, 229
Loofs, Friedrich 30
Louth, Andrew 226, 227
love 248
    of God for man 117, 122, 128, 130, 142, 154, 228, 261
    of man for neighbor 67, 242, 250–2, 261
Lubac, Henri de 7, 11, 13, 169, 267, 271, 275

Macedonius/Macedonians 25, 26, 32, 40, 42, 62, 83, 89, 90, 92, 93, 103, 113, 115, 116, 146, 149
"man on the red horse" 2, 3, 185, 186, 205, 254
Mani/Manichean 1, 126, 127, 161
Marcellus/Marcellan 212, 218, 220, 221
Marcian 25
Marcion/Marcionite 44
Martens, Peter 141
Maximus the Confessor 227, 228
mediation 17, 18, 46, 112, 188, 216, 217, 226, 227, 234, 242, 253, 268
meditation 204–6
Methodius of Olympus 182, 227, 229
miaphysite Christology 33
Michael, the archangel 32, 40
Migne, J.-P. 95
Mingarelli, J.A. 20, 21, 24, 26, 27, 41, 42, 47, 54–8, 60, 63, 64, 68, 79, 106, 118, 126, 145, 150
modalism 105
Moller, Philip 10
Montanists 105
moral life 16, 156, 157, 164, 165, 171, 178, 194, 250
    relation to contemplative life 150, 157, 158, 164–6, 190, 194, 197, 201
Moses 61, 139, 143, 148, 169, 230, 249, 255, 268, 277

Mother of God (*Theotokos*) 30, 33, 60, 63
Mühlenberg, Ekkehard 60
Müller-Wiener, Wolfgang 62
mutability 129, 159, 181, 185, 186, 188
mystery of Christ 10–13, 18, 234, 255, 267, 271, 275
mysteries of piety (see doctrines of piety)

Naaman the Syrian 50
nail-wounds 223–225
narrative coherence 256–9, 262
negation (see apophatic(ism))
Nelson, Anne Browning 2, 62
Neo-Arian(ism) 27, 28, 218
New Adam 140, 276
Nestorius/Nestorianism 2, 27, 30, 31, 38
Nicea/Nicene/pro-Nicene 36, 44, 71, 85, 87, 108, 111, 112, 208, 277
Nicodemus 93
Nile, the 45, 46
Noah 230
non-spatiality 35–36, 76, 82, 89, 92–93
Novatian 25, 26

O'Collins, Gerald 253
O'Keefe, John J. 10
obedience/disobedience 15, 18, 132–4, 140, 153, 168, 171, 173, 190, 192–4, 241, 246, 262, 263, 266, 278
"oil/oil conduits" 202, 204
Old Testament 10, 15, 18, 96, 155, 209, 210, 232, 241–3, 246, 254–6, 258, 259, 263, 271, 277
"olive trees" 202, 204–6
omnipresence 92, 93
Origen(ism) 3–5, 11, 44, 48, 62, 68, 112, 113, 169, 182, 188, 198, 213, 224–8
organically-one (*symphyēs/symphytōs*) 78, 79, 82, 101
Ὀρφανός, Μάρκος 59, 126, 158–161

Palestine 43, 44
Palladius of Galatia 20
parenesis 168, 175, 183, 189, 236
participation
    in divine life/virtue 15, 16, 100, 126–9, 135–7, 153, 157, 161, 162, 215–7, 228, 263

in Christ 170, 173, 175, 176, 178, 179, 184, 187, 189, 194, 195, 241
    in the Holy Spirit 138, 157, 175, 250
Passionei, Domenico 20
passions 64, 126, 140, 150, 159, 161, 190, 191
Paul, the apostle 96, 97, 115, 143, 145, 148–150, 169, 187, 208, 230
peace (see stability)
Pelagius/Pelagian 16, 195
Pelikan, Jaroslav 101
Pépin, Jean 213
Perczel, István 32–36
perfection 6, 17, 139, 171, 172, 222, 248, 251, 256, 263
    contemplative 17, 155, 156, 204, 213, 215, 216, 229, 233, 249
    moral 16, 18, 155–7, 184, 185, 194, 195, 216, 233, 261, 262
Peter, the apostle 30, 238, 242, 262
Philo 5
Plato/Platonism 33, 38, 39, 67, 159
Plaxco, Kellen 136, 162
Plotinus 112
Pneumatomachians 25
Porphyry 38, 67, 146, 147
practical virtue (see virtue, moral)
Prayer to the Angels (*DT*) 32, 40–2
Prayer to the Trinity (*DT*) 40–2, 45, 46
priesthood
    of Christ 18, 214, 235, 236, 238, 241–7, 249, 252–4, 256, 258–263, 265, 267, 268, 271
    of Levites/Joshua 187, 237, 242, 243, 246, 247, 254, 256, 258, 260, 261, 263, 265
    spiritual 249, 251, 261, 263, 265
"priestly garments" 241, 242, 244–246, 259, 260, 265
Prinzivalli, Emanuela 167, 195
Proclus 32, 34–36
progress 5, 17, 18, 172, 175, 181, 189, 193, 228
    final goal of 171, 172, 175, 179, 181, 184, 194, 196, 214, 216, 217, 222, 228, 229, 248, 251
property (*hypostatic*; see identity)
Prophets, the 10–12, 16, 17, 98, 141, 149, 151, 157, 168, 171, 186, 201, 229, 276

Pseudo-Athanasius 57, 63, 72, 86
Pseudo-Basil 21, 29, 57, 66, 68
Pseudo-Dionysius 32
Pseudo-Marcellus 57
purification/purity 182, 184, 202, 247–9, 251

Radde-Gallwitz, Andrew 6, 14, 30, 66, 144
recovery 1, 3, 7, 273
Reno, R.R. 10
repentance 18, 245, 246, 265, 266
rest (see stability)
Reuling, Hanneke 13
reverence (*eulabeia*) 166–8, 175, 185, 188, 190–2, 194
Reynolds, Stephen 64, 158–160, 211, 239
Risch, F.X. 21
Rousseau, Philip 22
Rufinus of Aquileia 20, 43
Russell, Norman 138, 139, 152

Sabbatius 25, 26
Sabellius/Sabellian 27, 105, 212
sanctification 15, 16, 100, 111, 124, 125, 129, 135–137, 149, 150, 154
Satan (See devil(s))
Schermann, Theodor 36
"seas" (as perils) 222, 231
"seers" 247, 249, 251, 252, 268, 269
Seiler, Ingrid 22, 40, 41, 62, 90, 103, 126, 136, 149, 150
sense(s) of Scripture
   allegorical 177, 180
   anagogical 5, 12, 18, 167, 180, 190, 200, 207, 222, 234
   applicative 18, 204, 247, 248, 261, 266, 267, 270, 277, 278
   figural 203, 204
   "*fuller*" (plenior) 266
   hidden 143
   historical/sensible 167, 176, 177, 180, 207, 230, 234, 241, 244, 264, 274
   immanent 169, 234, 243, 244
   literal 13, 18, 155, 167, 168, 177, 180, 183, 190, 207, 230, 234, 242–4, 247, 252–4, 256, 257, 259, 261–4, 267, 272, 274
   moral 12, 210
   plain 196, 233, 259, 271
   spiritual 11–3, 18, 167, 169, 176, 177, 179, 182, 183, 230, 234, 242–4, 247, 252, 253, 264–9, 274
"seven-eyed stone"/"stones" 50, 51, 173, 174–6, 247, 249, 250, 258, 259
Sheridan, Mark 5, 262
Silvas, Anna 22
Simonetti, Manlio 5, 13, 45, 51–53, 58, 159, 184, 197, 198, 262
simplicity (divine) 28, 29, 32, 34, 74, 77, 119
"simply" (*asyllogistōs*) 23, 24
sin/sinlessness 8, 18, 119, 121, 125–7, 131, 133, 140, 156, 176, 195, 231–243, 250, 259–263
skin tunics 159
Socrates Scholasticus 25, 26, 39, 54
Solari, Placid 159–161, 170, 178
Solomon 155, 233
Son, the
   activity of 70, 71, 90, 102, 103, 105, 122, 132, 243, 258, 259
   birth of 33, 63, 76, 122
   divinity/essence (ousia)/*nature* (physis) *of* 28, 29, 70, 73, 75, 79, 102, 186
   divine generation of 34–6, 63, 71, 74–80, 211
   giving the Spirit 16, 95, 133, 134, 139, 140, 153, 175
   identity of 70, 74, 79, 87–89
   Incarnation/Inhumanation/humanity of 6, 8, 9, 17, 28, 64, 65, 94, 114, 122, 124, 128, 130–3, 139, 140, 153, 158, 168, 170, 171, 173–6, 178, 179, 181, 184, 186, 197, 204, 205, 209, 217, 220, 221, 246, 253, 270, 278
   inspiring/interpreting Scripture 97, 141, 142, 147, 152, 153, 199, 233
   knowledge possessed by 23, 24, 44, 90–2, 109, 112, 113, 115, 116, 132
   mission(s) of 10, 89, 93, 94, 96, 232, 241
   name(s) of 71, 74, 75, 83, 84, 103, 104, 112, 121, 128, 137, 138, 254
   numerical unity of 28, 74, 75
   receiving the Spirit/baptism of 16, 132–4, 139, 174, 175, 204, 250, 252, 257, 261
   temptation of 237–9, 244, 261, 264, 265
   worship of 39, 71

Author and Subject Index

soteriology (see economy of recreation)
soul
    Christ's human 33, 64–6, 68, 168, 203–5, 207, 238, 239, 265
    dispositions/habits of 113, 147, 160–4, 185, 187
    enemies of the (See devil(s))
    parts/powers/properties of 126–9, 147, 158–160, 163, 171, 200, 203, 227
    pre-existence of the 17, 33, 158, 159, 172, 194, 196, 226, 227, 229, 239, 268
Spassky, Anatoly 21
speech
    contrasted with thought 201, 249
    divine 9, 92, 142, 143, 154, 200, 240, 241, 251
    human 7–9, 17, 70, 107, 108, 111, 120, 142–4, 154, 201, 202, 234
spiritual children 42, 43, 126, 213, 231
spiritual struggle (see temptation)
stability (*eustatheia*) 16, 131, 150, 157, 161, 177–9, 181–5, 188–194, 196, 217, 228–230, 237, 239, 248, 263
"standing" 237, 241, 242, 248, 251
Stefaniw, Blossom 2–4, 198
Steiger, Peter 5, 159, 167, 229
Stoic 178
"sun of righteousness" 189, 205, 210, 217
Swete, H.B. 73

teachers/teaching 165, 171, 187–9, 195, 201, 204, 217, 219, 220, 237, 238, 241, 244, 246
temptation 18, 173, 178, 190, 193, 236–8, 241, 244, 247, 252, 259, 261, 262
Tertullian 47, 129, 134
Theodore of Mopsuestia 2, 18, 47, 49–51, 219, 247, 252, 254–262, 266, 277
Theodoret of Cyrus 18, 48, 49, 51, 247, 252, 257, 259–263, 271
Theodosius I 25
"theology" (*theologia*) 29, 139, 208, 245
Theophilus of Alexandria 43, 44
thought (human) 8, 9, 84, 107, 108, 120, 143, 202
Tigcheler, Jo 4, 13, 167, 180, 243
"tin stone" 49
Thomas, the apostle 131

Tomus ad Antiochenos 52
Torrance, T.F. 7–9, 72, 73
"tower of Hananel" 193
Tranquillity (*apatheia*; see Stability)
Treier, Daniel 10
Trinity, the
    activity of 15, 70, 71, 82, 89, 98–107, 110, 111, 119–123, 130, 131, 133
    beatific vision of 1, 116
    consubstantiality of 35–6, 38, 39, 70, 71, 79, 83, 101, 106, 111
    doctrine of 13, 40, 41, 43, 53
    incorporeality of 76
    inspiring Scripture 9, 16, 141
    relations within 15
    unity of nature in 15, 70, 73, 74, 79, 91, 98, 104, 107, 115, 123, 212, 218
    unity of will 89, 91, 106, 107, 123
    worship of 106, 183
tropology (*tropologia*) 12, 49
Tura 6, 21, 51, 59–61, 64
Turcescu, Lucian 85
Tzamalikos, Panayiotis 23–7, 30, 31, 42, 43, 45–50

Vaggione, Richard Paul 29, 144
Valentinian Gnosticism 218
vice 129, 136, 190, 222
"vine and fig tree" 247, 250, 251
Virgin Mary, the 30, 32, 33, 95, 122, 170, 173, 174, 207
virtue 45, 136, 137
    contemplative (knowledge/wisdom) 46, 136, 137, 162–5, 177, 181, 197, 244
    definition of 161–3
    moral 46, 136, 162–4, 177, 181, 183, 244
Vogt, Hermann 25, 26

Webster, John 9, 10
Wickham, Lionel 86
Widdecombe, Peter 112
Williams, Frank 224–6
Williams, Frederick 86
Williams, Rowan 112
Word, the (see Son)

Young, Frances 2, 3, 108, 228

Zechariah, father of John 97
Zechariah, the prophet 61, 151, 152, 166, 186, 198, 278
Zerubbabel 50, 51, 256, 259
"Zion" 193, 201

SCRIPTURE INDEX

Gen 1:11–12 79
Gen 1:26 125
Gen 1:27 182
Gen 1:27–28 103
Gen 2:7 125
Gen 2:9 79
Gen 3:6 129
Gen 3:21 159
Gen 4:7 188
Gen 6:3 129, 134
Gen 15:17 271

Exod 7:1 139
Exod 26:3 246
Exod 33:13 116
Exod 33:19 209

Lev 23:39–40 180

Num 11:29 255

Deut 32:2 169

4 Kgdms 5:10 50
4 Kgdms 5:14 50
4 Kgdms 6:1–7 129

Job 33:4 255
Job 40:15–23 132

Ps 2:6 219
Ps 18:2 169
Ps 20 218
Ps 20:2 219
Ps 23 221, 245
Ps 23:3 222
Ps 23:3–4 222
Ps 23:3–6 221
Ps 23:6 222
Ps 23:7 222
Ps 23:7–8 221
Ps 23:7–10 221
Ps 26:10 132
Ps 31:7 192
Ps 32:6 95

Ps 33:10–11 191
Ps 70:3 192
Ps 70:18 42
Ps 89:17 215
Ps 108 143
Ps 108:27 144
Ps 109:1 255
Ps 117 174
Ps 117:22 174
Ps 118:103 276
Ps 127:5 177

Prov 2:6 191
Prov 2:8 191
Prov 3:18 181
Prov 7:11 188
Prov 8:22 147
Prov 8:25 78, 81
Prov 10:29 192
Prov 27:18 250

Cant 1:11–12 201

Isa 5:6 167
Isa 6:8–9 141
Isa 9:5 84, 187
Isa 11 51
Isa 11:1–3 50, 51, 174
Isa 19:1 168
Isa 26:1 192, 207
Isa 26:19 169
Isa 45:8 167
Isa 48:16 92
Isa 59:21 95
Isa 61:1 95
Isa 63:1–2 223
Isa 63:13–14 97

Jer 20:9 276

Ezek 36:26–27 83
Ezek 37:14 83

Joel 2:28 82, 83

Amos 4:11–13 55
Amos 4:13 49

Jonah 1:3 276
Jonah 1:9–10 276

Zech 1:1–6 188
Zech 1:3 185
Zech 1:5 186
Zech 1:7 186, 188
Zech 1:8 3, 186, 188, 254
Zech 1:9 187, 188
Zech 1:11 188
Zech 1:12–13 189
Zech 1:16 170
Zech 2:1 200
Zech 2:1–2 170
Zech 2:5 200
Zech 2:14–16 166
Zech 2:17 166, 191
Zech 3 4, 5, 11, 18, 19, 198, 235, 243, 252, 256, 257, 259, 264, 266, 271
Zech 3–4 51
Zech 3:1 236, 241
Zech 3:1–2 244
Zech 3:1–5 256
Zech 3:2 236, 240, 241
Zech 3:3–5 241, 244, 247, 256, 257, 264
Zech 3:4 242, 245, 259
Zech 3:5 245
Zech 3:6–7 247
Zech 3:7 248
Zech 3:8–9 50, 173, 247, 256, 268
Zech 3:8–4:10 49
Zech 3:9 50, 257
Zech 3:9–10 247
Zech 3:10 50
Zech 4 202, 203, 229
Zech 4:1 236
Zech 4:1–3 202
Zech 4:2 50
Zech 4:6 50, 51, 255
Zech 4:7 255
Zech 4:9 199
Zech 4:10 49, 50
Zech 4:11 206
Zech 4:11–14 202
Zech 4:12 206

Zech 4:14 206
Zech 5:1 200
Zech 5:9 200
Zech 6:1 164, 200
Zech 6:9 199
Zech 6:9–11 176
Zech 6:10 177
Zech 6:11 177, 200
Zech 8:9 171
Zech 8:10 213
Zech 8:11–12 168
Zech 9:7 190
Zech 9:9 201
Zech 9:9–10 255
Zech 9:11 191
Zech 9:12 191, 207
Zech 9:15–16 173, 175
Zech 10:1 208
Zech 11:1 199
Zech 12:7 172
Zech 14:5–7 214
Zech 14:9 179, 212
Zech 14:10 193
Zech 14:11 179
Zech 14:16 180

Mal 1:1 276
Mal 2 260
Mal 4:2 189

2 Esd 10:18 260

Sir 25:11 191

Wis 1:7 92
Wis 13:5 128

Matt 5:14 215
Matt 9:20–22 249
Matt 11:27 115
Matt 13:1–23 169
Matt 13:43 215
Matt 18:10 258
Matt 22:20 182
Matt 25:1–7 203

Mark 13:32 23, 24

Scripture Index

Luke 1:68 97
Luke 1: 70 97
Luke 4:18 95
Luke 9:26 262
Luke 12:9 262
Luke 14:28–30 193
Luke 15:8–10 182
Luke 20 224
Luke 20:42 255
Luke 22:31 238
Luke 22:32 262
Luke 22:54–62 262

John 1:1 86
John 1:2 92
John 1:14 31, 208
John 1:16 128
John 3:8 93
John 4:14 192
John 7:37–39 192
John 7:38 82
John 8:40 218
John 9:1–7 249
John 12:21 266
John 12:41 141, 255
John 12:49 55, 91
John 14:8 254
John 14:11 94
John 14:16 92, 100
John 14:28 85, 86, 94
John 15:1 181
John 15:15 116
John 16:13 55, 135
John 16:13–14 91
John 17:21 214
John 20:19 223
John 20:22 129, 133
John 20:22–23 90

Acts 2:36 27, 28, 29, 30, 31
Acts 28:25 141

Rom 1:1–4 209
Rom 8:15 130
Rom 8:29 127, 128, 169
Rom 14:17 104
Rom 16:27 55

1 Cor 1:24 178
1 Cor 2:10 115
1 Cor 3:1–2 165
1 Cor 5:4 182
1 Cor 8:4–6 104
1 Cor 10:4 97, 255
1 Cor 12:11 90
1 Cor 13:9 210
1 Cor 13:9–12 206
1 Cor 13:12 210
1 Cor 15:24 220
1 Cor 15:28 213
1 Cor 15:42–46 183
1 Cor 15:49 127, 169

2 Cor 1:22 95
2 Cor 4:4 80
2 Cor 5:16 209, 211
2 Cor 5:21 18, 243, 244, 245
2 Cor 13:3 97, 141

Gal 3:27 134, 244

Eph 1:13 95
Eph 2:2 222
Eph 2:5–6 127
Eph 2:6 183
Eph 4:6 105
Eph 4:11 248
Eph 4:13 213
Eph 4:30 104, 135
Eph 5:18 136
Eph 6:19 231

Phil 2:6–7 29, 131
Phil 2:11 183
Phil 3:12 263, 265

Col 1:15 80, 95, 127
Col 3:10 127, 131

1 Thess 5:19 136

1 Tim 5:6 55, 56

2 Tim 3:16 5, 141, 262
2 Tim 4:8 263

Heb 1:3 95
Heb 2:4 90
Heb 2:9 244
Heb 3:1 249
Heb 3:1–2 246, 268
Heb 4:15 178, 261
Heb 5:1–3 260
Heb 5:7 174
Heb 5:11–14 165
Heb 7:26–28 261
Heb 11:38 150

1 Pet 1:11 255
1 Pet 2:4–7 174
1 Pet 2:24 244

2 Pet 1:14 182

1 John 1:1 278
1 John 4:2 31
1 John 5:20 118

Jude 5 97, 255

Rev 10:10 276